SCARECROW AUTHOR BIBLIOGRAPHIES

1. John Steinbeck—1929–71 (Tetsumaro Hayashi). 1973. *See also no. 64.*
2. Joseph Conrad (Theodore G. Ehrsam). 1969.
3. Arthur Miller (Tetsumaro Hayashi). 2nd ed., 1976.
4. Katherine Anne Porter (Waldrip & Bauer). 1969.
5. Philip Freneau (Philip M. Marsh). 1970.
6. Robert Greene (Tetsumaro Hayashi). 1971.
7. Benjamin Disraeli (R.W. Stewart). 1972.
8. John Berryman (Richard W. Kelly). 1972.
9. William Dean Howells (Vito J. Brenni). 1973.
10. Jean Anouilh (Kathleen W. Kelly). 1973.
11. E.M. Forster (Alfred Borrello). 1973.
12. The Marquis de Sade (E. Pierre Chanover). 1973.
13. Alain Robbe-Grillet (Dale W. Frazier). 1973.
14. Northrop Frye (Robert D. Denham). 1974.
15. Federico García Lorca (Laurenti & Siracusa). 1974.
16. Ben Jonson (Brock & Welsh). 1974.
17. Four French Dramatists: Eugène Brieux, François de Curel, Emile Fabre, Paul Hervieu (Edmund F. Santa Vicca). 1974.
18. Ralph Waldo Ellison (Jacqueline Covo). 1974.
19. Philip Roth (Bernard F. Rodgers, Jr.). 2nd ed., 1984.
20. Norman Mailer (Laura Adams). 1974.
21. Sir John Betjeman (Margaret Stapleton). 1974.
22. Elie Wiesel (Molly Abramowitz). 1974.
23. Paul Laurence Dunbar (Eugene W. Metcalf, Jr.). 1975.
24. Henry James (Beatrice Ricks). 1975.
25. Robert Frost (Lentricchia & Lentricchia). 1976.
26. Sherwood Anderson (Douglas G. Rogers). 1976.
27. Iris Murdoch and Muriel Spark (Tominaga & Schneidermeyer). 1976.
28. John Ruskin (Kirk H. Beetz). 1976.
29. Georges Simenon (Trudee Young). 1976.
30. George Gordon, Lord Byron (Oscar José Santucho). 1977.
31. John Barth (Richard Vine). 1977.
32. John Hawkes (Carol A. Hryciw). 1977.
33. William Everson (Bartlett & Campo). 1977.
34. May Sarton (Lenora P. Blouin). 1978.
35. Wilkie Collins (Kirk H. Beetz). 1978.
36. Sylvia Plath (Lane & Stevens). 1978.
37. E.B. White (A.J. Anderson). 1978.
38. Henry Miller (Lawrence J. Shifreen). 1979.
39. Ralph Waldo Emerson (Jeanetta Boswell). 1979.
40. James Dickey (Jim Elledge). 1979.
41. Henry Fielding (H. George Hahn). 1979.
42. Paul Goodman (Tom Nicely). 1979.
43. Christopher Marlowe (Kenneth Friedenreich). 1979.
44. Leo Tolstoy (Egan & Egan). 1979.
45. T.S. Eliot (Beatrice Ricks). 1980.
46. Allen Ginsberg (Michelle P. Kraus). 1980.
47. Anthony Burgess (Jeutonne P. Brewer). 1980.

ANDREW M. GREELEY
An Annotated Bibliography

by
ELIZABETH HARRISON

Scarecrow Author Bibliographies, No. 92

The Scarecrow Press, Inc.
Metuchen, N.J., & London
1994

British Library Cataloguing-in-Publication Data available

Library of Congress Cataloging-in-Publication Data

Harrison, Elizabeth, 1929-
    Andrew M. Greeley: an annotated bibliography / by Elizabeth
Harrison.
      p.   cm. -- (Scarecrow author bibliographies ; no. 92)
    Includes index.
    ISBN 0-8108-2931-2 (acid-free paper)
    1. Greeley, Andrew M., 1928- Bibliography. I. Title.
II. Series.
    Z8368.95.H37 1994
    [PS3557.R358]
    016.813'54--dc20   94-25619

To Christine, Ron,

Arlene, and Jim

CONTENTS

PART ONE: PRIMARY SOURCES

PART TWO: SECONDARY SOURCES

INDEXES

APPENDIX

FOREWORD

I am pleased and honored to present this documentation of the writings of a remarkable man. Andrew Moran Greeley, a priest of the Roman Catholic Church, has made a significant contribution, over a period of almost forty years, to the study of education, ethnicity, the sociology of religion, and to the understanding of his Church and its people, particularly in the United States. For those who will study his work and his Church in the future I hope this book will be of some assistance.

The intended scope of the bibliography covers print material, written by and about Greeley, published in the United States in English between 1956 and 1993. Some books and articles published in England and Canada, found serendipitously, have been included, as well as a few sound recordings. No systematic search, however, has been made for audio-visual performances or for foreign editions of Greeley's books. There is also some ephemeral material (pamphlets written for teenagers in the late 1950s and dust jacket blurbs, for example) which has been excluded.

In the foreword to his fine Northrop Frye bibliography, Robert Denham writes of the bibliographer's "rage for order and completeness." I would hope to have achieved some measure of order, but, even within the above parameters, I cannot claim completeness. Nevertheless, I am reasonably confident that all original U. S. editions of primary and secondary books are included, and that nothing of major importance is missing from the balance of the work. Syndicated columns present some problems as records are no longer available, and there is a gap of almost two years in the secular ones where I did not have knowledge of, or access to, a newspaper which carried them for that period. A number of these are available in manuscript form in the Greeley archive described below.

I have personally verified most of the entries. Those not seen, indicated by an asterisk, were taken from authoritative sources.

The material is arranged by form, in the time-honored manner, and chronologically within each chapter so as to better delineate the different phases of Greeley's work. His books, however, are gathered together by year and then arranged alphabetically by title. Thus they may not be exactly in the order in which they were published within a given year.

The annotations are just that: descriptive notes with no critical analysis. The quotations in them are Greeley's words, taken, in most cases, from the work itself. Occasionally, in the unannotated entries, I have added a few words of clarification in parentheses.

A collection of unpublished scholarly papers, manuscripts and correspondence, primarily from the late 1960s to the mid-1980s, is housed at the Chicago Historical Society. It includes a few lengthy letters on topics such as student unrest in the 1960s, extensive memoranda (one on religio-ethnic pluralism, for example) grant proposals, survey questionnaires, and original manuscripts of some books written in the 1970s. Public access to this archive is prohibited during Greeley's lifetime without prior written permission from him.

With a few exceptions, the unpublished papers in Chapter Seven were seen in the Greeley archive. Those bearing the NORC label can, I am told, be found in the library at the National Opinion Research Center, University of Chicago, but I have not verified this personally. Many of these papers were presented at professional conferences and meetings, and I have included details of them where available.

I have selected the reviews of Greeley's books from the hundreds which have appeared in publications, scholarly and popular, Catholic and secular, across the United States. The majority are taken from national journals and newspapers readily accessible to the researcher. From some of these I have excerpted interesting or pertinent quotations.

The author index contains all authors and editors mentioned in the text except the writers of letters to the editors in reply to Greeley's articles, and, of course, Greeley himself. The reply letters are entered in the primary sources with references to and from the relevant articles. The titles of all primary books, essays, articles, short stories, and newsletters are indexed, as well as secondary books and essays.

Ten subject categories in the appendix provide some access to the principal areas of Greeley's work. It should be noted, however, that there is much overlapping between the different fields, and that all of his work is essentially religious and Catholic.

I am deeply indebted to many people and institutions whose professional knowledge and resources have helped to make this project possible. The first of these is Andrew Greeley himself. His gracious cooperation and unfailing patience when faced with endless questions have made my work much easier and more enjoyable. His administrative assistant, Mary Kotecki, has been a constant source of information and help.

I would also like to thank Archie Motley, Chicago Historical Society; Todd Brennan and John Sprague, Thomas More Association; Terri Golembiewski, *Chicago Sun Times* Library; Jean Blake, *National Catholic Reporter*; and Ceri Robinson, Rosner & Liss Public Relations. The following libraries have graciously made their facilities and resources available to me, for which I am especially grateful.

In Ontario: University of Guelph, Guelph Public Library (particular thanks to both their Interlibrary Loan Departments), McMaster University, University of St. Jerome's College, University of Waterloo, Wilfrid Laurier University, University of St. Michael's College, John Robarts Library--University of Toronto, Metropolitan Toronto Central Library.

In Chicago: Harold Washington Library Center, DePaul University, Illinois Benedictine College (at Lisle).

In Florida: Daytona Beach Public Library, Stetson University.

Finally, I would like to thank my children and their spouses, Christine Harrison and Ron MacKinnon, Jim Harrison and Arlene Vandersloot, for their encouragement, enthusiasm, patience, and help whenever needed. It is to them this book is affectionately dedicated.

Elizabeth Harrison
Guelph, Ontario

CHRONOLOGY

1928   Andrew Moran Greeley born in Oak Park, Illinois, on February
       5. Oldest child of Grace McNichols and Andrew Thomas
       Greeley. Grandson of Irish immigrants, raised in a devout Roman
       Catholic household, a child of the Great Depression, a native
       Chicagoan. These circumstances created the model for his future.

1935   In Grade 2 decided to be a priest, and never wavered from that
       decision.

1942   Entered Quigley Preparatory Seminary in downtown Chicago.

1947   Graduated from Quigley and entered St. Mary of the Lake
       Seminary, Mundelein, Illinois.

1954   Earned the S.T.L. degree from St. Mary of the Lake. On May 5
       was ordained a priest of the Roman Catholic Church. In June he
       was assigned as curate to the parish of Christ the King (St.
       Praxides in his stories) in Beverly Hills on the south-west side of
       Chicago.

1956   Published his first writings, two short stories, in the Catholic teen
       magazine *Hightime* using the pseudonym Laurence Moran, his
       confirmation and middle names. At this time was a member of the
       Sunday Night Group of "Catholic action" clergy. Also served as
       chaplain to Catholic Family Movement and Young Catholic
       Students groups.

1959   His first book, *The Church and the Suburbs*, was published.

1960   Assigned to part-time work toward the M.A. degree in sociology
       at the University of Chicago by Cardinal Albert Meyer. Con-
       sultant, Chicago Archdiocesan Conservation Council.

1961 Earned the M.A. degree in sociology, University of Chicago. Thesis: "Some aspects of interaction between religious groups in an upper middle class Roman Catholic parish."

1962 Earned the Ph.D. degree in sociology, University of Chicago. Thesis: "The influence of religion on the career plans and occupational values of June 1961 college graduates." Began work as senior study director at the National Opinion Research Center (NORC) of the University of Chicago, until 1968, while still serving as curate at Christ the King parish. Co-editor of *Apostolate*.

1963 Lecturer in sociology, University of Chicago, until 1972.

1964 Attended the third session of the Second Vatican Council as an observer and tourist. About this time his ill-fated small group church was formed.

1965 Released from parish work by Cardinal Meyer, and assigned to full-time work at NORC. Became associate editor of *Review of Religious Research*. Purchased a summer house in Grand Beach, Michigan.

1966 Published **The Education of Catholic Americans** which, after stories in *Time* and the *New York Times* and the resulting controversy, made him something of a national figure. In January, began his weekly column in the Catholic press which ran until January 1983. President American Catholic Sociological Society. Member of The Committee on the Student in Higher Education of the Hazen Foundation.

1968 In April, named program director in higher education at NORC, until 1970. Was appointed to the editorial boards of the *Journal of Higher Education*, *Concilium* until 1978, and the Confraternity of Christian Doctrine.

1969 Published **Why Can't They Be Like Us? facts and fallacies about ethnic differences and group conflicts in America**, reflecting his growing interest in ethnicity and ecumenical work with the American Jewish Committee. Professor of Higher Education at

University of Illinois, Chicago Circle, to March 1971. In March began the study of American priests for the National Conference of Catholic Bishops (NCCB). Named to editorial board of *Sociological Analysis*. Member planning committee National Conference on Higher Education; advisory committee on campus unrest and change, American Sociological Assn.; advisory committee for white ethnic groups, American Jewish Committee; Board of Trustees, Fontbonne College.

1970 Member National Public Advisory Committee on Regional Economic Development, U. S. Department of Commerce. Associate member Center for the Scientific Study of Religion.

1971 Founded the Center for the Study of American Pluralism at NORC. Member Board of Trustees Rosary College.

1972 Published *The Catholic Priest in the United States: sociological investigations* and *Priests in the United States: reflections on a survey*, the results of the priests' survey. Travelled to Australia to give a lecture series before the Eucharistic Congress in Melbourne. Breakup of his small group church.

1973 Around the world lecture tour for the U. S. State Department.

1974 In April, founded the journal, *Ethnicity*, and served as its first editor. In July, began his syndicated column in the secular press which ran until 1983. Series editor Sage Research Papers in the Social Sciences, Studies in Religion and Ethnicity.

1975 Began the research for *The Making of the Popes, 1978: the politics of intrigue in the Vatican* with many trips to Rome during the next three years.

1976 Published *Catholic Schools in a Declining Church*, which he has called "my most famous (or notorious) sociological work." Also published his first fiction book, *Nora Maeve and Sebi*, a children's story.

1978 Travelled to Rome to report on the two papal conclaves.

1979   Published his first novel, *The Magic Cup: an Irish legend*, and his first book of poetry, *Women I've Met*. Professor of Sociology, University of Arizona in Tucson for the winter semesters to date.

1981   Published *The Cardinal Sins*, the first of many best-selling novels. The controversy surrounding it brought him unwanted celebrity and he became a TV personality. His private files at Rosary College were "violated."

1984   Donated $1.5 million to the University of Chicago for a chair in Catholic studies named for his mother and father, Grace McNichols Greeley and Andrew Thomas Greeley.

1985   Research associate, Center for the Study of Politics and Society, NORC, to date.

1986   Published *Confessions of a Parish Priest: an autobiography*. In July began a weekly column in the *Chicago Sun-Times* which ran until October 1993. Created the $1 million Catholic Inner-City School Fund to provide scholarships for minority students in Chicago.

1988   In March, four sessions of the Popular Culture Association Meeting in New Orleans were devoted to his fiction. *The Incarnate Imagination: essays in theology, the arts and social sciences*, ed. by Ingrid H. Shafer, a festschrift in honor of his 60th birthday was published. Also in March, the first performance of *The Magic Cup*, an opera adapted from his first novel, composed by Edward McKenna, for which he wrote the libretto.

1991   Professor of Social Science, University of Chicago.

HONORS AND AWARDS

Thomas Alva Edison Award for radio broadcast on the *Catholic Hour* of excerpts from *Strangers in the House: Catholic Youth in America.* 1962.

Catholic Press Association Award for best book of the year for young people, for *Letters to Nancy: from Andrew M. Greeley.* 1965.

St. Joseph's College (Indiana) Honorary Doctor of Laws Degree. 1967.

St. Mary's College (Minnesota) Honorary Doctor of Letters Degree. 1967.

Thomas More Medal for the most distinguished contribution to Catholic literature. 1972.

Chosen by the editors of Interchurch Features as one of the eleven most influential Christian leaders. 1974.

St. Elizabeth Seton Award for the U. S. Catholic judged to have made the most important contribution to the promotion of Catholic education. 1976.

C. Albert Koob Award, National Catholic Education Association's highest honor. 1977.

Catholic Press Association Award for best Catholic column. 1977.

Thomas More Medal for the most distinguished contribution to Catholic literature, for *The American Catholic: a social portrait.* 1977.

Catholic Press Association Award for best short story, for "Ms. Carpenter." 1978.

Advertising Communications Times Accolade for professionalism in communications. 1983.

Bowling Green State University (Ohio). Honorary Doctor of Humane Letters Degree. 1986.

Mark Twain Award of the Society for the Study of Middle Western Literature. 1987.

Friends of the Chicago Public Library, Freedom to Read Award. 1989.

St. Louis University (Missouri). Honorary Doctor of Humanities Degree. 1991.

Northern Michigan University (Michigan). Honorary Doctor of Humane Letters Degree. 1993.

U. S. Catholic Award for Furthering the Cause of Women in the Church. 1993.

College of Lake County, Illinois, Outstanding Citizen Award. 1993.

ABBREVIATIONS

Assn.	Association
Dept.	Department
cm.	centimeter
ed.	edition, editor, edited
eds.	editions, editors
et al.	and others
G	Andrew Greeley
i.e.	that is
ms.	manuscript
NCCB	National Conference of Catholic Bishops
n.d.	no date
n.m.	no month
n.n.	no number
NORC	National Opinion Research Center
n.p.	no pagination, no place, no publisher
n.t.	no time
n.v.	no volume
n.y.	no year
p.	page
pp.	pages
q.v.	which see
rev.	revised
Univ.	University
vol.	volume
vols.	volumes
(251)	refers to code number assigned to each entry
*	item not seen by compiler

PART ONE:

PRIMARY SOURCES

CHAPTER ONE

BOOKS

NON-FICTION

1   *The Church and the Suburbs.* New York: Sheed & Ward, 1959.
    Parts appeared in *America, Ave Maria, Catholic World,
    Commonweal, Sign, Worship.*
        Rev. ed. New York: Paulist, 1963. *
    Nihil Obstat: Frederick E. Hillenbrand. Censor Deputatus.
    Imprimatur: Albert G. Meyer. Archbishop of Chicago.
    Chicago, June 8, 1959.
    Drawing from his experience as a curate in Christ the King parish
    in Chicago, G outlines some of the problems in suburbia:
    materialism, the family, community, leisure, liturgy, social
    action, "and their implication for the Catholic Church."

2   *Strangers in the House: Catholic youth in America.* New York:
    Sheed & Ward, 1961.
    Parts appeared in *America, The Critic, Marriage, Sign, Worship.*
        Rev. ed. Garden City, NY: Image, 1967. Paperbound. *
    Nihil Obstat: John A. McMahon. Censor Deputatus.
    Imprimatur: Albert Cardinal Meyer. Archbishop of Chicago.
    13 September 1960.
    In an attempt to initiate discussion on the subject, G presents his
    look at youth of the 1960 era. He discusses apathy, loss of self,
    the search for identity, as well as practical problems such as "why
    they drink . . . cheat . . . go steady." Bibliographical References.

3   *Religion and Career: a study of college graduates.* New York:
    Sheed & Ward, 1963.
    Published version of dissertation, "The influence of religion on
    the career plans and occupational values of June 1961 college
    graduates."

3

Nihil Obstat: Rt. Rev. Msgr. John A. McMahon. Censor
Librorum.
Imprimatur: Rt. Rev. Msgr. George J. Casey. Vicar General.
May 25, 1963.
Using data gathered by NORC from a survey of 40,000 seniors
graduating in June 1961, the author pursues "an investigation of
the alleged anti-intellectualism of American Catholics and an
explanation of the differences among the three major American
religious groups on certain dependent variables." His findings
question the myth that American Catholics cannot "do as well
. . . intellectually as other Americans." Appendixes include the
two survey questionnaires used (1961 and 1962) and 55 pages of
tables. Tables.

4   *And Young Men Shall See Visions: letters from Andrew M.
       Greeley.* New York: Sheed & Ward, 1964.
           Reprint. Garden City, NY: Image, 1968. Paperbound. *
       Nihil Obstat: Thomas F. Sullivan. Censor Librorium.
       Imprimatur: Cletus F. O'Donnell, D.D. Vicar General.
       July 10, 1963.
       Sixteen letters to a young man, John, which comprise "an essay
       in practical ascetics" and in which G presents his prescription for
       "a spiritual program or wisdom" for the Catholic layman. A
       companion volume to *Letters to Nancy: from Andrew M.
       Greeley.*

5   *Letters to Nancy: from Andrew M. Greeley.* New York: Sheed
       & Ward, 1964.
           Rev. ed. Garden City, NY: Image, 1967. Paperbound. *
       Nihil Obstat: Thomas F. Sullivan. Censor Librorum.
       Imprimatur: Cletus F. O'Donnell, D.D.
       July 10, 1963.
       Seventeen letters addressed to the young women of the 1960s in
       which the author remonstrates, prescribes and challenges as he
       presents his vision of the future for the dedicated Catholic
       laywoman. Winner of the 1965 Catholic Press Award for best
       book of the year for young people. A companion volume to *And
       Young Men Shall See Visions: letters from Andrew M. Greeley.*

6   *Priests for Tomorrow.* Notre Dame, IN: Ave Maria, 1964.

Parts appeared in *Ave Maria*.
Nihil Obstat: John L. Reedy, D.D. Censor Deputatus.
Imprimatur: Most Rev. Leo A. Pursley, D.D. Bishop of Fort
Wayne-South Bend.
March 1964.
In this brief booklet, G speaks to young priests, seminarians and
"to all alert Christians" (from the introduction) about the
problems and challenges to be faced. These include the virtues of
patience, chastity, poverty, obedience, as well as broader topics
such as professional competence and maturity. Recommended
Reading List.

7   *I Am with You*. Learn of Me Series. High School Confraternity
     Program: Book 4. Morristown, NJ: Silver Burdett, 1965. (NUC
     89-59731). *

8   and Peter H. Rossi. *The Education of Catholic Americans.*
     NORC Monographs in Social Research 6. Chicago: Aldine,
     1966.
     Reprint. Garden City, NY: Doubleday, 1968. Paperbound. *
     G and Rossi, his colleague and mentor, present a landmark study
     of the condition and effects of the American parochial school
     system. Both sides of the controversial question are considered
     with empirical objectivity using data from a two-year national
     survey by NORC. Extensive Tables. Bibliography. Index.

9   *The Hesitant Pilgrim: American Catholicism after the Council.*
     New York: Sheed & Ward, 1966. *
     Reprint. Garden City, NY: Image, 1969. Paperbound.
     Parts appeared in *America, Commonweal, The Critic, Homiletic
     & Pastoral Review, Sign.*
     A discussion from G's sociological viewpoint of, first, the
     American Catholic Church as institution including collegial
     authority, the pastor-curate relationship, and religious orders. And
     second, of American Catholic intellectual life and education. G's
     foreword is highly personal.

10   *The Catholic Experience: an interpretation of the history of
     American Catholicism.* Garden City, NY: Doubleday, 1967.
     Reprint. Garden City, NY: Image, 1969. Paperbound.
     Reprint. Garden City, NY: Doubleday, 1967. Microfilm

87/4001 (B). *
The author presents, from a sociological viewpoint, "a systematic treatment of major themes . . . with the necessary elimination of much detail," in the history of the American Catholic Church. Contains a chapter on "the Chicago experience" from the late thirties to the mid-sixties in which G himself played a small part.

11   *The Changing Catholic College.* NORC Monographs in Social Research 13. Chicago: Aldine, 1967.
With the assistance of William Van Cleve and Grace Ann Carroll. An investigation of thirty Catholic and six non-Catholic colleges and universities using data personally gathered by G and his team and from earlier NORC studies. It is an attempt to explain how and why Catholic colleges are changing and to what degree they are improving. Faculty, administration and students were studied and the conclusion reached that the leadership role of the president is paramount. An appendix presents "the objective correlates of academic improvement." Tables. Bibliography. Index.

12   *The Crucible of Change: the social dynamics of pastoral practice.* New York: Sheed & Ward, 1968.
From a sociological perspective, the author presents questions about, and problems in, pastoral work. He discusses the church in relation to society, community (including "the New Community"), its people, and the future, ending with his own "vision of the parish of the future."

13   *The Student in Higher Education.* New Haven, CT: Hazen Foundation, 1968. Paperbound.
Report of The Committee on the Student in Higher Education of the Hazen Foundation.
The Committee's Foreword states "Andrew M. Greeley . . . prepared the final draft of this report."
"This report was written to bring attention to the possibility of developmental higher education and to suggest the style and method with which colleges ought to attempt the possible." The Committee presents their concept of "education for individual development" (Nevitt Sanford) and some recommendations for implementing it.

14 *Uncertain Trumpet: the priest in modern America.* New York:
Sheed & Ward, 1968.
Adapted from retreats at Cardinal Stritch Retreat House.
Nihil Obstat: Leo J. Steady. Censor Librorum
Imprimatur: Robert F. Joyce. Bishop of Burlington.
October 3, 1967.
G presents "ideas for priestly reflection . . . consideration and
discussion" on subjects such as "the quest for maturity, learning
in the life of the priest, the priest and freedom, the priest and the
spiritual life, the priest and women."

15 Martin E. Marty and Stuart E. Rosenberg. *What Do We
Believe?* New York: Meredith, 1968.
Nihil Obstat: Lawrence A. Beeson J.C.D. Censor Deputatus.
Imprimatur: L.V. Lyons. Administrator, Diocese of Des Moines,
June 25, 1968.
G joins Protestant and Jewish representatives in analyzing the
results of identical Gallup Polls in 1952 and 1965 and a study
conducted for *The Catholic Digest.* (169 pages of results are
appended.) Topics covered include interreligious attitudes, youth,
Catholic schools and secularization. Tables. Bibliographic
References.

16 *From Backwater to Mainstream: a profile of Catholic higher
education.* New York: McGraw-Hill, 1969.
With a foreword by Clark Kerr and a commentary by David
Riesman.
A look at the past, present and future of Catholic colleges and
universities in the U. S., including "atmosphere . . . goals . . .
problems . . . prospects" and a long chapter of pertinent statistics.
An appendix contains a list of 388 Catholic institutions of higher
learning in the United States. Tables. Bibliography. Index.

17 and Martin E. Marty. *The Future of the Christian Churches in
the 1970's.* Fort George G. Meade, MD: U. S. Army Chaplain
Board, 1969. Paperbound. Typescript.
G's report covers American Catholicism, present and past, and
looks to the future as he predicts what the mid-1970's hold for the
Church. He concludes with advice for the military chaplain
dealing with young people in the middle seventies. Marty
envisions Protestantism in 1975. Tables. Bibliography.

18   *A Future to Hope In: socio-religious speculations.* Garden City,
        NY: Doubleday, 1969.
        Reprint. Garden City, NY: Image, 1970. Paperbound.
        "With very broad strokes" G outlines current problems of
        leadership, education, sex, community, work and play. He then
        prescribes his modest solutions as he pictures the possibilities for
        the future of society and the Church.

19   *Life for a Wanderer.* Garden City, NY: Doubleday, 1969.
        Reprint. Garden City, NY: Image, 1971. Paperbound. *
        "a series of reflections on what the Christian life seems to me to
        mean in the contemporary world . . . seen . . . through the
        perspective of a social scientist" but "profoundly shaped by the
        wisdom of years gone by." G presents his interpretation of the
        traditional concepts: faith, hope, charity, poverty, chastity,
        obedience, justice, temperance, fortitude and prudence.

20   *Religion in the Year 2000.* New York: Sheed & Ward, 1969.
        G considers what sociology sees for the future of religion,
        theology, the liturgy, clergy and churches. Using empirical
        evidence as well as theory he rejects the "secularization"
        hypothesis so prevalent at this time. Tables. Bibliographic
        References.

21   *Teenage World: its crises and anxieties.* Techny, IL: Divine
        Word, [1969]. Paperbound.
        A discussion of adolescence in which G delineates the inherent
        problems of that age group: peer pressure, religion, sex and
        drinking. He provides some general solutions, principally more
        parental responsibility and more enlightened instruction.

22   *Why Can't They Be Like Us? Facts and fallacies about ethnic
        differences and group conflicts in America.* Pamphlet Series
        Number 12. New York: Institute of Human Relations. American
        Jewish Committee, 1969. Paperbound.
        A new version published in 1971.
        Some chapters reprinted in *The White Majority, White Ethnics*,
        and *Overcoming Middle Class Rage*.
        In the foreword to this short study of ethnicity in the United
        States, Robert C. Wood describes G's work: "he provides
        definitions, concepts and statistics that define the essentials of the

contemporary ethnic condition . . . " and "takes us through an estimate of the current situation." Tables. Bibliographic References.

23 *A Fresh Look at Vocations.* Chicago: Claretian, 197?. (NUC 76-58623.) *

24 and William E. Brown. *Can Catholic Schools Survive?* New York: Sheed & Ward, 1970.
G contributes the 45 page Part I: a theology of Catholic education in the 1970s, in which he uses " 'education' in the narrow sense of the word, equating it with schools." He outlines the "crisis in Catholic education" and new directions for it under the headings innovation, love and comedy. Costs and financing of Catholic schools are tabled in six appendixes. Tables.

25 *The Friendship Game.* Garden City, NY: Doubleday, 1970. Reprint. Garden City, NY: Image, 1971. Paperbound. *
The author explores the possibilities and risks, the difficulties and pleasures, involved in friendship relationships including marriage. "My reflections are based in part on traditional wisdom (of the Christian Catholic variety), in part on the insights of social science, and in part . . . on my own experience."

26 *The Life of the Spirit (Also the Mind, the Heart, the Libido).* Kansas City, MO: National Catholic Reporter, 1970. Paperbound.
A version appeared in *National Catholic Reporter.*
A brief volume of essays adapted from G's column in the *National Catholic Reporter.* In an informal and common-sensible manner he discusses the Holy Spirit in five sections which cover: too busy, self-respect, other people, the people of God and the clergy.

27 *New Horizons for the Priesthood.* New York: Sheed & Ward, 1970.
Adapted from retreats at Cardinal Stritch Retreat House.
A short examination of the future of the priesthood through the virtues, such as hope, prudence, leadership, tolerance and enthusiasm, which will be required of priests in that future.

28   and Joe L. Spaeth. *Recent Alumni and Higher Education: a survey of college graduates.* New York: McGraw-Hill, 1970. With a commentary by Theodore M. Hesburgh.
Results and analysis of surveys of 40,000 graduates of 135 colleges and universities conducted by NORC from 1961 to 1968 to determine their views on higher education in general and their own colleges in particular. Tables. Bibliography.

29   *Youth Asks, Does God Still Speak?* Youth Forum Series. Camden, NJ: Thomas Nelson, 1970. Paperbound.
Writing for young people, G presents four "confused and overlapping issues": the graciousness of being, God, religion, and the Church. He then asks them to consider: "Does life have purpose, goodness, and beauty, or is it all a meaningless charade?" Bibliographical References.

30   *Come Blow Your Mind with Me.* Garden City, NY: Doubleday, 1971.
Parts appeared in *The Critic, Living Light, National Catholic Reporter, New York Times, Social Research, Sociological Analysis.*
A collection of essays dealing with the "mind-blowing" in the Catholic Church in the 1960s. In them, G outlines the need for humanly significant leadership and the importance of friendship. He concludes that if orthodoxy prevails "the mind-blowers will be a temporary aberration." Chapter 8 was originally given as part of the Thomas More Lectures at Yale University in 1970. Chapter 10 was G's presidential address to the American Catholic Sociological Society.

31   *Complaints against God.* Chicago: Thomas More, 1971. Paperbound. *
A new version published in 1989 *q.v.* for annotation.

32   *The Jesus Myth.* Garden City, NY: Doubleday, 1971.
Reprint. Garden City, NY: Image, 1971. Paperbound. *
Reprinted in *Myths of Religion* in 1989.
Defining myth in the social science sense as "a symbolic story which demonstrates . . . 'the inner meaning of the universe and of human life'," G presents "a popular description of the work of scripture scholars on the core of Jesus's message contained in the

parables." His reflections center on the life, teaching and personality of Jesus.

33   *The Touch of the Spirit.* New York: Herder and Herder, 1971.
Nihil Obstat: Leo J. Steady.
Imprimatur: Robert F. Joyce.
Burlington, July 27, 1971.
A series of spiritual reflections on the Spirit, commitment, community, sin and guilt, "based on a series of columns on spirituality . . . done for the *National Catholic Reporter.*"

34   *What a Modern Catholic Believes about God.* Chicago: Thomas More, 1971. Paperbound.
A part reprinted in *An Andrew Greeley Reader Vol.1.*
In this brief volume, the first of the Thomas More series *What a Modern Catholic Believes* . . . , G writes "about the 'images' of God and their implications" in chapters on The Father, The Son, and The Holy Spirit. He asserts "that God is man's mythological way of stating his faith about the nature of reality." (*See also What a Modern Catholic Believes about the Church.*)

35   *Why Can't They Be like Us? America's white ethnic groups.*
New York: Dutton, 1971.
Reprint. New York: Dutton, 1971. Book Club ed. *Psychology Today.* *
Reprint. New York: Dutton, 1975. Paperbound. *
An earlier version published in 1969 *q.v.* for annotation.

36   *The Catholic Priest in the United States: sociological investigations.* Washington, DC: United States Catholic Conference. Publications Office, 1972.
Erratum insert: "This entire report is the work of the National Opinion Research Center. The name of Reverend Andrew Greeley appears on the dust jacket and title page through an error."
One part of a study commissioned by the Committee on Pastoral Research and Practices of the National Conference of Catholic Bishops in 1967 which also includes theological, historical and psychological investigations. Directed by G, the study is "a description and analysis of the life and ministry of Roman Catholic priests in the United States of America." "This is a

research monograph, not a series of policy recommendations, and much less a political treatise." Includes main and resignee questionnaires. When asked about the erratum insert, G replied "it was agreed that no one's name would appear on the cover. Somebody at the bishops' office goofed up and put my name on it anyway. In fact, I wrote the whole report." Tables. Figures. Bibliography. Index.

37   *The Denominational Society: a sociological approach to religion in America.* Glenview, IL: Scott Foresman, 1972.
In this study of denominationalism in America the author attempts to improve our understanding of "the complex relationships between the denominations and the larger social structures . . . from a sociological perspective . . . " and thus our understanding of American religion. He examines the nature, function and organization of religion, as well as ethnicity and secularization, ending with a chapter of theories and predictions. Tables. Bibliography. Index.

38   *Jesus Now: meditations by a modern pilgrim.* Chicago: Thomas More, 1972.
Published anonymously.
Reprinted from *Markings*.
A part reprinted in *An Andrew Greeley Reader Vol.I.*

39   *Priests in the United States: reflections on a survey.* Garden City, NY: Doubleday, 1972.
G reflects on the study of the priesthood done by NORC for the NCCB (36). Under various topics: spirituality, celibacy, authority, morale, to name only a few, he provides 1) a summary of factual data from the report, 2) his own "speculations . . . about the causes, implications, and likely future effects of our findings," and 3) his personal policy recommendations. Tables.

40   *The Sinai Myth.* Garden City, NY: Doubleday, 1972. *
Reprint. Garden City, NY: Image, 1975. Paperbound.
Reprinted in *Myths of Religion* in 1989.
This, and *The Jesus Myth*, are, as Philip Gleason states in his review article "Greeley Watching," "personal syntheses of New and Old Testament themes developed from a reading of contemporary biblical scholarship." In *The Sinai Myth* G

discusses the experience of God on Sinai, and the Ten Commandments, emphasizing the importance of the first three. He reflects on the religious symbols in Exodus, Chapters 19 and 20, and their meaning. Bibliographical References.

41 *That Most Distressful Nation: the taming of the American Irish.* New York: Quadrangle, 1972.
Reprint. New York: Quadrangle, 1972. Paperbound. *
Foreword by Daniel P. Moynihan.
Parts appeared in *The Critic, Dissent, New Republic, New York Times Magazine.*
The author begins with historical background, the Celtic heritage, and the Irish American immigrant experience. Following are sociological discussions of politics, family and changing neighborhoods (a profile of Beverly in Chicago). Tables. Index.

42 *Unsecular Man: the persistence of religion.* New York: Schocken, 1972.
Rev. ed. New York: Schocken, 1985. With a new introduction by the author. Paperbound.
Reprint. New York: Dell, 1974. Paperbound. *
Reprint. *The Persistence of Religion.* London: S.C.M., 1973. *
"A volume of dissent" in which G, using sociology's research and theory, refutes the conventional wisdom of the day and identifies ∙ his understanding of human religious needs in areas such as faith, sex, community, leadership. Bibliographical References. Index.

43 *What a Modern Catholic Believes about the Church.* Chicago: Thomas More, 1972.
A part reprinted in *An Andrew Greeley Reader Vol.I.*
This is "an empirical book about the Church" in which the author discusses its relationship with God's Kingdom (or Power, to use the more modern term), the Vatican Council, and looks at "the Church as the People of God and as the Body of Christ." G tells of his own two parishes, St. Ursula and St. Praxides, and asserts that "the Spirit is capable of working through them."

44 *The New Agenda: a proposal for a new approach to fundamental issues in contemporary times.* Garden City, NY: Doubleday, 1973.

Reprint. Garden City, NY: Image, 1975. Paperbound. *
With a foreword by Gregory Baum.
One of G's most important books. In it, he does not provide new
answers to the old apologetic questions on matters such as faith,
community, ritual, education or sexuality, but presents entirely
new questions and the Christian responses to them. Baum's
foreword explains and critiques this new agenda.

45   and Gregory Baum, eds. *The Persistence of Religion.*
        Concilium: 81. New York: Herder and Herder, 1973.
        A collection of essays published by *Concilium*. G, senior editor,
        is on the Editorial Committee (Sociology of Religion) and the
        Editorial Board. His essay, "The Persistence of Community,"
        describes the communitarian movement, its dangers and how
        churches should respond to it. Not to be confused with the
        English edition of *Unsecular Man* which bears the same title.

46   *Sexual Intimacy.* Chicago: Thomas More, 1973.
        Reprint. New York: Seabury, 1975. Paperbound.
        Reprinted with *Love and Play* in 1988.
        A part reprinted in *An Andrew Greeley Reader Vol.I.*
        A lengthy essay "on the meaning of human sexuality" which the
        author states is "neither a sex manual nor a treatise on sexual
        ethics." In it he deals with concerns such as fidelity, conflict,
        friendship, reconciliation, and risk-taking as he relates them to the
        "Christian symbol system." Continued in *Love and Play.*

47   *Building Coalitions: American politics in the 1970s.* New York:
        New Viewpoints, 1974. Paperbound.
        Reprint. London: Croom Helm, 1974. *
        Reprint. London: Croom Helm, 1974. Paperbound. *
        A lengthy analysis of early 1970s American politics, largely
        Democratic, in which G advocates a return to "the reformist
        Democratic coalition inaugurated by Franklin Roosevelt" which,
        he says, must include the white ethnic working class. Tables.
        Index.

48   and Gregory Baum, eds. *The Church as Institution. Concilium*:
        91. New York: Herder and Herder, 1974.
        Reprint. New York: Seabury, 1974. *
        There is no contribution by G in this collection of thirteen essays

on the sociology of religion published by *Concilium*. G is a
member of the Editorial Committee (Sociology of Religion) and
the Editorial Board.

49   *The Devil, You Say! Man and his personal devils and angels.*
New York: Doubleday, 1974.
   Reprint. New York: Doubleday, 1976. Paperbound. *
   A version appeared in *New York Times Magazine*.
   G reflects on the mystery of evil. He examines human
weaknesses, the demons of today, and suggests angels which can
help overcome them. The greatest of these is the "Demon of
Fear," but he can be overpowered by the "Angel of Hope."

50   *Ecstasy: a way of knowing.*   Englewood Cliffs, NJ: Prentice-
Hall, 1974.
   Reprint. Englewood Cliffs, NJ: Prentice-Hall, 1974.
   Paperbound.
   An attempt "to provide a preliminary perspective for the study
and understanding of the ecstatic experience." The relationships
between mysticism and creative experience, madness, faddism and
Christianity are explored and examples of mystical experiences
included. Appendixes contain the questions asked in a national
survey and a list of Arnold Ludwig's altered states of
consciousness. Index.

51   *Ethnicity in the United States: a preliminary reconnaissance.*
Wiley Series in Urban Research. New York: John Wiley, 1974.
G reports on the two years of work at NORC's Center for the
Study of American Pluralism under an agreement with the Ford
Foundation. He begins a study of diversity in American society
and lays a foundation for further research in the field. William C.
McCready, Norman H. Nie and Barbara Currie make substantial
contributions. Tables. Extensive Bibliography. Index.

52   *Good News: further reflections by a modern pilgrim.*   Chicago:
Thomas More, 1974.
   Published anonymously.
   A version appeared in *Markings*.
   A part reprinted in *An Andrew Greeley Reader Vol.I.*

53   and Douglas J. Zeman. *Media: ethnic media in the United*

States. Hanover, NH: Project IMPRESS, 1974. Paperbound.
Typescript.
The two principal investigators present the data from a survey of
731 people from five ethnic media groups: Black, Spanish,
Italian, Polish and German. Subject areas covered were: demo-
graphics of the work force, news gathering and reporting, and
attitudes toward work. There is no analysis or commentary.

54   *Love and Play.* Chicago: Thomas More, 1975.
       Reprint. New York: Seabury, 1977. Paperbound.
       Reprint. London: W.H. Allen, 1984.
       Reprinted with *Sexual Intimacy* in 1988.
       A part reprinted in *An Andrew Greeley Reader Vol.I.*
       In this continuation of G's *Sexual Intimacy* he emphasizes the
       importance of playfulness and laughter in marital relations. He
       concludes with "Love is play; play is love. Both defy death."

55   *May the Wind Be at Your Back: the prayer of St. Patrick.* New
       York: Seabury, 1975. Paperbound.
       With photographs by the author.
       A series of nine personal meditations prompted by early Irish
       poems by St. Patrick, St. Brigid and St. Columcille. Photographs
       by the author are not labeled, but some are obviously of Ireland
       and Chicago.

56   *The Sociology of the Paranormal: a reconnaissance.* Sage
       Research Papers in the Social Sciences No. 90-023. Beverly
       Hills, CA: Sage, 1975. Paperbound.
       G studies paranormal, i.e., "psychic, mystic, and contact with the
       dead experiences, as they are described in the questions . . .
       asked in the NORC-Luce Foundation Basic Belief Study."
       (Questions included.) He finds that "the paranormal is normal"
       and that those who have such experiences are neither "sick" nor
       "deviants" nor "kooks." Paranormal experiences may be one way
       of dealing with "the fatal illness of life" and thus, G says, "are
       legitimate matters for social research." Tables. Figures.
       Bibliography.

57   William C. McCready and Kathleen McCourt. *Catholic Schools
       in a Declining Church.* Kansas City, MO: Sheed & Ward,
       1976.
       An updating of the 1963 NORC study which formed the basis for

The Education of Catholic Americans. It was done eleven years later in 1974 reflecting the changes in the post Vatican II Church. G calls it "my most famous (or notorious) sociological work." He presents his personal conclusions in an afterword. Questionnaires from the 1963 and 1974 NORC studies in Appendix II and III. Tables. Figures. Bibliography.

58   *The Communal Catholic: a personal manifesto.* New York: Seabury, 1976.
Parts in *National Catholic Reporter, New York Times, Public Interest.*
G sees the communal Catholic, one who is "strongly identified with the Catholic community but . . . rather uninterested in the organized church," as "probably the single best hope the church has of responding creatively to the crisis it presently faces." He deals with their problems, the resources available in the Catholic heritage and tradition, and describes "the kind of church which I think the communal Catholic would find attractive."

59   *Death and Beyond.* Chicago: Thomas More, 1976. Paperbound.
A part reprinted in *An Andrew Greeley Reader Vol.I.*
G discusses "limit--or horizon--experience . . . reassurance and reflection" as he contemplates death and life after death. Included are statistics on belief in life after death and contact with the dead experiences. Tables. Bibliographic References.

60   *Ethnicity, Denomination and Inequality.* Sage Research Papers in the Social Sciences No. 90-029. Studies in Religion and Ethnicity, edited by Andrew M. Greeley. Beverly Hills, CA: Sage, 1976.
The author discusses the question of inequality in the denominational, pluralist United States and analyzes data from twelve NORC surveys to show the surprising success of Polish, Italian and Slavic Catholics and the reversal of the Protestant ethic theory. He concludes that "we . . . can no longer afford to ignore the relationship between subculture and achievement. . . ." Tables. Bibliography.

61   *The Great Mysteries: an essential catechism.* New York: Seabury, 1976. *
Reprint. New York: Seabury, 1976. Paperbound.

Reprinted in 1985 with a new introduction by the author.
G presents the catechism in a new form as he deals with twelve
" . . . *great mysteries*, the core revelatory images of the Christian
tradition." Included is a "Guide for Discussion and Personal
Meditation" for each mystery. Recommended Reading List.

62   and William C. McCready. *The Ultimate Values of the
        American Population.* Sage Library of Social Research Vol. 23.
        Beverly Hills, CA: Sage, 1976. Paperbound.
        The authors report on ultimate values under several headings:
        typology, demography, familial background and relationships to
        religious and social behavior, the paranormal, quality of life, and
        value-oriented education. Appendix A contains the NORC
        Interview Schedule. Tables. Bibliographical References.

63   *The American Catholic: a social portrait.* New York: Basic,
        1977.
        Reprint. New York: Basic, 1977. Paperbound.
        "This book represents the summary of fifteen years of research
        on the latter stages of the acculturation of the Catholic ethnic
        immigrant groups into American society." G presents a landmark
        sociological study of the life of American Catholics in chapters on
        political behavior, prejudice, clergy, schools, family and others.
        Tables. Figures. Bibliographical References. Index.

64   and Nancy McCready. *Christ for All Seasons: fifty-two personal
        meditations.* Chicago: Thomas More, 1977.
        A version appeared in *Jesus Lives.*
        Weekly readings, following the four seasons, for meditation in an
        ordinary day-to-day environment.

65   and Gregory Baum, eds. *Ethnicity. Concilium*: 101. New
        York: Seabury, 1977.
        In an editorial, G summarizes the sociological data contained in
        the first section and comments briefly on ethnic heritage and
        diversity. Baum summarizes the theological essays in the second
        part. Tables. Bibliographical References.

66   *The Mary Myth: on the femininity of God.* New York: Seabury,
        1977.
        Reprinted in *Myths of Religion* in 1989.

G considers this one of his most important books in the development of his sociology of religion. With emphasis on art and poetry, he explores the religious symbolism of Mary as he develops a paradigm " . . . that represents four aspects of the Mary myth--Madonna, Sponsa, Virgo, and Pieta. . . . " He includes several original poems and classic illustrations of Marian and pagan art. Plates. Bibliographic References. Extensive Notes.

67   *Neighborhood.* New York: Seabury, 1977.
Based on his "social science research and theorizing on the subject" the author's "passionate defense of" neighborhoods looks at St. Angela's, Beverly, Bridgeport and the Stanislowowo, all in Chicago. From their beginnings, through the problems of urban renewal, to the possibilities for their future, he counters the prevailing wisdom and makes his case for neighborhoods. Includes G's photographs of Chicago. Bibliography.

68   *No Bigger than Necessary: an alternative to socialism, capitalism and anarchism.* New York: New American Library, 1977. Paperbound.
G continues Schumacher's *Small Is Beautiful* discussion. His alternative focuses on small, natural groups, e.g., neighborhood and family, and outlines Catholic social theory and its implications. Bibliographical References. Index.

69   *An Ugly Little Secret: anti-Catholicism in North America.* Kansas City, KA: Sheed, Andrews & McMeel, 1977.
A discussion of "the last remaining unexposed prejudice in American life, anti-Catholic nativism" which includes its history, some causes, and a chapter of examples. Chapter 6 contains the text of a controversial paper commissioned by the American Jewish Committee and delivered by G at its annual meeting in 1976. Bibliographical References.

70   and Gregory Baum, eds. *Communication in the Church. Concilium*: 111. New York: Seabury, 1978.
Papers presented at the 1977 annual meeting of the Editorial Board of *Concilium* at the Catholic Univ. of Notre Dame, South Bend, IN.
In G's contribution to this collection of essays, "The communal Catholic, the two churches: fitting a model," he discusses the

significance of the "new voluntarism" for the American Catholic Church. Using NORC data, he explains who the "neighbourhood communal Catholics" are, and declares that there is "a major communication 'gap' . . . " between them and the leadership of the Church. Table.

71 *Everything You Wanted to Know about the Catholic Church But Were Too Pious to Ask.* Chicago: Thomas More, 1978.
Reprint. New York: Harper & Row, 1979. Paperbound. *
A part reprinted in *An Andrew Greeley Reader Vol.I.*
Serious answers to religious, moral and social questions ranging from abortion and authorship of the Bible to freemasonry and genetic engineering, given from a Catholic perspective as well as the official Church position, and, on occasion, the author's own opinion.

72 *Crisis in the Church: a study of religion in America.* Chicago: Thomas More, 1979.
A part reprinted in *An Andrew Greeley Reader Vol.I.*
G outlines various kinds of religious dissidence and other factors that might have an impact as he discusses evangelization in the United States. He concludes that "a new agenda for intimacy" in the Church is essential. Tables. Figures.

73 ed. *The Family in Crisis or in Transition: a sociological and theological perspective. Concilium*: 121. New York: Seabury, 1979.
G contributes a brief editorial to this collection of essays on the family by predominantly American, indeed Chicago, sociologists and theologians. In it he notes that it is poverty, not "modernization" which is leading to the collapse of family life. Tables. Figures. Bibliographies.

74 *Fifty-Two Gospel Meditations: by a modern pilgrim.* Chicago: Thomas More, 1979.
Published anonymously.
Reprinted from *Markings*.
A part reprinted in *An Andrew Greeley Reader Vol.I.*

75 *The Making of the Popes 1978: the politics of intrigue in the Vatican.* Kansas City, KS: Andrews & McMeel, 1979.
Reprint. Kansas City, KS: Andrews & McMeel, 1979. Book

Club ed. Book of the Month Club. *

G's analysis, researched in Rome for over three years, of the conclaves which elected Popes John Paul I and II. He describes and evaluates the election process and pictures Rome and its people in the time before, during and after the conclaves. Photographs of contenders, the author, and some of Rome taken by the author. Appendix A: "Sociological Rationale for Papal Job Description." Appendix B: "Acceptance Messages of John Paul I and John Paul II." Index.

76   William C. McCready and Gary Theisen. *Ethnic Drinking Subcultures.* New York: Praeger, 1980.

The authors deal with three subjects: alcohol consumption, ethnic diversity, socialization, and their inter-relationship. Using a "socialization model" and applying "an ethnic-group perspective" they provide valuable insights for those engaged in the treatment and study of alcoholism. Tables. Figures. Bibliography. Index.

77   *The Young Catholic Family: religious images and marriage fulfillment.* Chicago: Thomas More, 1980.   Paperbound. Typescript.

Using data collected in a Knights of Columbus survey of Catholic young adults, and "based on an emerging theory of the sociology of religion" G shows that "religion and religious imagery will affect marital satisfaction and sexual fulfillment." Appendix A contains survey questions.

78   *The Irish Americans: the rise to money and power.* New York: Harper & Row, 1981.

Reprint. New York: Warner, 1981. Paperbound.

G asks the question "How can the Irish (Catholics) be American and still continue to be Irish?" In early chapters he discusses the Celtic heritage and the Irish immigrant experience and then the "present condition of Irish Catholics in America" including achievement, family, religion, politics and a chapter on Irish-American writers. Index.

79   *et al. Parish, Priest and People: new leadership for the local church.* Chicago: Thomas More, 1981.

A part reprinted in *An Andrew Greeley Reader Vol.I.*

G joins three theologians and sociologist colleague McCready in a multi-disciplinary study (past, present, and future) of the neighborhood Church (Parish, People) and its leader (Priest). The conclusion includes policy recommendations. Bibliography.

80   *The Religious Imagination.*   New York: Sadlier, 1981. Paperbound.
       One of G's most important works. "An empirical study . . . which tests the theory set down in *Religion: a secular theory* . . ." using five NORC surveys. He outlines the "stories of God" inherent in the religious imagery of American Catholics and the implications these may have for the development of religious faith. Tables. Bibliography.

81   *et al.   Young Catholics in the United States and Canada: a report to the Knights of Columbus.* New York: Sadlier, 1981.
       The results and analysis of a major sociological survey of Catholics, aged 14-29. Areas covered include apostasy, marriage, religious imagery, education, vocations and political beliefs. Tables. Figures. Bibliographic References.

82   *The Bottom Line Catechism for Contemporary Catholics.* Chicago: Thomas More, 1982. Paperbound.
       Reprint. London: W.H. Allen, 1983.
       Another version in *Bottom Line*.
       A part reprinted in *An Andrew Greeley Reader Vol.I.*
       G asks what do you *have* to believe to be a Catholic Christian, or, as he prefers to say, "what are we *privileged* to believe." He poses such questions as "Are prayers of petition appropriate?" and "Are we 'obliged' to attend mass?" He then provides his answers, the bottom line, on sin, resurrection, love, justice and temperance, to name only a few of the areas covered.

83   *Catholic High Schools and Minority Students.* New Brunswick, NJ: Transaction, 1982.
       Using NORC data, complex mathematical models, and in cooperation with the High School and Beyond study team, G studies the effect of Catholic secondary schools on their Black and Hispanic students. He concludes that more discipline, better teaching, and religious order ownership of some schools contribute to the successful performance of these students. Tables. Figures.

84   and Mary G. Durkin. *A Church to Come Home To.* Chicago: Thomas More, 1982.
      A part reprinted in *An Andrew Greeley Reader Vol.I.*
      G and theologian Durkin outline reasons and forces which motivate those who return to the Church. They offer "models of the vision to come home to" in chapters on aging and death, community, marriage, family, women, and others.

85   *Love in the Gospels: by a modern pilgrim.* Chicago: Thomas More, 1982.
      Published anonymously.
      Reprinted from *Markings.*
      A part reprinted in *An Andrew Greeley Reader Vol.I.*

86   *Religion: a secular theory.* New York: Free Press, 1982.
      Reprint. New York: Free Press, 1982. Paperbound. *
      "reflections upon religion as experience and religion as story." G presents his sociological model of religion, "a provisional and incomplete description of religious reality. . . . " Selected items from NORC Questionnaire. Bibliography. Index.

87   *The Catholic WHY? Book.* Chicago: Thomas More, 1983.
      A part reprinted in *An Andrew Greeley Reader Vol.I.*
      G answers questions "for those Catholics who are caught between the pre-Vatican and post-Vatican church" on topics ranging from liberation theology, world poverty and birth control to confession, homosexuality and ecumenism.

88   *et al. The Dilemma of American Immigration: beyond the golden door.* New Brunswick, NJ: Transaction, 1983.
      Reprint. New Brunswick, NJ: Transaction, 1983. Paperbound. *
      G and three NORC colleagues examine U. S. immigration and refugee experience. They discuss the consequences of immigration procedures in relation to both foreign and domestic policy and conclude with recommendations. Bibliography. Index.

89   *A Piece of My Mind . . . on just about everything.* New York: Doubleday, 1983.
      Reprint. New York: Doubleday, 1983. Book Club ed. Literary Guild. *

A collection of G's syndicated newspaper columns which appeared between 1980 and 1982 on women, politics, religion, marriage, family and sex, priesthood, church, youth, and the Pope. Each subject has a new introduction by the author.

90   and Mary G. Durkin. *Angry Catholic Women: a sociological investigation Andrew M. Greeley a theological reflection Mary G. Durkin.* Chicago: Thomas More, 1984. Paperbound. Typescript.
A part reprinted in *An Andrew Greeley Reader Vol.I.*
An interdisciplinary study in which G contributes an analysis of data from NORC's annual General Social Survey and a study of young Catholic adults done in 1979, in an attempt to explain the disaffection of some Catholic women. Theologian Durkin then reflects on this analysis in chapters on the issues of sexuality, femininity, marriage, and the domestic Church. Tables. Figures. Bibliographical References.

91   and Mary G. Durkin. *How to Save the Catholic Church.* New York: Viking, 1984.
Preface by David Tracy.
G joins with theologian Mary Durkin to produce this "book about the Catholic sensibility, the Catholic poetic intuition, the Catholic religious imagination. . . ." They emphasize these unique features of Catholicism in discussions of sex, women, the parish, art, social theory and more, but do not repudiate existing doctrine and ethics or propose changes to them. G wrote nine of the fourteen chapters as well as the introduction and conclusion.

92   *American Catholics Since the Council: an unauthorized report.* Chicago: Thomas More, 1985. Paperbound. Typescript.
A part reprinted in *An Andrew Greeley Reader Vol.I.*
This report "about the present condition of American Catholics, . . . mostly . . . the laity," based on data collected over the twenty years since Vatican II, covers a wide spectrum from sex, politics, schools, to family, women, anti-Catholicism and the religious imagination. G, still wearing his sociologist's hat, concludes with his own "cautious recommendations." Figures.

93   *The Great Mysteries: an essential catechism.* San Francisco: Harper & Row, 1985. Paperbound.

With a new introduction by the author.
First published in 1976.
In the new introduction to this edition, G explains the reasoning inherent in the writing of the original book in 1976.

94   *Confessions of a Parish Priest: an autobiography.* New York: Simon & Schuster, 1986.
Rev. ed. New York: Pocket, 1987. Paperbound.
G's memoir is essential to the understanding of the author and his work. In it, as well as chronicling his life, he presents a look at American Catholic social history pre-Vatican II up to the mid-1980s. A number of original poems are included. The 1987 paperbound edition adds a partly new chapter "Celibacy and Sexuality," and some additional material on the "theft" of his private papers (pp. 454-455).

95   *An Andrew Greeley Reader Volume I.* Ed. by John Sprague. Chicago: Thomas More, 1987.
A collection of excerpts from G's books which were published by the Thomas More Press in the 1970s and 1980s, and two from *The Critic.* Subjects covered range from the modern Catholic Church and its teaching, the vocation and celibacy of priests, and the position of women in the Church, to Christian devotions and the Church of the future.

96   and William McManus. *Catholic Contributions: sociology and policy.* Chicago: Thomas More, 1987. Paperbound.
G gives a sociologist's report: the results and analysis taken from several surveys outlining changes in Catholic contributions. He follows this with his own interpretation of, and speculation on, these changes. McManus contributes "A Bishop's Afterword" in which he discusses the subject in light of the data presented and adds his own recommendations. Figures.

97   *Conversations with Andrew Greeley.* Boston: Quinlan, 1988.
Interviewer: Ronald D. Pasquariello.
Pasquariello questions G on a full range of topics from writing to neighborhood to theology and priests. G's candid answers provide an excellent profile of his life, work and beliefs. G's portrait on the book jacket is by Chicago sculptor and artist John David Mooney.

98 *God in Popular Culture.* Chicago: Thomas More, 1988.
Paperbound.
Parts appeared in *America, Journal of Popular Culture, New York Times, Writer's Digest.*
A collection of twenty-five essays which explain G's theory of the religious imagination and illustrate it with examples from modern popular culture. These include the work of artists Bill Cosby, Bruce Springsteen, Madonna, Stephen King, Woody Allen and others, in popular music, TV, fiction, film, and comics. Index.

99 *Sexual Intimacy: Love and Play.* New York: Warner, 1988.
Paperbound.
With a new introduction by the author.
Originally published as two separate volumes *Sexual Intimacy* and *Love and Play.*
In the new introduction to this reissue of his two earlier essays, G reiterates his intention "to deal with human sexuality both in the context of the human propensity to seek meaning in behavior and from the viewpoint of a particular religious meaning system-- that of a schismatic Jewish sect founded by an obscure Galilean preacher named Jesus."

100 *When Life Hurts.* Chicago: Thomas More, 1988. *
Reprint. New York: Doubleday, 1989. Paperbound.
Previously published in different form in *Markings.*
A series of meditations, based on Gospel stories, for times of sorrow or stress. Each section contains the relevant Scripture citation.

101 *Andrew Greeley's Chicago.* Chicago: Contemporary, 1989.
In 175 black and white photographs, several essays, and extensive quotations from his novels, G portrays "his" Chicago and that of the characters in his stories. The pictures are of houses, churches, skyscrapers, interesting downtown signs, Lake Michigan and the waterfront, the Chicago river, and other scenes of the city which G has called one of the four most beautiful in the world.

102 *Complaints against God.* Chicago: Thomas More, 1989.
Paperbound.
A version published in 1971.
G is often humorous, but always serious, when he prays to God

about the earthly problems created by snowstorms, 747s, his friends, the end of summer, lovers, and more.

103   *Myths of Religion.* New York: Warner, 1989. Paperbound. Reprint containing: *The Jesus Myth, The Sinai Myth, The Mary Myth.*

104   *Religious Change in America. Social Trends in the United States.* Cambridge, MA: Harvard Univ. Press, 1989.
G makes "a modest attempt to ask how well religion has . . . fared in the United States since 1940. . . . " He studies religious social indicators in an attempt to prove that there has been "no major decline in American religious faith and devotion cannot be rejected." Sometimes referred to by the pre-publication title, Religious Indicators 1940-1985. Tables. Figures. Bibliography. Index.

105   and Jacob Neusner. *The Bible and Us: a priest and a rabbi read Scripture together.* New York: Warner, 1990.
Reprint. New York: Warner, 1991. Paperbound.
A Catholic social scientist and a Jewish humanist read portions of their respective Scriptures together, and each presents his interpretation. In conclusion, they ask the question, "Can religions carry on a dialogue?" Neusner answers that they cannot, G that they can. Index.

106   *The Catholic Myth: the behavior and beliefs of American Catholics.* New York: Scribner's, 1990.
Reprint. New York: Collier, 1991. Paperbound.
Appears in some library catalogs as The Greeley Report: the behavior and beliefs of American Catholics.
Using data from the NORC General Social Surveys and others, G reports and analyzes the attitudes and actions of Catholics in mid and late 20th Century America. One conclusion: Catholics, although often not agreeing with the Church, remain Catholics because they *like* being Catholic. An appendix contains a discussion of "Catholic, Capitalist, Socialist, and Anarchist Ideologies" based in part on *No Bigger Than Necessary: an alternative to socialism, capitalism and anarchism.* Index.

107   *The Irish: photographs by Andrew M. Greeley . . . along with*

poems, proverbs, and blessings. Chicago: Contemporary, 1990.
Reprint. Chicago: Contemporary, 1991. Paperbound. *
A collection of G's photographs of Irish men, women and
children, together with poems and blessings, many written by G,
and five original essays about the Irish. Also included are one of
his Mollie Whoopie stories and his well-known King of Kerry
tale.

108   *Year of Grace.* Chicago: Thomas More, 1990. Paperbound.
Reprint. Dublin: Mercier, 1991. Paperbound.
The author keeps a religious diary of prayers to God and reflects
on his spiritual reading and his daily life. The diary covers the
period from Apr. 14, 1989 to Apr. 15, 1990, and includes six
original poems. Continued in *Love Affair: a prayer journal.*

109   *A Book of Irish American Blessings & Prayers.* Chicago:
Thomas More, 1991. Paperbound.
A collection of original blessings--for friends, for confidence, for
first communion, for Christmas Day, for waterskiers, and many
more--and prayers, for the environment, for the church, for
forgiveness, for Ash Wednesday, for Ireland, among others.

110   *Faithful Attraction: discovering intimacy, love, and fidelity in
American marriage.* New York: Tor, 1991.
Reprint. New York: Tor, 1992. Paperbound.
Although the paperbound edition contains a fiction disclaimer, and
is often shelved in the fiction section in bookstores, this is a
sociological study of data on love and marriage, primarily from
two surveys done for *Psychology Today* by the Gallup
Organization. Topics covered include divorce, reconciliation,
forced sex, gender and generation gaps and others. An appendix
contains the two survey questionnaires. Figures. Bibliography.

111   *Love Affair: a prayer journal.* New York: Crossroad, 1992.
Beginning Sept. 11, 1990 G continues the diary begun in *Year of
Grace.* The entries are somewhat briefer and conclude Sept. 19,
1991. Of particular interest are his thoughts and prayers at the
time of the Persian Gulf war, and an appendix contains a reprint
of his article "How Just a War" from *The Critic*, Summer 1991.

NOVELS

112   *The Magic Cup: an Irish legend.* New York: McGraw-Hill,
        1979.
        Reprint. New York: Warner, 1979,* 1985, 1987.*
        Paperbound.
        Reprint. New York: Carroll & Graf, 1992. Paperbound.
        Drawings by Donald Dean Illustration Design.
        In this, G's first published novel, he retells the ancient Celtic
        legend of the quest for the Holy Grail. Young King Cormac
        MacDermot, the Irish Lancelot, seeks the Grail/girl, Princess
        Brigid, who actively helps him in his search. Together they
        overcome all obstacles. G concludes with a note, "The Irish Grail
        Cycle" which helps to explain the legend and his adaptation of it.
        Bibliography.

113   *Death in April.* New York: McGraw-Hill, 1980. *
        Reprint. New York: McGraw-Hill, 1980. Book Club ed.
        Reprint. New York: Dell, 1984. Paperbound. *
        Reprint. New York: Carroll & Graf, 1988. Paperbound. *
        Reprint. London: Macdonald, 1987.
        Successful novelist, Jim O'Neill rediscovers first love, Lynnie
        Slattery and the city of Chicago after 20 years away. In a bold
        and courageous ploy he rescues her from the shady machinations
        of Chicago's legal and political wheeler-dealers.

114   *The Cardinal Sins.* New York: Warner, 1981.
        Reprint. New York: Warner, 1981. Book Club ed. Literary
        Guild. *
        Reprint. New York: Warner, 1982, 1985,* 1987.
        Paperbound.
        Reprint. Boston: G.K. Hall, 1981. Large Print.
        Reprint. London: W.H. Allen, 1981. *
        Reprint. Anstey, Eng.: F.A. Thorpe, 1982. Large Print.
        Sound Recording. New York: Warner Audio, 1985. 2
        cassettes. Abridged. Read by Frank Langella. With a special
        introduction by the author.
        The first of G's best-selling novels which have earned him
        celebrity and wealth. This "comedy of grace" chronicles the lives
        of two Chicago priests, Kevin Brennan and Patrick Donahue, and
        the women they loved. Two prefatory notes describe the cardinal

sins and explain which characters are fictional. The paperbound editions contain "A Note on the Cover Design" and "A Personal Afterword" which attempt to answer critical questions raised when the book first appeared.

115   *Thy Brother's Wife.* New York: Warner, 1982.
       Reprint. New York: Warner, 1983,* 1987, 1989.*
       Paperbound.
       Reprint. Boston: G.K. Hall, 1982. Large Print. *
       Reprint. London: W.H. Allen, 1982. *
       Reprint. Anstey, Eng.: F.A. Thorpe, 1983. Large Print.
       The first part of the Passover trilogy, a Holy Thursday "meditation in story form," is about commitment--that of Paul and Sean Cronin and their adopted sister, Nora. Some commitments are kept, others are not. In "A Personal Afterword" G explains why a priest would "write a novel . . . about adultery, incest, and sacrilege." (*See also Ascent into Hell, Lord of the Dance*, and *The Passover Trilogy*.)

116   *Ascent into Hell.* New York: Warner, 1983. 21 cm. and 23 cm. eds.
       Reprint. New York: Warner, 1984,* 1987. Paperbound.
       Reprint. Boston: G.K. Hall, 1983. Large Print. *
       G's Good Friday meditation, the second book in the Passover trilogy, in which Hugh Donlon ends his "misguided crucifixion of himself" when he discovers a God of forgiveness and love. An expository afterword is included in which G gives the doctrinal basis for his story and states "it is documented in the Canon #179 of the Second Council of Orange, which is quoted below." The paperback reprinting included 25,000 business-reply card research questionnaires which G used to evaluate the readers' response to his novels. (*See also Thy Brother's Wife, Lord of the Dance*, and *The Passover Trilogy*.)

117   *Lord of the Dance.* New York: Warner, 1984.
       Reprint. New York: Warner, 1984. Book Club ed.
       Doubleday; Literary Guild; Mystery Guild. *
       Reprint. New York: Warner, 1985,* 1987, 1989.*
       Paperbound.
       Reprint. Boston: G.K. Hall, 1985. Large Print.
       Reprint. Bath: Chivers, 1985. Large Print. *

The story of Holy Saturday, the feast of resurrection and new beginnings, completes the Passover trilogy. Noele Marie Brigid Farrell, G's endearing heroine, rescues her family in this, arguably, his most popular novel. (*See also Thy Brother's Wife*, *Ascent into Hell*, and *The Passover Trilogy*.)

118   Blackie Ryan Mystery Series.
The titles in this series (five to date) are all taken from the Beatitudes from Jesus's Sermon on the Mount which G interprets in an introductory note to each story. Father Blackie Ryan, in his role as unassuming detective, is the central figure in each as he solves the crime and encourages the principal characters to find "God's passionate and implacable love." (*See* 119, 124, 126, 136, 139.)

119   *Happy Are the Meek.* New York: Warner, 1985. Paperbound.
Reprint. New York: Warner, 1985. Book Club ed.
Doubleday; Literary Guild. *
Reprint. Boston: G.K. Hall, 1986. Large Print.
Reprint. London: Macdonald, 1986.
After his introduction in *Virgin and Martyr*, Msgr. Blackie Ryan, now a detective-protagonist in his own series, solves the classic, locked-room murder of Wolfe Tone Quinlan and rescues the Quinlan family from the evils of incest and devil worship.

120   Time Between the Stars Series.
To date there are seven novels in this series set in Chicago between the 1933 World's Fair (represented by the 4th star in the city's flag) and the proposed 1992 World's Fair which did not happen (the potential 5th star in the flag). G chronicles the "social and religious evolution of Chicago Catholics" during this time in his stories of four families, particularly the Ryans. (*See* 121, 122, 128, 129, 131, 132, 137.)

121   *Virgin and Martyr.* New York: Warner, 1985.
Reprint. New York: Warner, 1985. Book Club ed.
Doubleday; Literary Guild. *
Reprint. New York: Warner, 1986. Paperbound.
Reprint. Boston: G.K. Hall, 1985. Large Print.
Reprint. Boston: G.K. Hall, 1985. Large Print. Paperbound.
Reprint. London: Macdonald, 1985. (This ed. adds the subtitle

"a Christmas legend.")
The first in the Time Between the Stars Series introduces G's most memorable character, Father Blackie Ryan, who solves the mystery of Cathy Collins's death in a story "about the dangers of religious enthusiasm, . . . traumatic times . . . in the Church and about God's grace. . . ."

122   *Angels of September.* New York: Warner, 1986. 21 cm. and 23 cm. eds.
      Reprint. New York: Warner, 1986. Book Club ed. Literary Guild. *
      Reprint. New York: Warner, 1987. Paperbound.
      Reprint. Boston: G.K. Hall, 1986. Large Print.
      Reprint. Boston: G.K. Hall, 1986. Large Print. Paperbound.
      Reprint. London: Macdonald, 1986. *
      A story of a love discovered after 40 years, and of powerful guilt. Anne Reilly is rescued by her angels of September, Mary Kate Ryan Murphy, Michael Casey, Patrol Officer Lopez, and the indomitable Blackie Ryan in this, the second of the Time Between the Stars Series.

123   *God Game.* New York: Warner, 1986.
      Reprint. New York: Tor, 1987. Paperbound.
      Reprint. Boston: G.K. Hall, 1987. Large Print.
      Reprint. London: Century Hutchinson, 1986.
      G's first venture into fantasy and speculative fiction is a metafictional, mixed tale of computer game-playing and creative story-telling. The narrator plays God as he grapples with an interactive fiction game run amok. His creatures, in their different world (or is it?) escape his control. All hell breaks loose as storms, violence and war take over, but, ultimately, he is able to achieve a happy ending.

124   *Happy Are the Clean of Heart.* New York: Warner, 1986. Paperbound.
      Reprint. New York: Warner, 1986. Book Club ed.
      Reprint. New York: Warner, 1988. Paperbound. *
      Reprint. Boston: G.K. Hall, 1987. Large Print.
      Reprint. London: Macdonald, 1987.
      Msgr. Blackwood Ryan, rector of Chicago's Holy Name Cathedral, saves his longtime love, movie star Lisa Malone, from

a particularly grisly torture and murder attempt. Second in the mystery series.

125   *The Final Planet.* New York: Warner, 1987.
      Reprint. New York: Warner, 1987. Book Club ed. Literary Guild; Science Fiction. *
      Reprint. New York: Tor, 1988. Paperbound. *
      Reprint. London: Century Hutchinson, 1988.
      Abbess Deirdre Cardinal Fitzgerald dispatches Seamus Finnbar O'Neill from the creaky, old spaceship Iona to check out the planet Zylong as a final resting place for her people. The bumbling Seamus has one frightening experience after another with the incomprehensible inhabitants, and falls in love with the magnificent Zylongi woman, Marjetta. As she and Seamus are about to be slain by the Hooded Ones, Deirdre and her crew arrive in the nick of time to save them and restore peace to Zylong.

126   *Happy Are Those Who Thirst for Justice.*   New York: Mysterious Press, 1987. *
      Reprint. New York: Mysterious Press, 1987. Book Club ed.
      Reprint. New York: Warner, 1988. Paperbound.
      Reprint. Boston: G.K. Hall, 1988. Large Print.
      Reprint. London: Severn, 1988. *
      In this third Blackie Ryan mystery, a "bloody and sordid tale of love run amok," Violet Enright is murdered on her luxury yacht, and all the members of her family are suspects. Msgr. Ryan, with help from sister, Mary Kate, and her husband, Joe Murphy, solves the locked-stateroom puzzle, and leads the family on the road to redemption.

127   *The Passover Trilogy.* New York: Avenel, 1987.
      Reprint containing: *Thy Brother's Wife*, *Ascent into Hell*, *Lord of the Dance*.
      This unabridged reprint contains an original introduction by G explaining Passover, its rituals and feasts, and relating it to the three novels.

128   *Patience of a Saint.* New York: Warner, 1987.
      Reprint. New York: Warner, 1987. Book Club ed. Doubleday. *

Reprint. New York: Warner, 1987. Paperbound.
Reprint. Boston: G.K. Hall, 1988. Large Print.
Reprint. Boston: G.K. Hall, 1988. Large Print. Paperbound.
Sound Recording. New York: Warner Audio, 1987. 2
cassettes. 2 hours. Abridged. Read by Ken Welsh. With a
special introduction by the author.
Redmond Peter Kane, protagonist in the third of G's Time
Between the Stars Series is struck by God's "cosmic baseball bat"
on his Road to Damascus, Wacker Drive in Chicago. Melodrama,
mystery, frustration, reconciliation and redemption follow. In "A
Theological Note" G explains and justifies his writing of the
story. "A Sociological Note" outlines G's sociology of intense
religious experiences.

129   *Rite of Spring.* New York: Warner, 1987.
       Reprint. New York: Warner, 1987. Book Club ed.
       Doubleday; Literary Guild. *
       Reprint. New York: Warner, 1988. Paperbound. *
       Reprint. Boston: G.K. Hall, 1988. Large Print.
       Reprint. Boston: G.K. Hall, 1988. Large Print. Paperbound.
       *
       Reprint. London: Macdonald, 1988. *
       Reprint. Bath: Chivers, 1989. Large Print.
       Brendan Ryan pursues his (imaginary?) love in this "Holy Grail
       legend . . . told in semicomic modern terms, with Blackie Ryan
       playing the Merlin role for all it is worth." G's note in conclusion
       deals with psychic phenomena and the novel's similarity to his
       Grail story, *The Magic Cup: an Irish legend.* Fourth in the Time
       Between the Stars Series.

130   *Angel Fire.* New York: Warner, 1988.
       Reprint. New York: Warner, 1988. Book Club ed. Literary
       Guild. *
       Reprint. New York: Tor, 1989. Paperbound.
       Reprint. Thorndike, ME: Thorndike, 1989. Large Print.
       Reprint. Thorndike, ME: Thorndike, 1989. Large Print.
       Paperbound. *
       Reprint. London: Legend, 1989. *
       The hero of this romantic fantasy, Sean Desmond, Chicago
       biology professor, travels to Stockholm to receive the Nobel prize
       and present his controversial evolutionary theory. On the way he

meets his guardian angel, the enchanting Gabriella Light. As they travel together, she protects him from the CIA, the KGB and assorted assassins. The story concludes in Ireland with a very human ending. G then adds several quotes about angels including two from Gabriella Light herself.

131   *Love Song.* New York: Warner, 1989.
Reprint. New York: Warner, 1989. Book Club ed. Book of the Month. *
Reprint. New York: Warner, 1989. Paperbound. *
Reprint. Boston: G.K. Hall, 1989. Large Print.
Reprint. London: Severn, 1990. *
Reprint. Bath: Chivers, 1990. Large Print.
The fifth novel in the Time Between the Stars Series, based on the Bible's Song of Songs, tells the modern day love story of assistant district attorney, Diana Lyons and Conor Clarke, whom she has been appointed to prosecute. With help from Judge Eileen Ryan Kane and her brother Blackie, all is resolved in a typical Greeley ending--hopeful and happy.

132   *St. Valentine's Night.* New York: Warner, 1989.
Reprint. New York: Warner, 1989. Book Club ed. Doubleday; Literary Guild. *
Reprint. New York: Warner, 1990. Paperbound.
Reprint. Thorndike, ME: Thorndike, 1990. Large Print.
Reprint. Thorndike, ME: Thorndike, 1990. Large Print. Paperbound. *
As a young boy Neil Connor rescued Megan Lane from her burning house. When he returns to Chicago 30 years later, he must save her again--this time from financial ruin, scandal, and murder. Number six in the Time Between the Stars Series is a love story full of mystery and mayhem.

133   *The Cardinal Virtues.* New York: Warner, 1990. 21 cm. and 23 cm. eds.
Reprint. New York: Warner, 1990. Book Club ed. Literary Guild. *
Reprint. New York: Warner, 1991. Paperbound.
Reprint. South Yarmouth, MA: Curley, 1991. Large Print.
Reprint. Wallington, Eng.: Severn, 1991.
Reprint. Bath: Chivers, 1991. Large Print. *

Sound Recording. New York: Harper Audio, ? CPN 2230.
*

G portrays life in a contemporary, suburban Chicago parish with
humor, outrage, and anguish. Old Priest Lar McAuliffe
anticipates conflict with New Priest Jamie Keenan, but finds
instead friendship and support from this "Michael Jordan of a
New Priest" as, together, they do battle with the adversaries (both
within and without) of the Archdiocese and the Church.

134   *An Occasion of Sin.* New York: G.P. Putnam's, 1991.
       Reprint. New York: G.P. Putnam's, 1991. Book Club ed.
       Doubleday; Literary Guild. *
       Reprint. New York: Jove, 1992. Paperbound.
       Reprint. Thorndike, ME: Thorndike, 1992. Large Print.
       Reprint. Thorndike, ME: Thorndike, 1992. Large Print.
       Paperbound. *
       Reprint. London: Piatkus, 1992. *
       Sound Recording. New York: Harper Audio, 1991. CPN
       2237. 2 cassettes. 180 minutes. Abridged. Performed by
       Philip Bosco.
       Is the late Chicago Cardinal John "Jumping Johnny" McGlynn an
       appropriate candidate for sainthood? Did he pursue a love affair
       with the beautiful Marbeth Quinlan? Was the unexplained cure of
       her grandson's cancer a miracle? Father Lar McAuliffe (from *The
       Cardinal Virtues*) is commissioned to investigate these and other
       questions in this suspenseful story, play devil's advocate, and
       present his recommendations. Along the way, the author provides
       insights into the canonization process.

135   *The Search for Maggie Ward.* New York: Warner, 1991. 21
       cm. and 23 cm. eds.
       Parts have appeared as the short stories: "Andrea" in *All about
       Women* and "The Dutchman's Ghost Town" in *Magazine of
       Fantasy & Science Fiction.*
       Reprint. New York: Warner, 1991. Book Club ed.
       Doubleday. *
       Reprint. New York: Warner, 1992. Paperbound.
       Reprint. Thorndike, ME: Thorndike, 1991. Large Print.
       Reprint. Thorndike, ME: Thorndike, 1991. Large Print.
       Paperbound. *
       Reprint. London: Severn, 1991. *

Sound Recording. ? Brilliance, ?. 10 cassettes. 14 hours.
Unabridged. 14 readers. *
Home from the Pacific theater of war in 1946, naval flier, Jerry
Keenan, meets a beautiful young woman in Arizona, but, after
they are together for a few days, she suddenly disappears. The
suspense mounts as his search for her ranges across the country.
It ends in Chicago where he finally finds his girl/Grail. As
background G presents an interesting picture of post-war
America. This novel is sometimes referred to by its working title,
War in Heaven.

136   *Happy Are the Merciful.* New York: Jove, 1992. Paperbound.
      Reprint. New York: G.P. Putnam's, 1992. Book Club ed.
      Doubleday; Mystery Guild. *
      Reprint. Thorndike, ME: Thorndike, 1992. Large Print.
      Reprint. London: Piatkus, 1993. *
      Blackie Ryan, now elevated to Bishop, solves another locked
      room mystery in which John and Mary Turner, wealthy
      inventors, are murdered in their bed in suburban Chicago.
      Interwoven is the love story of state's attorney Terry Scanlan and
      prime suspect, daughter Clare Turner, in this the fourth of G's
      mystery series.

137   *Wages of Sin.* New York: G.P. Putnam's, 1992.
      Reprint. New York: G.P. Putnam's, 1992. Book Club ed.
      Doubleday; Literary Guild. *
      Reprint. New York: Jove, 1993. Paperbound.
      Reprint. Thorndike, ME: Thorndike, 1993. Large Print.
      Reprint. Thorndike, ME: Thorndike, 1993. Large Print.
      Paperbound. *
      Sound Recording. New York: Harper Audio, 1992. CPN
      2275. 2 cassettes. 180 mins. Abridged. Performed by Fritz
      Weaver.
      The seventh in the Time Between the Stars series introduces the
      wealthy, talented Lorcan James Flynn and his family. Reunited
      with the lost love of his youth, Lorcan solves the mystery of the
      criminal explosion which had separated them thirty-five years
      before. As usual, psychiatrist Mary Kate Ryan Murphy has a part
      to play.

138   *Fall from Grace.* New York: G.P. Putnam's, 1993.
      Reprint. New York: G.P. Putnam's, 1993. Book Club ed.

Doubleday; Literary Guild; Mystery Guild. *
Reprint. Thorndike, ME: Thorndike, 1993. Large Print.
Sound Recording. New York: Harper Audio, 1993. n.n. 2
cassettes. 180 minutes. Performed by Philip Bosco.
Once again G presents the story of an influential Chicago family,
and of a lost love regained after many years. But major social
problems are featured this time--domestic abuse, alcoholism,
Satanic cults, and the sexual abuse of children by some clergy of
the Catholic Church. Andrew Greeley has been an outspoken
critic of the Church's handling of this crisis for many years (*See*
his *Chicago Sun Times* columns in Chapter Five.) In an afterword
to the novel he comments on Satanic rituals and the new,
improved Church procedures in Chicago for dealing with
pedophilia. Nine diocesan newspapers in major U. S. cities
refused to carry advertising for this book according to a *USA
Today* report.

139   *Happy Are the Peacemakers.*   New York: Jove, 1993.
        Paperbound.
        Reprint. New York: G.P. Putnam's, 1993. Book Club ed.
        Doubleday. *
        Reprint. Bath: Chivers, 1993. Large Print. *
        Sound Recording. Burlington, Ont.: Durkin Hayes, 1993. 2
        cassettes. Performed by Tom Bosley. *
        Bishop Blackie Ryan travels to Dublin for the Bloomsday
        celebrations. While there, he helps Tim Pat MacCarthy rescue the
        beautiful Nora MacDonaugh suspected, for the second time, of
        murdering her husband. G paints an engrossing picture of Dublin,
        James Joyce, and the Irish. Number five in the Blackie Ryan
        series.

SHORT STORIES

140   *Nora Maeve and Sebi.*   New York: Paulist Press, 1976. (Ms.
        only seen.)
        Pictures by Diane Dawson.
        G's only published children's story in which God and Archangel
        Michael help to find Nora Maeve (a three year old) and Sebi (a
        Labrador) when they are lost.

141   *All about Women.* New York: Warner, 1990.
       Reprint. New York: Tor, 1991. Paperbound.
       A collection of twenty-three short stories, all of them about
       women, which includes an introduction, by G, about storytelling.
       Fifteen have been published previously in various magazines.
       "Julie" appears in *Chicago Works: a collection of Chicago
       authors' best stories*, and "April Mae" in *The Seven Deadly Sins:
       stories of human weakness and virtue* as "Pride before a Fall."

142   and Michael Cassutt, eds. *Sacred Visions.* New York: Tor,
       1991.
       Reprint. New York: Tor, 1991. Paperbound.
       A collection of science fiction stories with Catholic themes. It
       includes an original story by G, "Xorinda the Witch" in which
       "we see again the eternal conflict between what is orthodox, and
       what is right."(from the foreword to the story.) G's introduction
       to the book presents his concept of the Catholic religious, or
       analogical, imagination and its presence in the stories.

POEMS

143   *Women I've Met.* Kansas City, MO: Andrews & McMeel, 1979.
       Paperbound.
       G's first book of poems, some of which have appeared elsewhere.
       He writes about women, Christmas, memories and Ireland. Some
       photographs by the poet are included.

144   *The Sense of Love: poems by Andrew M. Greeley.* Ashland,
       OH: Ashland Poetry, 1992. Paperbound.
       Using as section headings the three Greek words for different
       kinds of love: *eros, philos* and *agape*, G divides this collection of
       his poetry into the sexual, the social and the spiritual. Of
       particular interest are the twelve metaphors in which he compares
       God to a teenager, a homemaker, an Irish parent, etc., and
       "Christmas Carols, After the 'O' Antiphons based on symbols
       from the Jewish scriptures and sung at vespers the week before
       Christmas." Several of the poems have been published previously.

CHAPTER TWO

CONTRIBUTIONS TO BOOKS

ESSAYS

145   "The Catholic message and the American intellectual." *Pastoral Catechetics* ed. by Johannes Hofinger and Theodore C. Stone. New York: Herder and Herder, 1964. pp. 180-193.
Reprinted from *The Critic*, Apr./May 1964.
The author describes the reaction, or perhaps non-reaction, of secularist intellectuals to the philosophy of the Catholic Church. He concludes that they would be more inclined to believe this message if it produced "people who loved more."

146   "An exchange of views." *The Secular City Debate* ed.by Daniel Callahan. New York: Macmillan, 1966. pp. 101-126.
Reprinted from *Commonweal*, Nov. 12, 1965.
In this debate with Harvey Cox, Michael Novak and Daniel Callahan, generated by Cox's *The Secular City* and Callahan's subsequent article in *Commonweal*, G asks what proof (of a sociological nature) they have that urban man is becoming secular. Finally, he urges theologians to use "the most recent and the most factual and the most sophisticated sociology."

147   "How I see the issues." pp. 7-10. "The conversation." pp. 19-131. "Final position papers." pp. 139-141. *Issues That Divide the Church* ed. by Robert G. Hoyt. New York: Macmillan, 1967.
Proceedings of a symposium organized by the *National Catholic Reporter*, held in Kansas City, MO, Jan. 1967.
Appeared in *National Catholic Reporter* during Lent 1967.
G and five other prominent Catholics, on a panel moderated by Hoyt, discuss critical problems facing the Church. His initial paper considers "Can and ought the Church to trust the modern

world?," "Can the Church accept the basic orientations of American society?" and the "battle between evolutionists and revolutionists." His final position paper is roundly critical of the symposium: "a consummate waste of time . . . much-a-do about sublime nothings."

148   "The parish assistant." *Secular Priest in the New Church* ed. by Gerard S. Sloyan. New York: Herder and Herder, 1967. pp. 156-175.
An angry denunciation of the position held by the curate in relation to the pastor in many large dioceses in parts of the U. S. "The curate is a professional caught in a feudal structure" writes G. It is "an incredible abuse of human freedom and dignity." He is hopeful that the situation may improve, and appends to his essay the "Principles of Personnel Policy" developed by the personnel subcommittee of the Assn. of Chicago Priests as an example of the direction in which reform should proceed.

149   and Leonard J. Pinto. "The use of self-administered questionnaires." *Reducing the Costs of Surveys* by Seymour Sudman. NORC Monographs in Social Research 10. Chicago: Aldine, 1967. pp. 46-57.
The authors describe "leave-pick-up" methods of interviewing, including costs, and response differences with personal interviews. Tables.

150   and Donald A. Erickson. "Non-public schools and metropolitanism." *Metropolitanism: its challenge to education.* NSSE 67th Yearbook, Part 1. Chicago: National Society for the Study of Education, 1968. pp. 287-316.
After a brief look at the prevalence and distribution of non-public schools in America, the authors discuss their academic quality and whether there is a ghetto effect from them. The remainder of the essay deals with the controversial question of government support of, and policy concerning, these schools. Tables.

151   "The teaching of moral wisdom." *Stress and Campus Response* ed. by G. Kerry Smith. Current Issues in Higher Education, 1968. San Francisco: Jossey-Bass, 1968. pp. 209-213.
G discusses the morality of the youth of the 1960s and concludes

that it is "the responsibility of the colleges and universities" to teach "moral wisdom to young people."

152   "Catholic high schools and the secular city." *Trends and Issues in Catholic Education* ed. by Russell Shaw and Richard J. Hurley. New York: Citation, 1969. pp. 83-93.
Reprinted from *National Catholic Education Assn. Bulletin*, Aug. 1967.
The author proposes his "utopian plan for Catholic schools" in which large schools would be decentralized and students grouped together in small communities. He concludes that "Catholic schools should be different," and that in them "education . . . can be better, fuller, richer, more humane. . . ."

153   "The myths of secularity." *The World in the Church* ed. by Jordan Aumann. Chicago: Priory Press, [1969]. pp. 11-26. *

154   "Catholic scholars witness to freedom: a symposium." *The Catholic University: a modern appraisal* ed. by Neil G. McCluskey. Notre Dame, IN: Univ. of Notre Dame Press, 1970. pp. 307-320.
Appeared in *Commonweal*, June 2, 1967 as "Zeroing in on freedom: can the Charles Currans be freed."
In this brief essay, G supports the statement on academic freedom of the American Association of University Professors and its use in Catholic colleges. He reasons that it can be applied even to the teaching of theology.

155   "Sociology and Church structure." *Structures of the Church* ed. by Teodoro Jimenez. *Concilium*: 58. New York: Herder and Herder, 1970. pp. 26-35.
G offers "some reflections about the structure of Catholicism from the point of view of the sociology of human organizations." He presents six principles or guidelines by which he feels the Church can progress toward being a better human organization.

156   "The urban church." *Toward a National Urban Policy* ed. by Daniel P. Moynihan. New York: Basic, 1970. pp. 186-194.
A discussion of the need for extension of the community of neighborhoods in the modern city, as well as a call for the urban

churches to lead the way in "devising a vision of metropolitan urbanity."

157   "White against white: the enduring ethnic conflict." *The White Majority: between poverty and affluence* ed. by Louise K. Howe. New York: Random, 1970. pp. 111-118.
Excerpted from *Why Can't They Be like Us? Facts and fallacies about ethnic differences and group conflicts in America.*
G looks at ethnic competition in politics, housing, education, trade unions and small business. He then presents "some concrete findings about differences among ethnic groups in America" taken from NORC data gathered in the 1960s.

158   "Advantages and drawbacks of a centre of communication in the church: a sociological point of view." *Papal Ministry in the Church* ed. by Hans Kung. *Concilium* 64. New York: Herder and Herder, 1971. pp. 101-114.
G describes the types of religious leadership as distinguished by Joachim Wach. He then comments on that leadership in today's world and "the functions of a pope."

159   "The dynamics of Catholic opinion." *Reflections on Contemporary Catholic Problems* ed. by George A. Kelly. New York: St. John's Univ., 1971. pp. 19-28. *

160   "Ethnicity as an influence on behavior." *Ethnic Groups in the City: culture, institutions and power* ed. by Otto Feinstein. Lexington, MA: D.C. Heath, 1971. pp. 3-16.
Presented at the National Consultation on Ethnic America, Fordham Univ., June 21, 1968.
An expanded version appears in *Why Can't They Be like Us? Facts and fallacies about ethnic differences and group conflicts in America.*
G briefly describes the makeup of ethnic groups, and bemoans the lack of hard data about such groups. He concludes with a call for more research on American ethnics.

161   "Leadership and friendship: a sociologist's viewpoint." *Who Decides for the Church: studies in co-responsibility* ed. by James A. Coriden. Hartford, CT: Canon Law Society of America, 1971. pp. 266-279.
Also appeared in *Jurist*, Winter 1971.

From the perspective of sociology and theology, the author makes suggestions for a new leadership in the church under four headings: symbolic, ideological, interpersonal, and organizational.

162   "The new American religion." *The Concrete Christian Life* ed. by Christian Duquoc. *Concilium*: 69. New York: Herder and Herder, 1971. pp. 111-123.
A discussion of the counter-culture of this period in which G describes it as non-rational, simplistic, neo-pagan, emotional and dangerous. He concludes that it is "a substitute for the Christian view of the eschaton" prompted in part by "our failure to believe in the Real Eschaton."

163   "Priest, church and the future from a sociological viewpoint." *Future Forms of Ministry* ed. by Richard A. McCormick and George J. Dyer. n.p. National Federation of Priests' Councils and *Chicago Studies*, 1971. pp. 3-17.
G argues, contrary to the secularization theory of the time, that "ours is an age of profound religious questioning" in which the role of the priest is all-important. The low morale of clergy, he claims, is caused by poor communication between them and their people, the lack of religious conviction of some priests, and the lukewarm response of some laity. He concludes, on a "cautiously hopeful" note that these conditions can be changed.

164   "The redeeming of America according to Charles Reich." *The Con III Controversy: the critics look at The Greening of America* ed. by Philip Nobile. New York: Pocket, 1971. pp. 107-117. Reprinted from *America*, Jan. 9, 1971.
Drawing on religion and sociology, G analyzes Reich's portrait of America and his vision of the future. He likens him to the prophets Amos and Isaiah, and wonders if "Reich's rhetorical overkill had served the cause of serious discussion and planning." He concludes by questioning whether one would want to live in the future green America. "There's nothing more green than a graveyard."

165   and Galen L. Gockel. "The religious effects of parochial education." *Research on Religious Development: a comprehensive handbook* ed. by Merton P. Strommen. New York: Hawthorn, 1971. pp. 264-301.

A review of three studies which describe the effect of parochial schooling on the religious development of young people: 1) Johnstone, R. *The Effectiveness of Lutheran Elementary and Secondary Schools as Agencies of Christian Education.* St. Louis: Concordia Seminary, 1966. 2) Greeley, A.M. and Rossi, P.H. *The Education of Catholic Americans.* Chicago: Aldine, 1966. and 3) Erickson, D. Differential effects of public and sectarian schooling on the religiousness of the child. Unpublished doctoral dissertation, University of Chicago, 1962. It includes theoretical and practical conclusions and an outline of needed research. Tables. Figure. Bibliography.

166   "Religious symbolism, liturgy and community." *Liturgy in Transition* ed. by Herman Schmidt. *Concilium* 62. New York: Herder and Herder, 1971. pp. 59-69.
The author discusses "the sacred symbol . . . a conviction about the inherent structure of reality," rituals, as "perhaps the most important of religious symbols . . . ," including the Christian liturgy, and the community of the underground church which G calls the New Community.

167   "A social science model for the consideration of religious apostasy." *Perspectives of a Political Ecclesiology* ed. by Johannes B. Metz. *Concilium*: 66. New York: Herder and Herder, 1971. pp. 125-134.
G proposes an alternative model to the prevalent one which "sees apostasy as the result of fairly conscious, rational decision, made because Christianity has lost its credibility. . . . " He concludes that apostasy is complicated, involving "enormously powerful social, psychological, historical and cultural forces."

168   "Take heart from the heartland." *Overcoming Middle Class Rage* ed. by Murray Friedman. Philadelphia: Westminster, 1971. pp. 331-343.
Reprinted from *New Republic*, Dec. 12, 1970.
A discussion of ethnic politics in Middle West America following the 1970 election, with emphasis on Chicago and Mayor Richard J. Daley.

169   "'We' and 'they': the differences linger." *Overcoming Middle Class Rage* ed. by Murray Friedman. Philadelphia: Westminster, 1971. pp. 257-268.

Reprinted from *Why Can't They Be like Us? Facts and fallacies about ethnic differences and group conflicts in America.*
The author presents "some concrete data about differences among ethnic groups in America" taken from unpublished NORC data entitled Information About American Ethnic Groups. Tables.

170   "What is an ethnic?" *Overcoming Middle Class Rage* ed. by Murray Friedman. Philadelphia: Westminster, 1971. pp. 231-240.
Reprinted from *Why Can't They Be like Us? Facts and fallacies about ethnic differences and group conflicts in America.*
Also appears in *White Ethnics: their life in working class America.*
Following a description of ethnic groups and the reasons for their survival in the United States, G concludes that such groups enrich the culture, providing diversity, but also "the potential for conflict."

171   "Contemporary American romanticism." *Man in a New Society* ed. by Franz Bockle. *Concilium*: 75. New York: Herder and Herder, 1972. pp. 124-133.
G first outlines the reasons for the romanticism of this period: "the long years of non-productivity . . . " of the young, the disillusionment with empirical science, and the pervasiveness of Freudianism. He continues with its positive contributions including the emphasis on emotion, "the rediscovery of the sacred, the mystical and the ecstatic dimensions of the human personality . . . ," and the reexamination of cultural pluralism. He concludes with the liabilities: non-political and non-rational attitudes and the "*prejudiced* in the strict sense of the word . . . " manner in which humans are considered.

172   "New ethnicity and blue collars: cultural pluralism in the working class." *The World of the Blue Collar Worker* ed. by Irving Howe. New York: Quadrangle, 1972. pp. 285-296.
Excerpted from *That Most Distressful Nation: the taming of the American Irish.*
Reprinted in *The Study of Society: an integrated anthology*, *Ethnicity in the United States: a preliminary reconnaissance*, and *Dissent*, Winter 1972.
The author discusses ethnic diversity in the working class--the distrust of it, and the effect this distrust has particularly in the

political sphere--and the relationship between ethnicity and social class. He concludes with the assertion that diversity in the U. S. is not going to go away, and that someday it may even be regarded as desirable.

173   "Rethinking urban religious education." *Rethinking Urban Education* ed. by Herbert J. Walberg and Andrew T. Kopan. San Francisco: Jossey-Bass, 1972. pp. 165-172.
G presents three reasons for the lack of American academic research on religious education. 1) Social scientists in the education field may not be religious themselves. 2) American public education does not permit specific religious education. 3) The Catholic Church as the principal provider of religious education has not been that concerned with research on its education. He calls for more research as an aid in understanding and dealing with urban problems.

174   "A sex to love with." *Sex: thoughts for contemporary Christians* ed. by Michael J. Taylor. Garden City, NY: Doubleday, 1972. pp. 75-104.
Excerpted from *A Future to Hope In: socio-religious speculations*.
Reprinted from *The Critic*, Aug. 8, 1968.
G argues that the marriage relationship provides a model for the friendship necessary in all human relationships, and that the Church should set an example of this human friendship in its community. He concludes that the man/woman relationship will improve as new insights in psychology and psychiatry provide additional understanding. That, therefore, "man will become more loving and the world will become a more trusting, open, and peaceful place."

175   "Church marriage procedures and the contemporary family." *Divorce and Remarriage in the Catholic Church* ed. by Lawrence G. Wrenn. New York: Newman, 1973. pp. 105-113.
G presents a brief description of the American family and then examines the Church's marriage legislation. He poses a number of questions to canon lawyers and theologians, and suggests "that the matrimonial tribunals and the legal structures that support them are relics of another age."

176   "The Irish." *Through Different Eyes: black and white perspectives on American race relations* ed. by Peter I. Rose, Stanley Rothman and William J. Wilson. New York: Oxford, 1973. pp. 126-147.
A version appeared in *Dissent*, Oct. 1971 as "A most distressful nation: a portrait of the American Irish."
G takes a brief look at the Irish who emigrated to America in the 19th and early 20th centuries and their descendants. He then describes the Irish political style and presents "some tentative things about the relationships between the American Irish and the American blacks." Tables. Bibliographical References.

177   "What is an ethnic?" *White Ethnics: their life in working class America* ed. by Joseph Ryan. Englewood Cliffs, NJ: Prentice-Hall, 1973. pp. 11-16.
Reprinted from *Why Can't They Be like Us? Facts and fallacies about ethnic differences and group conflicts in America.*
Also appears in *Overcoming Middle Class Rage.*
Following a description of ethnic groups and the reasons for their survival in the United States, G concludes that such groups enrich the culture, providing diversity, but also "the potential for conflict."

178   and Paul B. Sheatsley. "Attitudes toward racial integration." *Social Problems and Public Policy: inequality and justice* ed. by Lee Rainwater. Chicago: Aldine, 1974. pp. 241-250.
The authors report the results of NORC surveys on White attitudes toward integration since 1970 as a follow-up to their article in *Scientific American*, Dec. 1971. Results are tabled by region, age, education, size of municipality, religion and ethnicity, and include attitudes toward the controversial busing issue. Tables. (*See also Scientific American*, June 1978.)

179   "Humour and ecclesiastical ministry." *Theology of Joy* ed. by Johannes B. Metz and Jean-Pierre Jossua. *Concilium*: 95. New York: Herder and Herder, 1974. pp. 134-140.
G considers ecclesiastical satire in Italian, French and Irish writings and films, and "the humour of the sacred and humour of faith." He concludes that the last of these "is the best guarantee of effective ecclesiastical ministry that can possibly exist."

180   "Implications for the sociology of religion of occult behavior in
       the youth culture." *On the Margin of the Visible: sociology, the
       esoteric, and the occult* ed. by Edward A. Tiryakian. New York:
       Wiley, 1974. pp. 295-302.
       Presented at the American Sociological Assn., Washington, DC,
       Aug. 31, 1970.
       Also appears in *Youth and Society*, Dec. 1970.
       A brief discussion of what the "neosacral" activities of upper-
       middle-class youth in the Sixties mean for those studying the
       sociology of religion and whether their perspectives "enable us to
       understand the phenomenon." Bibliographical References.

181   "Political attitudes among American white ethnics." *Sociological
       Essays and Research: introductory readings* ed. by Charles H.
       Anderson. Rev. ed. Homewood, IL: Dorsey, 1974. pp. 202-
       209.
       Reprinted from *Public Opinion Quarterly*, Summer 1972.
       Using survey results from several sources, G explores the
       attitudes of Jewish, Irish, Italian and other white ethnic groups
       toward the Vietnam war, the voting age, pollution, racial
       integration, etc. He concludes that most of those who label white
       ethnics as "hard hat" or "racist" are wrongly generalizing about
       a group of which they know almost nothing. Tables.

182   and William C. McCready. "Some notes on the sociological
       study of mysticism." *On the Margin of the Visible: sociology, the
       esoteric, and the occult* ed. by Edward A. Tiryakian. New York:
       Wiley, 1974. pp. 303-322.
       The authors describe ecstatic experiences with references to
       previous writings on the subject. They call for more serious
       research and outline a project in which they are currently
       engaged, directed by McCready. Tables. Bibliographical
       References.

183   "Nothing but a loud-mouthed Irish priest." *Journeys: the impact
       of personal experience on religious thought* ed. by Gregory
       Baum. New York: Paulist, 1975. pp. 167-209.
       Under the headings Twin Lakes, The Neighborhood, Seminary,
       Beverly Hills, The University, Grand Beach, G briefly chronicles
       his life and draws the pattern of his three present intellectual
       concerns, "ethnicity . . . in American society, the Catholic

experience in the United States and the coming together of religion and social science." Most of this material appears in his memoir, *Confessions of a Parish Priest: an autobiography.*

184   and William C. McCready. "The transmission of cultural heritages: the case of the Irish and the Italians." *Ethnicity: theory and experience* ed. by Nathan Glazer and Daniel P. Moynihan. Cambridge, MA: Harvard Univ. Press, 1975. pp. 209-235. Presented at the American Academy of Arts and Sciences, Brookline, MA, Oct. 26-28, 1972.
The authors ask "Does a knowledge of the cultural heritage of an immigrant group help us understand its present behavior?" From a study of the available literature under headings such as personality, political participation, moral issues and family structure attitudes, they conclude that, within some limits, it does. Tables. Bibliography.

185   "Why study ethnicity?" *The Diverse Society: implications for social policy* ed. by Pastora San Juan Cafferty and Leon Chestang. Washington, DC: National Assn. of Social Workers, 1976. pp. 3-12.
G describes the special characteristics of ethnicity in the United States, and answers the question "what direction will the ethnic revival take" as he discusses "diversity as a national resource."

186   "Freedom of choice: 'our commitment to integration'." *Parents, Teachers, and Children: prospects for choice in American education* by James S. Coleman *et al.* San Francisco: Institute for Contemporary Studies, 1977. pp. 183-205.
A study of educational choice and racial integration in which the author outlines changes in attitudes from 1963 to 1976, the effect of integration on education, and the effects of freedom of choice. Tables.

187   "Minorities: white ethnics." *Encyclopedia of Social Work* Vol. 2. 17th ed. Washington, DC: Assn. of Social Workers, 1977. pp. 979-984.
G's essay examines American cultural diversity or heterogeneity using two models: the melting-pot and the mosaic. He points out to helping professionals that "strengths of family and neighborhood ties" are greater among white ethnics than among British-American Protestants.

188 "New ethnicity and blue collars: cultural pluralism in the working class." *The Study of Society: an integrated anthology* ed. by Peter I. Rose. 4th ed. New York: Random, 1977. pp. 578-588. Excerpted from *That Most Distressful Nation: the taming of the American Irish.*
Reprinted from *The World of the Blue Collar Worker.*
The author discusses ethnic diversity in the working class--the distrust of it, and the effect this distrust has particularly in the political sphere--and the relationship between ethnicity and social class. He concludes with the assertion that diversity in the U. S. is not going to go away, and that someday it may even be regarded as desirable.

189 "Catholics and coalition: where should they go?" *Emerging Coalitions in American Politics* ed. by Seymour M. Lipset. San Francisco: Institute for Contemporary Studies, 1978. pp. 271-295.
A consideration of the position of Catholic ethnics in American politics, in which G attempts to show that they have not defected from the Democratic coalition either by ticket-switching or because of their stand on the social issues of abortion, sex and pornography. This, in spite of often being ignored by that coalition. He concludes with the suggestion that this will not change in the near future. Tables.

190 "American Catholics: the post-immigrant century." *The Third Century: America as a post-industrial society* ed. by Seymour M. Lipset. Stanford, CA: Hoover Institution, 1979. pp. 205-221.
G discusses the future of American Roman Catholics under three headings: Religious Change; Social, Economic, and Political Change; and Problems and Possibilities.

191 "Ethnic variations in religious commitment." *The Religious Dimension: new directions in quantitative research* ed. by Robert Wuthnow. New York: Academic, 1979. pp. 113-134.
Commenting on ethnicity and religious affiliation, and ethnicity and religious commitments, the author presents a preliminary analysis from NORC data of the "ethnicity of religious behavior." Tables. Figures. Bibliography.

192 "Why I remain a Catholic." *Why Catholic* ed. by John J. Delaney. Garden City, NY: Doubleday, 1979. pp. 53-69.

G gives four reasons for possibly leaving the Church: institutional, doctrinal, imaginative, and religious. By considering each of these he sets out his own reasons for staying in the Church.

193   "School desegregation and ethnicity." *School Desegregation: past, present and future* ed. by Walter G. Stephan and Joe R. Feagin. New York: Plenum, 1980. pp. 133-155.
G discusses "the impact of desegregation on current relations between Blacks and 'ethnics,' and whether desegregation promotes ethnic pluralism or cultural assimilation." Tables. Figure. Bibliography.

194   "Catholic high schools and minority students." *Private Schools and the Public Good: policy alternatives for the eighties* ed. by Edward M. Gaffney, Jr. Notre Dame, IN: Univ. of Notre Dame Press, 1981. pp. 6-16.
A report on NORC research comparing achievement and discipline in Catholic and public high schools from the High School and Beyond study directed by James S. Coleman. Tables.

195   "Religious musical chairs." *In Gods We Trust: new patterns of religious pluralism in America* ed. by Thomas Robbins and Dick Anthony. New Brunswick, NJ: Transaction, 1981. pp. 101-126.
A version was presented to the Ad Hoc Committee on Evangelization of the NCCB, Aug. 1977.
Reprinted from *Society*, May/June 1978.
The author studies three means by which people may leave the religious denomination in which they were raised: "secularization, family strain and religious intermarriage." He concludes that most Catholics who have left the Church have done so for the third reason. Tables. Figures. Bibliography.

196   "Priesthood." *Tomorrow's Church: what's ahead for American Catholics* ed. by Edward C. Herr. Chicago: Thomas More, 1982. pp. 92-106.
A part reprinted in *An Andrew Greeley Reader Vol. I.*
G comments on the present state of the priesthood, stressing the importance of priests' work and preaching, and condemning the "cheap grace" of their "instant social action militantism." He proposes "a limited term priesthood."

197 William C. McCready and Gary Theisen. "Ethnicity and nationality in alcoholism." *The Pathogenesis of Alcoholism. The Biology of Alcoholism.* Vol. 6 ed. by Benjamin Kissin and Henri Begleiter. New York: Plenum, 1983. pp. 309-340.
Using NORC data for their analysis, the authors consider the significance of ethnic and national origins in the use and abuse of alcohol under the headings: Drinking subcultures, A socialization model of drinking, and The effects of assimilation on ethnic drinking patterns. They conclude that alcoholism treatment can be much more effective if professionals are aware of "cultural variations" and how to deal with them. Tables. Figures. Bibliography.

198 "Andrew Greeley." *The Courage of Conviction* ed. by Phillip L. Berman. New York: Dodd, Mead, 1985. pp. 90-96.
Berman, founder of the Center for the Study of Contemporary Belief, edits a collection of thirty-two essays by a varied group of well-known men and women, among them Joan Baez, Robert Coles, the Dalai Lama, Elisabeth Kubler-Ross, and Norman Cousins, in which each answers "What do I believe" and "How have I put my beliefs into practice in daily life." G expounds his belief in love and hope--the Good News, and his Catholic Christian belief in sacramentality, the analogical imagination, and community. These, he states, have helped him to survive the turbulent years since the Vatican Council.

199 "Stephen King's horror has a healing power." *Kingdom of Fear: the world of Stephen King* ed. by Tim Underwood and Chuck Miller. San Francisco: Underwood-Miller, 1986. pp. 21-22.
Using King's *Cujo* as an example, G asks why do we read such horror stories. In agreement with King, he suggests that by doing so "we are reassured that there is hope that we may continue to survive the forces of evil a little bit longer." He concludes that such stories give us "tiny smidgens of hope" which "needs only to exist to finally win."

200 "The lay reaction." *The Church in Anguish: has the Vatican betrayed Vatican II?* ed. by Hans Kung and Leonard Swidler. San Francisco: Harper & Row, 1987. pp. 284-288.
Drawing on available empirical data, G suggests that Catholic laity, although not agreeing with Church doctrine on birth control and some other ethical questions, have not left the Church. They

have, however, protested by reducing their financial support. He concludes that Church leaders should be more aware of the reality of this situation, and should *listen* to their lay membership.

201   "Andrew Greeley 1928--" *Contemporary Authors: autobiography series* Vol.7 ed. by Mark Zadrozny. Detroit: Gale, 1988. pp. 37-53.
        G outlines his life story, emphasizing the influence of three parishes--St. Angela, Christ the King, and his mailbox parish. He writes of his seminary experience at Mundelein, early days at NORC, and his work on the religious imagination and the sociology of religion. In conclusion he tells how and why he began to write novels, and asserts that "one must be ready in life for surprises. . . ." Includes photographs of the author and his family. Bibliography.

202   "The novel as religious education." *Proceedings of the Center for Jewish-Christian Learning*, Vol. 3 ed. by Arthur E. Zannoni. St. Paul, MN: College of St. Thomas, 1988. pp. 24-28. *

203   "Imagination as a ragpicker." *Andrew Greeley's World: an anthology of critical essays 1986-1988* ed. by Ingrid Shafer. New York: Warner, 1989. pp. 341-349.
        The concluding essay in a collection of critical essays about G and his fiction. After commenting briefly on the essays, he explores his creativity using the *Phantasia/Ratio* model and the metaphor of the garbage-picker, collecting bits and pieces in the secret garden of his imagination.

204   "The crooked lines of God." *Authors of Their Own Lives: intellectual autobiographies by twenty American sociologists* ed. by Bennett M. Berger. Berkeley, CA: Univ. of California Press, 1990. pp. 131-151.
        As one might expect, much of this material duplicates that in G's memoir, *Confessions of a Parish Priest: an autobiography*. But, because he is writing here with and, probably, for other sociologists, the emphasis is on his sociological work. He outlines it succinctly, and includes some new, candid remarks about his battles with the University, and the Archdiocese, of Chicago. In closing, however, he avers "I am no longer of any mind to question the crooked lines of God."

205   "Why Catholics stay in the church." *In Gods We Trust: new patterns of religious pluralism in America* ed. by Thomas Robbins and Dick Anthony. 2d. ed. New Brunswick, NJ: Transaction, 1990. pp. 177-183.
Reprinted from *America*, Aug. 1, 1987.
Drawing, in part, on sociological data, the author suggests several factors which persuade Catholics to remain in the Church despite "the changes and the traumas of the last quarter-century." These include loyalty to their heritage comprised of "identity, community, and sacramentality."

206   "American exceptionalism: the religious phenomenon." *Is America Different? A new look at American exceptionalism* ed. by Byron E. Shafer. Oxford: Clarendon, 1991. pp.? *

207   "Andrew M. Greeley: sociologist, author, novelist." *The Last Priests in America: conversations with remarkable men* by Tim Unsworth. New York: Crossroad, 1991. pp. 116-123.
G offers his views on the priesthood, the Church, and Catholicism in this collection of interviews with American priests. He concludes with the declaration "that the parish and the home are where the religious action is." The material was compiled by Unsworth from an interview (questions not included), some of G's published articles, and *The Catholic Myth: the behavior and beliefs of American Catholics*.

208   "The demography of American Catholics: 1965-1990." *Vatican II and U. S. Catholicism* ed. by Helen R. Ebaugh. Religion and Social Order Series Vol. 2. Greenwich, CT: JAI Press, 1991. pp. 37-56. *

INTRODUCTIONS

209   "Editor's introduction." *Americans of Portuguese Descent* by Francis M. Rogers. Sage Research Papers in the Social Sciences, Studies in Religion and Ethnicity No. 90-013. Beverly Hills, CA: Sage, 1974. pp. 5-12.

210   Introduction to *The Napoleon of Notting Hill* by G.K. Chesterton. New York: Paulist, 1978. pp. vii-xvii.

211   Introduction to *The Varieties of Religious Experience* by William
        James. Garden City, NY: Image, 1978. pp. 9-20.

212   Foreword to *International Conflict in an American City: Boston's
        Irish, Italians, and Jews, 1935-1944* by John F. Stack, Jr.
        Contributions in Political Science Number 26. Westport, CT:
        Greenwood, 1979. pp. ix-xi.

213   Foreword to *Christian Families in the Real World: reflections on
        a spirituality for the domestic church* by Mitch and Kathy Finley.
        Chicago: Thomas More, 1984. pp. 7-8.

214   Introduction to *Quebec: the challenge of independence* by Anne
        Griffin. Cranbury, NJ: Associated Univ. Presses, 1984. pp. 11-
        13.

215   Afterword to *What I Believe: Catholic college students discuss
        their faith* ed. by David Murphy. Chicago: Thomas More, 1985.
        pp. 159-164.

216   Introduction to *The Robe* by Lloyd C. Douglas.   Boston:
        Houghton Mifflin, 1986. pp. vii-xi.

217   Foreword to *Priests: images, ideals and changing roles* by James
        A. Fischer. New York: Dodd, Mead, 1987. pp. xiii-xv.

218   Introductory poem "Blessing for the increase of love." n.p. "This
        is my beloved son." pp. 17-20. "A leap of love." pp. 34-38.
        "The love feast." pp. 39-42. *Let There Be Love: themes from
        the Bible* ed. by Kris Tuberty. Chicago: Thomas More, 1989.
        Appeared in different form in *Markings*.

219   Introduction to *Edge of Sadness* by Edwin O'Connor. Chicago:
        Thomas More, n.d. [1991]. n.p.

220   Introduction to *Lead Us Not into Temptation: Catholic priests and
        the sexual abuse of children* by Jason Berry. New York:
        Doubleday, 1992. pp. xiii-xiv.

SHORT STORIES

221 "Julie." *Chicago Works: a collection of Chicago authors' best stories* ed. by Laurie Levy. Chicago: Morton, 1990. pp.? *
Reprinted from *Literary Review* (Fairleigh Dickinson Univ.), Fall 1982 where it appeared as "Julie Quinn."
Also appears in *All about Women*.

222 "Pride before a Fall." *The Seven Deadly Sins: stories on human weakness and virtue*. Tarrytown, NY: Triumph, 1991. pp. 19-44.
Reprinted from *Catholic Herald*, Lent 1990.
Appeared in slightly different form in *All about Women* as "April Mae."

CHAPTER THREE

CONTRIBUTIONS TO PERIODICALS

ARTICLES

223   pseud. Laurence Moran. "The full life." *Today*, Vol. 11 Apr. 1956. pp. 24-25.

224   pseud. Laurence Moran. "Parish problem." *Today*, Vol. 11 May 1956. pp. 26-27.

225   pseud. Lawrence Moran. "The myth of machine-made leisure." *Social Order*, Vol. 6 Nov. 1956. pp. 434-439.

226   pseud. Laurence Moran. "How to 'say when'." *Today*, Vol. 12 Dec. 1956. pp. 18-19.

227   pseud. Laurence Moran. "Help wanted: visionaries." *Today*, Vol. 12 Mar. 1957. pp. 17-19.

228   "Road shows for Cana." *America*, Vol. 97 June 22, 1957. pp. 340-342.

229   "Revolution in the suburbs." *Ave Maria*, Vol. 86 Aug. 31, 1957. pp. 8-11.

230   "Games are not enough." *Today*, Vol. 13 Oct. 1957. pp. 14-16.

231   "What next?" *Worship*, Vol. 31 Nov. 1957. pp. 587-591. (Liturgical change.)

232   "Suburbia: a new way of life." *Sign*, Vol. 37 Jan. 1958. pp. 11-14.

233 "The Catholic suburbanite." *Sign*, Vol. 37 Feb. 1958. pp. 30-32.

234 "Ignored challenges." *Worship*, Vol. 32 Mar. 1958. pp. 218-224.

235 "Middle-range spirituality." *Today*, Vol. 13 June 1958. pp. 17-19.

236 "The religious revival: fact or fiction?" *Sign*, Vol. 37 July 1958. pp. 25-27.

237 "Should your daughter go to college?" *Grail*, Vol. 40 Sept. 1958. pp. 40-44.

238 "The suburban novel." *Catholic World*, Vol. 187 Sept. 1958. pp. 428-433.

239 "The waning of enthusiasm." *Worship*, Vol. 32 Oct. 1958. pp. 539-547.
Reprinted in *Catholic Mind*, Aug. 1959.

240 "Mass culture milieu." *Worship*, Vol. 33 Dec. 1958. pp. 19-26.
Excerpted in *Commonweal*, Jan. 9, 1959.

241 "The ordeal of the inside dopester." *Today*, Vol. 14 Dec. 1958. pp. 15-18.

242 "*Quadragesimo Anno* and 'new' problems." *America*, Vol. 100 Dec. 13, 1958. pp. 340-342.

243 "The parish, the teenager, and the liturgy." *North American Liturgical Week*, Vol. 20 n.m. 1959. pp. 197-198.

244 "Participation problems in the modern parish." *North American Liturgical Week*, Vol. 20 n.m. 1959. pp. 18-23.

245 "Liturgy and mass culture." *Commonweal*, Vol. 69 Jan. 9, 1959. pp. 387-389.
Excerpted from *Worship*, Dec. 1958.

246   "Beat, cool--and lonely." *Worship*, Vol. 33 Mar. 1959. pp. 204-
      209. (Apostolic commitment.)

247   "The changing city." *Catholic World*, Vol. 188 Mar. 1959. pp.
      481-487.

248   "The Super City." *Marriage*, Vol. 41 Mar. 1959. pp. 34-39.

249   "Going whose way?" *Worship*, Vol. 33 May 1959. pp. 354-358.
      (Priesthood.)

250   "The need for enthusiasm." *Marriage*, Vol. 41 May 1959. pp.
      55-58.

251   "Turning the slum tide." *Today*, Vol. 14 May 1959. pp. 10-12.

252   "How to make scholars at home." *Marriage*, Vol. 41 June 1959.
      pp. 40-44.

253   "Conformity or community?" *Sign*, Vol. 38 July 1959. pp. 18-
      19+.

254   "A new catechism: for the mature convert." *The Priest*, Vol. 15
      Aug. 1959. pp. 645-647.

255   "Treat them like people." *Marriage*, Vol. 41 Aug. 1959. pp.
      21-24.
      Reprinted in *Family Digest,* Nov. 1959.

256   "Waning of enthusiasm." *Catholic Mind*, Vol. 57 Aug. 1959.
      pp. 313-320.
      Reprinted from *Catholic World*, Oct. 1958.

257   "The urban parish under a microscope." *Social Order*, Vol. 9
      Sept. 1959. pp. 335-339.

258   "Suburban parish." *Commonweal*, Vol. 70 Sept. 25, 1959. pp.
      537-539.
      Adapted from **The Church and the Suburbs**.

259 "Organization man: hope for a halo." *Sign*, Vol. 39 Oct. 1959. pp. 48-50.

260 "Popular devotions friend or foe?" *Worship*, Vol. 33 Oct. 1959. pp. 569-573.

261 "Spirituality for the suburbanites." *Ave Maria*, Vol. 90 Oct. 3, 1959. pp. 23-25. *

262 "Maturity in the making." *Today*, Vol. 15 Nov. 1959. pp. 15-17.

263 "Optimistic thoughts." *Worship*, Vol. 33 Nov. 1959. pp. 628-633.

264 "Treat them like people." *Family Digest*, Vol. 15 Nov. 1959. pp. 28-32. *
Reprinted from *Marriage* Aug. 1959.

265 "The frustrating fifties." *Sign*, Vol. 39 Dec. 1959. pp. 33-39.

266 "The vanishing hero." *America*, Vol. 102 Dec. 12, 1959. pp. 350-352.
Continued in *America*, Mar. 19, 1960.

267 "Pioneers in suburbia." *Catholic Digest*, Vol. 24 Jan. 1960. pp. 20-23.
Condensed from **The Church and the Suburbs**.

268 "Serving Christ together." *Marriage*, Vol. 42 Feb. 1960. pp. 55-58.

269 "Pride." *Ave Maria*, Vol. 91 Feb. 27, 1960. pp. 8-9. *

270 "Psychology of worship." *Worship*, Vol. 34 Mar. 1960. pp. 188-195.

271 "No more 'radicals'?" *America*, Vol. 102 Mar. 19, 1960. pp. 733-735.
Continued from *America*, Dec. 12, 1959.

272   "Culture, contemplation and the religious revival." *The Critic*,
        Vol. 18 May 1960. pp. 17-18+.

273   "Prepare your child for college." *Marriage*, Vol. 42 June 1960.
        pp. 27-31.

274   "City life and the churches." *America*, Vol. 103 Aug. 27, 1960.
        pp. 573-574. (Study program: Community Life and Chicago's
        Housing.)

275   "The neurotic city." *Social Order*, Vol. 10 Sept. 1960. pp. 318-
        323.

276   "Why they cheat." *Sign*, Vol. 40 Oct. 1960. pp. 13-15.

277   "Let them make their own decisions." *Marriage*, Vol. 42 Dec.
        1960. pp. 7-11.

278   "Symbols for your family." *Catholic World*, Vol. 192 Dec.
        1960. pp. 171-175.
        Excerpted in *Commonweal*, Jan. 6, 1961.

279   "Man's need for symbols." *Commonweal*, Vol. 73 Jan. 6, 1961,
        pp. 388-390.
        Excerpted from *Catholic World*, Dec. 1960.

280   "Why they go steady." *Marriage*, Vol. 43 Feb. 1961. pp. 17-
        24.

281   "No more crusades." *Today*, Vol. 16 June 1961. pp. 25-26.

282   "Suburbia revisited." *Social Order*, Vol. 11 Oct. 1961. pp. 371-
        373.

283   "Myths, symbols and rituals in the modern world." *The Critic*,
        Vol. 20 Dec. 1961/Jan. 1962. pp. 18-25.

284   "Some aspects of interaction between religious groups in an upper
        middle class Roman Catholic parish." *Social Compass*, Vol. 9
        n.m. 1962. pp. 39-61. (Abstract in French.)

M. A. thesis submitted to Dept. of Sociology, Univ. of Chicago, Feb. 1961.

285 "The question of the parish as a community." *Worship*, Vol. 36 Feb. 1962. pp. 136-143.

286 "Give them back their revolutionary." *Marianist*, Vol. 53 Apr. 1962. pp. 4-8. *

287 "Catholic scholars of tomorrow: report on a survey." *The Critic*, Vol. 20 Apr./May 1962. pp. 24-26.

288 "The city and the church." *Catholic Digest*, Vol. 26 May 1962. pp. 100-115.

289 "Areas of research on religion and social organizations." *American Catholic Sociological Review*, Vol. 23 Summer 1962. pp. 99-112.

290 "Do they lose the faith at secular colleges?" *Catholic World*, Vol. 195 June 1962. pp. 143-148.

291 "The teen years: spiritual difficulties." *Ave Maria*, Vol. 95 June 2, 1962. pp. 21-23.

292 "New life for the ghost parish." *Information*, Vol. 76 July 1962. pp. 18-23. *

293 "White parish: refuge or resource?" *Interracial Review*, Vol. 35 July 1962. pp. 168-169. *

294 "New horizons in Catholic thought--II: sociology of religion." *The Critic*, Vol. 21 Aug./Sept. 1962. pp. 11-14+.

295 "Don't push them into marriage." *Marriage*, Vol. 44 Oct. 1962. pp. 34-38.
Reprinted in *Family Digest*, Mar. 1963.

296 "Housecleaning in the Negro community?" *Interracial Review*, Vol. 35 Nov. 1962. pp. 247-249. *

A version appears in *New City*, Nov. 1, 1962 and in *Catholic Mind*, June 1963.

297   and Robert D. Crain. "The Negro and his middle class leadership." *New City*, Vol. 1 Nov. 1, 1962. pp. 4-8. A version appears in *Interracial Review*, Nov. 1972 and in *Catholic Mind*, June 1963.

298   "Anti-intellectualism in Catholic colleges." *American Catholic Sociological Review*, Vol. 23 Winter 1962. pp. 350-368. (Reply Spring 1963.)

299   and James Casey. "An upper middle class deviant gang." *American Catholic Sociological Review*, Vol. 24 Spring 1963. pp. 33-41.

300   Lamanna, Richard A. "Greeley on anti-intellectualism." *American Catholic Sociological Review*, Vol. 24 Spring 1963. pp. 57-58. (Reply to Winter 1962.)

301   "American religious pluralism and social organization." *American Benedictine Review*, Vol. 14 Mar. 1963. pp. 69-78.

302   "Catholic colleges: system in transition." *Journal of Higher Education*, Vol. 34 Mar. 1963. pp. 158-163.

303   "Don't push them into marriage." *Family Digest*, Vol. 18 Mar. 1963. pp. 46-50. *
Reprinted from *Marriage* Oct. 1962.

304   "Letter to a young man." *Ave Maria*, Vol. 97 Mar. 16, 1963. pp. 5-9.

305   "Letter to a young woman." *Ave Maria*, Vol. 97 Mar. 23, 1963. pp. 8-12.

306   "Some information on the present situation of American Catholics." *Social Order*, Vol. 13 Apr. 1963. pp. 9-24.

307   "Church attendance among college graduates." *Catholic World*, Vol. 197 May 1963. pp. 95-99.

308 "Influence of the 'religious factor' on the career plans and occupational values of college graduates." *American Journal of Sociology*, Vol. 68 May 1963. pp. 658-671.

309 "Letter to a seminarian." *Ave Maria*, Vol. 97 May 4, 1963. pp. 5-8+.
Some material included in *Priests for Tomorrow*.

310 "Rejoinder to Lamanna." *American Catholic Sociological Review*, Vol. 24 Summer 1963. p. 167. (Rejoinder to Spring 1963.)

311 and Robert D. Crain. "What about this Negro community?" *Catholic Mind*, Vol. 61 June 1963. pp. 15-20.
A version appears in *Interracial Review*, Nov. 1962 and in *New City*, Nov. 1, 1962.

312 "Youth in the age of renewal. Part 1. The coward's trap." *Ave Maria*, Vol. 98 Sept. 21, 1963. pp. 5-7.

313 "Youth in the age of renewal. Part 2. God's rendezvous with man." *Ave Maria*, Vol. 98 Sept. 28, 1963. pp. 4-7.

314 "A note on the origins of religious differences." *Journal for the Scientific Study of Religion*, Vol. 3 Oct. 1963. pp. 21-31.

315 "Youth in the age of renewal. Part 3. Life is forever." *Ave Maria*, Vol. 98 Oct. 5, 1963. pp. 13-15.

316 "Youth in the age of renewal. Part 4. The importance of being yourself." *Ave Maria*, Vol. 98 Oct. 12, 1963. pp. 21-23.

317 "Youth in the age of renewal. Part 5. Out of the nest: lay people have a role in the church." *Ave Maria*, Vol. 98 Oct. 19, 1963. pp. 22-25.

318 "Youth in the age of renewal. Part 6. Your need to read." *Ave Maria*, Vol. 98 Oct. 26, 1963. pp. 8-11.

319 "Youth in the age of renewal. Part 7. Counterfeit husband." *Ave Maria*, Vol. 98 Nov. 2, 1963. pp. 12-14+.

320   "Youth in the age of renewal. Part 8. Look past the honeymoon."
       Ave Maria, Vol. 98 Nov. 9, 1963. pp. 9-11.

321   "Youth in the age of renewal. Part 9. Diplomas and diapers."
       Ave Maria, Vol. 98 Nov. 16, 1963. pp. 12-15.

322   "Youth in the age of renewal. Part 10. That extra dimension."
       Ave Maria, Vol. 98 Nov. 23, 1963. pp. 17-19+.

323   "Parish priest as administrator." *Apostolate*, Vol. 9 Winter 1963.
       pp. 25-31.

324   and Peter Rossi. "The effects of Catholic education. Part I."
       The Critic, Vol. 22 Dec. 1963/Jan. 1964. pp. 34-38.

325   and Peter H. Rossi. "Correlates of parochial school attendance."
       School Review, Vol. 72 Spring 1964. pp. 52-73.

326   and Peter H. Rossi. "The impact of the Roman Catholic
       denominational school." *School Review*, Vol. 72 Spring 1964.
       pp. 34-51.

327   "The Protestant ethic: time for a moratorium." *Sociological
       Analysis*, Vol. 25 Spring 1964. pp. 20-23.
       Presented at the American Catholic Sociological Society, Aug.
       1963.

328   "Conventional wisdom and the Catholic schools." *New City*, Vol.
       2 Mar. 15, 1964. pp. 7-9. (*Are Parochial Schools the Answer?*
       by Mary P. Ryan.) (Reply Mar. 15, 1964.)

329   Ryan, Mary P. "The real question: a reply." *New City*, Vol. 2
       Mar. 15, 1964. pp. 9-10. (Reply to Mar. 15, 1964.)

330   "Comment on Stark's 'On the incompatibility of religion and
       science; a survey of American graduate students'." *Journal for
       the Scientific Study of Religion*, Vol. 3 Apr. 1964. pp. 239-240.
       (Reply Apr. 1964.)

331   "Fraternal authority in the church." *Homiletic & Pastoral
       Review*, Vol. 64 Apr. 1964. pp. 561-570. (Replies May, June,
       July and Oct. 1964.)

332   Stark, Rodney. "Mr. Stark's reply to Father Greeley." *Journal for the Scientific Study of Religion*, Vol. 3 Apr. 1964. pp. 242-243. (Reply to Apr. 1964.)

333   "The Catholic message and the American intellectual." *The Critic*, Vol. 22 Apr./May 1964. pp. 34-35+. Reprinted in *Pastoral Catechetics*.

334   "A sociologist's view." *Catholic School Journal*, Vol. 64 May 1964. pp. 26-27.

335   Casey, George W. "Further thoughts on 'fraternal authority'." *Homiletic & Pastoral Review*, Vol. 64 May 1964. pp. 642+. (Reply to Apr. 1964.)

336   Grabowski, Stanley M. "Initiative . . . 'blind obedience' . . . 'subsidiarity'." *Homiletic & Pastoral Review*, Vol. 64 May 1964. pp. 637+. (Reply to Apr. 1964.)

337   Heide, Herman L. "Paternal vs. fraternal authority." *Homiletic & Pastoral Review*, Vol. 64 May 1964. pp. 647-648+. (Reply to Apr. 1964.)

338   McKenzie, John L. "The theory of authority." *Homiletic & Pastoral Review*, Vol. 64 May 1964. pp. 645+. (Reply to Apr. 1964.)

339   "A new breed." *America*, Vol. 110 May 23, 1964. pp. 706-709. Later published in pamphlet form by America Press. (Replies June 27, 1964.)

340   "Warmth from on high--authority in the church." *Homiletic & Pastoral Review*, Vol. 64 June 1964. p. 734. (Letter from a military chaplain.) (Reply to Apr. 1964.)

341   Polt, Walter J. *et al.* "The new breed arrives!" *America*, Vol. 110 June 27, 1964. pp. 863-865. (Replies to May 23, 1964.)

342   Cunningham, Thomas. "Fraternal authority: further searchings." *Homiletic & Pastoral Review*, Vol. 64 July 1964. pp. 822-823. (Reply to Apr. 1964.)

343 "Authority in the church." *Commonweal*, Vol. 80 July 24, 1964. pp. 515-516.
Excerpted from *Homiletic & Pastoral Review*, Apr. 1964.

344 "The contribution the behavioral sciences can make in seminary training." *National Catholic Educational Assn. Bulletin*, Vol. 61 Aug. 1964. pp. 47-53.

345 "American sociology and the study of ethnic immigrant groups." *International Migration Digest*, Vol. 1 Fall 1964. pp. 107-113.

346 Senlow, George. "The authority of sons." *Homiletic & Pastoral Review*, Vol. 65 Oct. 1964. p. 102. (Reply to Apr. 1964.)

347 "The new young people." *Catholic Digest*, Vol. 28 Oct. 1964. pp. 46-48.
Excerpted from *America*, May 23, 1964.

348 "Entering the mainstream." *Commonweal*, Vol. 81 Oct. 2, 1964. pp. 33-37.
(Intellectualism of American Catholics.) (Reply Oct. 16, 1964.)

349 Gordis, Robert. "Entering the mainstream." *Commonweal*, Vol. 81 Oct. 16, 1964. pp. 102-103. (Reply to Oct. 2, 1964.)

350 "U. S. Catholicism: growth or decline?" *America*, Vol. 111 Oct. 24, 1964. pp. 480-483.

351 Peter Rossi and Leonard Pinto. "The effects of Catholic education. Part II." *The Critic*, Vol. 23 Oct./Nov. 1964. pp. 49-52.

352 "Mirror of the minority?" *Extension*, Vol. 59 Nov. 1964. p. 10.
*

353 "Minds at work: conservative Catholics just a myth." *Catholic Mind*, Vol. 63 Feb. 1965. pp. 29-31.

354 Peter Rossi and Leonard Pinto. "The effects of Catholic education. Part III: are Catholic schools divisive?" *The Critic*, Vol. 23 Feb./Mar. 1965. pp. 57-62.

355 "Catholic education." *America*, Vol. 112 Apr. 17, 1965. pp. 522-524+.

356 "The temptation of the new breed." *America*, Vol. 112 May 22, 1965. pp. 750-752.

357 "Theories of American Catholicism." *The Critic*, Vol. 23 June/July 1965. pp. 28-32.

358 Seymour Sudman and Leonard Pinto. "The effectiveness of self-administered questionnaires." *Journal of Marketing Research*, Vol. 2 Aug. 1965. pp. 293-297.
A version appears in *Reducing the Costs of Surveys*.

359 "Authority and freedom." *Homiletic & Pastoral Review*, Vol. 65 Sept. 1965. pp. 999-1004.

360 "Some seminarians need to grow up." *St. Louis Review*, Sept. 24, 1965. n.p. (Reply Oct. 8, 1965.)

361 "The religious behavior of graduate students." *Journal for the Scientific Study of Religion*, Vol. 5 Oct. 1965. pp. 34-40.

362 Barnes, Michael. "Seminarians' dilemma." *St. Louis Review*, Oct. 8, 1965. n.p. (Reply to Sept. 24, 1965.)

363 *et al.* "'The secular city'." *Commonweal*, Vol. 83 Nov. 12, 1965. pp. 181-184.
Reprinted in *The Secular City Debate*.

364 "The real problems of the American church." *America*, Vol. 113 Nov. 13, 1965. pp. 571-572+.

365 "Criticism of undergraduate faculty by graduates of Catholic colleges." *Review of Religious Research*, Vol. 6 Winter 1965. pp. 96-106.

366 "Diaspora or pluralism?" *The Critic*, Vol. 24 Dec. 1965/Jan. 1966. pp. 56-58.

367 "Social-medical problems of youth." *Linacre Quarterly*, Vol. 33 Feb. 1966. pp. 12-16.

368   *et al.* "Catholicism Midwest style." *America*, Vol. 114 Feb. 12, 1966. pp. 222-223.

369   "What's RIGHT with American Catholics?" *Sign*, Vol. 45 Mar. 1966. pp. 9-12.

370   "The place of religion." *Commonweal*, Vol. 84 Apr. 1966. pp. 104-110. (Catholic colleges.)

371   "Organization or chaos." *Catholic Mind*, Vol. 64 June 1966. pp. 47-48.
       Reprinted from *St. Louis Review* Feb. 18, 1966.

372   and Seymour Warkov. "Parochial school origins and educational achievement." *American Sociological Review,* Vol. 31 June 1966. pp. 406-414.

373   "A farewell to the new breed." *America*, Vol. 114 June 4, 1966. pp. 801-804.

374   "The NEW community." *The Critic*, Vol. 24 June/July 1966. pp. 32-37.

375   "The lonely pastor and the expendable curate." *Homiletic & Pastoral Review*, Vol. 66 Aug. 1966. pp. 919-930.

376   "After secularity: the neo-gemeinschaft society: a post-Christian postscript." *Sociological Analysis*, Vol. 27 Fall 1966. pp. 119-127.
       Presidential address presented at the American Catholic Sociological Society Convention, Aug. 1966.

377   "The Catholic campus." *The Critic*, Vol. 25 Oct./Nov. 1966. pp. 84-89.

378   "Campus community: experiment in living." *America*, Vol. 115 Nov. 12, 1966. pp. 588-591.

379   "Issues in the teaching of religion in Catholic colleges and universities." *Living Light*, Vol. 3, No. 4 [1967]. pp. 77-92.

380   "Greeley on Fichter." *National Catholic Reporter,* Vol. 3 Jan. 4, 1967. p. 6. (Reply Jan. 4, 1967.)

381   Fichter, Joseph H. "Fichter on Greeley." *National Catholic Reporter,* Vol. 3 Jan. 4, 1967. p. 6. (Reply to Jan. 4, 1967.)

382   "The facts about Catholic schools." *Catholic Digest*, Vol. 31 Feb. 1967. pp. 14-16.
       Excerpted from *Our Sunday Visitor*, Nov. 1966.

383   "Issues that divide the Church: the discussion begins." *National Catholic Reporter,* Vol. 3 Feb. 8, 1967. pp. 1+.
       Also appears in *Issues That Divide the Church*.

384   "Laicization of Catholic colleges." *Christian Century*, Vol. 84 Mar. 22, 1967. pp. 372-375.

385   "Changing styles of Catholic spirituality." *Homiletic & Pastoral Review*, Vol. 67 Apr. 1967. pp. 557-565.

386   "Honesty in the church." *America*, Vol. 116 Apr. 1, 1967. p. 501.

387   "Religion and academic career plans: a note on progress." *American Journal of Sociology*, Vol. 72 May 1967. pp. 668-672. (Reply and rejoinder May 1968.)

388   *et al.* "Zeroing in on freedom: can the Charles Currans be freed?" *Commonweal*, Vol. 86 June 2, 1967. pp. 317-318.
       Reprinted in *The Catholic University: a modern appraisal*.

389   "Catholic high schools and the secular city." *National Catholic Educational Assn. Bulletin*, Vol. 64 Aug. 1967. pp. 78-81. *
       Reprinted in *Trends and Issues in Catholic Education*.

390   "Anti-clericalism in the American church." *American Ecclesiastical Review*, Vol. 157 Sept. 1967. pp. 180-188.

391   "A new urbanity." *New City*, Vol. 5 Oct. 1967. pp. 5-8.

392   "John Fitzgerald Kennedy, Doctor of the Church." *The Critic*,

Vol. 26 Oct./Nov. 1967. pp. 40-44 +.
Excerpted from *The Catholic Experience: an interpretation of the history of American Catholicism.*

393   "Myths and fads in Catholic higher education." *America*, Vol. 117 Nov. 11, 1967. pp. 542-545.

394   "Trouble makers haunt the church." *Theology Today*, Vol. 24 Jan. 1968. pp. 507-509.

395   "The problems of ex-priests." *Catholic Mind*, Vol. 66 Mar. 1968. pp. 8-9.

396   "The church in the suburbs: some afterthoughts." *New City*, Vol. 6 Apr. 1968. pp. 7-10.

397   Carr, Andrea and William J. Bowers. "On religion and academic career plans." *American Journal of Sociology*, Vol. 73 May 1968. pp. 768-769. (Reply to May 1967.)

398   "Reply." *American Journal of Sociology*, Vol. 73 May 1968. pp. 769-770. (Rejoinder to May 1967.)

399   "Greeley: it's faddish on revolution." *National Catholic Reporter,* Vol. 4 May 29, 1968. p. 8.

400   "A question of identity." *New City*, Vol. 6 July 1968. pp. 6-8. A version appeared in *The Priest*, Jan. 1969.

401   "A sex to love with." *The Critic*, Vol. 27 Aug. 8, 1968. pp. 32-43.
Excerpted from *A Future to Hope In: socio-religious speculations.*
Reprinted in *Sex: thoughts for contemporary Christians.*

402   "The college blight on idealism." *Educational Record*, Vol. 49 Fall 1968. pp. 429-434.

403   "Academe, my academe." *New City*, Vol. 6 Sept. 1968. pp. 15-18.

404   "What do the people say?" *Commonweal*, Vol. 89 Oct. 11, 1968.
p. 53. (*Humanae Vitae*.)

405   "The church as 'new community'." *Sign*, Vol. 48 Nov. 1968.
pp. 27-29.

406   "John Fitzgerald Kennedy, Doctor of the Church." *Catholic
Digest*, Vol. 33 Nov. 1968. pp. 17-19.
Reprinted from *The Critic* Oct./Nov. 1967.

407   "The psychedelic and the sacred." *Current Issues in Higher
Education*, Vol. 24 n.m. 1969. pp. 201-210.
A version appeared in *The Critic*, Apr. 1969.

408   "A question of identity." *The Priest*, Vol. 25 Jan. 1969. pp. 10-
12+.
A version appeared in *New City*, July 1968.

409   "Thoughts by the lake: interrupted by phones." *National Catholic
Reporter*, Vol. 5 Jan. 1, 1969. p. 10.   *

410   "The fear of being loved." *National Catholic Reporter*, Vol. 5
Jan. 8, 1969. p. 8.

411   "On the beach." *National Catholic Reporter*, Vol. 5 Jan. 15,
1969. p. 8.

412   "Solving problems for others." *National Catholic Reporter*, Vol.
5 Jan. 22, 1969. p. 8.

413   "Catholic alumni: seven years after." *America*, Vol. 120 Jan. 25,
1969. pp. 96-100.

414   "What will the younger generation do with the church?" *Catholic
Digest*, Vol. 33 Feb. 1969. pp. 34-37.
Excerpted from *What Do We Believe?*

415   "Gloom and doom don't fit into the Good News." *National
Catholic Reporter*, Vol. 5 Feb. 5, 1969. p. 8.

416   "Supermom." *National Catholic Reporter*, Vol. 5 Feb. 26, 1969.
p. 8.

417   "The first papal press conference: a vision." *The Critic*, Vol. 27
       Feb./Mar. 1969. pp. 14-19.

418   "Self-respect." *The Priest*, Vol. 25 Mar. 1969. pp. 140-144.

419   "The hardest virtue--tenderness." *National Catholic Reporter,*
       Vol. 6 Mar. 5, 1969. p. 6.

420   "The Blessed Mother's role in an otherwise male church."
       National Catholic Reporter, Vol. 5 Mar. 12, 1969. p. 8.

421   "Crisis of middle years--to keep on growing." *National Catholic
       Reporter*, Vol. 5 Mar. 26, 1969. p. 8.

422   "Leadership." *The Priest*, Vol. 25 Apr. 1969. pp. 208-213.

423   "The sacred and the psychedelic." *The Critic*, Vol. 27 Apr./May
       1969. pp. 25-32.
       A version appeared in *Current Issues in Higher Education*, 1969.

424   "Good worship." *Catholic Digest*, Vol. 33 May 1969. pp. 51-
       53.
       Excerpted from *A Future to Hope In: socio-religious
       speculations.*

425   "We can't walk alone." *Sign*, Vol. 48 May 1969. pp. 20-23.
       Excerpted from *Life for a Wanderer.*

426   "There's a new time religion on campus." *New York Times
       Magazine*, June 1, 1969. pp. 14-15+. (Replies June 29 and July
       13, 1969.)

427   Kruger, Annette. "Spellbound." *New York Times Magazine*,
       June 29, 1969. p. 28. (Reply to June 1, 1969.)

428   "We had better travel light." *Sign*, Vol. 48 July 1969. pp. 8-
       10+.
       Excerpted from *Like for a Wanderer.*

429   Witch, Cynthia. "Bewitched." *New York Times Magazine*, July
       13, 1969. p. 68. (Reply to June 1, 1969.)

430 "Overkill on celibacy." *The Tablet* (London), Vol. 223 July 19, 1969. pp. 712-713. (*Celibacy, Ministry, Church* by Joseph Blenkinsopp. Burns and Oates.)

431 "Ethnicity as an influence on behavior." *Integrated Education*, Vol. 7 July/Aug. 1969. pp. 33-41.

432 "May I borrow that computer you have in your pocket?" *Ave Maria*, Vol. 110 Aug. 9, 1969. pp. 24-29. Excerpted from *Life for a Wanderer*.

433 "The sociology of knowledge and the sociology of religion in the Catholic university." *Cross Currents*, Vol. 19 Fall 1969. pp. 481-492. Presented at the Sesquicentennial Conference, St. Louis Univ., St. Louis, MO, Oct. 17, 1968.

434 "The overcommitted man." *Sign*, Vol. 49 Sept. 1969. pp. 12-18. Excerpted from *Life for a Wanderer*.

435 "A fresh look at vocations." *Today*, Vol. 24 Oct. 1969. pp. 3-61. (This is the entire issue.)

436 "Why they leave." *American Ecclesiastical Review*, Vol. 161 Oct. 1969. pp. 251-257.

437 and Howard M. Bobren. "Comparative financial and employee data on Catholic institutions of higher education." *National Catholic Educational Assn. Bulletin*, Vol. 65 Nov. 1969. pp. 19-36.

438 "Continuities in research on the 'religious factor'." *American Journal of Sociology*, Vol. 75 Nov. 1969. pp. 355-359.

439 "A note on political and social differences among ethnic college graduates." *Sociology of Education*, Vol. 42 Winter 1969. pp. 98-103.

440 "The misunderstood minority." *Chicago Daily News*, Dec. 2, 1969. pp. 3+.

441   "Three ways to become more human." *U. S. Catholic and Jubilee*, Vol. 35 Jan. 1970. pp. 15-21.

442   "Come blow your mind with me." *The Critic*, Vol. 28 Jan./Feb. 1970. pp. 22-26.

443   "Beyond the secular city." *New York Times Book Review*, Mar. 15, 1970. Religious Book Supplement. pp. 7+.

444   "Our resurrection." *Catholic Digest*, Vol. 34 Apr. 1970. pp. 24-28.
        Excerpted from *Life for a Wanderer*.

445   "Religious intermarriage in a denominational society." *American Journal of Sociology*, Vol. 75 May 1970. pp. 949-952.

446   "Catholics and the sensitivity cult." *National Catholic Reporter*, Vol. 6 May 1, 1970. pp. 10-12.

447   "The new urban studies: a word of caution." *Educational Record*, Vol. 51 Summer 1970. pp. 232-236.

448   "Superstition, ecstasy and tribal consciousness." *Social Research*, Vol. 37 Summer 1970. pp. 203-211.

449   "Friendship is a risky game." *Sign*, Vol. 49 June 1970. pp. 12-18.
        Excerpted from *The Friendship Game*.

450   "Turning off the 'people': the war and white ethnic groups." *New Republic*, Vol. 162 June 27, 1970. pp. 14-16.
        Excerpted in *Current*, Aug. 1970.

451   "Fearless forecast for religion." *Catholic Digest*, Vol. 34 July 1970. pp. 14-16.
        Excerpted from *Religion in the Year 2000*.

452   "Intellectuals as an 'ethnic group'." *New York Times Magazine*, July 12, 1970. pp. 22-23+. (Replies July 26 and Aug. 9, 1970.)

453   Kauffmann, Stanley; Oxenhorn, Harvey. "Eggheads by the

bunch." *New York Times Magazine*, July 26, 1970. p. 49. (Replies to July 12, 1970.)

454   "Moral intelligence in a complicated society: the role of the college." *Univ. of Chicago Magazine*, Vol.? July/Aug. 1970. p.? *

455   "The risks of community." *The Critic*, Vol. 28 July/Aug. 1970. pp. 18-26.

456   Bughman, Robin R.; Chambers, Anne M.; Lloyd, Gerald D. "The intelligentsia." *New York Times Magazine*, Aug. 9, 1970. p. 58. (Replies to July 12, 1970.)

457   "The war and white ethnic groups." *Current*, n.v. No. 120 Aug. 1970. pp. 22-27. Excerpted from *New Republic*, June 27, 1970.

458   "Between 'tenuously in' and 'solidly in': a view from the borderland." *Educational Record*, Vol. 51 Fall 1970. pp. 413-418. (Commentary on "What's bugging the students?" by Kenneth Keniston. *Educational Record*, Spring 1970.)

459   "Malice in Wonderland: misperceptions of the academic elite." *Change*, Vol. 2 Sept./Oct 1970. pp. 32-39.

460   "The bread of faith." *The Critic*, Vol. 29 Sept./Oct. 1970. pp. 37-44.

461   "Comment on 'Educational expectations'." *American Sociological Review*, Vol. 35 Oct. 1970. pp. 917-918. (Article by Rhodes and Nam, *American Sociological Review*, Apr. 1970.)

462   "Religion still has tenure." *New York Times*, Oct. 17, 1970. p. 29.

463   and Joe L. Spaeth. "Research note: political change among college alumni." *Sociology of Education*, Vol. 43 Winter 1970. pp. 106-113.

464   "Implications for the sociology of religion of occult behavior in

the youth culture." *Youth and Society*, Vol. 2 Dec. 1970. pp.
131-140.
Revised version presented at the American Sociological Assn.,
Washington, DC, Aug. 31, 1970.
Reprinted in *On the Margin of the Visible*.

465   "Leadership in the church of the future." *Catholic Mind*, Vol. 68
Dec. 1970. pp. 11-18.

466   "Take heart from the heartland." *New Republic*, Vol. 163 Dec.
12, 1970. pp. 16-19. (Reply Dec. 26, 1970.)
Reprinted in *Overcoming Middle Class Rage*.

467   "Myths, meaning and Vatican III." *America*, Vol. 123 Dec. 19,
1970. pp. 538-542.

468   Kelly, Tom. "Mayor Daley's smart, but what else?" *New
Republic*, Vol. 163 Dec. 26, 1970. pp. 9-11. (Reply to Dec. 12,
1970.) (Rejoinder Jan. 2, 1971.)

469   "How to choose a friend." *Catholic Digest*, Vol. 35 Jan. 1971.
pp. 123-124.
Excerpted from *The Friendship Game*.

470   "Ethnic politics." *New Republic*, Vol. 164 Jan. 2, 1971. p. 43.
(Rejoinder to Dec. 26, 1970.)

471   "The redeeming of America according to Charles Reich."
America, Vol. 124 Jan. 9, 1971. pp. 14-17.
Reprinted in *The Con III Controversy: the critics look at the
Greening of America*.

472   "L'affaire Berrigan." *New York Times*, Feb. 19, 1971. p. 37.
(Reply Mar. 13, 1971.)

473   McGarry, Patrick S. "This is pluralism?" *New York Times*,
Mar. 13, 1971. p. 28. (Reply to Feb. 19, 1971.)

474   "The last of the American Irish fade away." *New York Times
Magazine*, Mar. 14, 1971. pp. 32-33+. (Replies Apr. 4, 1971.)

475   Clerkin, James *et al.* "The American Irish are alive and well."
        New York Times Magazine, Apr. 4, 1971. pp. 102-103. (Replies
        to Mar. 14, 1971.)

476   "The alienation of white ethnic groups." *Sign*, Vol. 50 May
        1971. pp. 16-21.
        Presented at the Conference on National Unity, Sterling Forest
        Gardens, NY, Nov. 19-20, 1969.
        Excerpted from *Why Can't They Be Like Us? Facts and fallacies
        about ethnic differences and group conflicts in America.*

477   "Catholic schools: survival or suicide?" *St. Anthony Messenger*,
        Vol. 78 May 1971. pp. 30-35.

478   "The American Irish since the death of Studs Lonigan." *The
        Critic*, Vol. 29 May/June 1971. pp. 27-33.

479   "Priest, church and the future from a sociological viewpoint."
        Chicago Studies, Vol. 10 Summer 1971. pp. 115-129.

480   "Two words to live by." *Sign*, Vol. 50 July 1971. pp. 5-8.
        Excerpted from *The Jesus Myth*.

481   "It has to be yes or no." *Sign*, Vol. 51 Aug.1971. pp. 10-13.

482   "Sociology as an art form." *American Sociologist*, Vol. 6 Aug.
        1971. pp. 223-225.

483   "The rediscovery of diversity." *Antioch Review*, Vol. 31 Fall
        1971. pp. 343-365.

484   "For a black vice president in 1972." *New York Times Magazine*,
        Sept. 19, 1971. pp. 28+. (Replies Oct. 17, 1971.)

485   "Portrait of the neighborhood, changing." *The Critic*, Vol. 30
        Sept./Oct. 1971. pp. 14-23.

486   " 'A most distressful nation': a portrait of the American Irish."
        Dissent, Vol. 18 Oct. 1971. pp. 450-459. (Reply Summer
        1972.)
        Expanded version in *Through Different Eyes: black and white
        perspectives on American race relations.*

487   *et al.* "The Newman Report: four comments." *Journal of Higher Education*, Vol. 42 Oct. 1971. pp. 610-623.

488   Boring, Phyllis Z.; Maltz, Charles. "A woman for V. P." *New York Times Magazine*, Oct. 17, 1971. pp. 8+. (Replies to Sept. 19, 1971.)

489   "After the synod." *America*, Vol. 125 Nov. 20, 1971. pp. 424-426. (Replies Jan. 15, 1972.)

490   "Leadership and friendship: a sociologist's viewpoint." *Jurist*, Vol. 31 Winter 1971. pp. 266-279.
       Also appears in *Who Decides for the Church: studies in co-responsibility*.

491   and Paul B. Sheatsley. "Attitudes toward racial integration." *Scientific American*, Vol. 225 Dec. 1971. pp. 10+. (*See also Social Problems and Public Policy: inequality and justice*, and *Scientific American*, June 1978.)
       Reprint. San Francisco: W.H. Freeman, 1971. *Scientific American* Offprints: 673. Microform. *

492   and William C. McCready. "An ethnic group which vanished--the strange case of the American Irish." *Social Studies: Irish Journal of Sociology*, Vol. 1 Jan. 1972. pp. 78-79.

493   Schall, James V. *et al.* "The bishops' role." *America*, Vol. 126 Jan. 15, 1972. pp. 37-38. (Replies to Nov. 20, 1971.)

494   "The uses of sociology." *The Month*, Vol. 5 Feb. 1972. pp. 48-53.

495   "The state of the priesthood." *National Catholic Reporter*, Vol. 8 Feb. 18, 1972. pp. 7-18.
       Presented at the Ad Hoc Committee on the Implementation of the Priesthood Study.

496   "Occupational choice among the American Irish: a research note." *Eire-Ireland*, Vol. 7 Spring 1972. pp. 3-9.

497   "A most distressful nation: the American Irish." *Intellectual Digest*, Vol. 11 Mar. 1972. pp. 23-24.

498   "Is Catholic sexual teaching coming apart?" *The Critic*, Vol. 30
        Mar./Apr. 1972. pp. 30-35.
        A part reprinted in *An Andrew Greeley Reader Vol.I.*

499   "Resurrection is real." *Catholic Digest*, Vol. 36 Apr. 1972. pp.
        113-114.
        Excerpted from *The Touch of the Spirit.*

500   "U. S. Catholics '72." *The Month*, Vol. 5 May 1972. pp. 135-
        138+.

501   "The new agenda." *The Critic*, Vol. 30 May/June 1972. pp. 36-
        42.
        A part reprinted in *An Andrew Greeley Reader Vol.I.*

502   "American Catholics--making it or losing it?" *Public Interest*,
        n.v. Summer 1972. pp. 26-37.

503   "Political attitudes among American white ethnics." *Public
        Opinion Quarterly*, Vol. 36 Summer 1972. pp. 213-220.
        Presented at the American Political Science Assn. Meetings, Sept.
        10, 1971.
        Reprinted in *Sociological Essays and Research.*

504   "War, morality & error." *Dissent*, Vol. 19 Summer 1972. pp.
        520-523.

505   Raleigh, John H. "The Irish as immigrants." *Dissent*, Vol. 19
        Summer 1972. pp. 542-543. (Reply to Oct. 1971.) (Rejoinder
        Summer 1972.)

506   "The Irish as immigrants: Andrew Greeley replies." *Dissent*,
        Vol. 19 Summer 1972. pp. 543-544. (Rejoinder to Summer
        1972.)

507   "Vandalism, suburban style." *U. S. Catholic*, Vol. 37 June 1972.
        pp. 33-38.

508   "Friendship and marriage." *Ecumenist*, Vol. 10 July/Aug. 1972.
        pp. 65-71.

509   "New questions." *Catholic Library World*, Vol. 44 July/Aug.

1972. pp. 8-10.
Excerpts from an address to the CLA Convention luncheon, Apr.
6, 1972.
(See also "Greeley: ask new questions." *National Catholic
Reporter*, Apr. 21, 1972.)

510   "The new agenda." *The Tablet* (London), Vol. 226 Aug. 26,
         1972. pp. 808-809.
         Part 1. (Part 2 *see* Sept. 2, 1972.)

511   "The ethnic and religious origins of young American scientists
         and engineers: a research note." *International Migration Review*,
         Vol. 6 Fall 1972. pp. 282-288.

512   "Comment   on   Hunt's   'Mythological-Symbolic   religious
         commitment: the LAM scales'." *Journal for the Scientific Study
         of Religion*, Vol. 11 Sept. 1972. pp. 287-289. (Reply Sept.
         1972.)

513   Hunt, Richard A. "Reply to Greeley." *Journal for the Scientific
         Study of Religion*, Vol. 11 Sept. 1972. pp. 290-292. (Reply to
         Sept. 1972.)

514   "The new agenda." *The Tablet* (London), Vol. 226 Sept. 2,
         1972. pp. 831-833.
         Part 2. (Part 1 *see* Aug. 26, 1972.)

515   and William C. McCready. "The end of American Catholicism?"
         America, Vol. 127 Oct. 28, 1972. pp. 334-338.

516   "Guide to conferencemanship: what to do when you don't know
         what to do." *College & University Business*, Vol. 53 Nov. 1972.
         pp. 49-52.
         Adapted from *University of Chicago Magazine*, Mar./Apr. 1972.
         Reprinted in *Nation's Schools*, Dec. 1972.

517   "The 'new politics' was big loser in election." *Catholic
         Messenger*, Nov. 16, 1972. p. 7.

518   "After exhaustion--taking a look at Catholic renewal." *National
         Catholic Reporter*, Vol. 9 Nov. 17, 1972. Christmas Book
         Report. pp. 7+. (Review essay.) (Replies Dec. 15, 1972.)

519 "The new ethnicity and blue collars: cultural pluralism in the working class." *Dissent*, Vol. 19 Winter 1972. pp. 270-277. Reprinted in *Ethnicity in the United States: a preliminary reconnaissance, The Study of Society*, and *The World of the Blue Collar Worker*.

520 "A guide to conferencemanship: what to do when you don't know what to do." *Nation's Schools*, Vol. 90 Dec. 1972. pp. 36-38. Reprinted from *College & University Business*, Nov. 1972.

521 Callahan, Daniel. "Coach Greeley fumbles." *National Catholic Reporter*, Vol. 9 Dec. 15, 1972. p. 10. (Reply to Nov. 17, 1972.)

522 "The civil religion of ethnic Americans: the viewpoint of a Catholic sociologist." *Vital Speeches of the Day*, Vol. 39 Dec. 15, 1972. pp. 145-150. A version was presented at the Colloquium on Civil Religion in America, Southeastern Baptist Seminary, Wake Forest, NC, Oct. 30-Nov. 1, 1972. A version appears in *Religious Education*, Sept. 1975 and in *Worldview*, Feb. 1973.

523 Dick, Daniel E. "In defense of O'Brien." *National Catholic Reporter*, Vol. 9 Dec. 15, 1972. p. 10. (Reply to Nov. 17, 1972.)

524 "Developing your sexuality." *The Critic*, Vol. 31 Jan./Feb. 1973. pp. 40-49. Excerpted from *Sexual Intimacy*.

525 "Civil religion and ethnic Americans." *Worldview*, Vol. 16 Feb. 1973. pp. 21-27. Presented at the Colloquium on Civil Religion in America, Southeastern Baptist Seminary, Wake Forest, NC, Oct. 30-Nov. 1, 1972. A version appears in *Religious Education*, Sept. 1975.

526 "Public and nonpublic schools: losers both." *School Review*, Vol. 81 Feb. 1973. pp. 195-206.

527 "A scrapyard for the Daley organization?" *Bulletin of Atomic Scientists*, Vol. 29 Feb. 1973. pp. 9-14.

528 "The Devil, you say." *New York Times Magazine*, Feb. 4, 1973. pp. 14-15+.
A version of *The Devil, You Say! Man and his personal devils and angels.*

529 "The end of religion?" *Religious Education*, Vol. 68 Mar. 1973. pp. 174-182.

530 "The 'religious factor' and academic careers: another communication." *American Journal of Sociology*, Vol. 78 Mar. 1973. pp. 1247-1255. (Reply July 1974.)

531 "The meaning of being Irish-American." *Chicago Tribune*, Mar. 17, 1973. p. 12.

532 "Reflections on politics and pluralism: a response to jeremiads." *Bulletin of Atomic Scientists*, Vol. 29 May 1973. pp. 31-34.

533 "Joys of sexuality." *Redbook*, Vol. 141 July 1973. pp. 67+.
*
Excerpted from *Sexual Intimacy*.

534 "More long weekends: a relatively modest proposal." *Christian Century*, Vol. 90 Sept. 5, 1973. pp. 852-855.

535 "Making it in America: ethnic groups and social status." *Social Policy*, Vol. 4 Sept./Oct. 1973. pp. 21-29.

536 "Catholic schools are committing suicide." *New York Times Magazine*, Oct. 21, 1973. pp. 40+. (Replies Dec. 2, 1973.)

537 "Fears too many men can't admit to their wives." *Redbook*, Vol. 142 Nov. 1973. pp. 96+. *
Excerpted from *Sexual Intimacy*.

538 "Word of dissent: America first revisited." *Bulletin of Atomic Scientists*, Vol. 29 Nov. 1973. pp. 50-51.

539 and William C. McCready. "Drop in churchgoing 'catastrophic'." *National Catholic Reporter*, Vol. 10 Nov. 16, 1973. pp. 1+.

540 "Leave John Kennedy in peace." *Christian Century*, Vol. 90 Nov. 21, 1973. pp. 1147-1151.

541 "The sexual revolution among Catholic clergy." *Review of Religious Research*, Vol. 14 Winter 1973. pp. 91-100.

542 "Father Greeley replies." *New York Times Magazine*, Dec. 2, 1973. p. 130. (Rejoinder to Dec. 2, 1973.)

543 McGuire, Michael A. "Unwholesome teachings?" *New York Times Magazine*, Dec. 2, 1973. pp. 129-130. (Reply to Oct. 21, 1973.) (Rejoinder Dec. 2, 1973.)

544 "A Christmas biography." *New York Times Magazine*, Dec. 23, 1973. pp. 8-9+. (Replies Jan. 20, 1974.)

545 "Theological table-talk: politics and political theologians." *Theology Today*, Vol. 30 Jan. 1974. pp. 391-397.

546 and William C. McCready. "Catholic education produces 'hopefuls'." *National Catholic Reporter*, Vol. 10 Jan. 11, 1974. p. 13.

547 "Rate of catastrophe may drop." *National Catholic Reporter*, Vol. 10 Jan. 11, 1974. pp. 7+.

548 Darst, Bette-Jean *et al.* "In His own time and ours." *New York Times Magazine*, Jan. 20, 1974. pp. 4+. (Replies to Dec. 23, 1973.) (Rejoinder Jan. 20, 1974.)

549 "In His own time and ours." *New York Times Magazine*, Jan. 20, 1974. p. 62. (Rejoinder to Jan. 20, 1974.)

550 and William C. McCready. "Does ethnicity matter?" *Ethnicity*, Vol. 1 Apr. 1974. pp. 91-108.
A version was presented to the American Academy of Arts and Sciences, Oct. 26, 1972.

551   "If Jesus were alive today would he be crucified?" *Chicago Daily News*, Apr. 6-7, 1974. pp. 1+. (Replies Apr. 13-14, 1974.) Appeared in *New York Times Magazine*, Dec. 23, 1973 as "A Christmas biography."

552   "Why priests stay." *National Catholic Reporter*, Vol. 10 Apr. 12, 1974. p. 24.

553   Mlincek, Jean *et al.* "The Holy Week biography: our readers respond." *Chicago Daily News*, Apr. 13-14, 1974. p. 8. (Replies to Apr. 6-7, 1974.)

554   "Marginal but not alienated:confessions of a loudmouthed Irish priest." *Social Policy*, Vol. 5 May/June 1974. pp. 4-11.

555   "Religion in a secular society." *Social Research*, Vol. 41 Summer 1974. pp. 226-240.

556   and Richard A. Schoenherr. "Role commitment processes and the American Catholic priesthood." *American Sociological Review*, Vol. 39 June 1974. pp. 407-426.
A version was presented at the 1971 American Sociological Assn. meetings in Denver, CO.

557   and Jim Miller. "Catholics and Democrats: an ethnic manifesto." *Village Voice*, June 6, 1974. pp. 8-10. (Reply *Wall Street Journal*, June 12, 1974.)

558   Editorial. "A Catholic manifesto." *Wall Street Journal*, June 12, 1974. p. 20. (Reply to *Village Voice*, June 6, 1974.)

559   "Bright new theology." *National Catholic Reporter*, Vol. 10 June 21, 1974. p. 9.

560   "Greeley replies to Humphreys." *American Journal of Sociology*, Vol. 80 July 1974. pp. 219-220. (Rejoinder to July 1974.)

561   Humphreys, Claire. "The religious factor: comment on Greeley's conclusion." *American Journal of Sociology*, Vol. 80 July 1974. pp. 217-219. (Reply to Mar. 1973.) (Rejoinder July 1974.)

562 "Political participation among ethnic groups in the United States: a preliminary reconnaissance." *American Journal of Sociology* Vol. 80 July 1974. pp. 170-204. Presented at the American Sociological Assn., New Orleans, Aug. 1972.

563 "Notes on a theology of pluralism." *Christian Century*, Vol. 91 July 3, 1974. pp. 696-700.

564 "The 'Catholic action' ideology: a non-nostalgic reappraisal." *The Critic*, Vol. 32 July/Aug./Sept. 1974. pp. 14-21.

565 "The demon of envy." *Sign*, Vol. 54 Sept. 1974. pp. 18-21. Excerpted from *The Devil, You Say! Man and his personal devils and angels.*

566 "The next 10 years." *National Catholic Reporter*, Vol. 11 Nov. 1, 1974. pp. 9-12. (Replies Nov. 22 and Dec. 6, 1974.)

567 "Antiwar fictions." *New York Times*, Nov. 6, 1974. p. 45.

568 Brown, Francis F. and Catherine Pinkerton. "Responses to Greeley." *National Catholic Reporter*, Vol. 11 Nov. 22, 1974. p. 10. (Replies to Nov. 1, 1974.)

569 Norman H. Nie and Barbara Currie. "Political attitudes among American ethnics: a study of perceptual distortion." *Ethnicity*, Vol. 1 Dec. 1974. pp. 317-343. Reprinted from *Ethnicity in the United States: a preliminary reconnaissance.*

570 Van Allen, Rodger. "Greeley drops out the middle." *National Catholic Reporter*, Vol. 11 Dec. 6, 1974. p. 7. (Reply to Nov.1, 1974.)

571 "Hail Mary." *New York Times Magazine*, Dec. 15, 1974. pp. 14-15+. (Replies Feb. 2, 1975.)

572 Dowling, Colette. "Barbie-doll virgin?" *New York Times Magazine*, Feb. 2, 1975. p. 52. (Reply to Dec. 15, 1974.) (Rejoinder Feb. 2, 1975.)

573   "Father Greeley replies." *New York Times Magazine*, Feb. 2, 1975. p. 52. (Rejoinder to Feb. 2, 1975.)

574   Riel, Arthur R., Jr. "Voice from the pews." *New York Times Magazine*, Feb. 2, 1975. p. 52. (Reply to Dec. 15, 1974.) (Rejoinder Feb. 2, 1975.)

575   "Ethnicity and racial attitudes: the case of the Jews and the Poles." *American Journal of Sociology*, Vol. 80 Jan. 1975. pp. 909-932.

576   "Is this suicide necessary?" *New York Times*, Jan. 15, 1975. p. 79. (Catholic schools.)

577   and William C. McCready. "Are we a nation of mystics?" *New York Times Magazine*, Jan. 26, 1975. pp. 12-13+. (Replies Feb. 23, 1975.)

578   *et al.* "American Catholics: ten years later." *The Critic*, Vol. 33 Jan./Feb. 1975. pp. 14-21.

579   "Catholic social activism--real or rad/chic?" *National Catholic Reporter*, Vol. 11 Feb. 7, 1975. pp. 7-8+. (Replies Feb. 28 and Mar. 7, 1975.)

580   Miller, Wesley. "Societal impact." *New York Times Magazine*, Feb. 23, 1975. pp. 72+. (Reply to Jan. 26, 1975.)

581   Ruskin, Asa P. "Mystical or physiological?" *New York Times Magazine*, Feb. 23, 1975. p. 72. (Reply to Jan. 26, 1975.)

582   Davis, William J. *et al.* "Andrew Greeley--real or rad/chic?" *National Catholic Reporter*, Vol. 11 Feb. 28, 1975. pp. 10-11. (Reply to Feb. 7, 1975.) (Rejoinder Mar. 14, 1975.)

583   O'Brien, David. "David O'Brien: Greeley's scenario features straw men." *National Catholic Reporter*, Vol. 11 Mar. 7, 1975. pp. 10-11. (Reply to Feb. 7, 1975.) (Rejoinder Mar. 14, 1975.)

584   "Greeley defends critique of bishops' booklet." *National Catholic Reporter*, Vol. 11 Mar. 14, 1975. p. 14. (Rejoinder to Feb. 28 and Mar. 7, 1975.)

585 "A model for ethnic political socialization." *American Journal of Political Science*, Vol. 19 May 1975. pp. 187-206.

586 "National Catechetical Directory: failure." *National Catholic Reporter*, Vol. 11 May 2, 1975. p. 11.

587 "In the neighborhood." *Human Behavior*, Vol. 4 June 1975. pp. 40-45.

588 "TV's Italian cops--trapped in old stereotypes." *New York Times*, July 27, 1975. Sec. II pp. 1+. (Replies Aug. 10, 1975.)

589 Spilotro, Nicholas *et al.* "Those stereotyped 'Italian' cops." *New York Times*, Aug. 10, 1975. Sec. II p. 23. (Replies to July 27, 1975.)

590 "The civil religion of ethnic Americans: the viewpoint of a Catholic sociologist." *Religious Education*, Vol. 70 Sept. 1975. pp. 499-514.
A version was presented at the Colloquium on Civil Religion in America, Southeastern Baptist Seminary, Wake Forest, NC, Oct. 30-Nov. 1, 1972.
A version appears in *Vital Speeches of the Day*, Dec. 15, 1972 and in *Worldview*, Feb. 1973.

591 "Too much ado about ethnicity? Church should rejoice in it." *Momentum*, Vol. 6 Oct. 1975. pp. 16-19. *

592 "Intellectuals." *The Tablet* (London), Vol. 229 Nov. 29, 1975. Tablet Educational Supplement pp. 1166-1168.

593 *et al.* "1975: 12 divergent views of a most frenzied year." *Chicago Tribune*, Dec. 28, 1975. Sec. 2 pp. 1-2.

594 "Why Hollywood never asks the God question." *New York Times*, Jan. 18, 1976. Sec. II pp. 1+.

595 "Coats of many colors. Photographs by Andrew M. Greeley." *Chicago Tribune Magazine*, Feb. 8, 1976. pp. 14-16. (Chicago domestic architecture.)

596   "A school report." *The Tablet* (London), Vol. 230 Mar. 27, 1976. Tablet Educational Supplement pp. 313-314.

597   "Birth control--a bitter pill for Catholics." *Chicago Tribune*, Mar. 28, 1976. pp. 1+. (*See also* Mar. 29 and 30, 1976.) Excerpted from *Catholic Schools in a Declining Church*.

598   "Catholics loyal to their schools, cite lack of them." *Chicago Tribune*, Mar. 29, 1976. p. 11. (*See also* Mar. 28 and Mar. 30, 1976.) Excerpted from *Catholic Schools in a Declining Church*.

599   "Supply of Catholic priests drops." *Chicago Tribune*, Mar. 30, 1976. p. 5. (*See also* Mar. 28 and Mar. 29, 1976.) Excerpted from *Catholic Schools in a Declining Church*.

600   "The spirit of pluralism." *Spiritual Life*, Vol. 22 Apr. 1976. pp. 2-9.

601   "Crisis in American Catholicism: ten years of declining loyalty and religious devotion in U. S." *Catholic Messenger*, Apr. 1, 1976. pp. 1+.

602   "The next pope." *New York Times Magazine*, Apr. 4, 1976. pp. 20-22+. (Replies May 30, 1976.)

603   "Crisis in American Catholicism Part II: the disastrous effect of Pope Paul's encyclical." *Catholic Messenger*, Apr. 8, 1976. p. 9.

604   "Crisis in American Catholicism Part III: fewer schools a mistake; CCD no substitute." *Catholic Messenger*, Apr. 15, 1976. p. 9.

605   "Crisis in American Catholicism Part IV: respect for the priesthood has been diminishing." *Catholic Messenger*, Apr. 22, 1976. p. 9.

606   "Crisis in American Catholicism Part V: despite what you hear, donations are down." *Catholic Messenger*, Apr. 29, 1976. p. 9.

607 "Crisis in American Catholicism Part VI: scenarios show some bad news on the horizon. *Catholic Messenger*, May 6, 1976. p. 9.

608 "The unwanted who proved indispensable." *Chicago Tribune Magazine*, May 23, 1976. pp. 26-31.

609 Murphy, Francis X. "In praise of Paul." *New York Times Magazine*, May 30, 1976. pp. 17+. (Reply to Apr. 4, 1976.) (Rejoinder May 30, 1976.)

610 O'Gorman, Ned. "Awesome event." *New York Times Magazine*, May 30, 1976. p. 17. (Reply to Apr. 4, 1976.) (Rejoinder May 30, 1976.)

611 "Back-pew spokesman." *New York Times Magazine*, May 30, 1976. p. 17. (Anonymous reply to Apr. 4, 1976.) (Rejoinder May 30, 1976.)

612 "Father Greeley replies." *New York Times Magazine*, May 30, 1976. p. 50. (Rejoinder to May 30, 1976.)

613 "Is ethnicity un-American?" *New Catholic World* Vol. 219 May/June 1976. pp. 106-112.

614 "Catholicism in America: two hundred years and counting: a personal interpretation." *The Critic*, Vol. 34 Summer 1976. pp. 14-47+.

615 "Is the American educational enterprise anti-Catholic?" *Origins*, Vol. 6 June 3, 1976. pp. 17+.
Presented at a meeting sponsored by the U. S. Office of Education, Washington, DC, May 14, 1976.

616 "Summer reading for candidates." *New York Times Book Review*, June 6, 1976. pp. 5-6.

617 "Anti-Catholic feeling among Jews." *New York Times*, June 19, 1976. p. 21. (*See* correction June 25, 1976. p. 27.) (Replies July 1 and Nov. 10, 1976.)

618   Mahoney, John P. *et al.* "Readers answer Father Greeley." *New York Times*, July 1, 1976. p. 29. (Replies to June 19, 1976.)

619   "If God loves diversity, shouldn't we?" *Sign*, Vol. 55 July/Aug. 1976. pp. 18-22.
       Excerpted from *The Communal Catholic: a personal manifesto*.

620   "Council or encyclical?" *Review of Religious Research*, Vol. 18 Fall 1976. pp. 3-24. (The H. Paul Douglass Lecture 1975.)

621   "The ethnic miracle." *Public Interest*, n.v., No. 45 Fall 1976. pp. 20-36.

622   "What is a liberal--who is a conservative?" *Commentary*, Vol. 62 Sept. 1976. pp. 65-67.

623   "Pop psychology and the gospel." *Theology Today*, Vol. 33 Oct. 1976. pp. 224-231.

624   "Heaven sets things right." *Sign*, Vol. 56 Nov. 1976. pp. 24-27.
       Excerpted from *The Great Mysteries: an essential catechism*.

625   Neusner, Jacob. "Interfaith dialogue." *New York Times*, Nov. 10, 1976. p. 28. (Reply to June 19, 1976.)

626   "Confessions of a storyteller." *New Review of Books and Religion*, Vol. 1 Feb. 1977. p. 3.

627   "Who controls Catholic education." *Education and Urban Society*, Vol. 9 Feb. 1977. pp. 147-166.

628   "Christian sex view persists." *National Catholic Reporter*, Vol. 13 Feb. 4, 1977. p. 15.

629   "*Humanae Vitae* and the sense of the faithful: some questions for theologians." *The Critic*, Vol. 35 Spring 1977. pp. 14-25.

630   "Dispelling myths about Catholics." *Chicago Tribune*, Apr. 3, 1977. Sec. 2 pp. 1+. (*See also* Apr. 4, 1977.)
       Excerpted from *The American Catholic: a social portrait*.

631 "The future of an ailing church." *Chicago Tribune*, Apr. 4, 1977. Sec. 4 p. 4. (*See also* Apr. 3, 1977.) Excerpted from *The American Catholic: a social portrait.*

632 "How conservative are American Catholics?" *Political Science Quarterly*, Vol. 92 Summer 1977. pp. 199-218.

633 "Anti-Catholicism in the academy." *Change*, Vol. 9 June 1977. pp. 40-43.

634 "On 'Is there an academic melting pot?'." (Comment on Wuthnow, SOE, January, 1977.) *Sociology of Education*, Vol. 50 July 1977. pp. 218-219. (Reply July 1977.)

635 Wuthnow, Robert. "Reply to Greeley." *Sociology of Education*, Vol. 50 July 1977. p. 219. (Reply to July 1977.)

636 "Neighbourhood and downtown." *The Tablet* (London), Vol. 231 July 9, 1977. Educational Supplement pp. 649-651. A version was presented to the National Catholic Education Assn.

637 "When religion cast off wonder, Hollywood seized it." *New York Times*, Nov. 27, 1977. Sec. II p. 1.

638 "A preliminary investigation: the 'profitability' of Catholic schools." *Momentum*, Vol. 8 Dec. 1977. pp. 43-49.

639 "Ethnic minorities in the United States: demographic perspectives." *International Journal of Group Tensions*, Vol. 7 Dec. 1977. pp. 64-97.

640 "Findings on Catholic abortion views shattering." *Anchor*, Vol.? Jan. 26, 1978. p. 6. *

641 "Debunking the role of social scientists in court." *Human Rights*, Vol. 7 Spring 1978. pp. 34-36+.

642 and Christian W. Jacobsen. "Editorial research note." *Ethnicity*, Vol. 5 Mar. 1978. pp. 1-13. (Occupational patterns of major U. S. ethnic groups.)

643   "The need for leadership: an outsider's viewpoint." *Liberal Education*, Vol. 64 May 1978. pp. 190-198.

644   "Religious musical chairs." *Society*, Vol. 15 May/June 1978. pp. 53-59.
Reprinted in *In Gods We Trust: new patterns of religious pluralism in America.*

645   D. Garth Taylor and Paul B. Sheatsley. "Attitudes toward racial integration." *Scientific American*, Vol. 238 June 1978. pp. 42-49. (*See also Scientific American*, Dec. 1971 and *Social Problems and Public Policy: inequality and justice.*)

646   "Role of the pope: no immediate change seen." *Chicago Sun Times*, Aug. 12, 1978. pp. 28+.

647   "Making of a pope: the critical issues cardinals must face." *Chicago Sun Times*, Aug. 13, 1978. Sec. 2 p. 1-3.

648   "You can expect some frantic campaigning in Rome." *Chicago Sun Times*, Aug. 13, 1978. Sec. V p. 2.

649   "Pope race giants too young, old." *Chicago Sun Times*, Aug. 14, 1978. pp. 5+.

650   "Papal vote to be most secretive in history." *Chicago Sun Times*, Aug. 15, 1978. p. 15.

651   "Trouble for Church? Rome not mourning Pope." *Chicago Sun Times*, Aug. 16, 1978. p. 29.

652   "An unprecedented delay in the election of a pope." *Chicago Sun Times*, Aug. 18, 1978. p. 24.

653   "Cardinals' jargon: reading between the lines." *Chicago Sun Times*, Aug. 19, 1978. p. 35.

654   "Choosing pope a human, often bitter, process." *Chicago Sun Times*, Aug. 20, 1978. p. 26.

655   "Papal electors unrepresentative." *Chicago Sun Times*, Aug. 21, 1978. p. 22.

656   "Little impact from 9 U. S. cardinals." *Chicago Sun Times*, Aug. 22, 1978. p. 25.

657   "Scant say by Yanks on pontiff." *Chicago Sun Times*, Aug. 22, 1978. pp. 4+.

658   "Conservative choice may become pope." *Chicago Sun Times*, Aug. 23, 1978. pp. 6+.

659   "Nonwhite bloc ready to alter papal conclave." *Chicago Sun Times*, Aug. 24, 1978. p. 8.

660   "Conclave: an exercise in vote getting." *Chicago Sun Times*, Aug. 25, 1978. pp. 17+.

661   "Italian power bloc isn't likely to lose." *Chicago Sun Times*, Aug. 26, 1978. pp. 4+.

662   "Pontiff seen as likeable, provincial." *Chicago Sun Times*, Aug. 27, 1978. p. 4.

663   "Pope John, sex, 2 issues they won't discuss." *Chicago Sun Times*, Aug. 27, 1978. p. 22.

664   "Pope must justify 'impulse' election." *Chicago Sun Times*, Aug. 29, 1978. p. 4.

665   "Pope faces plenty of problems; here are 7." *Chicago Sun Times*, Aug. 31, 1978. p. 36.

666   "To increase the enjoyment of sex in marriage." *Readers' Digest*, Vol. 113 Sept. 1978. pp. 111-114.
Excerpted from *Sexual Intimacy*.

667   "A charm and wit gone too soon." *Chicago Sun Times*, Sept. 30, 1978. p. 6.

668   "Unstable coalition of cardinals faces 2d test." *Chicago Sun Times*, Oct. 2, 1978. p. 12.

669   "John Paul's death a 'punishment'." *Chicago Sun Times*, Oct. 3, 1978. pp. 7+.

670 "Finding right 'Italian pastor' may not be a quick task." *Chicago Sun Times*, Oct. 4, 1978. pp. 44+.

671 "Who needs a pope? Reply of Christians is vigorous." *Chicago Sun Times*, Oct. 5, 1978. p. 42.

672 "Cardinals lack solid health data." *Chicago Sun Times*, Oct. 6, 1978. p. 22.

673 "New papal election puts strain on Vatican's purse." *Chicago Sun Times*, Oct. 7, 1978. pp. 22+.

674 "Vatican helped fuel rumors of plot to kill Pope." *Chicago Sun Times*, Oct. 8, 1978. p. 38.

675 "A pope from Sicily? It's possible." *Chicago Sun Times*, Oct. 9, 1978. p. 28.

676 "Pope maker Benelli emerging as candidate himself." *Chicago Sun Times*, Oct. 11, 1978. p. 20.

677 "Computer narrows pope race to 2." *Chicago Sun Times*, Oct. 12, 1978. p. 22. *

678 "Corner turning plan of the papacy." *Chicago Sun Times*, Oct. 13, 1978. p. 38.

679 "New pope must counter the curia." *Chicago Sun Times*, Oct. 14, 1978. p. 26.

680 "Two factions out to out-bluff in papal election." *Chicago Sun Times*, Oct. 15, 1978. p. 12.

681 "Cardinals cross up the soothsayers." *Chicago Sun Times*, Oct. 17, 1978. p. 10.

682 "2 significant papal revolutions." *Chicago Sun Times*, Oct. 19, 1978. p. 5. *

683 "New pope choice a big gamble." *Chicago Sun Times*, Oct. 20, 1978. p. 19.

684   "Making of a pope--how Wojtyla won." *Chicago Sun Times*, Oct. 22, 1978. p. 7.

685   "After Ellis Island: in praise of ethnic chauvinism." *Harper's*, Vol. 257 Nov. 1978. pp. 27-30.

686   "The sociology of American Catholics." *Annual Review of Sociology*, Vol. 5 n.m. 1979. pp. 91-111.

687   "Graced interludes of wonder." *Liturgy*, Vol. 24 Jan./Feb. 1979. pp. 30-33.
       An expanded version was presented at the East Coast Conference on Religious Education, Washington, DC, Spring, 1978.

688   "The American Irish: a report from Great Ireland." *International Journal of Comparative Sociology*, Vol. 20 Mar./June 1979. pp. 67-81.
       Another version was presented to the Cumann Merriman Summer School, Ennis, Ireland, Aug. 26, 1976, in commemoration of the American bicentennial.

689   "Varieties of apocalypse in science fiction." *Journal of American Culture*, Vol. 2 Summer 1979. pp. 279-287.
       A later version appeared in *God in Popular Culture*.

690   "Ethnic domestic architecture in Chicago." *Ethnicity*, Vol. 6 June 1979. pp. 137-146. (21 photographs of houses by the author.)

691   "Creativity in the Irish family: the cost of immigration." *International Journal of Family Therapy*, Vol. 1 Winter 1979. pp. 295-303.

692   *et al.* "Mary survives." *America*, Vol. 142 Feb. 23, 1980. pp. 135-137.

693   "U. S. Catholics grow up: a letter from America by Andrew Greeley." *The Tablet* (London), Vol. 234 Mar. 22, 1980. pp. 286-287.

694   "Religions's oldest scoop." *Psychology Today*, Vol. 13 Apr. 1980. pp. 86-88+. (Gnostics.) (Replies July 1980.)

695   "A post-Vatican II new breed? A report on contemporary Catholic
       teen-agers." *America*, Vol. 142 June 28, 1980. pp. 534-537.

696   Calvao, Maria; Hoeller, Stephen A.; Ray, Charles T.; "The
       controversial Gnostics." *Psychology Today*, Vol. 14 July 1980.
       p. 6. (Replies to Apr. 1980.) (Rejoinder July 1980.)

697   "Andrew M. Greeley replies." *Psychology Today*, Vol. 14 July
       1980. pp. 6+. (Rejoinder to July 1980.)

698   "Family patterns." *The Tablet* (London), Vol. 234 July 26, 1980.
       pp. 721-723.

699   "Comment on Newport article." (ASR, August, 1979) *American
       Sociological Review*, Vol. 45 Aug. 1980. p. 719. ("The
       religious switcher in the United States" by Frank Newport.)
       (Reply Aug. 1980.)

700   Newport, Frank. "Reply to 'Comment on Newport article, ASR,
       August, 1979'." *American Sociological Review*, Vol. 45 Aug.
       1980. p. 720. (Reply to Aug. 1980.)

701   "Church authority: beyond the problem." *National Catholic
       Reporter*, Vol. 16 Sept. 26, 1980. pp. 7-9.

702   *et al.* "A profile of the American Catholic family." *America*,
       Vol. 143 Sept. 27, 1980. pp. 155-160.

703   *et al.* "A sampler from past issues of *The Critic*." *The Critic*,
       n.v. n.d. [1981]. pp. 3-12.

704   "The state of the nations's happiness." *Psychology Today*, Vol.
       15 Jan. 1981. pp. 14+

705   "U. S. Catholics' crisis." *The Tablet* (London), Vol. 235 Jan.
       31, 1981. pp. 101-102.

706   "Tradition of church favors sex fulfillment." *National Catholic
       Reporter*, Vol. 17 Feb. 13, 1981. pp. 9+.

707   "The persistence of diversity." *Antioch Review*, Vol. 39 Spring

1981. pp. 141-155.
Reprinted in *Antioch Review*, Winter & Spring 1992.

708 "Catholics and the upper middle class: a comment on Roof."
Social Forces, Vol. 59 Mar. 1981. pp. 824-830. (Reply to
"Socioeconomic differentials among white socioreligious groups
in the United States." Sept. 1979.) (Rejoinder Mar. 1981.)

709 Roof, Wade C. "Unresolved issues in the study of religion and
the national elite: response to Greeley." *Social Forces*, Vol. 59
Mar. 1981. pp. 831-836. (Rejoinder to Mar. 1981.)

710 "Moral majority is liberal's fiction." *Detroit Free Press*, Mar.
22, 1981. Sec. B p. 4. *

711 "Minority students in Catholic secondary schools: the text of Fr.
Greeley's conclusions." *Chronicle of Higher Education*, Vol. 22
Apr. 13, 1981. pp. 15-16.

712 "Womanliness and the spiritual life of men." *America*, Vol. 144
Apr. 25, 1981. pp. 338-340.

713 "Schooling in the U. S. A." *The Tablet* (London), Vol. 235 May
9, 1981. pp. 448-449.

714 "*Quadragesimo Anno* after fifty years." *America*, Vol. 145 Aug.
1, 1981. pp. 46-49.

715 "The Pope and TV--why their relationship is a 'terrible mess'."
TV Guide, Vol. 29 Aug. 29, 1981. pp. 2-6.

716 "The religious imagination: a sociological approach." *Chicago
Studies*, Vol. 20 Fall 1981. pp. 267-280.

717 "The many meanings of Christmas." *Woman's Day*, n.v. Dec.
22, 1981. pp. 75+.

718 "Message from Chicago." *The Tablet* (London), Vol. 235 Jan.
16, 1982. pp. 54-55. (Theologians David Tracy and John Shea.)

719 "The failures of Vatican II after twenty years." *America*, Vol.
146 Feb. 6, 1982. pp. 86-89. (Replies June 12, 1982.)

720 "Social science sinners." *Society*, Vol. 19 Mar./Apr. 1982. pp. 62-65.

721 Weakland, Rembert, G. *et al.* "The 'failures of Vatican II' revisited." *America*, Vol. 146 June 12, 1982. pp. 454-460. (Replies to Feb. 6, 1982.) (Rejoinder June 12, 1982.)

722 "The 'failures of Vatican II' revisited." *America*, Vol. 146 June 12, 1982. pp. 460-461. (Rejoinder to June 12, 1982.)

723 "Catholics at the end of the century." *Literary Review* (Fairleigh Dickinson Univ.) Vol. 26 Fall 1982. pp. 5-11.

724 "Going their own way." *New York Times Magazine*, Oct. 10, 1982. pp. 28-29+.

725 "The year of the Catholic." *The Tablet* (London), Vol. 236 Oct. 23, 1982. pp. 1060-1061.

726 "Proposed: limited terms of priesthood." *National Catholic Reporter*, Vol. 19 Feb. 25, 1983. pp. 10-14+.

727 "Religion and social science." *National Forum*, Vol. 63 Spring 1983. pp. 21-23. *

728 "Do priests fall in love? Of course they do." *TV Guide*, Vol. 31 Mar. 26, 1983. pp. 4-7+.

729 "Selective Catholicism: how they get away with it." *America*, Vol. 148 Apr. 30, 1983. pp. 333-336.

730 "Overview exclusive: a sociologist on theology." *Overview*, n.v. May 1983. n.p.

731 "The Vatican: sacred and sovereign, formidable and fallible." *Travel & Leisure*, Vol. 13 May 1983. pp. 67-68+.

732 "Why Catholic higher learning is lower." *National Catholic Reporter*, Vol. 19 Sept. 23, 1983. pp. 1-6+.

733 "Seize the suburbs." *Chicago*, Vol. 33 Jan. 1984. p. 157.

734   "Summer festival in Bahia." *Travel & Leisure*, Vol. 14 May
       1984. pp. 182+.

735   "Who reads *those* books?" *America*, Vol. 150 May 26, 1984.
       pp. 393-397. (Replies June 16 and 23, 1984.)

736   Hughes, John J. *et al.* "The right stuff." *America*, Vol. 150
       June 16, 1984. p. 468. (Replies to May 26, 1984.)

737   "American Catholicism: 1909-1984." *America*, Vol. 150 June
       23, 1984. pp. 487-492. (Replies Aug. 4, 1984.)

738   Gallagher, Michael. " 'Those books' again." *America*, Vol. 150
       June 23, 1984. p. 504. (Reply to May 26, 1984.)

739   "Greeley responds." *America*, Vol. 151 July 21, 1984. p. 40.
       (Rejoinder to June 16 and 23, 1984.)

740   Gannon, Ann I.; Hughes, John J.   "Catholicism clarified."
       America, Vol. 151 Aug. 4, 1984. p. 60. (Replies to June 23,
       1984.)

741   The Editors. "The end of Catholicism: David Tracy and Andrew
       M. Greeley respond to Thomas Sheehan." *Commonweal*, Vol.
       111 Aug. 10, 1984. p. 425. (Reply to article in *New York.
       Review of Books*, June 14, 1984.) (*See* Aug. 10 and Oct. 5,
       1984.)

742   "The ways of knowing: neither fundamentalism nor agnosticism."
       Commonweal, Vol. 111 Aug. 10, 1984. pp. 431-433. *See also*
       Oct. 5, 1984 and discussion Sept. 21, 1984 (3183).

743   "How do Catholics vote?" *New York Times*, Aug. 12, 1984.
       Sec. IV p. 21.

744   "Catholic high schools: an effective inner-city ministry."
       National Catholic Reporter, Vol. 20 Aug. 31, 1984. pp. 11-12.

745   "The provisional path to mystery." *Commonweal*, Vol. 111 Oct.
       5, 1984. pp. 530-532. (*See also* Aug. 10, 1984.)

746 "Catholic intellectual life." *America*, Vol. 151 Nov. 24, 1984. p. 335.

747 "The making of a storyteller." *Thought*, Vol. 59 Dec. 1984. pp. 391-401.

748 "The bishops and the economy: a 'radical' dissent." *America*, Vol. 152 Jan. 5, 1985. pp. 19-25. (Replies Feb. 2 and 9, 1985.) *See also* discussion May 4, 1985 (3185).

749 Collesano, David. "Twenty years late." *America*, Vol. 152 Feb. 2, 1985. p. 96. (Reply to Jan. 5, 1985.) (Rejoinder Apr. 6, 1985.)

750 O'Connell, Brian J. "Poverty and the bishops." *America*, Vol. 152 Feb. 9, 1985. p. 115. (Reply to Jan. 5, 1985.) (Rejoinder Apr. 6, 1985.)

751 "A vision of grandeur for Navy Pier." *Chicago*, Vol. 34 Mar. 1985. pp. 148-149+.

752 "Who leads Catholics?" *New York Times*, Mar. 8, 1985. p. 35.

753 Hoffer, Thomas and James S. Coleman. "Achievement growth in public and Catholic schools." *Sociology of Education*, Vol. 58 Apr. 1985. pp. 74-97.

754 "Fiction and the religious imagination." *America*, Vol. 152 Apr. 6, 1985. pp. 274-277.

755 "Social analysis." *America*, Vol. 152 Apr. 6, 1985. p. 292. (Rejoinder to Feb. 2 and 9, 1985.)

756 "Why the peace pastoral did not bomb." *National Catholic Reporter*, Vol. 21 Apr. 12, 1985. p. 11.

757 "Stamp out sacramental tyranny." *U. S. Catholic*, Vol. 50 May 1985. pp. 13-18.

758 "Ellis Peters: another Umberto Eco?" *Armchair Detective*, Vol. 18 Summer 1985. pp. 238-245. A version in ***God in Popular Culture***.

759   "Films as sacrament." *The Critic*, Vol. 40 Fall 1985. pp. 23-39.

760   "What is subsidiarity? A voice from Sleepy Hollow." *America*, Vol. 153 Nov. 9, 1985. pp. 292-295.

761   "'We priests owe a debt of gratitude to Robert Blake'." *TV Guide*, Vol. 33 Dec. 14, 1985. pp. 6-10.

762   "'The Robe' and I: the making of a Christian storyteller." *New York Times Book Review*, Mar. 23, 1986. p. 3.
        Adapted from the introduction to *The Robe*.

763   "In defense of hopeful endings." *Writer's Digest*, Vol. 67 Jan. 1987. pp. 28-31.
        A version appears in *God in Popular Culture* as "In defense of comedy."

764   "Mysticism goes mainstream: Father Greeley's scientific survey." *American Health*, Vol. 6 Jan./Feb. 1987. pp. 47-49.

765   "Localism in Catholic fiction." *U. S. Catholic Historian*, Vol. 6 Spring/Summer 1987. pp. 240-247.

766   "Who reads book reviews anyway?" *Publishers Weekly*, Vol. 231 Apr. 10, 1987. p. 78. (Reply May 8, 1987.)

767   Bass, Judy. "In defense of book critics." *Publishers Weekly*, Vol. 231 May 8, 1987. p. 48. (Reply to Apr. 10, 1987.)

768   "Today's morality play: the sitcom." *New York Times*, May 17, 1987. Sec. II pp. 1+.
        Reprinted in *U. S. Catholic*, Feb. 1988 as "The best 30-minute sermon on TV."

769   and Michael Hout. "The center doesn't hold: church attendance in the United States, 1940-1984." *American Sociological Review*, Vol. 52 June 1987. pp. 325-345.
        A version was presented at the American Sociological Assn., New York, Aug. 30, 1986.

770   "What's in a name? Plenty." *U. S. Catholic*, Vol. 52 June 1987. p. 39.

771   "Hallucinations among the widowed." *Sociology and Social Research*, Vol. 71 July 1987. pp. 258-265.

772   "Why Catholics stay in the church." *America*, Vol. 157 Aug. 1, 1987. pp. 54-57.
Reprinted in *In Gods We Trust: new patterns of religious pluralism in America.*

773   "Community as social capital: James S. Coleman on Catholic schools." *America*, Vol. 157 Aug. 29, 1987. pp. 110-112.

774   "The fall of an archdiocese." *Chicago*, Vol. 36 Sept. 1987. pp. 128-131+.

775   *et al.* "If I had five minutes with the Pope." *America*, Vol. 157 Sept. 12, 1987. pp. 126-135.

776   *et al.* "Chords of a dissonant choir: leading American Catholics critique John Paul." *Newsweek*, Vol. 110 Sept. 21, 1987. p. 30.

777   "Empirical liturgy: the search for grace." *America*, Vol. 157 Nov. 21, 1987. pp. 379-383. (Reply Jan. 26, 1991.) *See also* comment in *Worship*, July 1988 (3216).

778   and Michael Hout. "Musical chairs: patterns of denominational change." *Sociology and Social Research*, Vol. 72 Jan. 1988. pp. 75-86.

779   "The best 30-minute sermon on TV." *U. S. Catholic*, Vol. 53 Feb. 1988. pp. 13-15. (The Cosby Show and other TV sitcoms.) Reprinted from *New York Times*, May 17, 1987, "Today's morality play: the sitcom."

780   "The Catholic imagination of Bruce Springsteen." *America*, Vol. 158 Feb. 6, 1988. pp. 110-115.

781   "Wasted opportunities: young people and religion." *The Critic*, Vol. 42 Spring 1988. pp. 15-29.

782   "Evidence that a maternal image of God correlates with liberal politics." *Sociology and Social Research*, Vol. 72 Apr. 1988. pp. 150-154.

783 "The success and assimilation of Irish Protestants and Irish Catholics in the United States." *Sociology and Social Research*, Vol. 72 July 1988. pp. 229-236.

784 "In defense of TV evangelism." *TV Guide*, Vol. 36 July 9, 1988. pp. 4-7.

785 "Defection among Hispanics." *America*, Vol. 159 July 23, 1988. pp. 61-62.

786 "'Christ' film offers challenge to faith." *Chicago Sun Times*, Aug. 14, 1988. pp. 7+.

787 "Love song." *Good Housekeeping*, Vol. 207 Sept. 1988. p. 229+.
Excerpted from *Love Song*.

788 "Correlates of belief in life after death." *Sociology and Social Research*, Vol. 73 Oct. 1988. pp. 3-8.

789 "Where have all the contributions gone? And why?" *National Catholic Reporter*, Vol. 25 Nov. 11, 1988. pp. 17-19.

790 "Don't scold Christmas Catholics." *U. S. Catholic*, Vol. 53 Dec. 1988. pp. 30-31.

791 "Sociology and the Catholic church: four decades of bitter memories." *Sociological Analysis*, Vol. 50 n.m. 1989. pp. 393-397.

792 "The declining morale of women." *Sociology and Social Research*, Vol. 73 Jan. 1989. pp. 53-58.

793 "Catholic schools: a golden twilight?" *America*, Vol. 160 Feb. 11, 1989. pp. 106-108+.

794 "Don't sell Catholic schools short." *U. S. Catholic*, Vol. 54 Mar. 1989. pp. 14-15.

795 "On the margins of the church: a sociological note." *America*, Vol. 160 Mar. 4, 1989. pp. 194-195+.

796   "Is there an American Catholic elite?" *America*, Vol. 160 May 6, 1989. pp. 426-429.

797   "Like a Catholic: Madonna's challenge to her church." *America*, Vol. 160 May 13, 1989. pp. 447-449.

798   and Michael Hout. "The secularisation myth." *The Tablet* (London), Vol. 243 June 10, 1989. pp. 665-667.

799   "How the other half writes." *Esquire*, Vol. 112 July 1989. p. 82.

800   "Protestant and Catholic: is the analogical imagination extinct?" *American Sociological Review,* Vol. 54 Aug. 1989. pp. 485-502.

801   "Celibacy as witness." *The Tablet* (London), Vol. 243 Aug. 26, 1989. pp. 968-970.

802   "St. Valentine's night." *Good Housekeeping*, Vol. 209 Oct. 1989. pp. 229-247+.
        Excerpted from *St. Valentine's Night.*

803   "Against R. C. I. A." *America*, Vol. 161 Oct. 14, 1989. pp. 231-234. (Replies Oct. 14 and Nov. 11, 1989.)

804   Duggan, Robert D. "A response to Andrew M. Greeley." *America*, Vol. 161 Oct. 14, 1989. pp. 235-237. (Reply to Oct. 14, 1989.)

805   "My research on Catholic schools." *Chicago Studies*, Vol. 28 Nov. 1989. pp. 245-263.

806   "Bishops paralyzed over heavily gay priesthood." *National Catholic Reporter*, Vol. 26 Nov. 10, 1989. pp. 13-14. *See also* comment Mar. 2, 1990 (3219).

807   Ivory, Thomas P. *et al.* "State of the question." *America*, Vol. 161 Nov. 11, 1989. pp. 328-330. (Replies to Oct. 14, 1989.)

808   "State of the question." *America*, Vol. 161 Nov. 11, 1989. p. 328. (Rejoinder to Oct. 14, 1989.)

809 *et al.* "Challenges facing U. S. Catholics: the next ten years." *Commonweal*, Vol. 116 Nov. 17, 1989. pp. 617-623.

810 Charles E. Case and Stephan Fuchs. "Social determinants of racial prejudice." *Sociological Perspectives*, Vol. 32 Winter 1989. pp. 469-483.

811 and Charles E. Case. "Attitudes toward racial equality." *Humboldt Journal of Social Relations*, Vol. 16 n.m. 1990. pp. 67-94.

812 "Good liturgy is little more than a good weave." *National Catholic Reporter*, Vol. 26 Mar. 16, 1990. pp. 12-13.

813 "Do Catholics have more fun?" *U. S. Catholic*, Vol. 55 Apr. 1990. pp. 29-30.

814 "Actions speak louder than doctrine in fueling dissent." *Chicago Sun Times*, May 6, 1990. p. 4.

815 "Angry Catholics: Poll finds key issues affect their generosity." *Chicago Sun Times*, May 6, 1990. pp. 1+.

816 "Parish priest holds key to solution of financial difficulties." *Chicago Sun Times*, May 6, 1990. p. 5.

817 "Catholics speak out: Many are angry, but few leave." *Chicago Sun Times*, May 7, 1990. p. 5.

818 "Family and faith are key reasons most Catholics remain in church." *Chicago Sun Times*, May 8, 1990. p. 8.

819 "Toughest church critics: Catholic women over 40." *Chicago Sun Times*, May 9, 1990. p. 14.

820 "Bernardin has favorable image with 70 percent." *Chicago Sun Times*, May 10, 1990. p. 14.

821 "Faithful attraction." *Good Housekeeping*, Vol. 210 June 1990. pp. 132-137.
Excerpted from *Faithful Attraction: discovering intimacy, love, and fidelity in American marriage*.

822   Robert T. Michael and Tom W. Smith. "Americans and their
       sexual partners." *Society*, Vol. 27 July/Aug. 1990. pp. 36-42.

823   "Some married men aren't faithful, but we don't say marriage is
       a failure." *Los Angeles Times*, Aug. 24, 1990. Sec. B p. 7.

824   *et al.* "Whodunit? Four top authors solve the *Twin Peaks*
       mystery." *TV Guide*, Vol. 38 Sept. 8, 1990. pp. 2-6.

825   "The Catholic novels of Jon Hassler." *America*, Vol. 163 Nov.
       17, 1990. pp. 366-367+.

826   *et al.* "Americans take sides." *Newsweek*, Vol. 116 Nov. 26,
       1990. pp. 31-34+. (Persian Gulf War.)

827   *et al.* "Dan Herr remembered:" *The Critic*, Vol. 45 Winter
       1990. pp. 3-13.

828   and Conor Ward. "'Development' and tolerance: the case of
       Ireland." *Eire-Ireland*, Vol. 25 Winter 1990. pp. 7-17.

829   and Michael Hout. "The cohort doesn't hold: comment on
       Chaves (1989)." *Journal for the Scientific Study of Religion*, Vol.
       29 Dec. 1990. pp. 519-524. ("Secularization and religious
       revival: evidence from U. S. church attendance rates, 1972-1986"
       by Mark Chaves. Dec. 1989.) (Rejoinder Dec. 1990.)

830   Chaves, Mark. "Holding the cohort: reply to Hout and Greeley."
       Journal for the Scientific Study of Religion, Vol. 29 Dec. 1990.
       pp. 525-530. (Rejoinder to Dec. 1990.)

831   "Hanukkah, Christmas--in the same light." *New York Times*,
       Dec. 11, 1990. p. 27.

832   "Healthy marriages are romantic ones, requiring mix of religion
       and sex." *National Catholic Reporter*, Vol. 27 Jan. 25, 1991. p.
       19. *See also* comment Mar. 22, 1991 (3224).

833   Yanitelli, Victor R. "Liturgy: giver of life." *America*, Vol. 164
       Jan. 26, 1991. p. 53. (Reply to Nov. 21, 1987.)

834   "The Catholic imagination and the Catholic university." *America*,
       Vol. 164 Mar. 16, 1991. pp. 285-288.

835   and John T. Durkin, Jr. "A model of religious choice under
       uncertainty: on responding rationally to the nonrational."
       Rationality and Society, Vol. 3 Apr. 1991. pp. 178-196. (Reply
       Jan. 1992.)

836   "Religion and attitudes towards AIDS policy." *Sociology and
       Social Research*, Vol. 75 Apr. 1991. pp. 126-132.

837   "Sacraments keep Catholics high on the church: survey findings
       pose challenge for liturgy. *National Catholic Reporter*, Vol. 27
       Apr. 12, 1991. p. 12.

838   "A God who plays it by ear: metaphors for God in recent films."
       Journal of Popular Film and TV, Vol. 19 Summer 1991. pp. 67-
       71.

839   "How just a war?" *The Critic*, Vol. 45 Summer 1991. pp. 33-
       40.
       Reprinted in *Love Affair: a prayer journal.*

840   "Comment on review of '*Ethnic Identity*'." *Contemporary
       Sociology*, Vol. 20 July 1991. p. 505. (Charles Hirschman's
       review of *Ethnic Identity* by Richard D. Alba.) (Rejoinder July
       1991.)

841   Hirschman, Charles. "Reply to Greeley." *Contemporary
       Sociology*, Vol. 20 July 1991. p. 505. (Rejoinder to July 1991.)

842   "Keeping the faith: Americans hold fast to the Rock of Ages."
       Omni, Vol. 13 Aug. 1991. p. 6.

843   "Who are the Catholic 'conservatives'?" *America*, Vol. 165 Sept.
       21, 1991. pp. 158-162. *See also* comment in *National Catholic
       Reporter*, Oct. 11, 1991 (3227).

844   "The paranormal is normal: a sociologist looks at parapsych-
       ology." *Journal of the American Society for Psychical Research*,
       Vol. 85 Oct. 1991. pp. 367-374. *

845   "The city that prays? 80% here do, study says." *Chicago Sun Times*, Oct. 27, 1991. p. 3. (*See also* Oct. 27, 28 and 29, 1991.)

846   "What is prayer?" *Chicago Sun Times*, Oct. 27, 1991. p. 3. (*See also* Oct. 27, 28 and 29, 1991.)

847   "Women, elderly pray the most, study of city says." *Chicago Sun Times*, Oct. 28, 1991. p. 18. (*See also* Oct. 27 and 29, 1991.)

848   "Prayer linked to happy marriage." *Chicago Sun Times*, Oct. 29, 1991. p. 18. (*See also* Oct. 27 and 28, 1991.)

849   "Rooting for--and rooted in--a city of neighborhoods." *Chicago Tribune Magazine*, Nov. 3, 1991. pp. 8+.

850   "Theology and sociology: on validating David Tracy." *Journal of the American Academy of Religion*, Vol. 59 Winter 1991. pp. 643-652.

851   "Have yourself a guilt-free little Christmas." *U. S. Catholic*, Vol. 56 Dec. 1991. pp. 12-13.

852   "Live and let die: changing attitudes." *Christian Century*, Vol. 108 Dec. 4, 1991. pp. 1124-1125.

853   "The persistence of diversity." *Antioch Review*, Vol. 50 Winter/Spring 1992. pp. 288-301.
        Reprinted from *Antioch Review*, Spring 1981.

854   Montgomery, James D. "Pascal's wager and the limits of rational choice: a comment on Durkin and Greeley." *Rationality and Society*, Vol. 4 Jan. 1992. pp. 117-121. (Reply to Apr. 1991.) (Rejoinder Jan. 1992.)

855   and John T. Durkin, Jr. "Response to Montgomery." *Rationality and Society*, Vol. 4 Jan. 1992. pp. 121-122. (Rejoinder to Jan. 1992.)

856   "The neglected Catholic vote is big one and may be returning to

the Democrats." *National Catholic Reporter*, Vol. 28 Jan. 10, 1992. pp. 5+

857   "The Catholic imagination of Bruce Springsteen." *Black Sacred Music*, Vol. 6 Spring 1992. pp. 232-243. *
Reprinted from *America*, Feb. 6, 1988.

858   "Like a Catholic: Madonna's challenge to her church." *Black Sacred Music*, Vol. 6 Spring 1992. pp. 244-247. *
Reprinted from *America*, May 13, 1989.

859   "Priestly silence on pedophilia." *New York Times*, Mar. 13, 1992. p. 31.

860   "A modest proposal for the reform of Catholic schools." *America*, Vol. 166 Mar. 21, 1992. pp. 234-238. (Reply July 25, 1992.) *See also* comment in *America*, June 20, 1992 (3228).

861   "Acting on the good news." *Momentum*, Vol. 23 Apr. 1992. pp. 32-35.

862   "Purgatory doesn't belong in limbo." *U. S. Catholic*, Vol. 57 Apr. 1992. pp. 29-30.

863   "The abortion debate and the Catholic subculture." *America*, Vol. 167 July 4, 1992. pp. 13-15.

864   Hurley, Mark J. "The easy way out?" *America*, Vol. 167 July 25, 1992. p. 47. (Reply to Mar. 21, 1992.)

865   "Churches should have an open-door policy." *U. S. Catholic*, Vol. 57 Aug. 1992. pp. 38-39.

866   "Catholics and sex: two sociological studies, Part 1. Sex and the married Catholic: the shadow of St. Augustine." *America*, Vol. 167 Oct. 31, 1992. pp. 318-323. (Replies Nov. 28 and Dec. 12, 1992.)

867   "Catholics and sex: two sociological studies, Part 2. Sex and the single Catholic: the decline of an ethic." *America*, Vol. 167 Nov.

7, 1992. pp. 342-347+. (Replies Nov. 28 and Dec. 12, 1992.) (Greeley's addition Nov. 28, 1992.)

868 Connolly, Ronald G. "Another reason why." *America*, Vol. 167 Nov. 28, 1992. p. 438. (Reply to Oct. 31, 1992.)

869 "Ethnic divergences." *America*, Vol. 167 Nov. 28, 1992. p. 438. (Addition to Nov. 7, 1992.)

870 Fisher, Philip C. "Graphic graphs." *America*, Vol. 167 Nov. 28, 1992. p. 438. (Reply to Oct. 31 and Nov. 7, 1992.)

871 O'Malley, William J. "After the age of reason." *America*, Vol. 167 Nov. 28, 1992. p. 438. (Reply to Nov. 7, 1992.)

872 "But Father, they're priests! Clerical culture and pedophilia." *The Critic*, Vol. 47 Winter 1992. pp. 43-51.

873 Ramstad, Philip S. "A friendly note." *America*, Vol. 167 Dec. 12, 1992. p. 486. (Reply to Oct. 31, 1992.)

874 Gallagher, John. "A misimpression perhaps." *America*, Vol. 167 Dec. 12, 1992. pp. 485-486. (Reply to Nov. 7, 1992.)

875 "Bricolage among the trash cans." *Society*, Vol. 30 Jan./Feb. 1993. pp. 70-75. (Reply July/Aug. 1993.)
Presented at the 50th anniversary of the National Opinion Research Center, Univ. of Chicago, Chicago, IL, 1991.

876 "Religion and attitudes toward the environment." *Journal for the Scientific Study of Religion*, Vol. 32 Mar. 1993. pp. 19-28.

877 "How serious is the problem of sexual abuse by clergy?" *America*, Vol. 168 Mar. 20, 1993. pp. 6-10. (Replies Apr. 17, 1993.)

878 Murnion, Philip J. "Regarding A. Greeley's data on sexual abuse by priests." *America*, Vol. 168 Apr. 17, 1993. p. 21. (Reply to Mar. 20, 1993.)

879 Pattan, Marianne. "Persons and personality." *America*, Vol. 168 Apr. 17, 1993. p. 22. (Reply to Mar. 20, 1993.)

880 Sherzer, William J. "Damning statistics." *America*, Vol. 168 Apr. 17, 1993. p. 22. (Reply to Mar. 20, 1993.)

881 Steinfels, Margaret O. "A misreading." *America*, Vol. 168 Apr. 17, 1993. p. 22. (Reply to Mar. 20, 1993.)

882 *et al.* "The forbidden books of youth." *New York Times Book Review*, June 6, 1993. pp. 13+.

883 "Religion not dying out around the world." *Origins*, Vol. 23 June 10, 1993. pp. 49-58.

884 Nugent, William R. "Wondrous muse." *Society*, Vol. 30 July/Aug. 1993. p. 4. (Reply to Jan./Feb. 1993.) (Rejoinder July/Aug. 1993.)

885 "Wondrous muse." *Society*, Vol. 30 July/Aug. 1993. p. 4. (Rejoinder to July/Aug. 1993.)

886 "A view from the priesthood: it's bigotry to blame celibacy for church problems." *Newsweek*, n.v. Aug. 16, 1993. p. 45.

887 "Why does the Church stand silent while women are abused?" *U. S. Catholic*, Vol. 58 Sept. 1993. pp. 28-29. *

888 "Necessity of feminism." *Society*, Vol. 30 Sept./Oct. 1993. pp. 12-15.

889 "The faith we have lost." *America*, Vol. 169 Oct. 2, 1993. pp. 14-16+. (*See also* Part 2, *America*, Oct. 9, 1993.)

890 "Magic in the age of faith." *America*, Vol. 169 Oct. 9, 1993. pp. 8-14. (*See also* Part 1, *America*, Oct. 2, 1993.)

INTERVIEWS

891 "Today's teenager." Interviewer: J. Gannon. *Family Digest*, Vol. 19 Jan. 1964. pp. 61-65. *

892 "Interview: the future of Catholic education." Interviewer:

Harold W. Herman. *College & University Business*, Vol. 42 May 1967. pp. 63-64.

893   "Catholics prosper while the church crumbles." Interviewer: T. George Harris. *Psychology Today*, Vol. 10 June 1976. pp. 44-51.

894   "Agree, disagree, other." Interviewer: Desmond O'Grady. *U. S. Catholic*, Vol. 41 Aug. 1976. pp. 28-32.

895   "A U. S. priest plays Teddy White in the Vatican, exposing the politics of picking a pope." Interviewer: Linda Witt. *People*, Vol. 12 July 9, 1979. pp. 69-70.

896   "The Catholic family, the school and the religious imagination." Interviewer: Bruno V. Manno. *Momentum*, Vol. 12 Feb. 1981. pp. 14-17+.

897   "Father Greeley: home, not Rome, is heart of church." Interviewer: Michael Schroeder. *Herald Examiner* (Los Angeles), July 18, 1981. pp. ?

898   "Father Greeley: new novel, new controversy." Interviewer: Edwin McDowell. *New York Times*, Mar. 22, 1982. Sec. III p. 11.

899   "Andrew Greeley: the most outspoken Catholic in America." Interviewers: the editors. *U. S. Catholic*, Vol. 49 Apr. 19, 1984. pp. 22-28.

900   "Cafeteria Catholicism: do you have to eat everything on your plate?" Interviewers: the editors. *U. S. Catholic*, Vol. 50 Jan. 1985. pp. 16-25.

901   "True Confessions, an interview with Father Andrew Greeley." *Irish America*, Vol. 2 June 1986. pp. 30-37. *

902   "The interview: Andrew Greeley." Interviewer: D. C. Denison. *Boston Globe Magazine*, Oct. 19, 1986. p. 2.

903   "Alienated laity must be won back, Greeley says." Interviewer:

Thomas C. Fox. *National Catholic Reporter,* Vol. 24 Jan. 15, 1988. pp. 7-8.

904   "Greeley: thoughts on Easter: an interview with Andrew Greeley." Interviewer: Anne K. Kaler. *Modern Liturgy,* Vol. 17 Apr. 1990. pp. 14-15.

905   "Liturgy as storytelling: an interview with Andrew Greeley." Interviewer: Anne K. Kaler. *Modern Liturgy,* Vol. 17 May 1990. pp. 15-17.

906   "'On the margins': a dialogue with Andrew Greeley." Interviewer: David M. Moss III. *Journal of Religion and Health,* Vol. 29 Winter 1990. pp. 261-283.

907   "What I watch." Interviewer: Ileane Rudolph. *TV Guide,* Vol. 40 Sept. 19, 1992. p. 3.

LETTERS

908   "Letters to the editor." (Re: "Freedom and Christian responsibility" by Robert Hoyt. *Social Order,* Sept. 1962.) *Social Order,* Vol. 12 Nov. 12, 1962. pp. 430-432.

909   "An exchange of views: Catholics in college." (Re: "Catholics in college" by Michael Novak. *Commonweal,* Jan. 25, 1963.) *Commonweal,* Vol. 78 Mar. 29, 1963. p. 17.

910   "A comment on Weigert's 'Immoral Rhetoric'." (Re: "The immoral rhetoric of scientific sociology" by Andrew J. Weigert. *American Sociologist,* May 1970.) *American Sociologist,* Vol. 5 Nov. 1970. p. 371.

911   Letter to editor. (Re: "On being deradicalized" by Nathan Glazer. *Commentary,* Oct. 1970.) *Commentary,* Vol. 51 Jan. 1971. p. 20.

912   Letter to editor. "The Galbraith-Kuh-Thurow plan." (Re: "The Galbraith plan to promote the minorities" by John K. Galbraith, Edwin Kuh and Lester C. Thurow. *New York Times Magazine,*

Aug. 22, 1971.) *New York Times Magazine*, Sept. 12, 1971. pp. 92-94.

913　　Letter. (Re: Ethnicity.) *Commentary*, Vol. 54 Oct. 1972. pp. 16+.

914　　"Labels." (Re: "On original sin and conservatives" by Andrew Hacker. *New York Times Magazine*, Feb. 25, 1973.) *New York Times Magazine*, Apr. 1, 1973. p. 78.

915　　"To the editor." (Re: "Jewish self-interest in black pluralism" by Oliver C. Cox. *Sociological Quarterly*, Spring 1974.) *Sociological Quarterly*, Vol. 16 Winter 1975. p. 134.

916　　"Public and private schools." (Re: "Standards of research" by Robert Cain and Willis Hawley. *Society*, Jan./Feb. 1982.) *Society*, Vol. 19 July/Aug. 1982. pp. 6-7.

917　　"Catholic sociology." (Re: research on Catholic schools.) *New Republic*, Vol. 187 Dec. 13, 1982. p. 40.

918　　"Father Healy besieged by friends and foes." (Re: Timothy Healy as director of the New York Public Library.) *New York Times*, Apr. 21, 1989. p. 30.

919　　"What I saw at the revolution." (Re: Wilfrid Sheed's review of *What I Saw at the Revolution* by Peggy Noonan. *New York Times Book Review*, Feb. 4, 1990.) *New York Times Book Review*, Mar. 4, 1990. p. 40.

920　　"Not much of a blip." (Re: "Coming to grips with losses" by Mark Christensen. *America*, Jan. 26, 1991.) *America*, Vol. 164 Mar. 9, 1991. pp. 277-278.

SHORT STORIES

921　　"Ms. Carpenter." *U. S. Catholic*, Vol. 43 May 1978. pp. 17-20.
Reprinted in *All about Women*.
Winner of the Catholic Press Association award for best short story of 1978.

922 "Julie Quinn." *Literary Review* (Fairleigh Dickinson Univ.),
Vol. 26 Fall 1982. pp. 12-22.
Reprinted in *All about Women* as "Julie."

923 "Anne Marie." *U. S. Catholic*, Vol. 49 Mar. 1984. pp. 18-24.

924 "The priest and Jenny Martin." *Redbook*, Vol. 162 Apr. 1984.
pp. 60-64+.
Reprinted in *All about Women* as "Jenny."

925 "A handful of tinsel." *Ladies Home Journal*, Vol. 101 Dec.
1984. pp. 84+.
Reprinted in *All about Women* as "Marge."

926 "How Father Grinch stole Christmas." *U. S. Catholic*, Vol. 49
Dec. 1984. pp. 32-37.

927 "Count the ways." *U. S. Catholic*, Vol. 51 June 1986. pp. 26-
32.

928 "Between times: three short stories." *The Critic*, Vol. 41 Fall
1986. pp. 3-34. (Short stories: "Peggy," "Paula," "Dierdre.")
Reprinted in *All about Women*. *

929 "The dutchman's ghost town." *Magazine of Fantasy & Science
Fiction*, Vol. 72 Feb. 1987. pp. 118-140.
Reprinted in *All about Women* as "Andrea."

930 "Sionna Marie." *U. S. Catholic*, Vol. 53 Jan. 1988. pp. 30-34.
Reprinted in *All about Women*.

931 "Martina." *Literary Review* (Fairleigh Dickinson Univ.), Vol. 31
Spring 1988. pp. 333-342.
Reprinted in *All about Women*.

CHAPTER FOUR

NEWSPAPER COLUMNS: CATHOLIC

Andrew Greeley wrote a weekly column in the Catholic press from 1966 until 1983 (bi-weekly until Oct. 13, 1966 with a few exceptions). It was widely syndicated to a number of papers--no one is sure just how many, and records are no longer available. The following columns were seen in the *Catholic Messenger* (Davenport, Iowa) recorded on microfilm by The Forman Co., Monmouth, IL. Notes in parentheses are the compiler's.

932   "Listen closely to protesters." Jan. 20, 1966. p. 10.

933   "Dr. Rosemary Lauer is wrong." Feb. 3, 1966. p. 10.

934   "Don't dump institutional Church." Feb. 17, 1966. p. 10.

935   "The least important Catholics." Mar. 3, 1966. p. 10.

936   "Bringing back the 'boondoggle'." Mar. 17, 1966. p. 10. (Public works program of WPA.)

937   "Censors discourage scholarship." Mar. 31, 1966. p. 14.

938   "The Chancery & the University." Apr. 14, 1966. p. 10.

939   "Freedom in the Church is growing." Apr. 28, 1966. p. 12.

940   "Fr. Greeley on today's seminarians." May 12, 1966. p. 12.

941   "Just don't label it 'sociology'." May 26, 1966. p. 12. (*The De-Romanization of the American Catholic Church* by Joseph Scheuer and Edward Wakin. Macmillan.)

942   "The threat of compulsory service." June 9, 1966. p. 12.

943   "Seminarians: no laughing matter." June 23, 1966. p. 10.

944   "Sometimes silence is wisdom." June 30, 1966. p. 10+.

945   "The minority needs the majority." July 7, 1966. p. 12. (Civil rights.)

946   "Church needs study commissions." July 14, 1966. p. 10.

947   "A 'triumphalist' talks back." July 21, 1966. p. 10.

948   "Is Martin Luther King to blame?" Aug. 4, 1966. p. 12. (Chicago West Side race riots.)

949   "Charges reporting distorted study." Aug. 18, 1966. p. 14. (*The Education of Catholic Americans*.)

950   "The making of American slaves." Sept. 1, 1966. p. 10. (National Service.)

951   "What makes the sisters run?" Sept. 15, 1966. p. 10.

952   "Who are the real traditionalists?" Sept. 29, 1966. p. 10.

953   "Church's biggest giant would be out of place." Oct. 13, 1966. p. 12. (John England.)

954   "Raps demand for racial balance in schools." Oct. 20, 1966. p. 12.

955   "Dry stereotype of canon lawyer is dead." Oct. 27, 1966. p. 14.

956   "ACP--significant for American Catholics." Nov. 3, 1966. p. 16. (Assn. of Chicago Priests.)

957   "Administration without leadership is useless." Nov. 10, 1966. p. 12.

958   "Foresees change in selection of bishops." Nov. 17, 1966. p. 12.

959   "The battle begins: Irish vs. American Irish." Nov. 24, 1966.
        p. 12.

960   "Bishop's meeting was 'a smashing success'." Dec. 1, 1966. p.
        12. (NCCB request for vernacular liturgy.)

961   "Faith, Pat, but aren't the colored shameful!" Dec. 8, 1966. p.
        12.

962   "Church needs protection from crackpots." Dec. 15, 1966. p.
        12. (Reply Dec. 29, 1966.)

963   "Church has overlooked new breed's idealism." Dec. 22, 1966.
        p. 10.

964   "Some observations on Fr. Fichter's survey." Dec. 29, 1966.
        p. 10.

965   McMillan, Joseph. "Fr. Greeley's column on crackpots praised."
        Dec. 29, 1966. p. 12. (Reply to Dec. 15, 1966.)

966   "Secular humanists are evasive but nice." Jan. 5, 1967. p. 10.

967   "Liberals, conservatives show lack of charity." Jan. 12, 1967.
        p. 12.

968   "Finds problem in 'contemporary reality'." Jan. 19, 1967. p.
        10.

969   "Reservations greet Webster's secularization." Jan. 26, 1967. p.
        10. (Webster College.)

970   "American Church has ignored its talent." Feb. 2, 1967. p. 10.

971   "The religious garb helps define a social role." Feb. 9, 1967.
        p. 12.

972   "Celibacy and human love are not alternatives." Feb. 16, 1967.
        p. 10.

973   "Goodness gracious: Doyle, Bradley, now Davis." Feb. 23,
        1967. p. 10.

974 "Once again, 10 least important Catholics." Mar. 2, 1967. p. 10.

975 "Teachers treated like glorified babysitters." Mar. 9, 1967. p. 10.

976 "Ecumenism is a casualty of Vietnam war." Mar. 16, 1967. p. 10.

977 "It's time (for some) of second thoughts." Mar. 23, 1967. p. 10.

978 "Harris poll gives clear mandate for change." Mar. 30, 1967. p. 12.

979 "Style of renewal needs change." Apr. 6, 1967. p. 12.

980 "Church needs studies of bigotry." Apr. 13, 1967. p. 14.

981 "The Pope, obviously, is a Marxist." Apr. 20, 1967. p. 10.

982 "NAPR begs the celibacy question." Apr. 27, 1967. p. 12. (National Association for Pastoral Renewal.) (Replies May 11,1967.)

983 "C. U. case marks fateful choice." May 4, 1967. p. 10. (Catholic Univ. and Charles Curran.)

984 Francoeur, Robert. "Priests respond to Father Greeley's column on celibacy." May 11, 1967. p. 12. (Reply to Apr. 27, 1967.)

985 Best, Patrick K. "Iowan defends NAPR." May 11, 1967. p. 12+. (Reply to Apr. 27, 1967.)

986 "Protest is a two-edged sword." May 11, 1967. p. 12. (Bigotry.)

987 "All you gr'ups are out of it." May 18, 1967. p. 10. (New Breed want New Church.)

988   "Church must face public opinion." May 25, 1967. p. 12. (Report of Birth Control Commission leaked.)

989   "Needed: a rhetoric of confidence." June 1, 1967. p. 12.

990   "All hail to a grotesque book." June 8, 1967. p. 12. (*A Modern Priest Looks at His Outdated Church* by James Kavanaugh. Trident.)

991   "The new democracy in the Church requires patience." June 15, 1967. p. 10.

992   "Seminarians can go home again." June 22, 1967. p. 10.

993   "The time is not right for a change to optional celibacy." June 29, 1967. p. 10.

994   "Hypothesis: recruiters, not celibacy, kill vocations." July 6, 1967. p. 12.

995   "Rising expectations race renewal." July 13, 1967. p. 10.

996   "Educators have blown their cool." July 20, 1967. p. 10.

997   "Fanatic rebels are at it again." July 27, 1967. p. 10.

998   "Prophets of doom are still hoping." Aug. 3, 1967. p. 12.

999   "Renewal efforts too often are too little too late." Aug. 10, 1967. p. 10.

1000   "'The other Church' is heard from." Aug. 17, 1967. p. 12. ('Kavanaugh Phenomenon'.)

1001   "Glenmary's collapse--a tragedy for the Church." Aug. 24, 1967. p. 10.

1002   "Callahan asks impossible goals." Aug. 31, 1967. p. 10.

1003   "Father John Courtney Murray: last of the old breed." Sept. 7, 1967. p. 10.

1004   "Curia reform is still in doubt." Sept. 14, 1967. p. 12.

1005   "Fascists in blackface strut down street of ironies." Sept. 21, 1967. p. 10.

1006   "New topics for Catholic educators." Sept. 28, 1967. p. 10.

1007   "Small Catholic high school provides important advantage." Oct. 5, 1967. p. 10.

1008   "Popular election of bishops coming." Oct. 12, 1967. p. 10.

1009   "Catholic underground groups are a sign of great vitality." Oct. 19, 1967. p. 12.

1010   "The Church as teacher is losing." Oct. 26, 1967. p. 12.

1011   "Racist anti-clericalism is coming in the American Church." Nov. 2, 1967. p. 14.

1012   "Mass apostasy not in sight." Nov. 9, 1967. p. 12.

1013   "Future of celibacy, schools, liturgy, new communities." Nov. 16, 1967. p. 10.

1014   "A 'Protestantized' Church coming." Nov. 23, 1967. p. 12.

1015   "Will Church leadership permit a persecution of nuns?" Nov. 30, 1967. p. 10.

1016   "On looking back we look blind." Dec. 7, 1967. p. 12.

1017   "Is there a place where the 'alien' go to register?" Dec. 14, 1967. p. 12. (Alienation in the Church.)

1018   "Consultation is the best antidote for alienation." Dec. 21, 1967. p. 18.

1019   "The Church and change in the U. S." Dec. 28, 1967. p. 10.

1020   "Two specials top 'most unimportant' awards of 1967." Jan. 4, 1968. p. 10.

1021   "Column on Irish produces some pious bigots." Jan. 11, 1968. p.12.

1022   "The 'kiddy apostolate' requires real adults." Jan. 18, 1968. p. 10.

1023   "Tired of hearing about ex-priests." Jan. 25, 1968. p. 10.

1024   "A tragedy that may be underway." Feb. 1, 1968. p. 10. (End of liturgical change.)

1025   "Intolerance is aggravating a tense situation." Feb. 8, 1968. p. 12.

1026   "Self-haters love to hate the past." Feb. 15, 1968. p. 10.

1027   "Amateurism: instant answers, simple solutions." Feb. 22, 1968. p. 10.

1028   "Authority may require resistance, but it is still essential." Feb. 29, 1968. p. 10.

1029   "Present draft law is one equity among many." Mar. 7, 1968. p. 12.

1030   "Does it take a woman to make sense about celibacy?" Mar. 14, 1968. p. 10.

1031   "Let them hear, who have ears to hear--or else!" Mar. 21, 1968. p. 10. (Report of Kerner Commission on racial riots.)

1032   "No loss of faith; but confidence in leadership gone." Mar. 28, 1968. p. 12.

1033   "Kerner report produced no 'sound and fury' nor action." Apr. 4, 1968. p. 12.

1034   "Major problem?--not to be able to fulfill the call." Apr. 11, 1968. p. 12.

1035   "'Theology of hope' replaces 'death of God' theology." Apr. 18, 1968. p. 10.

1036   "Objective study doesn't have predetermined results." Apr. 25, 1968. p. 10. (Commission for the Study of the Life and Ministry of the Priest.)

1037   "'Peace & race' put United States in political crisis." May 2, 1968. p. 12.

1038   "A first: Church renewal of religious life from within." May 9, 1968. p. 12.

1039   "Father Greeley does not like 'posturing' revolutionaries." May 16, 1968. p. 10.

1040   "Rebukes press for misinformation on research project." May 23, 1968. p. 10. (NCCB priests' study.)

1041   "Consistent action vs. obedience as an 'elastic virtue'." May 30, 1968. p. 10.

1042   "Who are the most disgusting in university uprisings?" June 6, 1968. p. 10.

1043   "Irish political wisdom also good ecclesiastical wisdom." June 13, 1968. p. 12.

1044   "The paranoid style of our politics: hatred in all seasons." June 20, 1968. p. 10.

1045   "Phenomenon: Church catches up when others give it up." June 27, 1968. p. 10.

1046   "A 'non-controversy' on obligation to schools and poverty." July 4, 1968. p. 12.

1047   "Romantics choose myth over realistic social change." July 11, 1968. p. 10.

1048   "American Catholicism needs no 'prophets of gloom'." July 18, 1968. p. 10.

1049   "Revolt against intellectualism produces new witchcraft." July 25, 1968. p. 10.

1050   "Study of priesthood is more than study of celibacy." Aug. 1, 1968. p. 12.

1051   "Today's Christians aren't different." Aug. 8, 1968. p. 12.

1052   "Encyclical is really about papacy." Aug. 15, 1968. p. 12. (*Humanae Vitae.*)

1053   "Strange case of non-hero worship." Aug. 22, 1968. p. 10. (Charles Davis.)

1054   "To be or to do: that is the question for Christian people." Aug. 29, 1968. p. 10.

1055   "If the bishops try repression, reaction will be explosive." Sept. 5, 1968. p. 10. (*Humanae Vitae.*)

1056   "It was a summer for the self-righteous: the hard-liners." Sept. 12, 1968. p. 12.

1057   "Looking at the birth control controversy as an outsider." Sept. 19, 1968. p. 10.

1058   "Sensitivity training valued by enthusiasm, not evidence." Sept. 26, 1968. p. 10.

1059   "Positions have way of reversing, if one can be patient." Oct. 3, 1968. p. 10.

1060   "The 'free' Church and the official: must they be at war?" Oct. 10, 1968. p. 10.

1061   "Foreign visitors become 'experts' on American culture." Oct. 17, 1968. p. 10.

1062   "Is it really necessary to condemn a newspaper today?" Oct. 24, 1968. p. 10. (*National Catholic Reporter.*)

1063   "Critical questions yet unanswered." Oct. 31, 1968. p. 12. (Birth control.)

1064   "Managing foolishness all around." Nov. 7, 1968. p. 10.

1065   "Is Vatican II about to be repealed?" Nov. 14, 1968. p. 10.

1066   "'Call me Jim' goes on and on and on and on and on." Nov. 21, 1968. p. 12. (James Kavanaugh.)

1067   "The bishops' pastoral letter is ambiguous--is that bad?" Nov. 28, 1968. p. 10.

1068   "Quickie Greeley liberal trap test on Catholic colleges." Dec. 5, 1968. p. 10.

1069   "Catholics always seem willing to throw the first stone." Dec. 12, 1968. p. 10. (Reply Jan. 16, 1969.)

1070   "Recognition for the 14 outstanding long-sufferers of 1968." Dec. 19, 1968. p. 10.

1071   "Colleges must prove worth." Dec. 26, 1968. p. 10.

1072   "Star Trek teaches friendship, trust." Jan. 2, 1969. p. 10.

1073   "Students out to destroy schools." Jan. 9, 1969. p. 10.

1074   "'Schism' is just a created demon." Jan. 16, 1969. p. 10.

1075   Fanning, Samuel J. "Questions envy & jealousy as an 'Irish specialty'." Jan. 16, 1969. p. 10. (Reply to Dec. 12, 1968.)

1076   "Parental hang-ups can explain much so-called 'apostasy'." Jan. 23, 1969. p. 10.

1077   "Some elements which produce a crisis of leadership." Jan. 30, 1969. p. 10.

1078   "The last of the Irish headushers." Feb. 6, 1969. p. 10. (Reply to John Cogley.)

1079   "More than Irish pride required." Feb. 13, 1969. p. 10.

1080   "'Nice guys' don't get protested." Feb. 20, 1969. p. 10.

1081   "1969 seems off to a bad start." Feb. 27, 1969. p. 10.

1082   "No one asks if parents will pay." Mar. 6, 1969. p. 10.

1083   "Free associations lacking goals." Mar. 13, 1969. p. 10.

1084   "The panic in Catholic education." Mar. 20, 1969. p. 10.

1085   "The 'sensitivity' cult is dangerous." Mar. 27, 1969. p. 10.

1086   "What is our 'family' doing for us?" Apr. 3, 1969. p. 10.

1087   "Laity have changed their minds." Apr. 10, 1969. p. 12. (Catholic schools.)

1088   "Science is dead, myth now lives." Apr. 17, 1969. p. 10.

1089   "God is found alive in classrooms." Apr. 24, 1969. p. 10.

1090   "Clergy in politics no simple issue." May 1, 1969. p. 10.

1091   "'Call me Jim' has written again." May 8, 1969. p. 10. (James Kavanaugh.)

1092   "Miss Devlin 'the Irish Julian Bond'." May 15, 1969. p. 10.

1093   "Vatican II: the successful council." May 22, 1969. p. 10.

1094   "Celibacy debate hasn't been useful." May 29, 1969. p. 10.

1095   "The sweet misery up in suburbia." June 5, 1969. p. 10.

1096   "Religious life will survive again." June 12, 1969. p. 10.

1097   "Today's family is in great shape." June 19, 1969. p. 10.

1098   "The Church must honor prophets." June 26, 1969. p. 10.

1099   "Crisis in the Church's credibility." July 3, 1969. p. 10.

1100   "Gap between reality & desire." July 10, 1969. p. 10.

1101   "What war? Was there a war?" July 17, 1969. p. 10.

1102   "Father Greeley becomes worried." July 24, 1969. p. 10.

1103   "Self-annointed crusaders continue." July 31, 1969. p. 10.
        (Sensitivity training.)

1104   "Real issue of education is values." Aug. 7, 1969. p. 10.

1105   "American theologians are hiding." Aug. 14, 1969. p. 10.

1106   "'Sensitivity' cult should be stopped." Aug. 21, 1969. p. 10.

1107   "Calls Shannon departure betrayal." Aug. 28, 1969. p. 10.

1108   "We may be riding the 'J curve'." Sept. 4, 1969. p. 10.

1109   "Suggests three factors to ease danger of revolution." Sept. 11,
        1969. p. 10.

1110   "Will we reject a strong asset in the name of foolish fad?" Sept.
        18, 1969. p. 10.

1111   "New style leadership is needed to stop the revolution." Sept.
        25, 1969. p. 10.

1112   "Is 'age of laity' able to offer much improvement?" Oct. 2,
        1969. p. 10.

1113   "Danielou: victim of misinterpretation, now guilty of same."
        Oct. 9, 1969. p. 10.

1114   "Theological ideas on demise while emotionalism on rise." Oct.
        16, 1969. p. 10.

1115   "Why do Americans like titles?" Oct. 23, 1969. p. 10.

1116   "The 'prophets of doom' won't win." Oct. 30, 1969. p. 10.

1117   "Memo to 'Time': choose Suenens." Nov. 6, 1969. p. 10.

1118   "Disagree without being disloyal." Nov. 13, 1969. p. 10.

1119   "Youth is nice, but so temporary." Nov. 20, 1969. p. 10.

1120   "Catholic U, and Father Murphy."   Nov. 27, 1969.   p. 10.

1121   "Still a 'no' vote on 'sensitivity'."   Dec. 4, 1969.   p. 10.

1122   "Problems with instant reformers."   Dec. 11, 1969.   p. 10.

1123   "The 20 who moved us in the 60s."   Dec. 18, 1969.   p. 18.

1124   "A few of our 1960s disasters."   Dec. 25, 1969.   p. 10.

1125   "This is an honest revolutionary."   Jan. 1, 1970.   p. 10.
            (Bernadette Devlin.)

1126   "Caricature of the peace movement."   Jan. 8, 1970.   p. 10.

1127   "Muddling through to nowhere."   Jan. 15, 1970.   p. 10.

1128   "Be careful with Mr. Gallup's poll."   Jan. 22, 1970.   p. 10.
            (Declining Church attendance.)

1129   "Study destroys 'youth culture' myth."   Jan. 29, 1970.   p. 10.

1130   "Attention followers of fashion: the times are changing."   Feb. 5,
            1970.   p. 10.

1131   "Celibacy is not the right issue."   Feb. 12, 1970.   p. 10.

1132   "Two sad stories IHMs and C.U."   Feb 19, 1970.   p. 10.

1133   "Celibacy counterattack 'offensive'."   Feb. 26, 1970.   p. 10.

1134   "Are we compelled to categorize?"   Mar. 5, 1970.   p. 10.

1135   "Why the gloom among clergy?"   Mar. 12, 1970.   p. 10.

1136   "Priests leaving lose constituency."   Mar. 19, 1970.   p. 10.

1137   "Why is Pat Moynihan a 'devil'?"   Mar. 26, 1970.   p. 10.

1138   "Are the 'best' priests in or out?"   Apr. 2, 1970.   p. 10.

1139   "Anti-war mood is in the 'silent'."   Apr. 9, 1970.   p. 12.

1140   "Research: long, complicated, costly." Apr. 16, 1970. p. 10.

1141   "Don't talk peace and make war." Apr.23, 1970. p. 10.

1142   "Today's election winning formula." Apr. 30, 1970. p. 10.

1143   "Are we forgetting the good news?" May 7, 1970. p. 10.

1144   "Priests' senates have promise." May 14, 1970. p. 10.

1145   "'Bomb' offers irresponsible solution." May 21, 1970. p. 10.
        (Overpopulation.)

1146   "Voting should be last, not first, resort." May 28, 1970. p. 10.

1147   "Young new left can't go it alone--allies are needed." June 4,
        1970. p. 12.

1148   "The new 'conventional wisdom'." June 11, 1970. p. 12.

1149   "This class of people is 'thriftless and less desirable'." June 18,
        1970. p. 10.

1150   "If you don't look around you'd think the sky was falling on us."
        June 25, 1970. p. 10.

1151   "The college campus crisis will probably get worse." July 2,
        1970. p. 10.

1152   "Cognizance of American politics is 'strictly academic'." July 9,
        1970. p. 10.

1153   "'Degree game' characterizes universities' unreality." July 16,
        1970. p. 10.

1154   "Ethnic identification not social problem, but social asset." July
        23, 1970. p. 10.

1155   "College 'under trees' no worse than present system." July 30,
        1970. p. 10.

1156 "Second-rate education may, at least, not destroy poets." Aug. 6, 1970. p. 10.

1157 "Collegiality becomes real only by use in controversy." Aug. 13, 1970. p. 12.

1158 "Father Greeley confesses: he's a populist." Aug. 20, 1970. p. 10.

1159 "The people can be trusted in the long run." Aug. 27, 1970. p. 10.

1160 "The populist is tempted to see conspiracies around him." Sept. 3, 1970. p. 12.

1161 "What would have happened if Martin Luther had stayed?" Sept. 10, 1970. p. 10.

1162 "Self-righteous fanatics heading revolutions are not new." Sept. 17, 1970. p. 10.

1163 "Catholic journals are in trouble." Sept. 24, 1970. p. 10.

1164 "Clerical goodness isn't the same as political goodness." Oct. 1, 1970. p. 10.

1165 "Let us now praise intelligent, competent men." Oct. 8, 1970. p. 10. (George Higgins.)

1166 "Youth worship: the peculiar sect." Oct. 15, 1970. p. 10.

1167 "'There will be another council sometime before 1980'." Oct. 22, 1970. p. 12.

1168 "Opinions of youth cannot be sole criteria of faith." Oct. 29, 1970. p. 12.

1169 "A scholar isn't necessarily also a prophet." Nov. 5, 1970. p. 10.

1170 "It is very risky being a leader in this time." Nov. 12, 1970. p. 10.

1171   "One honest project is underway." Nov. 19, 1970. p. 10. (NCCB priests' study.)

1172   "If the Vatican trusted bishops, liturgy would improve." Nov. 26, 1970. p. 10.

1173   "The balanced ticket is still winning elections." Dec. 3, 1970. p. 10.

1174   "Cardinal Greeley would be the Midway's flashiest man." Dec.10, 1970. p. 10.

1175   "It's hard to tell how we're best classified." Dec. 17, 1970. p. 18.

1176   "The great athletics conspiracy goes on." Dec. 24, 1970. p. 10.

1177   "Help! I'm surrounded by incompetent romantic amateurs." Dec. 31, 1970. p. 10.

1178   "We need decentralization for freedom at the top." Jan. 7, 1971. p. 10.

1179   "Pentacostalism: is it a bridge?" Jan. 14, 1971. p. 10.

1180   "Playing the game of Catholic writer-fighter." Jan. 21, 1971. p. 10.

1181   "Scholarship counts: conservative, liberal labels irrelevant." Jan. 28, 1971. p. 10.

1182   "Why are our radicals the only ones the FBI catches?" Feb. 4, 1971. p. 10.

1183   "Destruction is not the way to educate people." Feb. 11, 1971. p. 10.

1184   "Is school aid opposition rooted in nativist suspicions?" Feb. 18, 1971. p. 10.

1185   "Looking back with Gary Wills as he ridicules the past." Feb. 25, 1971. p. 10.

1186   "Don't expect the synod to solve 'priesthood' issues." Mar. 4, 1971. p. 10.

1187   "Casting stones at people is no way to convert them." Mar. 11, 1971. p. 10.

1188   "Theologians need room in which to work on questions." Mar. 18, 1971. p. 10.

1189   "Some questions on team ministry." Mar. 25, 1971. p. 12.

1190   "Society won't be changed by denial of its complexity." Apr. 1, 1971. p. 14.

1191   "Critic does away with schools but offers no alternative." Apr. 8, 1971. p. 10.

1192   "Courage comes out strongest at the top at Notre Dame." Apr. 15, 1971. p. 10. (Theodore M. Hesburgh.)

1193   "Selective defense of the rule of law isn't working out." Apr. 22, 1971. p. 10.

1194   "Studier of priesthood is both optimistic and pessimistic." Apr. 29, 1971. p. 10.

1195   "Why Eberhart went to jail to protest our corruption." May 6, 1971. p. 12.

1196   "Beautiful people--the best years are still ahead." May 13, 1971. p. 10.

1197   "Why researchers expect little." May 20, 1971. p. 12.

1198   "Celibacy is not the main issue for priests: power is." May 27, 1971. p. 10.

1199   "This is the season to pick on Mayor Richard A.[*sic*] Daley." June 3, 1971. p. 10. (*Boss: Richard J. Daley of Chicago* by Mike Royko. Dutton.)

1200 "Research report on priesthood given insulting treatment." June 10, 1971. p. 10.

1201 "Hoyt leaves NCR under pressure: the end of an era." June 17, 1971. p. 10.

1202 "A man with a clippings file uses it against 'radicals'." June 24, 1971. p. 10. (*The Decline and Fall of Radical Catholicism* by James Hitchcock. Herder & Herder.)

1203 "There's no one way to be an authentic liberal Catholic." July 1, 1971. p. 10.

1204 "Discovering again that people are more than labels." July 8, 1971. p. 10.

1205 "A foolish, worthless exercise in Chicago." July 15, 1971. p. 10.

1206 "All kinds of people go to jail--some for sensible reasons." July 22, 1971. p. 10.

1207 "'Absurd' school aid decisions smell of anti-Catholicism." July 29, 1971. p. 10.

1208 "The politics of selecting bishops should become public." Aug. 5, 1971. p. 10.

1209 "The 'official' Church should quit the school business." Aug. 12, 1971. p. 10.

1210 "Priest nominee to bishops synod asks questions on the process." Aug. 19, 1971. p. 10.

1211 "What has happened now to the priesthood survey?" Aug. 26, 1971. p. 10.

1212 "Put no limitations on the exercise of priestly ministry." Sept. 2, 1971. p. 10.

1213 "It's so easy to blame everything, even inflation on the 'hard hats'." Sept. 9, 1971. p. 10.

1214   "The bishops now have a tool for ignoring their priesthood study." Sept. 16, 1971. p. 10.

1215   "Minnesota's St. John's Abbey is a remarkable place." Sept. 23, 1971. p. 10.

1216   "The U. S. chair should be vacant." Sept. 30, 1971. p. 10. (At Synod of Bishops.)

1217   "Now you can be an ethnic American." Oct. 7, 1971. p. 10.

1218   "Curia vendetta with Kung is near showdown." Oct. 14, 1971. p. 10.

1219   "Reform in the Church hasn't failed; it hasn't been tried." Oct. 21, 1971. p. 10.

1220   "Newsweek report shows Church's slow rate of change." Oct. 28, 1971. p. 10.

1221   "Some guilt-ridden writers want all of us to join them." Nov. 4, 1971. p. 10.

1222   "If a senator is a priest can his judgment be trusted?" Nov. 11, 1971. p. 10.

1223   "Can anything good come from someone named Novak?" Nov. 18, 1971. p. 10.

1224   "The Nazi mentality in some movements." Nov. 25, 1971. p. 10.

1225   "The late synod: 'We had a disaster and no one noticed'." Dec. 2, 1971. p. 10.

1226   "Some people seem to enjoy feeling guilty." Dec. 9, 1971. p. 10.

1227   "It's easy to forget that Jesus is no one's monopoly." Dec. 16, 1971. p. 16.

1228　"Few care about the Cardinal's job." Dec. 23, 1971. p. 10.
(Cardinal John Krol.)

1229　"Sophisticated discrimination now seems to be rampant." Dec.
30, 1971. p. 10.

1230　"A sad defense of the indefensible." Jan. 6, 1972. p. 10.

1231　"Pat Moynihan for man of the year." Jan. 13, 1972. p. 10.

1232　"A new realism hits Church unity move." Jan. 20, 1972. p. 10.

1233　"Unfair attacks on a good scholar." Jan. 27, 1972. p. 10.

1234　"Setting rules so you always win." Feb. 3, 1972. p. 10.

1235　"Watch out for those non-events." Feb. 10, 1972. p. 10.

1236　"Busing works in a special case." Feb. 17, 1972. p. 10.

1237　"Some people can admit failure." Feb. 24, 1972. p. 10.

1238　"It's time for the British to get out of Ireland." Mar. 2, 1972.
p. 10.

1239　"Card. Suenens--a victim of 'clerical envy'." Mar. 16, 1972. p.
10.

1240　"Women's lib has points--especially for men." Mar. 23, 1972.
p. 10.

1241　"To call Ireland a theocracy is 'nonsense'." Mar. 30, 1972. p.
10.

1242　"The ethnic 'thing' is not a fraud." Apr. 6, 1972. p. 10.

1243　"How Christians meet hopelessness." Apr. 13, 1972. p. 10.
(Reply Apr. 27, 1972.)

1244　"How the Irish are fashionable--in a bad way." Apr. 20, 1972.
p. 10.

1245   "A little garbage goes a long way." Apr. 27, 1972. pp. 10+.

1246   Kane, Esther. "The saints, not the bishops." Apr. 27, 1972. p.
         10. (Reply to Apr.13, 1972.)

1247   "The IRA are brutal murderers." May 4, 1972. pp. 10+.

1248   "We, of all people, should laugh." May 11, 1972. p. 10.

1249   "The pain of a Slavic intellectual." May 18, 1972. pp. 10+.
         (*The Rise of the Unmeltable Ethnic* by Michael Novak.
         Macmillan.)

1250   "Is it better to play hockey or to sleep well?" May 25, 1972. p.
         10.

1251   "Won't the lying about the war ever stop?" June 1, 1972. p. 10.

1252   "How to express distrust of almost everyone." June 8, 1972. p.
         10.

1253   "Christianity should aid political commitment." June 15, 1972.
         p. 10.

1254   "Leadership could be the trouble." June 22, 1972. p. 10.

1255   "Planning for a world for perfect beings only." June 29, 1972.
         p. 10.

1256   "What Faddists say about the family isn't so." July 6, 1972. p.
         10.

1257   "Reasons for the clergy to stay out of politics." July 13, 1972.
         p. 10.

1258   "The rational way to care for a small planet." July 20, 1972. p.
         10.

1259   "The angels are not on one side in busing controversy." July 27,
         1972. p. 10.

1260 "Catholics are going to decide the '72 election." Aug. 3, 1972. p. 10.

1261 "Extremist Catholics lack sense of humor." Aug. 10, 1972. p. 10.

1262 "Political reformers deceive us." Aug. 17, 1972. p. 10.

1263 "New pack of purists pursuing political power." Aug. 24, 1972. p. 10.

1264 "The young and educated were war backers." Aug. 31, 1972. p. 10.

1265 "It's so easy to blame the Church for every old problem." Sept. 7, 1972. p. 10.

1266 "Some of us aren't consistent in judgments." Sept. 14, 1972. p. 10.

1267 "Death loses its sting." Sept. 21, 1972. p. 10.

1268 "We must insist on having a longer summer." Sept. 28, 1972. p. 10.

1269 "Our schools will not lead the way to equality." Oct. 5, 1972. p. 10. (*Inequality: a reassessment of the effect of family and schooling in America* by Christopher Jencks. Basic.) (*See also* Oct. 12 and 19, 1972.)

1270 "Must we learn to live with some inequality?" Oct. 12, 1972. p. 10. (*See also* Oct. 5 and 19, 1972.)

1271 "Practical solutions beat waiting for a Utopia." Oct. 19, 1972. p. 10. (*See also* Oct. 5 and 12, 1972.)

1272 "It's fashionable--but unfair--to flog 'ethnics'." Oct. 26, 1972. p. 10.

1273 "We seem to know little about the 'ethnics'." Nov. 2, 1972. p. 12.

1274   "A fresh ally of the Catholic school." Nov. 9, 1972. p. 10.

1275   "How the people lost the right to elect bishops." Nov. 16, 1972. p. 10.

1276   "European countries hide a system of slavery." Nov. 23, 1972. p. 10.

1277   "The election was not a victory for racism." Nov. 30, 1972. p. 10.

1278   "Why doesn't the Roman principle apply to all." Dec. 7, 1972. p. 10.

1279   "At least one sports book is really about God." Dec. 14, 1972. p. 10. (*When All the Laughter Died in Sorrow* by Lance Rentzel. Saturday Review.)

1280   "Without technology most of us would be dead." Dec. 21, 1972. p. 14.

1281   "The act of faith is not so easy these days." Dec. 28, 1972. p. 10.

1282   "The trouble with selective quotas." Jan. 4, 1973. p. 10.

1283   "The firing of a good Republican." Jan. 11, 1973. p. 10. (Robert A. Podesta.)

1284   "Liberal elitists work to despise the ethnics." Jan. 18, 1973. p. 10.

1285   "Trouble with 'what Jesus would'." Jan 25, 1973. pp. 10+.

1286   "Must only some of the bigots be denounced?" Feb. 1, 1973. p. 10.

1287   "There are three kinds of Irish revolutionaries." Feb. 8, 1973. p. 10.

1288   "A room mother who might find peace in jail." Feb. 15, 1973. p. 10.

1289 "The Vietnam war will go the way of the Great Depression." Feb. 22, 1973. p. 10.

1290 "Curia 'no win' tactics." Mar. 1, 1973. p. 10.

1291 "Three problems for liberals to work on." Mar. 8, 1973. p. 10.

1292 "Don't have strange names for God." Mar. 15, 1973. p. 10.

1293 "Vatican tokenism degrades Papacy." Mar. 22, 1973. p. 10.

1294 "Can everyone be a war criminal?" Mar. 29, 1973. p. 10.

1295 "Blame Wilson for interventionism." Apr. 5, 1973. p. 10.

1296 "Awful sermons feed a new anticlericalism." Apr. 12, 1973. p. 10.

1297 "History for anti-abortion fanatics." Apr. 19, 1973. p. 10.

1298 "The 'sexual revolution' is a myth." Apr. 26, 1973. p. 10.

1299 "Sisters, please quote in context." May 3, 1973. p. 10+.

1300 "Why collective decisions are often not good." May 10, 1973. p. 10.

1301 "The dumbest crooks in history?" May 17, 1973. p. 10. (Watergate).

1302 "The Jesuits are OK, but I wouldn't be one." May 24, 1973. p. 10.

1303 "Truth is stranger than fiction--and more frightening." May 31, 1973. p. 10.

1304 "For the Ordinandi: being a priest is more fun." June 7, 1973. p. 10.

1305 "If religious are returning to old habits, is that bad?" June 14, 1973. p. 10.

1306 "We need a few new Msgr. Egans." June 21, 1973. p. 10.

1307 "Watergate shows that Madison's plan works." June 28, 1973. p. 10.

1308 "Can a priest's aunt stop calling him Father?" July 5, 1973. p. 10.

1309 "More confusion by the romantics." July 12, 1973. p. 10.

1310 "Anti-Catholicism survives among the elites." July 19, 1973. p. 10.

1311 "Let's ordain women and get to real issues." July 26, 1973. p. 10.

1312 "The Church is a fraternity of local churches." Aug. 2, 1973. p. 10.

1313 "Think of Dan Berrigan as poet, not politician." Aug. 9, 1973. p. 10.

1314 "'We need fair trials for politicians too'." Aug. 16, 1973. p. 10.

1315 "Some people have the critic's responsibility." Aug. 23, 1973. p. 10.

1316 "It is time to consider presidential candidates." Aug. 30, 1973. p. 10.

1317 "Those Sunday sermons are hard to improve." Sept. 13, 1973. p. 10.

1318 "Theologians should not speak from ignorance." Sept. 20, 1973. p. 10.

1319 "To the new--and different--Apostolic Delegate." Sept. 27, 1973. p. 10.

1320 "Have we gotten rid of the new barons?" Oct. 4, 1973. p. 8.

1321 "If a priest knows, he's peeked." Oct. 11, 1973. p. 8.

1322 "Don't kid yourself when the kids question you." Oct. 18, 1973. p. 8.

1323 "Was Cogley gone before he left?" Oct. 25, 1973. p. 8.

1324 "Liberation won't come from vulgar Marxism." Nov. 1, 1973. p. 10.

1325 "Searching of youth is no surprise." Nov. 8, 1973. p. 10.

1326 "A case of too radical and too reactionary heretics." Nov. 15, 1973. p. 8.

1327 "Anti-Catholicism still serves the need for a handy scapegoat." Nov. 22, 1973. p. 8.

1328 "The liberal heretics are murdering the faith." Nov. 29, 1973. p. 8.

1329 "Conservative heretics love the strictly verbal." Dec. 6, 1973. p. 8.

1330 "Messing around vs. making rules." Dec. 13, 1973. p. 8.

1331 "They need reconciliation theology." Dec. 20, 1973. p. 14.

1332 "Keep the comic gang." Dec. 27, 1973. p. 8. (*Wanderer.*)

1333 "Notice the celibate heroes on TV." Jan. 3, 1974. p. 8.

1334 "Priests' senates seem to be slipping into a tyranny of the majority." Jan. 10, 1974. p. 8.

1335 "Ecumenism isn't the only priority." Jan. 17, 1974. p. 8.

1336 "Colleges, Franciscans may need liberating." Jan. 24, 1974. p. 8.

1337 "The 'wounded black' is one more stereotype." Jan. 31, 1974. p. 8.

1338   "'Accountability' is not going to happen soon." Feb. 7, 1974. p. 8.

1339   "Personnel boards are not bringing salvation." Feb. 14, 1974. p. 8.

1340   "You have rights--or you don't." Feb. 21, 1974. p. 8.

1341   "A reconsideration of John Cogley's move." Feb. 28, 1974. p. 8.

1342   "Church structure reflects society." Mar. 7, 1974. p. 8.

1343   "What do they want?" Mar. 14, 1974. p. 8.

1344   "A man named Ireland didn't fear our idea." Mar. 21, 1974. p. 8.

1345   "The strange selectivity of liberals." Mar. 28, 1974. p. 8.

1346   "Greeley writes 'too much' because it's fun." Apr. 4, 1974. p. 8.

1347   "Greeley is relieved: he's still in trouble." Apr. 25, 1974. p. 8.

1348   "The perfectionist misses the point." May 2, 1974. p. 8.

1349   "Everyone agrees: we need Popes." May 9, 1974. p. 8.

1350   "Something good for a bicentennial." May 16, 1974. p. 8.

1351   "Bishops are important but they are not God." May 23, 1974. p. 8.

1352   "An extraordinary bishop retires." May 30, 1974. p. 8. (Ernest Primeau.)

1353   "Why don't priests ask the folks in the pews?" June 6, 1974. p. 8.

1354   "A disgusting episode in American history." June 13, 1974. p. 8.

1355   "The Catholic non-Catholics hear." June 20, 1974. p. 8. (Theodore Hesburgh.)

1356   "Why pick on politics as a despiritualizer?" June 27, 1974. p. 8.

1357   "Anti-Catholic bigotry flies high on the left." July 4, 1974. p. 8.

1358   "To be a Catholic is to be both strict and lax." July 11, 1974. p. 8.

1359   "Holy Year 1975: relic of an archaic past or an extraordinarily exciting idea." July 18, 1974. p. 8.

1360   "Catholic schools are the 'community schools'." July 25, 1974. p. 8.

1361   "Shouldn't Catholics resent bias?" Aug. 1, 1974. pp. 8+.

1362   "Religious communities must support talent." Aug. 8, 1974. p. 8.

1363   "Bankruptcy is around the corner." Aug. 15, 1974. p. 8.

1364   "What does life mean? That is the problem." Aug. 22, 1974. p. 8.

1365   "They expiate for all but Catholics." Aug. 29, 1974. p. 8.

1366   "New contest: lousiest sermons." Sept. 5, 1974. p. 8.

1367   "People are fed up with carrying blame." Sept. 12, 1974. p. 8.

1368   "That so-called document of the U. S. bishops isn't really." Sept. 26, 1974. p. 8.

1369   "The day the FBI came for a visit." Oct. 3, 1974. p. 8.

1370   "New reasons why men are leaving the priesthood." Oct. 10, 1974. p. 8.

1371   "It's odd the way the new liturgy is blamed." Oct. 17, 1974. p. 8.

1372   "How important the Transcendent?" Oct. 24, 1974. p. 8.

1373   "We are people who don't despair." Oct. 31, 1974. p. 10.

1374   "No need for homogenization when present system works." Nov. 7, 1974. p. 8.

1375   "If the Pope cries out who can blame him?" Nov. 14, 1974. p. 8.

1376   "The old neighborhood still provides a fellowship of faith." Nov. 21, 1974. p. 8.

1377   "Anyone think where the slums came from?" Nov. 28, 1974. p. 8.

1378   "There must be a middle ground." Dec. 5, 1974. p. 8.

1379   "Well-to-do sit in suburbs and call the city poor racists." Dec. 12, 1974. p. 14.

1380   "Should we be taken seriously?" Dec. 26, 1974. p. 8.

1381   "What's happening to Episcopalians?" Jan. 2. 1975. p. 8.

1382   "Those who pay should have a say." Jan. 9, 1975. p. 8.

1383   "The earth's most successful event." Jan. 16, 1975. p. 8+.

1384   "Do right-to-lifers want gun control and worker safety?" Jan. 23, 1975. p. 8.

1385   "We get a show of hands rather than rational discussion." Jan. 30, 1975. p. 8.

1386   "They're tearing down America." Feb. 6, 1975. p. 8.

1387   "Let's not use the Spirit as excuse." Feb. 13, 1975. p. 8.

1388   "Anti-Catholicism is alive and well." Feb. 20, 1975. p. 8.

1389   "Campion joins fight against ethnicity." Feb. 27, 1975. p. 7.

1390   "Do Catholics need a new anathema?" Mar. 6, 1975. p. 7.

1391   "Pat Crowley was an authentic man." Mar. 13, 1975. p. 7.

1392   "Is the priesthood still respectable?" Mar. 20, 1975. p. 7.

1393   "Our past is useful, but not as escape." Mar. 27, 1975. p. 7.

1394   "The Catholic elites seem ashamed of us." Apr. 3, 1975. p. 7.

1395   "Gregorian chants still prospering." Apr. 10, 1975. p. 7.

1396   "It seems to be time to beat up the Irish." Apr. 17, 1975. p. 7.

1397   "The qualified laity aren't appreciated." Apr. 24, 1975. p. 7.

1398   "Monsignor practices reverse McCarthyism." May 1, 1975.
        p. 7. (George Higgins.)

1399   "An excellent movie made in Madison." May 8, 1975. p. 8.

1400   "The Church should give some answers." May 15, 1975. p. 8.

1401   "You need a Church to stay in the race." May 22, 1975. p. 7.

1402   "Ethnicity bothers some Catholics." June 5, 1975. p. 7.

1403   "Movies are better made by Catholics." June 12, 1975. p. 7.

1404   "If it's going to hurt, what do you say?" June 19, 1975. p. 7.

1405   "This kind of 'loyalty' doesn't help bishops." June 26, 1975.
        p. 7.

1406   "Catholic socialism is the latest fashion." July 3, 1975. p. 7.

1407   "The Gini ratio says we're not so bad." July 10, 1975. p. 7.

1408   "We've failed them and no one cares." July 17, 1975. p. 7.

1409   "Saving the Church from Christianity." July 24, 1975. p. 7.

1410   "The U. S. Church is in dire crisis." July 31, 1975. p. 7.

1411   "The U. S. produces a new theologian." Aug. 7, 1975. p. 7. (David Tracy.)

1412   "If Catholics stop it others pick it up." Aug. 14, 1975. p. 7.

1413   "An ethnicity story to break your heart." Aug. 21, 1975. p. 7.

1414   "Women's ordination: the great non-issue." Aug. 28, 1975. p. 7.

1415   "Caution abandoned for enthusiasms." Sept. 4, 1975. p. 7.

1416   "A surge of piety among the editors." Sept. 11, 1975. p. 7.

1417   "Commonweal to get the stupidity award." Sept. 18, 1975. p. 7.

1418   "Catholicism in U. S. not hopeful picture." Sept. 25, 1975. p. 7.

1419   "'Protestant ethic' might be a help." Oct. 2, 1975. p. 7.

1420   "A little learning still isn't enough." Oct. 9, 1975. p. 7.

1421   "Is anyone going to Church today?" Oct. 16, 1975. p. 7.

1422   "Are sisters now seekers of power?" Oct. 23, 1975. p. 7.

1423   "Get the stories from old folks." Oct. 30, 1975. p. 7.

1424   "The liberationists bring on laughter." Nov. 6, 1975. p. 7.

1425   "Anti-semitic binge at United Nations." Nov. 13, 1975. p. 7.

1426   "Laity needs strong independent voice." Nov. 20, 1975. p. 7.

1427   "Our social theory is being ignored." Nov. 27, 1975. p. 7.

1428   "The TV Catholics aren't very real." Dec. 4, 1975. p. 7.

1429   "Catholics should be better givers." Dec. 11, 1975. p. 7.

1430   "The horror stories of anti-Catholicism." Dec. 18, 1975. p. 7.

1431   "The Curia wins despite its loss." Dec. 25, 1975. p. 7.

1432   "Why no priests in kiddy apostolate?" Jan. 1, 1976. p. 7.

1433   "Lock the barn! the horse is out." Jan. 8, 1976. p. 7.

1434   "Neighborhoods have education influence." Jan. 15, 1976. p. 7.

1435   "Do liberals want an end to liberty?" Jan. 22, 1976. p. 7.

1436   "Kung's big mistake: he is successful." Jan. 29, 1976. p. 7.

1437   "Blowing the whistle on Michael Novak." Feb. 5, 1976. p. 7.

1438   "The Church could say more on sex." Feb. 12, 1976. p. 7.

1439   "A Pole downplays education of Poles." Feb. 19, 1976. p. 7.

1440   "Where have all the women gone?" Feb. 26, 1976. p. 7.

1441   "Liberation theology gives up freedom." Mar. 4, 1976. p. 7.

1442   "Can't we forget liberal faddism?" Mar. 11, 1976. p. 7.

1443   "Superficial studies of Catholic history." Mar. 18, 1976. p. 7.

1444   "Empirical evidence or 'trend sniffing'." Mar. 25, 1976. p. 7.

1445   "Sisters don't reflect spirit of founders." May 13, 1976. p. 6.

1446   "Why won't Church heed the evidence?" May 20, 1976. p. 6.

1447   "When tide turns, nobody is ready." May 27, 1976. p. 6.

1448   "Schools don't drain Church's finances." June 3, 1976. p. 6.

1449   "Church's teachings subject to change." June 10, 1976. p. 6.

1450   "Social action style is only ideological." June 17, 1976. p. 6.

1451   "Fifteen rules for book reviewing." June 24, 1976. p. 6.

1452   "Research center would do little." July 1, 1976. p. 6.

1453   "Phony statistics on religious ed." July 8, 1976. p. 7

1454   "Bishops still care about popularity." July 15, 1976. p. 6.

1455   "Church 'parades' ignore lost sheep." July 22, 1976. p. 7.

1456   "I detest policies, but I like people." July 29, 1976. p. 7.

1457   "Correction for 'phantom study'." Aug. 5, 1976. p. 6.

1458   "This column may be purged." Aug. 12, 1976. p. 7.

1459   "Where gone, Madonna?" (Poem.) Aug. 19, 1976. p. 6.

1460   "Demo ticket spells trouble." Aug. 26, 1976. p. 7. (Replies
        Sept. 9, 16 and 23, 1976.)

1461   "Persistence of anti-Catholicism." Sept. 2, 1976. p. 6.

1462   "Some outrage is selective." Sept. 9, 1976. p. 7.

1463   Eberdt, Kathleen. "Greeley's faulty history." Sept. 9, 1976. pp.
        8+. (Reply to Aug. 26, 1976.)

1464   Rolene, Marcy. "Greeley does not promote responsible study of
        issues." Sept. 9, 1976. p. 8. (Reply to Aug. 26, 1976.)

1465   Howe, William B. "Greeley like Spiro Agnew: the slashing lacks
        research." Sept. 16, 1976. pp. 8+. (Reply to Aug. 26, 1976.)

1466   McCormally, John. "Greeley's misstatement no slip of pen."
        Sept. 16, 1976. p. 8. (Reply to Aug. 26, 1976.)

1467   "Documenting anti-Catholicism." Sept. 16, 1976. p. 10.

1468   Bishop, Jean. "Dismayed by the prejudice." Sept. 23, 1976.
        p. 8. (Reply to Aug. 26, 1976.)

1469   McGreevy, Gene F. "Are bishops being fair?" Sept. 23, 1976.
        p. 8. (Reply to Aug. 26, 1976.)

1470   "Success story for ecumenism." Sept. 30, 1976. p. 7.

1471   "Amateurism at the USCC." Oct. 7, 1976. p. 6.

1472   "Demented drivel in 'The Critic'." Oct. 14, 1976. p. 7.

1473   "No way to run a meeting." Oct. 21, 1976. p. 6.

1474   "Xeroxed songs a major scandal." Oct. 28, 1976. p. 10.

1475   "Garbage in the 'Village Voice'." Nov. 4, 1976. p. 6. (*See
        also* Dec. 16, 1976.)

1476   "1,500 better than 800,000." Nov. 11, 1976. p. 6.

1477   "Detroit was an act of oppression." Nov. 18, 1976. p. 8.

1478   "What do 'the people' want." Nov. 25, 1976. p. 6.

1479   "Incompetency at the USCC." Dec. 2, 1976. p. 6.

1480   "Should faculties have the power?" Dec. 9, 1976. p. 6.

1481   "An exchange of letters." Dec. 16, 1976. p. 11. (*Village Voice.
        See also* Nov. 4, 1976.)

1482   "Lack of study is a tragedy." Dec. 23, 1976. p. 6.

1483   "Priest limits ethnic label." Dec. 30, 1976. p. 7.

1484   "Hatchet job in 'Commonweal'." Jan. 6, 1977. p. 7. (Daniel
        P. Moynihan.)

1485   "Baum affair an ugly act." Jan. 13, 1977. p. 8. (Reply Jan. 27, 1977).

1486   "Mayor Daley." Jan. 20, 1977. p. 7. (Poem.)

1487   "'Call to Action'." Jan. 27, 1977. p. 7. (Poem.)

1488   Popson, Martha. "Decent man is getting 'Baumed'." Jan. 27, 1977. p. 8. (Reply to Jan. 13, 1977.)

1489   "Inept amateurs in both wings." Feb. 3, 1977. p. 6.

1490   "Misstatements badly printed." Feb. 10, 1977. p. 6.

1491   "More flak on Detroit." Feb 17, 1977. p. 7.

1492   "NCR's vicious review of Kung." Feb. 24, 1977. p. 6. (*On Being a Christian* by Hans Kung. Doubleday.)

1493   "The politics of the neighborhood." Mar. 3, 1977. p. 6.

1494   "The AJC affair has ended." Mar. 10, 1977. p. 7. (Controversy with American Jewish Committee.)

1495   "Risking fanaticism." Mar. 17, 1977. p. 8. (Reply Mar. 31, 1977.)

1496   "Cogley cultists are at it again." Mar. 24, 1977. p. 6.

1497   "No Catholic scholarship." Mar. 31, 1977. p. 6. (*Evangelization in the American Context* by David Burrell and Franzita Kane. Univ. of Notre Dame Press. And *Religion and Self-Acceptance* by John Haught. Paulist/Newman.)

1498   Madden, Loretto A. "Greeley is unfair." Mar. 31, 1977. p. 8. (Reply to Mar. 17, 1977.)

1499   "Church staff should get out." Apr. 7, 1977. p. 7.

1500   "New language called 'Nunnish'." Apr. 14, 1977. p. 6.

1501   "Accountability for Church $$$." Apr. 21, 1977. p. 6.

1502   "Reclaiming lost sheep." Apr. 28, 1977. p. 6.

1503   "DePaul parents should be told." May 5, 1977. p. 7. (*Raid on the Articulate* by John D. Crossan. Harper.)

1504   "A report that says little." May 12, 1977. p. 6.

1505   "It's constitutional to be anti-Catholic." May 19, 1977. p. 9.

1506   "Why did our attitude change?" May 26, 1977. p. 9.

1507   "The snobbishness is mind-boggling." June 2, 1977. p. 9.

1508   "Good riddance to Call to Action." June 9, 1977. p. 9.

1509   "Clergy and religious attack the families." June 16, 1977. p. 9.

1510   "Catholic snobs dislike ethnics." June 23, 1977. p. 9.

1511   "It was, thank God, a nice meeting." June 30, 1977. p. 9. (Vatican III - The Work To Be Done.)

1512   "The U. S. is taking theological lead." July 7, 1977. p. 9.

1513   "How to learn to be a priest." July 14, 1977. p. 9.

1514   "Do we encourage anti-Catholicism." July 21, 1977. p. 9.

1515   "Ballade Pour Une Archeveque Nordamerican and A Ballade for Rosemary Radford Reuther." July 28, 1977. p. 9. (Poems.)

1516   "Back to the impact of Humanae Vitae." Aug. 4, 1977. p. 9.

1517   "Something to watch in New York City." Aug. 11, 1977. p. 9. (Mario Cuomo.)

1518   "A suggestion for Knights of Columbus." Aug. 18, 1977. p. 9.

1519   "They won a battle but lost the war." Aug. 25, 1977. p. 9.

1520   "It is now clear that celibates need friends." Sept. 1, 1977. p. 9.

1521   "How Catholics leave the Church." Sept. 8, 1977. p. 9.

1522   "Lack of intimacy is a religious problem." Sept. 15, 1977. p. 9.

1523   "The work is so bad it can't be believed." Sept. 22, 1977. p. 9. (*Catechetical Directory*.)

1524   "Evidence for the shift to the right." Sept. 29, 1977. p. 9.

1525   "Why don't we study anti-Catholicism?" Oct. 6, 1977. p. 9.

1526   "They still come in the night." Oct. 13, 1977. p. 9.

1527   "Catholic schools mean lots of money." Oct. 20, 1977. p. 9.

1528   "Some quality work is still being done." Oct. 27, 1977. p. 9.

1529   "Have the blind followed the blind." Nov. 3, 1977. p. 9.

1530   "Our bishops were ready." Nov. 10, 1977. p. 9.

1531   "Poor staff work hurts the bishops." Nov. 17, 1977. p. 9.

1532   "The synod was a waste of time." Nov. 24, 1977. p. 9.

1533   "A good bill that won't pass." Dec. 1, 1977. p. 9. (Packwood-Moynihan bill re college tuition credits.)

1534   "The evidence won't go away." Dec. 8, 1977. p. 9.

1535   "Is there criticism in the Church?" Dec. 15, 1977. p. 9.

1536   "How to offend absolutely everyone." Dec. 22, 1977. p. 9.

1537   "The mush is running heavy." Dec. 29, 1977. p. 9.

1538   "It makes sense to be bitter." Jan. 5, 1978. p. 9.

1539   "There is bad news and more bad news." Jan. 12, 1978. p. 9.

1540   "The evidence for the crisis of decline." Jan. 19, 1978. p. 9.

1541   "Gather the folks, break bread, tell the stories." Jan. 26, 1978.
        p. 9. (*Stories of God: an unauthorized biography* by John Shea.
        Thomas More.)

1542   "Get back into the religion business." Feb. 2, 1978. p. 9.

1543   "Style and class are missing." Feb. 9, 1978. p. 9. (*National
        Catholic Reporter.*)

1544   "Carter is betraying Catholic education." Feb. 16, 1978. p. 9.

1545   "Bishops' committee no help to priests." Feb 23, 1978. p. 9.

1546   "How not to look at 'Close Encounters'." Mar. 2, 1978. p. 9.

1547   "This is not pious pleading." Mar. 9, 1978. p. 9.

1548   "The odd case of the 'bigoted' friend." Mar. 16, 1978. p. 9.

1549   "Professor doesn't know his subject." Mar. 23, 1978. p. 9.
        (Dr. Stephen Schmidt.)

1550   "Some Catholics try to please." Mar. 30, 1978. p. 9.

1551   "Modern vocabulary for a modern world." Apr. 6, 1978. p. 9.

1552   "Anti-Catholicism is 'in' in Washington." Apr. 13, 1978. p. 9.

1553   "Do surveys show good or bad news?" Apr. 20, 1978. p. 9.
        (Gallup/Catholic Press Assn. study.)

1554   "Moral theology is mostly worthless." Apr. 27, 1978. p. 9.

1555   "Why Americans beat Germans." May 4, 1978. p. 9.

1556   "A nasty farewell to Phyllis McGinley." May 11, 1978. p. 9.

1557   "Readers deserve better reporting." May 18, 1978. p. 9.
(*National Catholic Reporter*.)

1558   "A radical defense of Catholic schools." May 25, 1978. p. 9.

1559   "Religious bigotry making comeback?" June 1, 1978. p. 9.

1560   "Good thought flows again." June 8, 1978. p. 9.

1561   "It's time to write to the President." June 15, 1978. p. 9.

1562   "The tuition credit stirs up old fires." June 22, 1978. p. 9.

1563   "The PTA against freedom of choice." June 29, 1978. p. 9.

1564   "Chicago old-timers strike a chord." July 6, 1978. p. 9.

1565   "Sometimes 1,000 is better than 6,000." July 13, 1978. p. 9.
(CORPUS study of priesthood.)

1566   "They aren't first to get involved." July 20, 1978. p. 9.

1567   "Signs that Greeley does not exaggerate." July 27, 1978. p. 9.
(Anti-Catholicism.)

1568   "This election is grisly business." Aug. 3, 1978. p. 9.

1569   "The 'dynamic duo' needs careful watch." Aug. 10, 1978. p. 9.
(Peter Berger and Richard J. Neuhaus.)

1570   "Catholic intellectuals snubbed by Church." Aug. 17, 1978.
p. 9.

1571   "Why priests don't learn to preach." Aug. 24, 1978. p. 9.

1572   "'With it' theologians sound a bit flaky." Aug. 31, 1978. p. 9.

1573   "The anti-Catholicism comes unawares." Sept. 7, 1978. p. 9.
(Letters between Ben Bradlee and Andrew Greeley).

1574   "The Knights take the lead." Sept. 14, 1978. p. 9.

1575   "God, give thanks, is not a theologian." Sept. 21, 1978. p. 9.

1576   "If we don't work, how can the Spirit?" Sept. 28, 1978. p. 9.

1577   "A great beginning for Papa Gianpablo." Oct. 5, 1978. p. 9.

1578   "More insults to Catholics." Oct. 12, 1978. p. 9.

1579   "We have variety in religious styles." Oct. 19, 1978. p. 9.

1580   "The advice is poor." Oct. 26, 1978. p. 9.

1581   "The only reason for having religion." Nov. 2, 1978. p. 9.

1582   "The worst stupidity in a long time." Nov. 9, 1978. p. 9. (George Higgins's dismissal.)

1583   "The professionals get the axe." Nov. 16, 1978. p. 9.

1584   "Why do we abuse our best people." Nov. 23, 1978. p. 9. (Dan Lord and John Courtney Murray.)

1585   "The guerrilla war in Washington." Nov. 30, 1978. p. 9.

1586   "The guilt revolt among the bishops." Dec. 7, 1978. p. 9.

1587   "The conspiracy is informal but real." Dec. 14, 1978. p. 9.

1588   "Dear Holy Father: Don't let them get to you." Dec. 21, 1978. p. 9.

1589   "Another 'plan' without evidence." Dec. 28, 1978. p. 9.

1590   "Betrayal hurts." Jan. 4, 1979. p. 8.

1591   "A closer look at 'liberation'." Jan. 11, 1979. p. 9.

1592   "The last man to be anti-Polish." Jan. 18, 1979. p. 9.

1593   "Entering nasty times in American politics." Jan. 25, 1979. p. 9.

1594   "How to have a 'perfect' Church." Feb. 1, 1979. p. 9.

1595   "In defense of the first John Paul." Feb. 8, 1979. p. 9.

1596   "Still listening to traveling men." Feb. 15, 1979. p. 9.

1597   "Bungling amateurs in communications." Feb. 22, 1979. p. 9.

1598   "Even popes need good information." Mar. 1, 1979. p. 9.

1599   "Why the Irish don't feel well." Mar. 8, 1979. p. 9.

1600   "Acceptable groups and unacceptable." Mar. 15, 1979. p. 9.

1601   "Bill McCready is no 'assistant'." Mar. 22, 1979. p. 9.

1602   "Melancholy man looking at himself." Mar. 29, 1979. p. 9.

1603   "We are definitely in a new era." Apr. 5, 1979. p. 9.

1604   "A little bit of good news." Apr. 12, 1979. p. 9.

1605   "The tide turns against abortion." Apr. 19, 1979. p. 9.

1606   "The G-men get their man." Apr. 26, 1979. p. 9. (Renard Koehnemann.)

1607   "Needed: a better anthropology of sex." May 3, 1979. p. 9.

1608   "We need more, not less, talent." May 10, 1979. p. 9.

1609   "The pope's first serious blunder." May 17, 1979. p. 9.

1610   "The paper is dull and trivial." May 24, 1979. p. 9.

1611   "A Church NLRB should be set up." May 31, 1979. p. 9.

1612   "The drifters rush back home." June 7, 1979. p. 9.

1613   "Young writers should beware." June 14, 1979. p. 9.

1614 "A special style of sensitivity." June 21, 1979. p. 9. (Celibacy.)

1615 "Marriage Encounter is different." June 28, 1979. p. 9.

1616 "The trouble in the priesthood." July 5, 1979. p. 9.

1617 "Teaching Church vs. learning Church?" July 12, 1979. p. 9.

1618 "Not all bishops are Irish." July 19, 1979. p. 9.

1619 "A handy guide to Vaticanology." July 26, 1979. p. 9.

1620 "The most creative group of priests." Aug. 2, 1979. p. 9.

1621 "Catholic myths still persist." Aug. 9, 1979. p. 9.

1622 "The year's worst Catholic book." Aug. 16, 1979. p. 9. (*Gyn/Ecology* by Mary Daly. Beacon.)

1623 "A memo to the U. S. delegation to the Synod of Bishops." Aug. 23, 1979. p. 9.

1624 "Homework is needed on the family." Aug. 30, 1979. p. 9.

1625 "Jesus taught in 'table talk'." Sept. 6, 1979. p. 9.

1626 "To pull and push simultaneously is dumb." Sept. 13, 1979. p. 9.

1627 "Notre Dame should be No. 1." Sept. 20, 1979. p. 9.

1628 "Who cares about Chicago?" Sept. 27, 1979. p. 15.

1629 "There is a sickness in the Church." Oct. 4, 1979. p. 9.

1630 "Guidelines violate God's love affair." Oct. 11, 1979. p. 9.

1631 "We now have a Catholic novel." Oct. 18, 1979. p. 9. (*Land's End* by Kevin Starr. McGraw-Hill.)

1632   "Proud to be on enemies' list." Oct. 25, 1979. p. 9.

1633   "What is important in a pope?" Nov. 1, 1979. p. 9.

1634   "Ordinary people, extraordinary lives." Nov. 8, 1979. p. 9.
        (*Simple Gifts* by John Kotre. Andrews & McMeel.)

1635   "Scare stories are in fashion." Nov. 15, 1979. p. 9.

1636   "How the pope upset the liberals." Nov. 22, 1979. p. 9.

1637   "The Inquisition has no clothes." Nov. 29, 1979. p. 9.

1638   "Selective obedience becomes a habit." Dec. 6, 1979. p. 9.

1639   "Some Catholics are turncoats." Dec. 13, 1979. p. 9. (Gary
        Wills and Jim Castelli.)

1640   "Is this why the laity is so dissatisfied?" Dec. 20, 1979. p. 11.

1641   "Two sonnets on Christmas." Dec. 27, 1979. p. 9. (Poems.)

1642   "A prediction for the 1980s." Jan. 3, 1980, p. 9.

1643   "Is this pope a dangerous man?" Jan. 10, 1980. p. 9.

1644   "The God who fell has found a poet." Jan. 17, 1980. p. 9.

1645   "There is power in clerical envy." Jan. 24, 1980. p. 9.

1646   "The new inquisition hurts the dialogue." Jan. 31, 1980. p. 9.

1647   "The Catholic revival fondly remembered." Feb. 7, 1980. p. 9.

1648   "We are more than you think." Feb. 14, 1980. p. 9.

1649   "How the pope is misrepresented." Feb. 21, 1980. p. 9.

1650   "Hans Kung is a man of true faith." Feb. 28, 1980. p. 9.

1651   "How to get a kick in the teeth." Mar. 6, 1980. p. 9.

1652 "'Poor dears, they mean well'." Mar. 13, 1980. p. 9. (Reply Mar. 20, 1980.)

1653 Barker, Barnabas. "Trouble with Father Greeley's view." Mar. 20, 1980. p. 8. (Reply to Mar. 13, 1980.)

1654 "We need women deacons." Mar. 20, 1980. p. 9.

1655 "Intellectuals are no longer scarce." Mar. 27, 1980. p. 9.

1656 "Is anyone paying attention to the questions?" Apr. 3, 1980. p. 9.

1657 "On the odyssey of Michael Novak." Apr. 10, 1980. p. 9.

1658 "Three 'educations' that raise doubts." Apr. 17, 1980. p. 9.

1659 "The authority of the Church is collapsing." Apr. 24, 1980. p. 9.

1660 "The poet pope understands." May 1, 1980. p. 9.

1661 "How the family educates." May 8, 1980. p. 9.

1662 "Hans Kung is not an egotist." May 15, 1980. p. 9.

1663 "The Church is not an army." May 22, 1980. p. 9.

1664 "There's little new about the family." May 29, 1980. p. 9.

1665 "Catholic women are 'feminists'." June 5, 1980. p. 9.

1666 "Our freedom is indivisible." June 12, 1980. p. 9.

1667 "Some hope in the woman issue." June 19, 1980. p. 9.

1668 "A book for all who find Jesus irresistible." June 26, 1980. p. 9. (*Stories of Faith* by John Shea. Thomas More.)

1669 "A decision done in the wrong way." July 3, 1980. p. 9.

1670 "Catechetics is in a mess." July 10, 1980. p. 9.

1671   "Who 'deserves' the sacraments." July 17, 1980. p. 9.

1672   "A truth-teller is leaving us." July 24, 1980. p. 9. (Archbishop Jean Jadot.)

1673   "Why the Church avoids parties." July 31, 1980. p. 9.

1674   "The jury is out on the pope." Aug. 7, 1980. p. 9.

1675   "Where can you get a good statue of Mary?" Aug. 14, 1980. p. 9.

1676   "We listen and link." Aug. 21, 1980. p. 9.

1677   "Is she not a gift . . . a sign of the giver?" Aug. 28, 1980. p. 9.

1678   "Talented people come from God." Sept. 4, 1980. p. 9.

1679   "The pope teaches sexual equality." Sept. 11, 1980. p. 9.

1680   "Loyalty to the pope is not enough." Sept. 18, 1980. p. 9.

1681   "The pope, yes; the synod, no." Sept. 25, 1980. p. 9.

1682   "Naturally, priests fall in love." Oct. 2, 1980. p. 9.

1683   "How to improve a short homily." Oct. 9, 1980. p. 9.

1684   "A feeling of pride in being American." Oct. 16, 1980. p. 9.

1685   "Does the Church ever change?" Oct. 23, 1980. p. 9.

1686   "Authority needs new style." Oct. 30, 1980. p. 9.

1687   "One man knows how to dialogue." Nov. 6, 1980. p. 9. (*Does God Exist?* by Hans Kung. Doubleday.)

1688   "The Holy Spirit was sent packing by the synod." Nov. 13, 1980. p. 9.

1689   "Something good at the synod went unnoticed." Nov. 20, 1980. p. 9.

1690   "An image problem affects Catholics." Nov. 27, 1980. p. 9.

1691   "There is evidence of anti-Catholicism." Dec. 4, 1980. p. 9.

1692   "Women have a friend in Jesus." Dec. 11, 1980. p. 9.

1693   "Who are the real lovers?" Dec. 18, 1980. p. 9.

1694   "Irish blessings for greetings." Dec. 25, 1980. p. 9.

1695   "Catholic schools do what others don't." Jan. 1, 1981. p. 7.

1696   "Is anything more important than the Bible?" Jan. 8, 1981. p. 9.

1697   "How are we doing as a sacrament?" Jan. 15, 1981. p. 9.

1698   "Be good, but be competent, also." Jan 22, 1981. p. 9.

1699   "Erotic love has its place in the Bible." Jan 29, 1981. p. 9.

1700   "Before dialogue can occur . . . " Feb. 5, 1981. p. 9.

1701   "Graham Green's [sic] Catholic vision." Feb. 12, 1981. p. 9.

1702   "Be careful of a poke in the nose." Feb. 19, 1981. p. 9.

1703   "Anti-Catholicism continues to live." Feb. 26, 1981. p. 9.

1704   "If it weren't for sexual attraction." Mar. 5, 1981. p. 9. (*Marital Intimacy* by Joan Anzia and Mary Durkin. Andrews & McMeel.)

1705   "Catholic novels are coming back." Mar. 12, 1981. p. 9.

1706   "Watch out for secret societies." Mar. 19, 1981. p. 9.

1707   "New law code will be ignored." Mar. 26, 1981. p. 9.

1708   "If Ms. Lucy had attended the synod." Apr. 2. 1981. p. 9.

1709   "Let's not deny the Incarnation." Apr. 9, 1981. p. 9.

1710   "Telling stories can be perilous." Apr. 16, 1981. p. 9.

1711   "Schools work; CCD doesn't." Apr. 23, 1981. p. 9.

1712   "Why the hatred of Catholic schools?" Apr. 30, 1981. p. 9.

1713   "New imperialists from Maryknoll?" May 7, 1981. p. 9.

1714   "Greeley feels got; he gets getter." May 14, 1981. p. 9. (Reply
        to Philip Nobile's review of *The Cardinal Sins*.)

1715   "Perfect leadership is not scriptural." May 21, 1981. p. 9.

1716   "Grandparents are something special." May 28, 1981. p. 9.

1717   "When listening was not on the agenda." June 4, 1981. p. 9.

1718   "They would jump for joy if they had these results." June 18,
        1981. p. 9.

1719   "Tradition without the track record." June 25, 1981. p. 9.

1720   "American Catholics are troubled but not simple." July 2, 1981.
        p. 9.

1721   "Not a matter of lack of experience." July 9, 1981. p. 9.

1722   "On being stung from all sides." July 16, 1981. p. 9.

1723   "Hyper papal style isn't traditional." July 23, 1981. p. 9.

1724   "How to improve the preaching." July 30, 1981. p. 9.

1725   "Taking aim at liberation theology." Aug. 6, 1981. p. 9.

1726   "Catholic scholars won't be helped by new rule." Aug. 13, 1981.
        p. 9.

1727 "Greeley reviews his reviewers reviewing him." Aug. 20, 1981. p. 9.

1728 "Delighted not to be a folk hero." Aug. 27, 1981. p. 9.

1729 "Fraternity among priests?" Sept. 3, 1981. p. 9.

1730 "Tempted to believe that status is enough." Sept. 10, 1981. p. 9.

1731 "When a priest becomes pastor." Sept. 17, 1981. p. 9.

1732 "Amateurism tolerates poor performance." Sept. 24, 1981. p. 9.

1733 "Self-esteem: missing ingredient among priests." Oct. 1, 1981. p. 9.

1734 "How not to revive religious life." Oct. 8, 1981. p. 9.

1735 "Explaining why Catholic is better." Oct. 15, 1981. p. 9.

1736 "Make room for teenagers." Oct. 22, 1981. p. 9.

1737 "Investigation needed, but not this one." Oct. 29, 1981. p. 11. . (Of seminaries.)

1738 "An iceberg is bearing down." Nov. 5, 1981. p. 9.

1739 "We don't follow our own teaching." Nov. 12, 1981. p. 9.

1740 "Marxism doesn't end poverty." Nov. 19, 1981. p. 9.

1741 "Jesus had to be divine--look at his treatment of women." Nov. 26, 1981. p. 9.

1742 "Tearing down a piece of our history." Dec. 3, 1981. p. 9. (Holy Family Church, Chicago.)

1743 "Hans Kung is popular in Chicago." Dec. 10, 1981. p. 9.

1744 "The author's mixed mailbag." Dec. 17, 1981. p. 9.

1745   "Liturgy is meant to touch our experience." Dec. 24, 1981. p. 11.

1746   "Love works as main motivation against sin." Jan. 7, 1982. p. 9.

1747   "'Cold sexuality' puzzles him." Jan. 14, 1982. p. 9.

1748   "Some work is not worthwhile." Jan. 21, 1982. p. 9.

1749   "An open letter to the next bishop." Jan. 28, 1982. p. 9.

1750   "'Irreplaceable' laity were replaceable." Feb. 4, 1982. p. 9.

1751   "Something to learn from the laity." Feb. 11, 1982. p. 9.

1752   "What is 'the consent of the faithful'?" Feb. 18, 1982. p. 9.

1753   "20 questions for men who would be bishop." Feb. 25, 1982. p. 9.

1754   "The facts are unpleasant." Mar. 4, 1982. p. 9.

1755   "Greeley's law confirmed again." Mar. 11, 1982. p. 9.

1756   "Don't worry about 'disturbing' the laity." Mar. 18, 1982. p. 9.

1757   "But pride is the chief sin." Mar. 25, 1982. p. 9.

1758   "Can humor mix with religion?" Apr. 1, 1982. p. 9.

1759   "What schools can, can't do." Apr. 8, 1982. p. 9. (Reply Apr. 22, 1982.)

1760   "Greeley's parody of his reviewers." Apr. 15, 1982. p. 9.

1761   Seifert, Edward. "Fr. Greeley is reaching 'new heights of absurdity'." Apr. 22, 1982. p. 8. (Reply to Apr. 8, 1982.)

1762   "Where the Church was wrong." Apr. 22, 1982. p. 9. (Reply May 13, 1982.)

1763 "Write no patronizing columns about me." Apr. 29, 1982. p. 9. (Replies May 6, 1982.)

1764 Fiedler, R. A., II. "He wants to add a hearty Amen." May 6, 1982. p. 8. (Reply to Apr. 29, 1982.)

1765 Fugate, Elizabeth. "Reader feels cheated over Greeley defensiveness." May 6, 1982. p. 8. (Reply to Apr. 29, 1982.)

1766 "It sounds like feelings were hurt." May 6, 1982. p. 8. (Anonymous reply to Apr. 29, 1982.)

1767 "This 'teaching' raises questions." May 6, 1982. p. 9. (Reply May 27, 1982.)

1768 Colonnese, Louis. "Father Greeley's view is the wrong one." May 13, 1982. p. 8. (Reply to Apr. 22, 1982.)

1769 Hagner, Rita. "Father Greeley for truth-seekers." May 13, 1982. p. 8. (Letter.)

1770 "Choose between violence and peace." May 13, 1982. p. 9.

1771 "They'll want Cody back." May 20, 1982. p. 9.

1772 Van Winkle, Charles. "Reader looking for logic." May 27, 1982. p. 8. (Reply to May 6, 1982.)

1773 "Sexual neuterism is not a virtue." May 27, 1982. p. 9.

1774 "Another change in Catholic thinking." June 3, 1982. p. 9.

1775 "Serious study: no easy answer." June 10, 1982. p. 9. (Immigration.)

1776 "Let's get back to competence." June 17, 1982. p. 9.

1777 "Try prudence before acting." June 24, 1982. p. 9.

1778 "A bishop-critic is not necessarily an unbeliever." July 1, 1982. p. 9.

1779   "A new cathedral in a modern city?" July 8, 1982. p. 9.

1780   "The pope isn't selling well." July 15, 1982. p. 9.

1781   "Those mysterious men in black." July 22, 1982. p. 9.

1782   "Admirable work by the bishops." July 29, 1982. p. 9.

1783   "Bishops are for non-Catholics." Aug. 5, 1982. p. 9.

1784   "God as woman has been around for a long time." Aug. 12, 1982. p. 9.

1785   "Open letter to a priest." Aug. 19, 1982. p. 9.

1786   "Can some people really be sexless?" Aug. 26, 1982. p. 9.

1787   "This tradition ought to be rediscovered." Sept. 2, 1982. p. 9.

1788   "A little advice for the archbishop." Sept. 9, 1982. p. 9.

1789   "The culture is a-changing." Sept. 16, 1982. p. 9.

1790   "They should have stayed home." Sept. 23, 1982. p. 9.

1791   "Bishops are human too." Sept. 30, 1982. p. 9.

1792   "Is the Church a democracy?" Oct. 7, 1982. p. 9.

1793   "Time for another look at ourselves." Oct. 14, 1982. p. 9.

1794   "Research shows how we are." Oct. 21, 1982. p. 9.

1795   "How to do cheap research." Oct. 28, 1982. p. 15.

1796   "If politicians can do it, why not priests?" Nov. 4, 1982. p. 9.

1797   (Not titled. Column about Church history.) Nov. 11, 1982. p. 9.

1798   "'Supercardinal' is painfully bad." Nov. 18, 1982. p. 9.

1799   "Questions about that letter on nuclear arms." Nov. 25, 1982.
        p. 9.

1800   "A question for theologians." Dec. 2, 1982. p. 9.

1801   "When columnists miss the mark." Dec. 9, 1982. p. 9.

1802   "Stir conscience, don't 'bind' it." Dec. 16, 1982. p. 9.

1803   "A certain oddity in that letter by the bishops." Dec. 23, 1982.
        p. 9.

1804   "Story-telling beats column writing: Father Greeley's final
        column." Jan. 6, 1983. p. 9. (Replies Jan. 13 and 20, 1983.)

1805   Ruiz, Armando. "Greeley column will be missed." Jan. 13,
        1983. p. 8. (Reply to Jan. 6, 1983.)

1806   Handley, R. W. "Thanks for the reading." Jan. 20, 1983. p.
        8. (Reply to Jan. 6, 1983.)

CHAPTER FIVE

NEWSPAPER COLUMNS: SECULAR

Andrew Greeley wrote a syndicated column, at first twice and then three times a week, from July 1974 until January 1983. It appeared in many newspapers across the United States which published it at various times and frequencies. Syndication records are no longer available. The following columns, from July 16, 1974 to August 10, 1978, were seen in the *Chicago Tribune* recorded on microfilm by University Microfilms, Inc., Ann Arbor, MI.

1807   "Is America over the hill?" July 16, 1974. p. 10.

1808   "End economic imperialism!" July 18, 1974. p. 18.

1809   "Virtuous man? God spare us." July 23, 1974. p. 10.

1810   "Luring youth into church." July 25, 1974. p. 14.

1811   "Those middle Americans." July 30, 1974. p. 10.

1812   "Expecting 'stands' by Church." Aug. 1, 1974. p. 16.

1813   "Call your precinct captain." Aug. 6, 1974. p. 14.

1814   "Richard Nixon's worst fault." Aug. 8, 1974. p. 18.

1815   "Deciding who 'got' Nixon." Aug. 15, 1974. p. 22.

1816   "A dispensable motivation." Aug. 20, 1974. p. 12. (Guilt.)

1817   "Watergate not a cosmic event." Aug. 22, 1974. p. 18.

1818   "Kerner is a political prisoner." Aug. 27, 1974. p. 10. (Otto Kerner.)

1819   "Is Ford future that bright?" Aug. 29, 1974. p. 14. (Gerald Ford.)

1820   "Summer can't be over yet." Sept. 3, 1974. p. 12.

1821   "It's easier to go on fighting." Sept. 5, 1974. p. 16.

1822   "Patty Hearst's real crime." Sept. 10, 1974. p. 10.

1823   "Amnesty a political bargain." Sept. 12, 1974. p. 22.

1824   "The fix is in--and engraved on a stonewall." Sept. 17, 1974. Sec. 2 p. 4.

1825   "The FBI checks new suspect--me." Sept. 19, 1974. Sec. 2 p. 6.

1826   "Reform's okay but clout's what it takes." Sept. 24, 1974. Sec. 2 p. 3.

1827   "Church and state on head of a pin." Sept. 26, 1974. Sec. 2 p. 6.

1828   "Save Chicago Bears the American way." Oct. 1, 1974. Sec. 2 p. 4.

1829   "Ford's plan--much ado about nothing. Oct. 3, 1974. Sec. 2 p. 6.

1830   "Upon this Moon, build a church?" Oct. 8, 1974. Sec. 2 p. 5. (Sun Myung Moon.)

1831   "Charisma a candidate's magic?" Oct. 10, 1974. Sec. 2 p. 4. (Senator Edward Kennedy.)

1832   "Sorry, Chris, but no ethnic revival." Oct. 15, 1974. Sec. 2 p. 4.

1833   "'Nixanalysis'--an obscene scene." Oct. 17, 1974. Sec. 2 p. 5.

1834   "Sex and more sex, but family still here." Oct. 22, 1974. Sec. 2 p. 4.

1835   "Lots of luck to you bullet biters." Oct. 24, 1974. Sec. 2 p. 6.

1836   "'Chic Think' cool, but only for a fool." Oct. 29, 1974. Sec. 2 p. 5.

1837   "Poor devils, you, no haunted houses." Oct. 31, 1974. Sec. 2 p. 6.

1838   "Cries of atrocity, but still war." Nov. 5, 1974. Sec. 2 p. 5.

1839   "A question: who watches the FBI?" Nov. 7, 1974. Sec. 2 p. 5.

1840   "Of course, that's it--blame Catholics." Nov. 12, 1974. Sec. 2 p. 4.

1841   "Stop stinging the WASPS." Nov. 14, 1974. Sec. 2 p. 4.

1842   "Our basic need for original sin." Nov. 19, 1974. Sec. 2 p. 4.

1843   "The issue is busing, not racism." Nov. 21, 1974. Sec. 2 p. 4.

1844   "One man's busing solution." Nov. 26, 1974. Sec. 2 p. 4.

1845   "Lord's laughing rejoinder." Nov. 28, 1974. Sec. 2 p. 4.

1846   "The biggest weapon: food." Dec. 3, 1974. Sec. 2 p. 4.

1847   "A prayer to St. Nicholas." Dec.5, 1974. Sec. 2 p. 4.

1848   "U. S. tops--that's the trouble." Dec. 10, 1974. Sec. 2 p. 4.

1849   "Butz needs to learn charity." Dec. 12, 1974. Sec. 2 p. 4. (Secretary of Agriculture Earl Butz.)

1850   "A merry Saturnalia to all!" Dec. 17, 1974. Sec. 2 p. 3.

1851   "A new cross for Catholics." Dec. 19, 1974. Sec. 2 p. 4.

1852   "A prayer for Christmas Day." Dec. 24, 1974. p. 9.

1853   "Levi: dignity as victim." Dec. 26, 1974. Sec. 2 p. 4. (Edward Levi.)

1854 "Beware! Moral infants on loose." Dec. 31, 1974. p. 12.

1855 "Dems find disaster formula." Jan. 2, 1975. Sec. 2 p. 4.

1856 "Socialism at the gas pump?" Jan. 7, 1975. Sec. 2 p. 3.

1857 "A symbolic rebirth of death." Jan. 9, 1975. Sec. 2 p. 4.

1858 "Arabs bail out our failures?" Jan. 14, 1975. Sec. 2 p. 3.

1859 "America speaks: 'Tax us!'" Jan. 16, 1975. Sec. 2 p. 4.

1860 "Telling them off for 'Boss'." Jan. 21, 1975. Sec. 2 p. 4.

1861 "A view of the Irish colony." Jan. 23, 1975. Sec. 2 p. 4.

1862 "Just join in at the chorus." Jan. 28, 1975. Sec. 2 p. 4.

1863 "Neighbor, police thyself." Jan. 30, 1975. Sec. 2 p. 4.

1864 "The search for common good." Feb. 4, 1975. Sec. 2 p. 4.

1865 "Real anti-Semitism is envy." Feb. 6, 1975. Sec. 2 p. 4.

1866 "Hot cross buns, anyone?" Feb. 11, 1975. Sec. 2 p. 4.

1867 "Martyrdom on love's day." Feb. 13, 1975. Sec. 2 p. 3.

1868 "An essay: hail to the chief." Feb. 18, 1975. Sec. 2 p. 4.

1869 "Godfather, give us a break." Feb. 20, 1975. Sec. 2 p. 4.

1870 "Bury my blood in Gresham." Feb. 25, 1975. Sec. 2 p. 4.

1871 "Requiem for a lost generation." Feb. 27, 1975. Sec. 2 p. 4.

1872 "New season for churchmen." Mar. 4, 1975. Sec. 2 p. 4.

1873 "Politics of the great debate." Mar. 6, 1975. Sec. 2 p. 4.

1874 "The Royko syndrome at work." Mar. 11, 1975. Sec. 2 p. 4.

1875   "Patronizing patron Patrick." Mar. 13, 1975. Sec. 2 p. 4.

1876   "America, you're no soft touch." Mar. 18, 1975. Sec. 2 p. 4.

1877   "The drive is on to get the Irish." Mar. 20, 1975. Sec. 2 p. 4.

1878   "The crime of pushing a mop." Mar. 25, 1975. Sec. 2 p. 3.

1879   "Men need liberation, too." Mar. 27, 1975. Sec. 2 p. 3.

1880   "Clothes don't make a religion." Apr. 1, 1975. Sec. 2 p. 3.

1881   "Debacle in the Third World." Apr. 3, 1975. Sec. 2 p. 4.

1882   "A fetus is a baby--call it that." Apr. 8, 1975. Sec. 2 p. 3.

1883   "Selective morality is bunk." Apr. 10, 1975. Sec. 2 p. 3.

1884   "The moral issue of Viet Nam." Apr. 15, 1975. Sec. 2 p. 4.

1885   "The porch of '46 still a special spot." Apr. 17, 1975. Sec. 2 p. 4.

1886   "Recognizing Selma's progress." Apr. 22, 1975. Sec. 2 p. 4.

1887   "Now the Catholics are conspiring." Apr. 24, 1975. Sec. 2 p. 4.

1888   "Are we really worth saving?" Apr. 29, 1975. Sec. 2 p. 4.

1889   "A command to get rid of pesky people." May 1, 1975. Sec. 2 p. 3.

1890   "Anarchy can't be all bad." May 6, 1975. Sec. 2 p. 4.

1891   "Viet Nam was a big victory." May 13, 1975. Sec. 2 p. 3.

1892   "Hypocrisy camps with refugees." May 15, 1975. Sec. 2 p. 4.

1893   "Making the worst of a good situation." May 20, 1975. Sec. 2 p. 4.

1894 "'Da mare' and 'the mayua'." May 22, 1975. Sec. 2 p. 4.

1895 "How bores give faith a bad name." May 27, 1975. Sec. 2 p. 4.

1896 "Hollywood likes its spaghetti underdone." May 29, 1975. Sec. 2 p. 3.

1897 "A tea drinker's unquenched thirst." June 3, 1975. Sec. 2 p. 4.

1898 "Halt a burocrat, kill a colossus." June 10, 1975. Sec. 2 p. 4.

1899 "Let's market U. S. citizenship." June 12, 1975. Sec. 2 p. 4.

1900 "Where are the storytellers?" June 17, 1975. Sec. 2 p. 4.

1901 "Mr. Moynihan, you're right on." June 19, 1975. Sec. 2 p. 4.

1902 "The enigma of the Irish isle." June 24, 1975. Sec. 2 p. 4.

1903 "The Irish style has slipped away." June 26, 1975. Sec. 2 p. 4.

1904 "A cardinal's commandment." July 1, 1975. Sec. 2 p. 4.

1905 "World waits on the Pope." July 3, 1975. Sec. 2 p. 3.

1906 "The bottom-line Christians." July 8, 1975. Sec. 2 p. 4.

1907 "An American in Poland." July 10, 1975. Sec. 2 p. 4.

1908 "Piecing together puzzle of Poland." July 15, 1975. Sec. 2 p. 3.

1909 "Dear Mr. Airline President:" July 17, 1975. Sec. 2 p. 4.

1910 "Comparisons that fall short." July 22, 1975. Sec. 2 p. 3.

1911 "Breakdown on busing road." July 24, 1975. Sec. 2 p. 4.

1912 "Just who are we to believe?" July 29, 1975. Sec. 2 p. 3.

1913   "'Nashville' is ripe for reform." July 31, 1975. Sec. 2 p. 4.

1914   "How to fill world's food gap." Aug. 5, 1975. Sec. 2 p. 4.

1915   "Why can't summer last?" Aug. 7, 1975. Sec. 2 p. 4.

1916   "Erasing poverty for $8 a year." Aug. 12, 1975. Sec. 2 p. 3.

1917   "If Hubert were President. . . . " Aug. 14, 1975. Sec. 2 p. 4.

1918   "A kid's revolt against love?" Aug. 19, 1975. Sec. 2 p. 3.

1919   "They just love to hate America." Aug. 21, 1975. Sec. 2 p. 4.

1920   "God save the metropolis." Aug. 26, 1975. Sec. 2 p. 3.

1921   "What we need is men's lib." Aug. 28, 1975. Sec. 2 p. 3.

1922   "All the world's a padre's pulpit." Sept. 2, 1975. Sec. 2 p. 4.

1923   "Why do they hate America?" Sept. 4, 1975. Sec. 2 p. 3.

1924   "A question nobody can answer." Sept. 9, 1975. Sec. 2 p. 4.

1925   "The bigot in the trash heap." Sept. 11, 1975. Sec. 2 p. 4.

1926   "Beware the energy puritans." Sept. 16, 1975. Sec. 2 p. 4.

1927   "The bourgeoisie's big secret." Sept. 18, 1975. Sec. 2 p. 3.

1928   "Do mystics psych out science?" Sept. 23, 1975. Sec. 2 p. 4.

1929   "A look at what we've lost." Sept. 25, 1975. Sec. 2 p. 4.

1930   "Ideological chic has had its day." Sept. 30, 1975. Sec. 2 p. 4.

1931   "A forum for hate-U.S. naivete." Oct. 2, 1975. Sec. 3 p. 4.

1932   "The Cleaver cure for kooks." Oct. 7, 1975. Sec. 2 p. 4.

1933   "The cartel drills into the poor." Oct. 14, 1975. Sec. 2 p. 4.

1934   "Emperor still has no clothes." Oct. 16, 1975. Sec. 3 p. 4.

1935   "U. S. gets second billing on victory." Oct. 21, 1975. Sec. 2
        p. 4.

1936   "Patty loser in FBI-SLA war." Oct. 23, 1975. Sec. 2 p. 4.

1937   "Why God is not always available." Oct. 28, 1975. Sec. 2 p. 4.

1938   "It's the year of the professor." Oct. 30, 1975. Sec. 2 p. 3.

1939   "A junket in the name of the Lord." Nov. 4, 1975. Sec. 2 p. 4.

1940   "The American dream is true." Nov. 6, 1975. Sec. 2 p. 4.

1941   "A cup full of nothing for poor." Nov. 11, 1975. Sec. 2 p. 4.

1942   "Give us freedom and decency." Nov. 13, 1975. Sec. 2 p. 4.

1943   "Rape book a feminist Ms.-take." Nov. 18, 1975. Sec. 2 p. 4.

1944   "Ford plays politics of default." Nov. 20, 1975. Sec. 2 p. 4.

1945   "How to be guilty but innocent." Nov. 25, 1975. Sec. 2 p. 4.

1946   "A chance to redeem the past." Nov. 27, 1975. Sec. 2 p. 4.

1947   "Challenge to the culture thief." Dec. 2, 1975. Sec. 2 p. 3.

1948   "The integration everyone ignores." Dec. 4, 1975. Sec. 2 p. 4.

1949   "Who said Naziism is dead?" Dec. 9, 1975. Sec. 2 p. 3.

1950   "Does the ax man cometh?" Dec. 11, 1975. Sec. 2 p. 4.

1951   "But who will fight the Goths?" Dec. 16, 1975. Sec. 2 p. 4.

1952   "Is world just a giant bribe?" Dec. 18, 1975. Sec. 2 p. 4.

1953   "The United States of Great Britain?" Dec. 23, 1975. p. 18.

1954   "God better have a sense of humor." Dec. 25, 1975. Sec. 3 p. 4.

1955   "Too late for our redemption?" Dec. 30, 1975. p. 8.

1956   "Moynihan's the critics' choice." Jan. 1, 1976. Sec. 3 p. 4.

1957   "'Throw the dirty tricksters out'." Jan. 6, 1976. Sec. 2 p. 4.

1958   "If New York would lose a war." Jan. 8, 1976. Sec. 2 p. 4.

1959   "Stone throwers aim at Camelot." Jan. 13, 1976. Sec. 2 p. 4.

1960   "Poles' pride permeates TV fog." Jan. 15, 1976. Sec. 2 p. 4.

1961   "Political homilies from the pious." Jan. 20, 1976. Sec. 2 p. 4.

1962   "Liberals' creature may take the lead." Jan. 22, 1976. Sec. 2 p. 4.

1963   "A lesson of history is forgotten." Jan. 27, 1976. Sec. 2 p. 4.

1964   "Plea for reforming political reformers." Jan. 29, 1976. Sec. 2 p. 4.

1965   "American tourists get tough." Feb. 3, 1976. Sec. 2 p. 4.

1966   "Freedom scores a breakthrough." Feb. 5, 1976. Sec. 2 p. 3.

1967   " . . . to punish those who form majority." Feb. 10, 1976. Sec. 2 p. 3.

1968   "Making the system work." Feb. 12, 1976. Sec. 2 p. 4.

1969   "Women's right to rat race." Feb. 17, 1976. Sec. 2 p. 3.

1970   "Blind justice is exactly that." Feb. 19, 1976. Sec. 2 p. 4.

1971   "A united Ireland the only solution." Feb. 24, 1976. Sec. 2 p. 4.

1972   "Unearned hate a common bond." Feb. 26, 1976. Sec. 2 p. 4.

1973   "Cost of freedom is worth it." Mar. 2, 1976. Sec. 2 p. 3.

1974   "Kingly conduct ill fits the role." Mar. 4, 1976. Sec. 2 p. 4.

1975   "In defense of Polish pride." Mar. 9, 1976. Sec. 2 p. 4.

1976   "World famine: a feast of lies." Mar. 11, 1976. Sec. 2 p. 4.

1977   "In search of new morality." Mar. 16, 1976. Sec. 2 p. 3.

1978   "Hope makes Irish eyes smile." Mar. 18, 1976. Sec. 2 p. 3.

1979   "What the country needs now is a big yawn." Mar. 23, 1976. Sec. 2 p. 3.

1980   "Italy ought to know better." Mar. 25, 1976. Sec. 2 p. 4.

1981   "'Chicago 7' fooled no one but the media." Mar. 30, 1976. Sec. 2 p. 4.

1982   "Patty 'convicted' before trial began." Apr. 1, 1976. Sec. 2 p. 4.

1983   "Don't judge Carter on religion." Apr. 6, 1976. Sec. 2 p. 4.

1984   "Image not enough for Walker." Apr. 8, 1976. Sec. 2 p. 4.

1985   "Bishops stonewall on birth-control findings." Apr. 13, 1976. Sec. 2 p. 4.

1986   "Less can be so much more." Apr. 15, 1976. Sec. 2 p. 3.

1987   "Putting cities together again." Apr. 20, 1976. Sec. 2 p. 4.

1988   "Films censor life's meaning." Apr. 22, 1976. Sec. 2 p. 3.

1989   "Media message falls on deaf ears." Apr. 27, 1976. Sec. 2 p. 4.

1990   "If only they could win . . . " Apr. 29, 1976. Sec. 2 p. 3.

1991   "'Older' is not always 'wiser'." May 4, 1976. Sec. 2 p. 4.

1992   "Plot can't crumble Cookie Monster." May 6, 1976. Sec. 2 p. 4.

1993   "Ireland is 'A Terrible Beauty'." May 11, 1976. Sec. 2 p. 3.

1994   "It's time to integrate the suburbs." May 13, 1976. Sec. 2 p. 3.

1995   "Self-help is black battle cry." May 18, 1976. Sec. 2 p. 4.

1996   "Military academies flunk out." May 20, 1976. Sec. 2 p. 4.

1997   "The vendetta against Moynihan." May 25, 1976. Sec. 2 p. 4.

1998   "Watergate, Chicago-style." May 27, 1976. Sec. 2 p. 4.

1999   "No, I won't leave the priesthood." June 1, 1976. Sec. 2 p. 3.

2000   "Giving research a dirty name." June 3, 1976. Sec. 2 p. 3.

2001   "Catholic or not, he's still a Jesuit." June 8, 1976. Sec. 2 p. 4.

2002   "Liberals' labels don't fit the facts." June 10, 1976. Sec. 2 p. 4.

2003   "'Right' is wrong for Midwest." June 15, 1976. Sec. 2 p. 4.

2004   "They've taken a vow of silence." June 17, 1976. Sec. 2 p. 4.

2005   "Inquisitors take on psychics." June 29, 1976. Sec. 2 p. 4.

2006   "If films are right, we're nuts." July 1, 1976. Sec. 2 p. 4.

2007   "Farewell to a man of vision." July 6, 1976. Sec. 2 p. 4.

2008   "Even 'liberals' fear freedom." July 8, 1976. Sec. 2 p. 4.

2009   "U. S. press is eager to hurt Italy." July 13, 1976. Sec. 2 p. 3.

2010   "Signs of the times unheeded. July 15, 1976. Sec. 2 p. 4.

2011   "Quotes hinder more than help." July 20, 1976. Sec. 2 p. 4.

2012   "Judges should not be legislators." July 22, 1976. Sec. 2 p. 4.

2013   "Problems without solutions." July 27, 1976. Sec. 2 p. 4.

2014   "Don't divorce religion, ethics." July 29, 1976. Sec. 2 p. 4.

2015   "Jimmy asked for trouble." Aug. 5, 1976. Sec. 2 p. 4.

2016   "Benefits of being a victim." Aug. 10, 1976. Sec. 2 p. 3.

2017   "Olympics a vicious con game." Aug. 12, 1976. Sec. 2 p. 4.

2018   "'I'm tired of being a Democrat'." Aug. 17, 1976. Sec. 2 p. 4.

2019   "Why there are fewer Chinese." Aug. 19, 1976. Sec. 2 p. 4.

2020   "Try these solutions, Jimmy." Aug. 24, 1976. Sec. 2 p. 3.

2021   "'Ethnics' is code word for Catholics." Aug. 26, 1976. Sec. 2
        p. 3.

2022   "Food doesn't just grow on trees." Aug. 31, 1976. Sec. 2 p. 3. `

2023   "'Permissiveness' got an early start." Sept. 2, 1976. Sec. 2
        p. 4.

2024   "New politics: a plains sweep." Sept. 7, 1976. Sec. 2 p. 4.

2025   "Europe's forgotten people." Sept. 9, 1976. Sec. 2 p. 4.

2026   "Seamus McGinity finds a key issue." Sept. 14, 1976. Sec. 2
        p. 4.

2027   "Jimmy can win Catholics." Sept. 16, 1976. Sec. 2 p. 4.

2028   "The real miracle isn't life on Mars." Sept. 21, 1976. Sec. 3
        p. 3.

2029   "Gospel according to St. Marx." Sept. 23, 1976. Sec. 3 p. 4.

2030   "Unseal the cork on Ireland's agony." Sept. 28, 1976. Sec. 3 p. 3.

2031   "The Irish have much to learn about us." Sept. 30, 1976. Sec. 3 p. 4.

2032   "How could a 'Yank' be Irish?" Oct. 5, 1976. Sec. 3 p. 4.

2033   "The conversation at gate 14." Oct. 7, 1976. Sec. 3 p. 3.

2034   "Why the Left hates Moynihan." Oct. 12, 1976. Sec. 3 p. 3.

2035   "Carter is humble and devout." Oct. 14, 1976. Sec. 3 p. 4.

2036   "If bigots are bounced, who's left?" Oct. 19, 1976. Sec. 3 p. 4.

2037   "Nations the hypocrites forget." Oct. 26, 1976. Sec. 3 p. 3.

2038   "Carter may end Civil War." Oct. 28, 1976. Sec. 3 p. 4.

2039   "Phone addicts a pain in the ear." Nov. 2, 1976. Sec. 3 p. 4.

2040   "Catholic sermons are a shame." Nov. 4, 1976. Sec. 3 p. 4.

2041   "The reign that fell on Plains." Nov. 9, 1976. Sec. 3 p. 4.

2042   "Wanted: new ideas for liberals." Nov. 11, 1976. Sec. 3 p. 4.

2043   "How did Greeks do so well?" Nov. 16, 1976. Sec. 3 p. 4.

2044   "Chicago machine still rolling." Nov. 18, 1976. Sec. 3 p. 4.

2045   "The power of a straight ticket." Nov. 23, 1976. Sec. 3 p. 3.

2046   "Patty will have place in history." Nov. 25, 1976. Sec. 3 p. 4.

2047   "Who can vote for immorality?" Nov. 30, 1976. Sec. 3 p. 4.

2048   "We're not wealthy at their expense." Dec. 2, 1976. Sec. 3 p. 4.

2049   "Stop blaming the farmers for world's hunger." Dec. 7, 1976. Sec. 3 p. 3.

2050   "Churches should meet on abortion." Dec. 9, 1976. Sec. 3 p. 4.

2051   "Speaking for most Catholics. . . . " Dec. 14, 1976. Sec. 3 p. 3.

2052   "Jimmy isn't a King James." Dec. 16, 1976. Sec. 3 p. 4.

2053   "Institutions for the aged. . . . " Dec. 21, 1976. Sec. 3 p. 4.

2054   "Daley: the first of a new breed." Dec. 23, 1976. p. 11.

2055   "Poland is ready to explode." Dec. 28, 1976. Sec. 3 p. 3.

2056   "Daley haters couldn't keep quiet." Dec. 30, 1976. Sec. 3 p. 4.

2057   "A memory of cruel injustice." Jan. 4, 1977. Sec. 3 p. 4.

2058   "The forgotten minorities." Jan. 6, 1977. Sec. 3 p. 4.

2059   "Report written in doublethink." Jan. 11, 1977. Sec. 3 p. 3.

2060   "The customer be damned." Jan. 13, 1977. Sec. 3 p. 3.

2061   "Taxing the poor to aid the rich." Jan. 18, 1977. Sec. 3 p. 3.

2062   "If things are a mess, blame U. S." Jan. 25, 1977. Sec. 3 p. 3.

2063   "Soak the poor, save the rich." Jan. 27, 1977. Sec. 3 p. 4.

2064   "Waiting for the Pope to die." Feb. 1, 1977. Sec. 2 p. 3.

2065   "There is fear in the Vatican." Feb. 3, 1977. Sec. 3 p. 4.

2066   "Our immigrants catch up fast." Feb. 8, 1977. Sec. 3 p. 4.

2067   "The chilly truth about gas crisis." Feb. 10, 1977. Sec. 3 p. 3.

2068   "A baby boom on the kibbutz." Feb. 15, 1977. Sec. 2 p. 3.

2069   "When blacks oppress blacks." Feb. 17, 1977. Sec. 3 p. 4.

2070   "Catholics cling to tradition." Feb. 22, 1977. Sec. 3 p. 3.

2071   "'Universal service' means jail." Mar. 1, 1977. Sec. 3 p. 3.

2072   "Suffer the little children. . . ." Mar. 3, 1977. Sec. 3 p. 4.

2073   "Why can't women be priests?" Mar. 8, 1977. Sec. 3 p. 3.

2074   "We all have a right to roots." Mar. 10, 1977. Sec. 3 p. 4.

2075   "Third World murders are holy." Mar. 15, 1977. Sec. 3 p. 3.

2076   "Youthful ambition still blind." Mar. 17, 1977. Sec. 3 p. 4.

2077   "Equality for whites?" Mar. 22, 1977. Sec. 3 p. 4.

2078   "A welcome to illegal aliens." Mar. 24, 1977. Sec. 3 p. 4.

2079   "How sweet the abuse of power." Mar. 29, 1977. Sec. 3 p. 3.

2080   "A puritan view: conserve energy." Mar. 31, 1977. Sec. 3 p. 3.

2081   "Outrageous lies sell the best." Apr. 5, 1977. Sec. 3 p. 3.

2082   " . . . and a service for mankind." Apr. 7, 1977. Sec. 3 p. 4.

2083   "Competition, egalitarianism, and envy." Apr. 12, 1977. Sec. 3 p. 4.

2084   "Why terrorists attacked Jews." Apr. 14, 1977. Sec. 3 p. 4.

2085   "The Russians still baffle us." Apr. 19, 1977. Sec. 2 p. 3.

2086   "Why Chicagoans picked Bilandic." Apr. 21, 1977. Sec. 3 p. 3.

2087   "Phony symbols in the Capitol." Apr. 26, 1977. Sec. 3 p. 3.

2088   "A better plan for volunteers." Apr. 28, 1977. Sec. 3 p. 4.

2089   "Mr. Carter, meet Congress." May 3, 1977. Sec. 3 p. 3.

2090   "Bishops and the bureaucrats." May 5, 1977. Sec. 3 p. 4.

2091   "An energy crisis? No kidding?" May 10, 1977. Sec. 3 p. 3.

2092   "The view from upstairs." May 12, 1977. Sec. 2 p. 4.

2093   "That old-time brainwashing." May 17, 1977. Sec. 3 p. 3.

2094   "Foreign policy at least is funny." May 19, 1977. Sec. 3 p. 4.

2095   "The real problem of our cities." May 24, 1977. Sec. 3 p. 3.

2096   "They're out to get the cities." May 26, 1977. Sec. 3 p. 4.

2097   "How the Vatican fights unity." May 31, 1977. Sec. 3 p. 3.

2098   "Have black gains been kept?" June 2, 1977. Sec. 3 p. 4.

2099   "Catholic youth has a prayer." June 7, 1977. Sec. 3 p. 3.

2100   "Novelists of the madhouse." June 9, 1977. Sec. 3, p. 4.

2101   "The devil's back in business." June 14, 1977. Sec. 3 p. 3.

2102   "The quality of life is not a product." June 16, 1977. Sec. 3
         p. 4.

2103   "Troubled cities baffle a Martian." June 21, 1977. Sec. 3 p. 4.

2104   "The vicious liberal bigots." June 28, 1977. Sec. 3 p. 3.

2105   "Riots and political blackmail." June 30, 1977. Sec. 3 p. 4.

2106   "Is 1977 the turning point for freedom?" July 5, 1977. Sec. 3
         p. 4.

2107   "Unmoved by 'movements'." July 7, 1977. Sec. 3 p. 4.

2108   "The unisexists are puritans." July 12, 1977. Sec. 3 p. 3.

2109   "Another Catholic sex squabble." July 14, 1977. Sec. 3 p. 4.

2110   "Most agree: God is not mad." July 19, 1977. Sec. 3 p. 4.

2111   "Don't give an inch to metrics." July 21, 1977. Sec. 3 p. 3.

2112   "Are some roots inferior?" July 26, 1977. Sec. 3 p. 3.

2113   "A weak spot in Soviet armor." July 28, 1977. Sec. 3 p. 4.

2114   "Death rays in the real world." Aug. 2, 1977. p. 7.

2115   "Has Bella blown her fuse?" Aug. 4, 1977. Sec. 3 p. 3.

2116   "Loneliness is the deadliest disease." Aug. 9, 1977. Sec. 3
         p. 3.

2117   "Tut-tut! Too much of a tomb." Aug. 11, 1977. Sec. 3 p. 4.

2118   "Is heaven going to be a drag?" Aug. 16, 1977. Sec. 3 p. 3.

2119   "'Leaders' without followers." Aug. 18, 1977. Sec. 3 p. 4.

2120   "Refugees: no room at the inn." Aug. 23, 1977. Sec. 3 p. 4.

2121   "The rich speak for the poor." Aug. 25, 1977. Sec. 3 p. 3.

2122   "Education experts flunk out." Aug. 30, 1977. Sec. 3 p. 3.

2123   "The family is far from dead." Sept. 1, 1977. Sec. 3 p. 4.

2124   "Catholic teachers could call it hypocrisy." Sept. 8, 1977. Sec.
         3 p. 3.

2125   "Can only the rich be honest?" Sept. 13, 1977. Sec. 3 p. 3.

2126   "Should the elitists tell us how to live?" Sept. 15, 1977. Sec. 3
         p. 4.

2127   "Daley's real pals won't talk." Sept. 20, 1977. Sec. 3 p. 4.

2128   "'Majority' rule and genocide." Sept. 22, 1977. Sec. 3 p. 4.

2129   "Sex and violence in the family." Sept. 27, 1977. Sec. 3 p. 3.

2130   "Everybody has ethics problems." Sept. 29, 1977. Sec. 3 p. 4.

2131   "Catholic schools doing a job." Oct. 4, 1977. Sec. 3 p. 4.

2132   "Voluntary busing makes sense." Oct. 6, 1977. Sec. 3 p. 4.

2133   "Let's ditch the Panama Canal." Oct. 11, 1977. Sec. 3 p. 3.

2134   "The ghost of radicalism past." Oct. 13, 1977. Sec. 3 p. 3.

2135   "A jailer's heartrending book." Oct. 18, 1977. Sec. 3 p. 4.

2136   "Quotas would legalize bias." Oct. 20, 1977. Sec. 3 p. 4.

2137   "A hypothesis that falls short." Oct. 25, 1977. Sec. 3 p. 3.

2138   "All's well that ends quickly." Oct. 27, 1977. Sec. 3 p. 3.

2139   "England's peculiar economy." Nov. 3, 1977. Sec. 3 p. 4.

2140   "French Marxism in trouble." Nov. 8, 1977. Sec. 3 p. 4.

2141   "Many fear Polish uprising." Nov. 10, 1977. Sec. 3 p. 4.

2142   "Ulster a medieval nightmare." Nov. 15, 1977. Sec. 3 p. 4.

2143   "Irish feminists Europe's toughest." Nov. 17, 1977. Sec. 3 p. 4.

2144   "Quotas cannot right past wrongs." Nov. 22, 1977. Sec. 3 p. 4.

2145   "Getting a kick out of outrage." Nov. 24, 1977. Sec. 3 p. 4.

2146   "Youth today: sweet and sane." Nov. 29, 1977. Sec. 3 p. 4.

2147   "If Patty had been a radical. . . ." Dec. 1, 1977. Sec. 3 p. 3.

2148   "Life after death vs. scientific dogma." Dec. 6, 1977. Sec. 3 p. 4.

2149   "What the New News gave up." Dec. 8, 1977. Sec. 3 p. 4.

2150   "Church leaders blunder on." Dec. 13, 1977. Sec. 3 p. 3.

2151   "The real key to teen drinking." Dec. 15, 1977. Sec. 3 p. 4.

2152   "Right or wrong, policies work." Dec. 20, 1977. Sec. 3 p. 3.

2153   "The things that didn't happen." Dec. 22, 1977. Sec. 3 p. 4.

2154   "Of course, it really was Santa." Dec. 27, 1977. Sec. 3 p. 4.

2155   "The darkness of midwinter." Dec. 29, 1977. Sec. 3 p. 4.

2156   "Religion sells--if not in church." Jan. 3, 1978. Sec. 3 p. 4.

2157   "The feminists who envy men." Jan. 5, 1978. Sec. 3 p. 4.

2158   "Catholic attendance still falling." Jan. 10, 1978. Sec. 3 p. 3.

2159   "A crisis that some can't see." Jan. 12, 1978. Sec. 3 p. 4.

2160   "New priests are nowhere." Jan. 17, 1978. Sec. 3 p. 4.

2161   "False alarms about the family." Jan. 19, 1978. Sec. 3 p. 4.

2162   "Diplomats keep Poles apart." Jan. 24, 1978. Sec. 3 p. 3.

2163   "Finding a 'Teaching Authority'." Jan. 26, 1978. Sec. 3 p. 4.

2164   "New sex code is an old game." Jan. 31, 1978. Sec. 3 p. 3.

2165   "Busing and the end of the city." Feb. 2, 1978. Sec. 3 p. 3.

2166   "Our yearnings for a family." Feb. 7, 1978. Sec. 3 p. 3.

2167   "Symbolism discriminates." Feb. 9, 1978. Sec. 3 p. 4.

2168   "Filmmakers hate Italians." Feb. 14, 1978. Sec. 3 p. 4.

2169   "Corruption as a way of life." Feb. 16, 1978. Sec. 3 p. 4.

2170   "New Liberalism a hollow mockery." Feb. 21, 1978. Sec. 3
          p. 3.

2171   "Tough women fail to tenderize men." Feb. 23, 1978. Sec. 3
          p. 4.

2172   "Arrogance killed a college." Feb. 28, 1978. Sec. 3 p. 3.

2173   "A new kick for naive nuns." Mar. 2, 1978. Sec. 3 p. 4.

2174   "The myth of the Italian Mafia." Mar. 7, 1978. Sec. 3 p. 4.

2175   "They don't print what we think." Mar. 9, 1978. Sec. 3 p. 4.

2176   "A Marxist view of the family." Mar. 14, 1978. Sec. 3 p. 4.

2177   "Let's pass laws, not judgments." Mar. 16, 1978. Sec. 3 p. 4.

2178   "Racism fading, but poverty isn't." Mar. 21, 1978. Sec. 3 p. 4.

2179   "Why Daley's story is untold." Mar. 23, 1978. Sec. 3 p. 4.

2180   "Danger of moral principles." Mar. 28, 1978. Sec. 3 p. 4.

2181   "Catholics in Washington." Mar. 30, 1978. Sec. 3 p. 4.

2182   "A shabby book about prelates." Apr. 4, 1978. Sec. 3 p. 3.

2183   "Catholics steaming in silence." Apr. 11, 1978. Sec. 3 p. 3.

2184   "Call time out to love your kids." Apr. 13, 1978. Sec. 3 p. 4.

2185   "Physicists, atoms, and God." Apr. 18, 1978. Sec. 3 p. 4.

2186   "Equal rights for ugly people." Apr. 25, 1978. Sec. 3 p. 4.

2187   "Racial tensions on campus rising." Apr. 27, 1978. Sec. 3 p. 3.

2188   "Mystics and official skeptics." May 2, 1978. Sec. 3 p. 3.

2189   "Offensive films about women." May 4, 1978. Sec. 3 p. 3.

2190   "The 'softening' of education." May 9, 1978. Sec. 3 p. 4.

2191   "The cultural vice of selective outrage." May 11, 1978. Sec. 3 p. 3.

2192   "Closing the Catholic schools." May 16, 1978. Sec. 3 p. 4.

2193   "Apes who learn to share food and to love." May 18, 1978. Sec. 3 p. 4.

2194   "Busing and 'white flight'." May 23, 1978. Sec. 3 p. 4.

2195   "Should we elect a Cabinet?" May 25, 1978. Sec. 3 p. 4.

2196   "Beware of nonpolitical hacks." May 30, 1978. Sec. 3 p. 4.

2197   "Commissions of absurdities." June 1, 1978. Sec. 3 p. 4.

2198   "Americans still don't trust Russia." June 6, 1978. Sec. 3 p. 4.

2199   "Feeling sorry for only a few." June 8, 1978. Sec. 3 p. 4.

2200   "Providence-St. Mel's mission." June 13, 1978. Sec. 3 p. 4.

2201   "Califano's cheap trick." June 15, 1978. Sec. 3 p. 3.

2202   "Taking the sense out of census." June 20, 1978. Sec. 3 p. 3.

2203   "Vultures around Patty Hearst." June 22, 1978. Sec. 3 p. 4.

2204   "Who will pick the next Pope?" June 27, 1978. Sec. 3 p. 3.

2205   "Let's save the family from HEW." June 29, 1978. Sec. 3 p. 4.

2206   "Here's your jet but what's your hurry." July 4, 1978. Sec. 3 p. 3.

2207   "On rights, Left can do no wrong." July 6, 1978. Sec. 3 p. 4.

2208   "Two languages and four issues." July 11, 1978. Sec. 3 p. 4.

2209   "Some care about next Pope." July 13, 1978. Sec. 3 p. 4.

2210   "Illegitimacy and the liberals." July 18, 1978. Sec. 3 p. 3.

2211   "Affirmative action must have some victims." July 20, 1978. Sec. 3 p. 4.

2212   "Academic mockery of freedom." July 27, 1978. Sec. 3 p. 4.

2213   "The insolence of public office." Aug. 1, 1978. Sec. 3 p. 3.

2214   "Blacks and anti-Catholicism." Aug. 3, 1978. Sec. 3 p. 4.

2215   "Collective guilt and damnation." Aug. 8, 1978. Sec. 3 p. 3.

2216   "No news isn't good news." Aug. 10, 1978. Sec. 3 p. 4.

The following columns, from Oct. 31, 1978 to February 13, 1981, were seen in the *Chicago Sun Times* recorded on microfilm by Bell and Howell, Wooster, OH.

2217   "Why do men dominate women?" Oct. 31, 1978. p. 35.

2218   "The two crucial years in a marriage." Nov. 2, 1978. p. 61.

2219   "The smug generation." Nov. 7, 1978. p. 34.

2220   "Poppycock about Pope." Nov. 9, 1978. p. 74.

2221   "No kidding, Ms. Norton." Nov. 14, 1978. p. 50.

2222   "The busing charade." Nov. 16, 1978. p. 78.

2223   "What energy crisis?" Nov. 21, 1978. p. 38.

2224   "Political vs. moral leaders." Nov. 23, 1978. p. 82.

2225   "Thoughts on moral vision." Nov. 28, 1978. p. 40.

2226   "Boycott the Olympics." Dec. 1, 1978. p. 50.

2227   "So a little brainwashing never hurt anybody, eh?" Dec. 7, 1978.
         p. 74.

2228   "New career: housewife." Dec. 12, 1978. p. 44.

2229   "Blasphemy's in fashion." Dec. 14, 1978. p. 78.

2230   "Dear John Paul: Don't let 'em get to you." Dec. 19, 1978.
         p. 34.

2231   "The hated Hispanics." Dec. 21, 1978. p. 62.

2232   "Carter's cheap shot." Dec. 28, 1978. p. 58.

2233   "What's OPEC doing with all that money?" Jan. 2, 1979. p. 30.

2234   "A hard look at Teddy." Jan. 4, 1979. p. 54.

2235   "Don't give Asia's 'boat people' a thought." Jan. 8, 1979.
         p. 36.

2236   "Progress on integration." Jan. 11, 1979. p. 52.

2237   "Ripping off the elderly." Jan. 16, 1979. p. 30.

2238   "In defense of Woody Hayes." Jan. 25, 1979. p. 46.

2239   "All smoke and no fire." Jan. 29, 1979. p. 30.

2240   "Our odd way of learning truth about Ireland." Feb. 12, 1979.
         p. 36.

2241   "Better Marxism than Islam." Feb. 22, 1979. p. 51.

2242   "Vatican health is myth." Mar. 23, 1979. p. 52.

2243   "Ignoring anti-Catholic bias." Apr. 10, 1979. p. 36.

2244   "Pope opens door to his soul." Apr. 17, 1979. p. 42.

2245   " . . . but let's not revive the draft." Apr. 19, 1979. p. 63.

2246   "What's wrong with the Irish." May 1, 1979. p. 36.

2247   "Sneaky survivor of '60s." May 8, 1979. p. 46.

2248   "Better nuclear risk than gas shortages?" May 17, 1979. p. 49.

2249   "Russia's secret empire." May 22, 1979. p. 42.

2250   "Catholics and 'guidelines'." May 24, 1979. p. 62.

2251   "Cruel exploitation of politicians' relatives." May 31, 1979.
        p. 58.

2252   "Cardinal-watching." June 8, 1979. p. 56.

2253   "It doesn't make any census." June 12, 1979. p. 42.

2254   "On enjoying more than sex with the opposite sex." June 27,
        1979. p. 60.

2255   "Our new era of doom and gloom." July 4, 1979. p. 42.

2256   "Duck! That UFO's a bit of Skylab." July 10, 1979. p. 34.

2257   "Why do the feminists play macho games?" July 27, 1979.
        p. 44.

2258   "Revive draft? Most arguments for it are phony." July 30, 1979.
        p. 26.

2259   "What will Pope tell us?" Aug. 3, 1979. p. 46.

2260   "Winning his feminist merit badge at 30,000 feet." Aug. 11,
        1979. p. 28.

2261   "The orgy began at Woodstock." Aug. 24, 1979. p. 54.

2262   "Many bloody hands responsible for world terrorism." Sept. 3,
        1979. p. 16.

2263   "Oldsters 'out of it'?" Sept. 21, 1979. p. 50.

2264   "Because he is a Kennedy." Sept. 24, 1979. p. 37.

2265   "We just won't let young people grow up." Sept. 28, 1979.
        p. 44.

2266   "Whence the magic of this man?" Oct. 6, 1979. p. 40.

2267   "He's going to be a great Pope." Oct. 10, 1979. p. 47.

2268   "Pope's visit marred by his insensitivity to problems." Oct. 12,
        1979. p. 47.

2269   "Must we be fashionable and pooh-pooh hope." Oct. 19, 1979.
        p. 50.

2270   "Is it too risky to love?" Oct. 23, 1979. p. 46.

2271   "Don't blame pig-headed princess." Oct. 24, 1979. p. 61.

2272   "Nightmare remains." Oct. 26, 1979. p. 52.

2273   "A flip-flop in 'living together'." Nov. 2, 1979. p. 49.

2274   "What's Pope up to?" Nov. 8, 1979. p. 70.

2275   "May Catholics dissent?" Nov. 15, 1979. p. 74.

2276   "The 'us' and 'them' fallacy." Nov. 16, 1979. p. 44.

2277   "Quiet diplomacy with ayatollah? Impossible!" Nov. 20, 1979.
        p. 29.

2278   "Is U. S. helpless giant? No, self-restrained." Nov. 23, 1979.
        p. 75.

2279   "Let Iran self-destruct." Nov. 29, 1979. p. 66.

2280 "Life in Washington has gotten to William Miller." Dec. 4, 1979. p. 48.

2281 "Misreading the Pope." Dec. 13, 1979. p. 82.

2282 "John Paul's the real loser in Kung affair." Dec. 25, 1979. p. 50.

2283 "70s weren't so bad." Dec. 28, 1979. p. 32.

2284 "This complex Pope." Jan. 8, 1980. p. 32.

2285 "'How could we know he'd get tough, comrade Leonid?'" Jan. 10, 1980. p. 55.

2286 "Schools' 3 impossible tasks." Jan. 16, 1980. p. 54.

2287 "What's up? Dock workers sure know . . . " Jan. 19, 1980. p. 18.

2288 "Hang on till 9th year, your marriage may rebound." Jan. 26, 1980. p. 22.

2289 "Getting a bit drafty." Jan. 30, 1980. p. 58.

2290 "Whoever said work is all that rewarding?" Feb. 14, 1980. p. 56.

2291 "Let's not convert teen girls into infantrypersons." Feb. 15, 1980. p. 43.

2292 "Do women manipulate men? Does sun rise?" Feb. 22, 1980. p. 42.

2293 "Carter blusters and blunders through crises." Mar. 1, 1980. p. 24.

2294 "Sharing blame for terror." Mar. 5, 1980. p. 52.

2295 "Answer 'no' to polls." Mar. 7, 1980. p. 46.

2296   "Catholic and uncatholic." Mar. 11, 1980. p. 36.

2297   "La difference." Mar. 15, 1980. p. 28.

2298   "St. Patrick and remnants of a mystic past." Mar. 17, 1980. p. 50.

2299   "One last fling for Anderson--and chaos." Mar. 21, 1980. p. 48.

2300   "Close-minded Pope?" Mar. 24, 1980. p. 30.

2301   "Keeping Ron's finger off the atomic trigger." Mar. 28, 1980. p. 44.

2302   "Limerance ain't so grand." Mar. 31, 1980. p. 34.

2303   "Of course Reagan's age should be issue." Apr. 11, 1980. p. 39.

2304   "Have women ever served as priests?" Apr. 19, 1980. p. 26.

2305   "Yes, he can win." Apr. 23, 1980. p. 67.

2306   "We're lucky if aborted early." May 2, 1980. p. 48.

2307   "In her image . . . " May 9, 1980. p. 50.

2308   " . . . and makes the church look dumb." May 10, 1980. p. 28.

2309   "Refugee surge spurs epidemic of nativism." May 16, 1980. p. 62.

2310   "No polygamy deals." May 19, 1980. p. 34.

2311   "Who cares about kids?" May 22, 1980. p. 66.

2312   "Elect him! He can laugh at himself." May 23, 1980. p. 45.

2313   "The Catholic church riles its women." May 26, 1980. p. 24.

2314 "Cubans cry out--but we stutter, stumble." May 29, 1980. p. 48.

2315 "A religious classic: All That Jazz." June 2, 1980. p. 36.

2316 "Politicizing can poison personal relationships." June 6, 1980. p. 65.

2317 "Anderson was the real victor June 3." June 11, 1980. p. 74.

2318 "Cowardice on gas tax." June 14, 1980. p. 28.

2319 "Those purgatorial June graduation ceremonies." June 18, 1980. p. 57.

2320 "Priests and married women: subtle chemistry." June 23, 1980. p. 32.

2321 "Election '80: comic tragedy." June 27, 1980. p. 43.

2322 "Is God like sensuous woman?" June 30, 1980. p. 32.

2323 "Registration is the first step." July 4, 1980. p. 22.

2324 "A loss for pope--and U. S. Catholicism." July 9, 1980. p. 60.

2325 "Peace role for IRA?" July 11, 1980. p. 40.

2326 "2 questions for draft supporters." July 12, 1980. p. 22.

2327 "A harsh birth-control solution for Catholics." July 21, 1980. p. 26.

2328 "The up-tight GOP: permanent minority." July 23, 1980. p. 68.

2329 "Put Olympic lunacy to rest." July 31, 1980. p. 62.

2330 "Get the kids!" Aug. 6, 1980. p. 52.

2331 "Ron won't have to slay Democratic dragon." Aug. 9, 1980. p. 26.

2332   "Dodging the draft." Aug. 19, 1980. p. 36.

2333   "Poland could spark another world crisis." Aug. 23, 1980.
        p. 28.

2334   "Pope repudiates male domination." Aug. 25, 1980. p. 34.

2335   "Reagan confused about Genesis . . . " Aug. 30, 1980. p. 24.

2336   " . . . and it should last until Columbus Day." Sept. 1, 1980.
        p. 22.

2337   "Is teen sex rooted in self-contempt?" Sept. 12, 1980. p. 50.

2338   "Of course priests fall in love." Sept. 15, 1980. p. 34.

2339   "Carter's debate stand defies logic." Sept. 18, 1980. p. 71.

2340   "Jealousy killing ERA?" Sept. 25, 1980. p. 66.

2341   "Guess what? That's census." Sept. 27, 1980. p. 28.

2342   "My God, it's difficult to be a woman." Oct. 4, 1980. p. 28.

2343   "Should church never mix in politics?" Oct. 11, 1980. p. 26.

2344   "Immigrants go home." Oct. 14, 1980. p. 38. *

2345   "So what's so bad about job favoritism?" Oct. 20, 1980. p. 37.

2346   "Halloween mystery." Oct. 22, 1980. p. 76.

2347   "Must human males go through ape stage?" Oct. 24, 1980. p.
        41.

2348   "Sure I'm liberated, but I still hold door open for women." Nov.
        8, 1980. p. 30.

2349   " . . . maybe, but liberals can salvage lost issues." Nov. 19,
        1980. p. 61.

2350   "A birth-control message Catholic leaders ignore." Nov. 26, 1980. p. 29.

2351   "No. 1 tax problem: the cash economy." Dec. 3, 1980. p. 51.

2352   "Why teen pregnancy is raging." Dec. 9, 1980. p. 39.

2353   "A bad year for Catholic church." Dec. 11, 1980. p. 71.

2354   "Let's move Christmas." Dec. 15, 1980. p. 46.

2355   "They talk funny: So what?" Dec. 23, 1980. p. 24.

2356   "Richard Nixon for the Supreme Court!" Dec. 31, 1980. p. 17.

2357   "Religion's hard, fanatical edge hogs the spotlight." Jan. 3, 1981. p. 16.

2358   "Lennon's death marked end of '60s values." Jan. 10, 1981. p. 22.

2359   "Crisis showed our best and worst." Jan. 23, 1981. p. 27.

2360   "The dog, Watson, is still not barking." Jan. 30, 1981. p. 31.

2361   "Love and sex: Truths the Bible teaches us." Feb. 13, 1981. p. 38.

Andrew Greeley wrote a column in the *Chicago Sun Times* which was published almost every Sunday from July 13, 1986 until October 31, 1993. The following were seen recorded on microfilm by University Microfilms, Inc., Ann Arbor, MI. At the time of writing his column appears weekly, on Sundays, in the *Daily Southtown* (Chicago).

2362   "Church time bomb: Pederast priests." July 13, 1986. Sec. V p. 43.

2363   "The Ulster issue that counts." July 20, 1986. Sec. V p. 54.

2364   "Snub of beauty is an insult to God." July 27, 1986. Sec. V p. 51.

2365   "Archdiocese vigilantes riding high." Aug. 3, 1986. Sec. V p. 46.

2366   "City-suburban dividing line nothing but an evil fiction." Aug. 10, 1986. Sec. V p. 50.

2367   "Language not nation's social glue." Aug.17, 1986. Sec. V p. 56.

2368   "Hold that school, summer's still on." Aug. 24, 1986. Sec. V p. 58.

2369   "Cardinal perched on a powder keg." Aug. 31, 1986. Sec. V p. 51.

2370   "Red Baron of Vatican at it again." Sept. 14, 1986. Sec. C p. 53.

2371   "Bernardin ship still dead in the water." Sept. 21, 1986. Sec. C p. 50.

2372   "Another depression? Don't rule it out." Sept. 28, 1986. Sec. C p. 60.

2373   "Church leaders have obligation to decry violation of women." Oct. 5, 1986. Sec. C p. 64.

2374   "Making it happen in Chicago." Oct. 12, 1986. Sec. C p. 59.

2375   "Soviets have grounds to fear war." Oct. 19, 1986. Sec. C p. 68.

2376   "'Genocidal' aspects to immigration bill." Oct. 26, 1986. Sec. C p. 67.

2377   "Naive clergymen and radical chic." Nov. 2, 1986. Sec. C p. 65.

2378   "Timid leadership at root of priests' morale plunge." Nov. 9, 1986. Sec. C p. 70.

2379   "Key issue for 1988: how to revitalize nation's capitalism." Nov. 16, 1986. Sec. C p. 59.

2380   "A sad performance by Catholic bishops." Nov. 23, 1986. Sec. C p. 65.

2381   "Iran deal can make case for impeachment." Nov. 30, 1986. Sec. C p. 57.

2382   "Farm slump might spawn a new global depression." Dec. 7, 1986. Sec. C p. 64.

2383   "It's the party that matters, not the man." Dec. 14, 1986. Sec. C p. 65.

2384   "What Jesus thought about God." Dec. 21, 1986. Sec. C p. 57.

2385   "Don't blame selves for kids." Dec. 28, 1986. Sec. C p. 51.

2386   "Unguided missile in the Holy Land." Jan. 4, 1987. Sec. C p. 47.

2387   "Viet lesson: avoid draft in peacetime." Jan. 11, 1987. Sec. C p. 45.

2388   "Catholic teachers downtrodden." Jan. 18, 1987. Sec. C p. 53.

2389   "Film critics vs. book reviewers." Jan. 25, 1987. Sec. C p. 35.

2390   "The election issue that no one will address: our schools." Feb. 1, 1987. Sec. C p. 47.

2391   "Blood on our hands in Iran-Iraq war." Feb. 15, 1987. Sec. C p. 56.

2392   "Church must look to its own sexism." Feb. 22, 1987. Sec. C p. 49.

2393   "Slim pickings without Cuomo." Mar. 1, 1987. Sec. C p. 51.

2394   "Reagan should quit--but he won't." Mar. 8, 1987. Sec. C p. 67.

2395   "Sex education debate awash in naivete." Mar. 15, 1987. Sec. C p. 49.

2396   "13th century style serves Vatican ill." Mar. 22, 1987. Sec. C p. 13.

2397   "Anti-Irish prejudice a safe one for liberals." Mar. 29, 1987. Sec. C p. 13.

2398   "Of surrogate mothers and concubines." Apr. 5, 1987. Sec. C p. 11.

2399   "Catholics need not revel over PTL scandal." Apr. 12, 1987. Sec. C p. 11.

2400   "Religious share spring festivals celebrating life." Apr. 19, 1987. Sec. C p. 11.

2401   "Drug testing--why single out athletes?" Apr. 26, 1987. Sec. C p. 11.

2402   "Suburbia's children opt for the city." May 3, 1987. Sec. C p. 11.

2403   "Rape epidemic making a hoax of civilization." May 10, 1987. Sec. C p. 13.

2404   "Don't close that valuable parish school." May 17, 1987. Sec. C p. 11.

2405   "Should a man be denounced at his funeral." May 24, 1987. Sec. C p. 11.

2406   "Remembering steel massacre and its legacy." May 31, 1987. Sec. C p. 11.

2407   "If one man's privacy is lost, all will suffer." June 7, 1987. Sec. C p. 11.

2408   "Why friendly skies and other things got ugly." June 21, 1987. Sec. C p. 11.

2409   "No Vatican message on Waldheim--it's just bungling by curia."
        June 28, 1987. Sec. C p. 11.

2410   "U. S. should leap at chance of Soviet deal." July 5, 1987. Sec.
        C p. 11.

2411   "Turncoats won't swell GOP ranks." July 12, 1987. Sec. C p.
        11.

2412   "Catholic Church was democratic--for its first 1,200 years. July
        19, 1987. Sec. C p. 11.

2413   "Our chickens of 1960s come home to roost." July 26, 1987.
        Sec. C p. 15.

2414   "Summer fun obscures big news on arms." Aug. 2, 1987. Sec.
        C p. 13.

2415   "Get smart--bet against the experts." Aug. 9, 1987. Sec. C p.
        13.

2416   "Incompetence behind a lot of gold braid." Aug. 16, 1987. Sec.
        C p. 13.

2417   "Easy divorce is no blessing for women." Aug. 23, 1987. Sec.
        C p. 13.

2418   "Legalization may be only hope on drugs." Aug. 30, 1987. Sec.
        C p. 13.

2419   "Liberals oblivious to union busting." Sept. 6, 1987. Sec. C p.
        14.

2420   "Catholics may protest, but they're loyal." Sept. 13, 1987. Sec.
        C p. 11.

2421   "Wall-building: when will we see folly of it?" Sept. 20, 1987.
        Sec. C p. 13.

2422   "Means become ends in flawed Reagan policy." Sept. 27, 1987.
        Sec. C p. 13.

2423   "Notre Dame ought to be an academic powerhouse, too." Oct. 4, 1987. Sec. C p. 15.

2424   "Wyeth's puritanism deprives poor Helga of joys of eroticism." Oct. 11, 1987. Sec. C p. 13.

2425   "Soviet change a great victory for our system." Oct. 18, 1987. Sec. C p. 13.

2426   "Youth drain disaster hits Ireland again." Oct. 25, 1987. Sec. C p. 17.

2427   "U. S.-European alliance just a one-way street." Nov. 1, 1987. Sec. C p. 15.

2428   "NFL strike's worst aspect--fan's envy." Nov. 8, 1987. Sec. C p. 13.

2429   "Where blame falls in our school mess." Nov. 15, 1987. Sec. C p.13.

2430   "Wrigleyville, like Cubs, a sure loser." Nov. 22, 1987. Sec. C p. 14.

2431   "Media's double standard exposed in Ginsburg case." Nov. 29, 1987. Sec. C p. 14.

2432   "Vatican's Red Baron helps widen split with Judaism." Dec. 6, 1987. Sec. C p. 14.

2433   "Mussolini-style politics rears its ugly head in Chicago." Dec. 13, 1987. Sec. C p. 14.

2434   "Urgent steps needed to lure new priests." Dec. 20, 1987. Sec. C p. 13.

2435   "Presidential timber out--wooden men in." Dec. 27, 1987. Sec. C p. 17.

2436   "Gorbachev's dedication may pay off." Jan. 3, 1988. Sec. C p. 11.

2437   "Why Catholic Church has financial woes." Jan. 10, 1988. Sec. C p. 14.

2438   "Man relearns an old lesson in AIDS crisis." Jan. 17, 1988. Sec. C p. 13.

2439   "'Belfast Diary'--a vivid portrait of Ulster's troubles." Jan. 24, 1988. Sec. C p. 14.

2440   "He dares to challenge the accepted wisdom on race, poverty." Jan. 31, 1988. Sec. C p. 12.

2441   "Outlay for art at Old St. Pat's a hopeful sign." Feb. 7, 1988. Sec. C p. 13.

2442   "St. Valentine's meaning lost on churchmen." Feb. 14, 1988. Sec. C p. 13.

2443   "Reformers change tune on patronage when they get into office." Feb. 21, 1988. Sec. C p. 14.

2444   "Ethical systems change as mankind acquires new wisdom." Feb. 28, 1988. Sec. C p. 14.

2445   "Church needs symbol with true impact." Mar. 6, 1988. Sec. C p. 13.

2446   "British remain blind to their genocidal mentality on Ireland." Mar. 13, 1988. Sec. C p. 13.

2447   "City's reform regime has winning average lower than Cubs'." Mar. 20, 1988. Sec. C p. 15.

2448   "No, Jackson can't win--but neither can any other Dems in race." Mar. 27, 1988. Sec. C p. 13.

2449   "The time is approaching for the Yankee to, indeed, go home." Apr. 3, 1988. Sec. C p. 13.

2450   "What the pope's encyclical on social justice chooses to ignore." Apr. 10, 1988. Sec. C p. 14.

2451   "Blacks and Poles--it all falls together for Aurelia Pucinski."
        Apr. 17, 1988. Sec. C p. 16.

2452   "Strange new elite in party of Scarface Al." Apr. 24, 1988. Sec.
        C p. 13.

2453   "Catholic Church not facing up to problem of homosexual
        priests." May 1, 1988. Sec. C p. 13.

2454   "Our skyline under attack by the uglies." May 8, 1988. Sec. C
        p. 13.

2455   "Blacks can't be indulged on anti-Semitism." May 15, 1988.
        Sec. C p. 13.

2456   "Illegals taking jobs scorned by Americans." May 22, 1988.
        Sec. C p. 13.

2457   "Why there's anger among some blacks." May 29, 1988. Sec.
        C p. 13.

2458   "Hopes of many perished along with Bobby." June 5, 1988.
        Sec. C p. 15.

2459   "Jahn's design would be one L of a library." June 12, 1988.
        Sec. C p. 13.

2460   "Archdiocese out of touch with people of Holy Family parish."
        June 19, 1988. Sec. C p. 13.

2461   "'Liberals' needn't fret--black-Jewish coalition remains intact."
        June 26, 1988. Sec. C p. 14.

2462   "Art deco all the way--let's bring back the Black Horse Troop."
        July 3, 1988. Sec. C p. 14.

2463   "Bishops have nothing to contribute to the 'star wars' debate."
        July 10, 1988. Sec. C p. 16.

2464   "Why the Vatican tried so hard to appease Marcel Lefebvre."
        July 17, 1988. Sec. C p. 14.

2465   "Catholics in the forefront of white support for Jesse Jackson." July 24, 1988. Sec. C p. 16.

2466   "'68 protesters fail to claim bitter legacy." July 31, 1988. Sec. C p. 13.

2467   "The Left takes a turn toward the practical." Aug. 7, 1988. Sec. C p. 13.

2468   "Catholicism hit by flight of Hispanics." Aug. 14, 1988. Sec. C p. 13.

2469   "Anglican bishops caught with their hypocrisy showing on Ulster." Aug. 21, 1988. Sec. C p. 14.

2470   "Distinction between lust, desire lost in 'Last Temptation' furor." Aug. 28, 1988. Sec. C p. 14.

2471   "Bishops could use Ebert's insights on 'Last Temptation,' but . . . " Sept. 4, 1988. Sec. C p. 13.

2472   "Tax issue cries for discussion, but Bush stonewalls." Sept. 11, 1988. p. 57.

2473   "Bickering on bias--let's get the facts." Sept. 18, 1988. p. 51.

2474   "Burying 'Diggy'--and Catholic schools." Sept. 25, 1988. p. 49.

2475   "Voters caught between the devil and the deep blue sea." Oct. 2, 1988. p. 53.

2476   "Black or white, our next mayor faces impossible job." Oct. 9, 1988. p. 63.

2477   "His message on women not the last word." Oct. 16, 1988. p. 49.

2478   "Height of political folly." Oct. 23, 1988. p. 49.

2479   "Detroit cardinal discovers parishioners aren't so docile." Oct. 30, 1988. p. 51.

2480 "Worthy education plan gets the brushoff from Bush." Nov. 6, 1988. p. 59.

2481 "The low road proves the one to take to White House." Nov. 13, 1988. p. 53.

2482 "Dems ignored Catholics." Nov. 20, 1988. p. 51.

2483 "Anger at vote polls comes mostly from the losers." Nov. 27, 1988. p. 55.

2484 "Repression not the answer in Catholic tragicomedy." Dec. 4, 1988. p. 67.

2485 "Clipper fortunately is keeping a piece of Chicago history afloat." Dec. 11, 1988. p. 59.

2486 "Harold Washington's legacy turning into hatred." Dec. 18, 1988. p. 69.

2487 "All our abuses cannot quell the Christmas spirit." Dec. 25, 1988. p. 53.

2488 "Daley name not the asset everyone seems to think it is." Jan. 1, 1989. p. 55.

2489 "Public school 'reform'? It's all a charade." Jan. 8, 1989. p. 54.

2490 "Scorched earth for schools." Jan 15, 1989. p. 51.

2491 "Why Reagan was popular despite mediocre presidency." Jan. 22, 1989. p. 51.

2492 "Clerics offer platitudes as solutions." Jan. 29, 1989. p. 56.

2493 "Mayors come and go; city remains almost ungovernable." Feb. 5, 1989. p. 53.

2494 "TV news leaves us in the dark." Feb. 12, 1989. p. 57.

2495   "End can't justify the means in commodity trader sting." Feb. 19, 1989. p. 73.

2496   "Don't knock political compromise." Feb. 26, 1989. p. 57.

2497   "Race the only issue in mayoral primary? Not quite." Mar. 5, 1989. p. 47.

2498   "Khomeini must be quarantined." Mar. 12, 1989. p. 67.

2499   "Pity the poor U. S. archbishops." Mar. 19, 1989. p. 49.

2500   "Freedom of expression under assault from all sides." Mar. 26, 1989. p. 45.

2501   "No shortage of scoundrels draping themselves in flag." Apr. 2, 1989. p. 45.

2502   "Let's hear it for a dull Chicago election." Apr. 9, 1989. p. 55.

2503   "Ban assault weapons now." Apr. 16, 1989. p. 45.

2504   "Rights crusaders of '64 wrought better than they knew." Apr. 23, 1989. p. 57.

2505   "Sex survey foes in error." Apr. 30, 1989. p. 58.

2506   "Hitler birthday surveys give Germany ominous look." May 7, 1989. p. 59.

2507   "How the powerful fall victim to their own arrogance." May 14, 1989. p. 57.

2508   "Priests' morale sagging--but what can you expect?" May 21, 1989. p. 55.

2509   "Daley scores with savvy Irish politics." May 28, 1989. p. 51.

2510   "If you were Gorbachev--" June 4, 1989. p. 50.

2511   "Momentous events of '89 leave Marxism in shambles." June 11, 1989. p. 57.

2512 "Renounce butchers of Beijing." June 18, 1989. p. 51.

2513 "Chicago can't escape stereotype." June 25, 1989. p. 52.

2514 "Democratic China? Don't hold breath." July 2, 1989. p. 48.

2515 "Catholics hit with 'tithing' hammer." July 9, 1989. p. 46.

2516 "School 'reform'--it's tall order." July 16, 1989. p. 47.

2517 "Much-touted immigration 'reform' proves a fizzle." July 23, 1989. p. 51.

2518 "Parasitism spawns some guilty consciences in suburbs." July 30, 1989. p. 52.

2519 "Why Marxism holds appeal." Aug. 6, 1989. p. 48.

2520 "Women the big losers in 'sexual revolution'." Aug. 13, 1989. p. 47.

2521 "How did Daley pull it off?" Aug. 20, 1989. p. 52.

2522 "What a Catholic thinks about tithing." Aug. 27, 1989. p. 50.

2523 "Cardinal Glemp outburst gives Jews cause to wonder." Sept. 3, 1989. p. 47.

2524 "Affirmative action creates new victims: white males." Sept. 10, 1989. p. 43.

2525 "Brave Poles get short shrift from Bush administration." Sept. 17, 1989. p. 57.

2526 "Catholic church isn't racist." Sept. 24, 1989. p. 57.

2527 "Chicago's exciting experiments in democracy." Oct. 1, 1989. p. 57.

2528 "Some of Chicago's 'racial tensions' are more rhetoric than real." Oct. 8, 1989. p. 63.

2529 "Sen. Helms might be stupid, but don't call him a censor." Oct. 15, 1989. p. 51.

2530 "Reforms needed to solve archdiocese's money pinch." Oct. 22, 1989. p. 61.

2531 "1980s making their exit on a wave of self-indulgence." Oct. 29, 1989. p. 55.

2532 "Double standard on celibacy." Nov. 5, 1989. p. 63.

2533 "Irish most tolerant people--but they'll never believe it." Nov. 12, 1989. p. 59.

2534 "Irish put it all in perspective." Nov. 19, 1989. p. 57.

2535 "2 ways to ease archdiocese financial bind." Nov. 26, 1989. p. 59.

2536 "Jesuit murders don't justify support of Salvador rebels." Dec. 3, 1989. p. 63.

2537 "New Europe emerges in momentous year." Dec. 10, 1989. p. 55.

2538 "Pedophile priests--clergy can't sweep them under the rug." Dec. 17, 1989. p. 61.

2539 "No Christmas spirit toward boat people of Vietnam." Dec. 24, 1989. p. 33.

2540 "Archdiocese sorely in need of another Arnold Damen." Dec. 31, 1989. p. 47.

2541 "Was Bush afraid of Swiss Guard?" Jan. 7, 1990. p. 49.

2542 "Dramatic moves could lift Bernardin out of fiscal crisis." Jan. 14, 1990. p. 45.

2543 "Four gates to victory in nation's battle against drugs." Jan. 21, 1990. p. 43.

2544   "Parish sacred to Catholics." Jan. 28, 1990. p. 43.

2545   "Fearsome foursome denied equal justice." Feb. 4, 1990. p. 47.

2546   "Cardinal not listening to rumbling volcano." Feb. 11, 1990.
          p. 55.

2547   "Catholic church must clean out the pedophile priests." Feb. 25,
          1990. p. 47.

2548   "Leftist clergy, journalists running out of 'good guys'." Mar. 4,
          1990. p. 51.

2549   "What ever happened to presumption of innocence?" Mar. 11,
          1990. p. 43.

2550   "Helmut Kohl a master of the Big Lie." Mar. 18, 1990. p. 47.

2551   "Pincham and Partee--ideology loses, pragmatism wins." Mar.
          25, 1990. p. 43.

2552   "Bernardin points way in the abortion debate." Apr. 1, 1990.
          p. 56.

2553   "Germans also knew the horrors of war." Apr. 8, 1990. p. 46.

2554   "Brilliant airport plan encounters instant negativism." Apr. 15,
          1990. p. 45.

2555   "Nothing wrong with church PR; we could use it here." Apr. 22,
          1990. p. 49.

2556   "Whither Ireland's vibrant youth?" May 6, 1990. p. 53.

2557   "Ancient rivalries still plague Middle Europe." May 13, 1990.
          p. 45.

2558   "Hungary has head start on the rest of Eastern Europe." May 20,
          1990. p. 53.

2559   "Where's church sense of justice?" May 27, 1990. p. 49.

2560 "Collective guilt? No, judge everyone as an individual." June 3, 1990. p. 55.

2561 "Archbishop Weakland leads the way by listening." June 10, 1990. p. 53.

2562 "Affirmative action offers minorities only token gains." June 17, 1990. p. 41.

2563 "Excommunicate Cuomo? It's just a grandstand play." June 24, 1990. p. 53.

2564 "Lake bottom for NU but not Loyola?" July 1, 1990. p. 47.

2565 "Bishops move on pedophilia--for the wrong motives." July 8, 1990. p. 45.

2566 "Suburb protests on O'Hare noise have a hollow ring." July 15, 1990. p. 43.

2567 "Gorbachev a Chicago-style pol." July 22, 1990. p. 43.

2568 "Archdiocese fiscal woes took root in the Cody era." July 29, 1990. p. 41.

2569 "Irresponsible TV treatment of the W. Side blackout." Aug. 5, 1990. p. 47.

2570 "Liberals can hardly complain of high court choices." Aug. 12, 1990. p. 47.

2571 "Ambitious prosecutors get their lumps." Aug. 19, 1990. p. 47.

2572 "Celibate priests no less content than married men." Aug. 26, 1990. p. 51.

2573 "High hopes for world order if Bush can keep his cool." Sept. 2, 1990. p. 55.

2574 "Freedom of expression cuts 2 ways." Sept. 9, 1990. p. 53.

2575   "Employees still enemy to many managements." Sept. 16, 1990. p. 54.

2576   "Don't be fooled: War with Iraq would be costly." Sept. 23, 1990. p. 45.

2577   "Blundering toward war." Sept. 30, 1990. p. 54.

2578   "Judge Pincham finds a whipping boy--the Irish, no less." Oct. 7, 1990. p. 52.

2579   "The Great 1990 Budget Debacle // Snake oil and 'free lunch'." Oct. 14, 1990. p. 38.

2580   "Don't cover up sex charges against priests." Oct. 21, 1990. p. 40. (Reply Nov. 2, 1990.)

2581   "Halloween a time to laugh away our worst fears." Oct. 28, 1990. p. 40.

2582   Ruiz, Joseph B. "Greeley column on fellow priest was unfair." Nov. 2, 1990. p. 42. (Reply to Oct. 21, 1990.)

2583   "Archdiocese direct-mail drive only a short-run solution." Nov. 4, 1990. p. 42.

2584   "Democracy paralyzed." Nov. 11, 1990. p. 41.

2585   "The folly of the Harold Washington Party." Nov. 18, 1990. p. 46.

2586   "No American should die for Kuwait." Nov. 25, 1990. p. 48.

2587   "High noon in the desert // Bush's war not justifiable." Dec. 2, 1990. p. 44.

2588   "Irish catch up with Collins' insights into the troubles." Dec. 9, 1990. p. 42.

2589   "Twisted concepts of nation's prestige." Dec. 16, 1990. p. 44.

2590   "Maximum force, minimum sense." Dec. 23, 1990. p. 42.

2591   "A war in the gulf is unlikely--and here's why." Dec. 30, 1990. p. 38.

2592   "Who'll say nay to erring Bush?" Jan. 6, 1991. p. 40.

2593   "Bush swept toward war by force of own rhetoric." Jan. 13, 1991. p. 36.

2594   "Bush gets his war--and the price may be terrible." Jan. 20, 1991. p. 46.

2595   "Holy Family lesson lost." Jan. 27, 1991. p. 34.

2596   "History ignored, endless war looms in gulf." Feb. 3, 1991. p. 44.

2597   "Why a ground war looms." Feb. 10, 1991. p. 46.

2598   "Desperate cities // Maybe they should just declare war . . . " Feb. 17, 1991. p. 44.

2599   "Catholic Church can't exist only for clergy." Feb. 24, 1991. p. 52.

2600   "It's no wonder the Mideast hates us." Mar. 3, 1991. p. 50.

2601   " . . . and the selection is an inherently political process." Mar. 10, 1991. p. 40.

2602   "What Paddy's Day is all about // Let there be friendship, forgiveness and reconciliation." Mar. 17, 1991. p. 40.

2603   "Voters know big-city mayors can't work miracles." Mar. 24, 1991. p. 40.

2604   "Common territory for Christians, Jews." Mar. 31, 1991. p. 38.

2605   "Truth might set archdiocese free from its financial woes." Apr. 7, 1991. p. 40.

2606   "Gulf victory less than moral." Apr. 14, 1991. p. 36.

2607   "Exorcist contingent bedevils sophisticated Catholics." Apr. 21, 1991. p. 36.

2608   "Catholic schools do the best with problem students." Apr. 28, 1991. p. 32.

2609   "There's a better way to deal with pedophile cases, but . . . " May 5, 1991. p. 42.

2610   "Real issue in Ulster talks: Will Protestants share power?" May 12, 1991. p. 36.

2611   "Can Ireland leave grim past behind?" May 19, 1991. p. 32.

2612   "Make the public schools compete." May 26, 1991. p. 38.

2613   "Hardball not the answer." June 2, 1991. p. 48.

2614   "A plea for tuition vouchers--for black Baptist schools." June 9, 1991. p. 42.

2615   "Archdiocese policy puts 'fink' firms over unions." June 16, 1991. p. 38.

2616   "Parades of self-deception." June 23, 1991. p. 38.

2617   "Cardinal loses 'referendum'." June 30, 1991. p. 34.

2618   "Yugoslavia a fiction; Croats, Slovenes deserve freedom." July 7, 1991. p. 36.

2619   "Ironies abound on Thomas." July 14, 1991. p. 36.

2620   "Archdiocese violating church's labor tradition." July 21, 1991. p. 36.

2621   "Wilder reflects liberals' bias against Catholicism." July 28, 1991. p. 32.

2622   "Teachers our best hope; give them that pay hike." Aug. 11, 1991. p. 40.

2623   "The Democrats can win in '92." Aug. 18, 1991. p. 42.

2624   "Religion must launch crusade against rape." Aug. 25, 1991. p. 40.

2625   "Unionism victim of 'liberal' snobs." Sept. 1, 1991. p. 38.

2626   "Let's judge 'natural law' on its philosophical merits." Sept. 8, 1991. p. 46.

2627   "Misguided compassion on pedophiles." Sept. 15, 1991. p. 36.

2628   "TV film shows Catholics how much they're hated." Sept. 22, 1991. p. 40.

2629   " . . . But you can't let the city blow away." Sept. 29, 1991. p. 30.

2630   "Democrats can win--and Cuomo's the man." Oct. 6, 1991. p. 40.

2631   "The folly of political correctness." Oct. 13, 1991. p. 42.

2632   "A special prosecutor needed on pedophilia." Oct. 20, 1991. p. 40.

2633   "Public played fair in Thomas case." Oct. 27, 1991. p. 43.

2634   "Response on pedophiles welcome--but it's only a start." Nov. 3, 1991. p. 38.

2635   " . . . But party's liberal elite lie in wait." Nov. 10, 1991. p. 52.

2636   "Let Irish share in multicultural bounty." Nov. 17, 1991. p. 52.

2637   "Daley lacks the powers that his father had." Nov. 24, 1991. p. 44.

2638   "In Ireland, kids are to enjoy." Dec. 1, 1991. p. 42.

2639   "The negatives of promiscuity." Dec. 8, 1991. p. 42.

2640   "Dublin has its charms." Dec. 15, 1991. p. 50.

2641   "Discovering the night." Dec. 22, 1991. p. 50.

2642   "Cuomo's exit disastrous for Democrats." Dec. 29, 1991. p. 41.

2643   "'Cold turkey'--can Eastern Europe handle the pain?" Jan. 5, 1992. p. 44.

2644   "Answering *Time's* query: God's love both masculine, feminine." Jan. 12, 1992. p. 36.

2645   "Short-term profit focus sinks U. S. auto industry." Jan. 19, 1992. p. 40.

2646   "Facing up to hard times." Jan. 26, 1992. p. 32.

2647   "Cardinal does the right thing--thrice." Feb. 2, 1992. p. 34.

2648   "Tolerance, yes--but not for neglect of our children." Feb. 9, 1992. p. 38.

2649   "Things cardinal's sex-abuse commission should know." Feb. 16, 1992. p. 46.

2650   "Strange conspiracy shackles the war against breast cancer." Feb. 23, 1992. p. 38.

2651   "We can't go on strangling the cities." Mar. 1, 1992. p. 34.

2652   "Myths about Irish Catholics endure in face of facts." Mar. 8, 1992. p. 38.

2653   "Mayor lets tears flow--what's wrong with that?" Mar. 15, 1992. p. 42.

2654   "Put the pols back in candidate choice." Mar. 22, 1992. p. 41.

2655   "An ignorant assault on 'Postwar World'." Mar. 29, 1992. p. 34.

2656   "Why Braun has to be a long shot." Apr. 5, 1992. p. 30.

2657   "Archdiocese spins its wheels on pedophile priest problem." Apr. 12, 1992. p. 46.

2658   "3rd airport, runways crucial to city status." Apr. 19, 1992. p. 38.

2659   "Many urban holes to plug--give cities the power to do it." Apr. 26, 1992. p. 38.

2660   "Marching in under a cloud." May 3, 1992. p. 38.

2661   "Blacks the victims--in more than one way." May 10, 1992. p. 40.

2662   "Sometimes there are no solutions." May 17, 1992. p. 34.

2663   "Casey's failing human--church ciphers worse." May 24, 1992. p. 36.

2664   "Mindless populism boosts Perot--and fascist specter." May 31, 1992. p. 34.

2665   "Liberal-left snobs fret over owls, don't give a hoot about workers." June 7, 1992. p. 40.

2666   "Civil authorities must act on cases involving priests." June 14, 1992. p. 42.

2667   "Cardinal merits praise for move toward reform." June 21, 1992. p. 37.

2668   "White House hardly the place for CEO with own secret police." June 28, 1992. p. 34.

2669   "Casino complex distasteful prospect, but let's face it: jobs, funds needed." July 5, 1992. p. 34.

2670   "Our South Side Irish Mayor bluffing on airport? No way." July 12, 1992. p. 40.

2671   "Priestly discontent greatly exaggerated." July 19, 1992. p. 38.

2672   "Fascism still tempts many in our nation." July 26, 1992. p. 34.

2673   "What a ticket of 2 southern Baptists must do to reassure Catholic voters." Aug. 2, 1992. p. 42.

2674   "Laity oppose cover-up of pedophile charges." Aug. 9, 1992. p. 42.

2675   "Nation's anger coming from the wrong sources." Aug. 16, 1992. p. 40.

2676   "President, GOP put their faith in imagemakers." Aug. 23, 1992. p. 42.

2677   "Cardinal gets blind-sided by one slick pol." Sept. 6, 1992. p. 48.

2678   "It's impossible to separate God, politics." Sept. 13, 1992. p. 54.

2679   "Sexual abuse of children an epidemic." Sept. 20, 1992. p. 42.

2680   "Debates defeat Bush's strength--sound bite." Sept. 27, 1992. p. 46.

2681   "Cardinal's review board answers need." Oct. 4, 1992. p. 44.

2682   "Bush will pay price for jobs, senseless war." Oct. 18, 19 92. p. 52.

2683   "Voting ticket eases paralysis of government." Oct. 25, 1992. p. 50.

2684   "Danger lurks in strength of Perot appeal." Nov. 1, 1992. p. 52.

2685   "Election '92: sadly it was a real scream." Nov. 8, 1992. p. 50.

2686   "Galileo OK; now women wait turn." Nov. 15, 1992. p. 42.

2687   "Disillusionment killing hope of new Europe." Dec. 6, 1992. p. 56.

2688   "Ireland wears changes like an old shoe." Dec. 13, 1992. p. 46.

2689   "Grinches fit the faithful for hair shirts." Dec. 20, 1992. p. 58.

2690   "Archdiocese owes laity an apology." Dec. 27, 1992. p. 50.

2691   "Clinton lied to us about his cabinet." Jan. 3, 1993. p. 39.

2692   "Priests' 'conduct code' ignores laity's rights." Jan. 10, 1993. p. 40.

2693   "Clinton backs school choice--for Chelsea." Jan. 17, 1993. p. 36.

2694   "Clinton aims to please--and probably won't." Jan. 24, 1993. p. 38.

2695   "Baird rejection reflects deep anger in U. S." Jan. 31, 1993. p. 40.

2696   "Clinton settles for less in bid to lift gay ban." Feb. 7, 1993. p. 46.

2697   "Clinton shows cowardliness in Wood fiasco." Feb. 14, 1993. p. 46.

2698   "Clinton shows society's bias against Moms." Feb. 21, 1993. p. 46.

2699   "Priests' silence on sex cases deepens agony." Feb. 28, 1993. p. 38.

2700   "Tracking source of 'witch-hunt'." Mar. 7, 1993. p. 37.

2701   "Serbian voters share blame for 'cleansing'." Mar. 14, 1993.
        p. 46.

2702   "Only truth can save Church in dealing with sex charges." Mar.
        21, 1993. p. 45.

2703   "Saints preserve us all from parading Irish." Mar. 28, 1993. p.
        44.

2704   "Loss of respect increases risk run by women." Apr. 4, 1993.
        p. 42.

2705   "Painful lesson for businesses--small is good." Apr. 11, 1993.
        p. 32.

2706   "Moynihan is often right but usually ignored." Apr. 18, 1993.
        p. 46.

2707   "Sum of Kinsey, other 'reports': statistical trash." Apr. 25,
        1993. p. 42.

2708   "Priests should heed call for code of ethics." May 2, 1993. p.
        46.

2709   "Prissy Harvard rewrites rules of date game." May 9, 1993. p.
        44.

2710   "Bosnia mission is moral--but also impossible." May 16, 1993.
        p. 44.

2711   "Three-peat rates high on looters' protest agenda." May 23,
        1993. p. 42.

2712   "Moral cesspool brings decay of human rights." May 30, 1993.
        p. 40.

2713   "Kids felt pain of Catholic 'discipline'." June 6, 1993. p. 36.

2714   "Catholic reforms can't cancel out cruelty of abuse." June 13,
        1993. p. 40.

2715   "Economic salvation of poor rests with unions." June 20, 1993.
        p. 35.

2716   "Church leaders in U. S. refuse to face abuse." June 27, 1993.
        p. 34.

2717   "Marxists escape indictment for killing millions." July 4, 1993.
        p. 42.

2718   "Cynical press corps does hatchet job on Clinton." July 11,
        1993. p. 38.

2719   "'Frankenstein' reduces T-Rex to a pale tale." July 18, 1993.
        p. 36.

2720   "Importance of abuse issue eludes Church." July 25, 1993. p.
        44.

2721   "Searching for nature's 'message'." Aug. 1, 1993. p. 40.

2722   "Custody battles treat children like trophies." Aug. 8, 1993. p.
        38.

2723   "Papal visit brings out worst in media." Aug. 15, 1993. p. 37.

2724   "Cubs vs. Sox: our cultural phenomenon." Aug. 22, 1993. p.
        42.

2725   "Catholic partner rates as a prize in sexual survey." Aug. 29,
        1993. p. 44.

2726   "'68 Dem Convention rioters leave a legacy of failure." Sept. 5,
        1993. p. 44.

2727   "Peace: an act of courage." Sept. 12, 1993. p. 48.

2728   "Society puts lowly teachers in strike mood." Sept. 19, 1993.
        p. 48.

2729   "Clinton shares gifts that made Lincoln great." Sept. 26, 1993.
        p. 48.

2730   "History shows Pope's teaching can be altered." Oct. 3, 1993.
         p. 52.

2731   "1,000% bullet tax targets the killers." Oct. 10, 1993. p. 50.

2732   "Revenge deepens pain." Oct. 17, 1993. p. 50.

2733   "Laity's anger hits church in pocketbook." Oct. 24, 1993. p.
         50.

2734   "Time to give parents options on education." Oct. 31, 1993. p.
         48.

CHAPTER SIX

BOOK AND FILM REVIEWS

BOOKS

2735   "The Counter-Reformation comes to an end." Review of *The Mind of the Catholic Layman* by Daniel Callahan. Scribner's. *Reporter*, Vol. 29 Nov. 21, 1963. pp. 56+.

2736   Review of *The Radical Right* by Daniel Bell. Doubleday. *American Catholic Sociological Review*, Vol. 24, Winter 1963. pp. 367-369.

2737   "Michael Novak: review of *A New Generation, American and Catholic*." Review of *A New Generation, American and Catholic* by Michael Novak. Herder and Herder. *U. S. Catholic*, Vol. 29 Apr. 1964. pp. 56-58. *

2738   "Four views of Rome." Reviews of *The Pilgrim* by Michael Serafian, Farrar, Straus; *The Second Session* by Xavier Rynne, Farrar, Straus; *The Open Church* by Michael Novak, Macmillan; and *Observer in Rome* by Robert M. Brown, Doubleday. *Reporter*, Vol. 31 Sept. 24, 1964. pp. 64+.

2739   "Divine Spark." Review of *The Mandelbaum Gate* by Muriel Spark. Knopf. *Reporter*, Vol. 34 Mar. 24, 1966. pp. 56-58.

2740   Review of *The De-Romanization of the American Catholic Church* by Edward Wakin and Joseph F. Scheuer. Macmillan. *American Sociological Review*, Vol. 31 Aug. 1966. pp. 573-574.

2741   "Age of innocents." Reviews of *The New Left* by Phillip A. Luce, McKay; and *The New Student Left* ed. by Mitchell Cohen and Dennis Hale, Beacon. *Reporter*, Vol. 35 Sept. 8, 1966. pp. 52-54.

2742   Reviews of *Academic Freedom in the Catholic University* by
        Edward Manier and John Houck, Fides; and *The Shape of
        Catholic Higher Education* ed. by Robert Hassenger, Univ. of
        Chicago Press. *Harvard Educational Review*, Vol. 37 n.m. 1967.
        pp. 500-502.

2743   "A chap in his place." Review of *Letters of C. S. Lewis* ed. by
        W. H. Lewis. Harcourt, Brace & World. *Reporter*, Vol. 36
        Jan. 12, 1967. p. 64.

2744   "Wonderful town." Review of *Division Street: America* by Studs
        Terkel. Pantheon. *Reporter*, Vol. 36 Apr. 20, 1967. pp. 53-54.

2745   Review of *Catholic Action in Italy: the sociology of a sponsored
        organization* by Gianfranco Poggi. Stanford Univ. Press. *Social
        Forces*, Vol. 46 Sept. 1967. pp. 119-120.

2746   and Peter Riga. "The Church against itself: two assessments."
        Review of *The Church Against Itself* by Rosemary Ruether.
        Sheed & Ward. *Jubilee*, Vol. 15 Nov. 1967. p. 17.

2747   "Review Symposium." Review of *Christian Beliefs and Anti-
        semitism* by Charles Y. Glock and Rodney Stark. Harper &
        Row. *American Sociological Review*, Vol. 32 Dec. 1967. pp.
        1007-1009.

2748   "Making what?" Review of *Making It* by Norman Podhoretz.
        Random House. *Reporter*, Vol. 38 Mar. 7, 1968. pp. 46-47.

2749   "Moynihan and Drucker--Demythologizers." Review-commentary
        on *Maximum Feasible Misunderstanding* by Daniel P. Moynihan,
        Free Press; and *The Age of Discontinuity* by Peter F. Drucker,
        Harper & Row. *Educational Record*, Vol. 50 Summer 1969. pp.
        319-326. *See also* (2751).

2750   "Curing the Curia." Reviews of *The Politics of the Vatican* by
        Peter Nichols, Praeger; and *The Catholic Crisis* by Thomas
        O'Dea, Beacon. *Transaction*, Vol. 6 June 1969. pp. 74-75.

2751   Reviews of *Maximum Feasible Misunderstanding* by Daniel P.
        Moynihan, Free Press; and *The Age of Discontinuity* by Peter

F. Drucker. Harper & Row. *The Critic*, Vol. 27 June/July 1969. pp. 86-89. *See also* (2749).

2752 Review of *Divine Disobedience: profiles in Catholic radicalism* by Francine du Plessix Gray. Knopf. *New York Times Book Review*, May 31, 1970. pp. 2+.

2753 Review of *The Real Majority: an extraordinary examination of the American electorate* by Richard M. Scammon and Benjamin J. Wattenberg. Coward-McCann. *The Critic*, Vol. 29 Nov./Dec. 1970. pp. 82-84.

2754 Review of *Catholics/U.S.A.: perspectives on social change* ed. by William T. Liu and Nathaniel J. Pallone. Wiley. *Social Forces*, Vol. 49 Dec. 1970. pp. 323-324.

2755 Review of *Beyond Belief* by Robert N. Bellah. Harper & Row. *American Journal of Sociology*, Vol. 76 Jan. 1971. pp. 754-755.

2756 Review of *Charles Carroll of Carrollton: the making of a revolutionary gentleman* by Thomas O. Hanley. Catholic Univ. of America Press. *America*, Vol. 124 Mar. 13, 1971. p. 266.

2757 Review of *Daley of Chicago* by Bill Gleason. Simon & Schuster. *The Critic*, Vol. 29 May/June 1971. pp. 75-77.

2758 Review of *The Fragmented Layman* by Thomas Campbell and Yoshio Fukuyama. Pilgrim. *Religious Education*, Vol. 66 May/June 1971. pp. 237-238.

2759 Review of *Ethnic Politics in America* by Edgar Litt. Scott, Foresman. *International Migration Review*, Vol. 5 Fall 1971. pp. 392-393.

2760 "Another look at Mike Royko's 'Boss'." Review of *Boss: Richard J. Daley of Chicago* by Mike Royko. Dutton. *Chicago History*, Vol. 1 Fall 1971. pp. 250-251.

2761 Review of *Sociology and the Study of Religion* by Thomas F. O'Dea. Basic. *Church History*, Vol. 40 Sept. 1971. p. 353.

2762   Review of *The Autobiography of Lincoln Steffens*. Harcourt
          Brace Jovanovich. *New Republic*, Vol. 165 Nov. 6 1971. pp.
          29-31.

2763   Review of *The Middle Americans* by Robert Coles. Atlantic,
          Little, Brown. *The Critic*, Vol. 30 Nov./Dec. 1971. pp. 76-79.

2764   Review of *Irish/Charles G. Halpine in Civil War America* by
          William Hanchett. Syracuse Univ. Press. *International
          Migration Review*, Vol. 6 Spring 1972. p. 91.

2765   Review of *The Occult Revolution: a Christian meditation* by
          Richard Woods. Herder & Herder. *The Critic*, Vol. 30
          Mar./Apr. 1972. pp. 90-91.

2766   Review of *American Mosaic; social patterns of religion in the
          United States* ed. by Phillip E. Hammond and Benton Johnson.
          Random House. *Religious Education*, Vol. 67 Mar./Apr. 1972.
          pp. 152-153.

2767   "Image voting." Review of *The Ticket-splitter: a new force in
          American politics* by Walter Devries and Lance Tarrance, Jr.
          Eerdmans. *Commentary*, Vol. 53 Apr. 1972. pp. 91-93.

2768   "Cultural repertoires." Review of *Ethnic Enterprise in America:
          business and welfare among Chinese, Japanese, and Blacks* by
          Ivan H. Light. Univ. of California Press. *Monthly Labor
          Review*, Vol. 95 May 1972. pp. 73-74. *See also* (2787).

2769   "Jewish identity." Review of *A Bias of Reflections* by Nathan
          Perlmutter. Arlington House. *Commentary*, Vol. 54 Nov. 1972.
          p. 100.

2770   "After exhaustion--taking a look at Catholic renewal." Reviews
          of *Bare Ruined Choirs: doubt, prophecy and radical religion* by
          Gary Wills,   Doubleday; and *The Renewal of American
          Catholicism* by David O'Brien, Oxford Univ. Press. *National
          Catholic Reporter*, Vol. 9 Nov. 17, 1972. Christmas Book
          Report pp. 7+. *See also* (2771).

2771   Review of *Bare Ruined Choirs: doubt, prophecy and radical religion* by Gary Wills. Doubleday. *Commentary*, Vol. 55 Feb. 1973. pp. 90-92. *See also* (2770).

2772   Review of *Religious Liberty in the United States: the development of church-state thought since the revolutionary era* by Elwyn A. Smith. Fortress. *Journal of American History*, Vol. 59 Mar. 1973. pp. 997-998.

2773   "The clergyman as political animal: a reassessment." Review of *Father Coughlin: the tumultuous life of the priest of the little flower* by Sheldon Marcus. Little, Brown. *Chicago Tribune*, June 3, 1973. Sec. 7 p. 1.

2774   Review of *The Seduction of the Spirit: the use and misuse of people's religion* by Harvey Cox. Simon & Schuster. *New York Times Book Review*, Sept. 16, 1973. pp. 7-8.

2775   "Greeley on Greeley and bishops: reflections on priest surveys." Review of *Organizational Climates and Careers: the work lives of priests* by Douglas T. Hall and Benjamin Schneider. Seminar. *National Catholic Reporter,* Vol. 9 Sept. 28, 1973. p. 15.

2776   Review of *Prejudice and Tolerance in Ulster* by Rosemary Harris. Rowman & Littlefield. *Social Science Quarterly*, Vol. 54 Dec. 1973. pp. 650-651.

2777   Review of *Beleaguered Minorities: cultural politics in America* by S. J. Makielski, Jr. Freeman. *Political Science Quarterly*, Vol. 89 n.m. 1974. pp. 401-402.

2778   Review of *The Remaking of the Church: an agenda for reform* by Richard P. McBrien. Harper & Row. *National Catholic Reporter,* Vol. 10 Jan. 25, 1974. p. 10.

2779   Review of *The Irish: marriage, emigration, and fertility* by Robert E. Kennedy, Jr. Univ. of California Press. *International Migration Review*, Vol. 8 Spring 1974. pp. 95-96. *See also* (2784).

2780   Reviews of *Ethnic and Social Segregation in the New York Metropolis: residential patterns among white ethnic groups, blacks and Puerto Ricans* by Nathan Kantrowitz, Praeger; and *The White Ethnic Movement and Ethnic Politics* by Perry L. Weed, Praeger. *Social Forces*, Vol. 52 Mar. 1974. pp. 429-430.

2781   "Papas Ratti and Pacelli." Review of *The Vatican in the Age of the Dictators (1922-1945)* by Anthony Rhodes. Holt, Rinehart & Winston. *New Republic*, Vol. 170 Mar. 30, 1974. pp. 24-25.

2782   Review of *Real Lace: America's Irish rich* by Stephen Birmingham. Harper & Row. *The Critic*, Vol. 32 Mar./Apr. 1974. pp. 59-61.

2783   Review of *Liberalization of American Protestantism: a case study in complex organizations* by Henry J. Pratt. Wayne State Univ. Press. *American Journal of Sociology*, Vol. 79 May 1974. pp. 1574-1575.

2784   Review of *The Irish: emigration, marriage and fertility* by Robert E. Kennedy. Univ. of California Press. *American Journal of Sociology*, Vol. 80 July 1974. pp. 289-291. *See also* (2779).

2785   Review of *Is the Way of the Denomination Dead?* by Elmer L. Towns. Nelson. *Journal of Ecumenical Studies*, Vol. 11 Fall 1974. pp. 691-692.

2786   Review of *The Academic Melting Pot: Catholics and Jews in American higher education* by Stephen Steinberg. McGraw-Hill. *Journal of Higher Education*, Vol. 46 Jan./Feb. 1975. pp. 121-123.

2787   Review of *Ethnic Enterprise in America: business and welfare among Chinese, Japanese and Blacks* by Ivan H. Light. Univ. of California Press. *American Journal of Sociology*, Vol. 80 Mar. 1975. pp. 1264-1266. *See also* (2768).

2788   Review of *Bonds of Pluralism: the form and substance of urban social networks* by Edward O. Laumann. Wiley. *American Political Science Review*, Vol. 69 June 1975. pp. 711-712.

2789   "Scoop." Review of *The Life and Politics of Henry M. Jackson* by Peter J. Ognibene.   Stein & Day.   *New York Times Book Review*, Jan. 11, 1976.   p. 2.   (Reply Mar. 7, 1976.)

2790   Ognibene, Peter J.   "Scoop."   *New York Times Book Review*, Mar. 7, 1976.   p. 28.   (Reply to Jan. 11, 1976.)   (Rejoinder Mar. 7, 1976.)

2791   Rejoinder to Mar. 7, 1976.   *New York Times Book Review*, Mar. 7, 1976.   p. 28.

2792   Review of *The Catholic Cult of the Paraclete* by Joseph Fichter. Sheed & Ward.   *Social Forces*, Vol. 54 June 1976.   p. 953.

2793   Review of *The Immigrant Church: New York's Irish and German Catholics, 1815-1865* by Jay P. Dolan.   Johns Hopkins Univ. Press.   *Journal of American History*, Vol. 63 June 1976.   pp. 121-122.

2794   Reviews of *The Roman Catholic Church and the Creation of the Modern Irish State, 1878-1886* by Emmet Larkin, American Philosophical Society; and *The Irish Diaspora in America* by Lawrence J. McCaffrey, Indiana Univ. Press.   *New York Times Book Review*, June 27, 1976.   p. 8.

2795   "Two views of Muggeridge's Jesus."   Review of *Jesus: the man who lives* by Malcolm Muggeridge.   Harper & Row.   *The Alternative*, Vol. 9 June/July 1976.   pp. 26-27.

2796   "Hans Kung: embattled teacher and priest."   Review of *On Being a Christian* by Hans Kung.   Doubleday.   *New York Times Book Review*, Dec. 19, 1976.   pp. 5+.

2797   Review of *Ethnic Families in America: patterns and variations* ed. by Charles H. Mindel and Robert L. Habenstein.   Elsevier. *Social Forces*, Vol. 55 Mar. 1977.   pp. 841-843.

2798   "Jonathan Livingston Shimoda."   Review of *Illusions: the adventures of a reluctant Messiah* by Richard Bach.   Delacorte. *New York Times Book Review*, Apr. 10, 1977.   p. 11.

2799   "A welcome double shot of saloon philosophy."   Reviews of *Mr.*

Dooley and the Chicago Irish ed. by Charles Fanning, Arno; and *Mr. Dooley's Chicago* by Barbara Schaaf, Doubleday. *Chicago Tribune*, May 22, 1977. Sec. 7 p. 3.

2800   Review of *Polish-American Politics in Chicago* by Edward R. Kantowicz. Univ. of Chicago Press. *American Political Science Review*, Vol. 71 June 1977. pp. 719-720.

2801   Review of *A Hair of the Dog: Irish Drinking and American Stereotype* by Richard Stivers. Pennsylvania State Univ. Press. *Society*, Vol. 14 July/Aug. 1977. pp. 88-89. *See also* (2807).

2802   "Making a cult of it." Review of *All God's Children* by Carroll Stoner and Jo Anne Parke. Chilton. *New York Times Book Review*, Aug. 14, 1977. pp. 13+.

2803   Review of *The Fall of Public Man* by Richard Sennett. Knopf. *Theology Today*, Vol. 34 Oct. 1977. pp. 324+.

2804   "Cruel treatment." Review of *Karen-Ann: the Quinlans tell their story* by Joseph Quinlan and Julia Quinlan. Doubleday. *New York Times Book Review*, Oct. 9, 1977. p. 10.

2805   "Time to proceed." Review of *Human Sexuality: new directions in American Catholic thought* by Anthony Kosnik *et al.* Paulist. *Family Planning Perspectives*, Vol. 9 Nov./Dec. 1977. p. 296.

2806   Review of *Immigrants and Religion in Urban America* ed. by Randall M. Miller and Thomas D. Marzik. Temple Univ. Press. *Journal of American History*, Vol. 64 Mar. 1978. pp. 1133-1134.

2807   Review of *A Hair of the Dog: Irish drinking and American stereotype* by Richard Stivers. Pennsylvania State Univ. Press. *Social Forces*, Vol. 56 June 1978. pp. 1268-1269. *See also* (2801).

2808   "Listen to the Survivors." Review of *A Jew Today* by Elie Wiesel. Random House. *New York Times Book Review*, Jan. 21, 1979. p. 10.

2809   Review of *Anti-semitism in the New Testament?* by Samuel Sandmel. Fortress. *Journal of Ecumenical Studies*, Vol. 16 Spring 1979. pp. 328-329.

2810   Review of *Evangelization in the American Context* ed. by David B. Burrell and Franzita Kane. Univ. of Notre Dame Press. *Journal of Higher Education*, Vol. 49 Mar./Apr. 1978. pp. 196-197.

2811   Review of *A General Theory of Secularization* by David Martin. Harper & Row. *Catholic Historical Review*, Vol. 65 Apr. 1979. pp. 328-330.

2812   "Symposia." "Who's a chauvinist?" Review of *Ethnic Chauvinism: the reactionary impulse* by Orlando Patterson. Stein & Day. *Contemporary Sociology*, Vol. 8 July 1979. pp. 517-519.

2813   "Fulminations and great good fun." Review of *The Battle for the American Church* by George A. Kelly. Image. *National Catholic Reporter*, Vol. 17 May 29, 1981. p. 15.

2814   "Ethnics' progress: is data fact?" Review of *Ethnic America: a history* by Thomas Sowell. Basic. *Psychology Today*, Vol. 15 Sept. 1981. pp. 90-92+.

2815   Review of *Northern Ireland: between civil rights and civil war* by Liam O'Dowd, Bill Rolston and Mike Tomlinson. Humanities. *Contemporary Sociology*, Vol. 11 Sept 1982. pp. 591-592. (Reply Mar. 1983.)

2816   O'Dowd, Liam. "Comment on Greeley's review of *Northern Ireland*." *Contemporary Sociology*, Vol. 12 Mar. 1983. p. 125. (Reply to Sept. 1982.) (Rejoinder Mar. 1983.)

2817   "Reply to O'Dowd." *Contemporary Sociology*, Vol. 12 Mar. 1983. pp. 125-126. (Rejoinder to Mar. 1983.)

2818   Review of *Countercultures: the promise and peril of a world turned upside down* by J. Milton Yinger. Free Press. *Sociology and Social Research*, Vol. 67 Apr. 1983. pp. 339-340.

2819   "The woman in Pius XII's life. . . . " Reviews of *La Popessa* by
         Paul I. Murphy and R. Rene Arlington, Warner; and *St. Peter's
         Banker* by Luigi DiFonzo, Franklin Watts. *National Catholic
         Reporter,* Vol. 19 May 6, 1983. pp. 22-23.

2820   "A trial never attended." Review of *Pontiff* by Max Morgan-
         Witts and Gordon Thomas. Doubleday. *National Catholic
         Reporter,* Vol. 19 July 15, 1983. pp. 11+.

2821   "Catholic nostalgia novels: the best is yet to come." Reviews of
         Prince of Peace by James Carroll, Little, Brown; and *Virgins* by
         Caryl Rivers, St. Martin's. *National Catholic Reporter,* Vol. 20
         Oct. 19, 1984. pp. 14-15.

2822   "Methods." Review of *Social Values and Social Change: adapt-
         ation to life in America* ed. by Lynn R. Kahle. Praeger.
         Contemporary Sociology, Vol. 14 Jan. 1985. pp. 105-106.

2823   "The moles of the Vatican." Review of *The Noonday Devil* by
         Ralph McInerny. Atheneum. *New York Times Book Review,*
         Mar. 31, 1985. p. 19.

2824   Reviews of *The Spirit of Democratic Capitalism* by Michael
         Novak, Simon & Schuster; and *Confession of a Catholic* by
         Michael Novak, Harper & Row. *Journal of Religion,* Vol. 65
         Oct. 1985. pp. 557-558.

2825   Review of *Habits of the Heart: individualism and commitment in
         American life* by Robert N. Bellah *et al.* Univ. of California
         Press. *Sociology and Social Research,* Vol. 70 Oct. 1985. p.
         114. *See also* (2856).

2826   Review of *Religion in Public Life* by A. James Reichley.
         Brookings Institution. *Political Science Quarterly,* Vol. 101 n.m.
         1986. pp. 479-480.

2827   Review of *The Politics of Sex and Religion* by Robert B. Kaiser.
         Leaven. *America,* Vol. 154 Jan. 25, 1986. pp. 55-56.

2828   Review of *Religious Assortative Marriage in the United States* by
         Robert A. Johnson. Academic. *Sociology,* Vol. 20 Feb. 1986.
         pp. 129-130.

2829   "Tedious novel takes cockeyed view of Vatican." Review of
        Vatican by Malachi Martin. Harper & Row. *Chicago Tribune*,
        Feb. 2, 1986. Sec. 14 p. 39.

2830   Review of *Religion and the Presidential Election* by Paul Lopatto.
        Praeger. *Contemporary Sociology*, Vol. 15 Mar. 1986. pp. 289-
        290.

2831   "Race and ethnic groups." Review of *The Transformation of the
        Jews* by Calvin Goldscheider and Alan S. Zuckerman. Univ. of
        Chicago Press. *Contemporary Sociology*, Vol. 15 Sept. 1986.
        pp. 769-770.

2832   Review of *The Madonna of 115th Street: faith and community in
        Italian Harlem 1880-1950* by Robert A. Orsi. Yale Univ. Press.
        Journal of Religion, Vol. 67 Jan. 1987. pp. 102-103. *See also*
        (2834).

2833   Review of *The American Catholic People: their beliefs, practices,
        and values* by George H. Gallup, Jr. and Jim Castelli.
        Doubleday. *America*, Vol. 156 Feb. 7, 1987. pp. 104-107.

2834   "Review essay: the cult of the Virgin Mary." Reviews of *The
        Cult of the Virgin Mary: psychological origins* by Michael P.
        Carroll, Princeton Univ. Press; and *The Madonna of 115th
        Street: faith and community in Italian Harlem, 1880-1950* by
        Robert A. Orsi, Yale Univ. Press. *Sociology and Social
        Research*, Vol. 71 Apr. 1987. pp. 172-173. *See also* (2832).

2835   Review of *Being Had: historians, evidence and the Irish in North
        America* by Donald Akenson. P.D. Meany. *International
        Migration Review*, Vol. 21 Summer 1987. p. 440.

2836   Reviews of *Catholic Immigrants in America* by James S. Olson,
        Nelson Hall; and *Familiar Strangers: Gypsy life in America* by
        Marlene Sway, Univ. of Illinois Press. *International Migration
        Review*, Vol. 22 Winter 1988. pp. 662-663.

2837   Review of *Women Clergy in England: sexism, modern
        consciousness and church viability* by Edward C. Lehman, Jr.

Edwin Mellon. *Contemporary Sociology*, Vol. 17 Mar. 1988. pp. 231-232.

2838   Review of *The Catholic Church in World Politics* by Eric O. Hanson. Princeton Univ. Press. *Journal of Religion*, Vol. 68 Apr. 1988. p. 325.

2839   Review of *The Future of Catholic Leadership: responses to the priest shortage* by Dean R. Hoge. Sheed & Ward. *Theology Today*, Vol. 45 Apr. 1988. pp. 130+.

2840   Review of *The Irish in Chicago* by Lawrence J. McCaffrey *et al.* Univ. of Illinois Press. *Contemporary Sociology*, Vol. 17 May 1988. p. 293.

2841   Review of *Religious Diversity and Social Change: American cities 1890-1906* by Kevin Christiano. Cambridge Univ. Press. *American Journal of Sociology*, Vol. 94 May 1989. pp. 1438-1440.

2842   "Not a conspiracy, just incompetence." Review of *A Thief in the Night: the mysterious death of Pope John Paul I* by John Cornwell. Simon & Schuster. *The Tablet* (London), Vol. 243 June 3, 1989. pp. 643-644.

2843   Review of *Modern Ireland: 1600-1972* by R. F. Foster. Allen Lane/Penguin. *New York Times Book Review*, June 4, 1989. p. 3.

2844   Review of *Rainbow's End: Irish Americans and the dilemmas of urban machine politics, 1840-1985* by Steven P. Erie. Univ. of California Press. *Contemporary Sociology*, Vol. 19 Jan. 1990. pp. 66-68.

2845   Review of *The Bicentennial History of the Catholic Church in America: historical studies of the Catholic people in America 1789-1989* ed. by Christopher J. Kauffman. Macmillan. *Theology Today*, Vol. 47 Apr. 1990. pp. 88-89.

2846   Review of *Sex and Morality in the United States: an empirical inquiry under the auspices of the Kinsey Institute* by Albert D.

Klassen, Colin Williams and Eugene E. Levitt. Wesleyan Univ. Press. *Society*, Vol. 27 May/June 1990. pp. 103-105.

2847 Review of *American Catholic Laity in a Changing Church* by William D'Antonio *et al.* Sheed & Ward. *Social Forces*, Vol. 68 June 1990. pp. 1355-1357.

2848 Review of *The People's Religion: American faith in the 90's* by George Gallup, Jr. and Jim Castelli. Macmillan. *Political Science Quarterly*, Vol. 105 Fall 1990. pp. 491-492.

2849 Review of *North of Hope* by Jon Hassler. Ballantine. *America*, Vol. 163 Nov. 17, 1990. p. 366.

2850 Review of *Under God: religion and American politics* by Gary Wills. Simon & Schuster. *Political Science Quarterly*, Vol. 106 Summer 1991. p. 366.

2851 Review of *Culture Wars: the struggle to define America* by James D. Hunter. Basic. *New York Times Book Review*, Nov. 24, 1991. pp. 13+.

2852 Review of *Ethnic Identity: the transformation of white America* by Richard D. Alba. Yale Univ. Press. *Political Science Quarterly*, Vol. 106 Winter 1991-92. pp. 754-756.

2853 Review of *A Sociological Study of Secularization Trends in the American Catholic University: decatholicizing religious curriculum* by Frank D. Schubert. Edwin Mellon. *Journal of Church and State*, Vol. 33 Winter 1991. pp. 143-144.

2854 Review of *The Distancing of God: Catholic bishops in American politics* by Timothy A. Byrnes. Princeton Univ. Press. *America*, Vol. 165 Dec. 7, 1991. pp. 440-441.

2855 Review of *Seeing Things* by Seamus Heaney. Random. *Commonweal*, Vol. 119 Mar. 13, 1992. p. 27.

2856 "Habits of the head." Reviews of *The Good Society* by Robert N. Bellah *et al.*, Knopf; and *Habits of the Heart: individualism and commitment in American life* by Robert N. Bellah *et al.*,

Univ. of California Press. *Society*, Vol. 29 May/June 1992. pp. 74-81. *See also* (2825).

2857   Review of *God's Warriors: the Christian right in Twentieth-Century America* by Clyde Wilcox. Johns Hopkins Univ. Press *Political Science Quarterly*, Vol. 107 Summer 1992. pp. 356-358.

2858   Review of *Opus Dei: an investigation into the secret society struggling for power within the Roman Catholic Church* by Michael Walsh. Harper Collins. *National Catholic Reporter*, Vol. 28 Nov. 20, 1992. p. 35.

2859   Review of *Madonnas That Maim: popular Catholicism in Italy since the Fifteenth Century* by Michael P. Carroll. Johns Hopkins Univ. Press. *Contemporary Sociology*, Vol. 22 Jan. 1993. pp. 121-122.

2860   Review of *Textures of Irish America* by Lawrence J. McCaffrey. Syracuse Univ. Press. *Catholic Historical Review*, Vol. 79 Apr. 1993. pp. 362-364.

2861   Review of *What Does the Lord Require?* by Stephen Hart. Oxford Univ. Press. *Public Opinion Quarterly*, Vol. 57 Summer 1993. pp. 286-287.

2862   Review of *Conscience First, Tradition Second: a study of young American Catholics* by Patrick H. McNamara. SUNY. *Social Forces*, Vol. 71 June 1993. pp. 1090-1091.

FILMS

2863   "How to get a red hat." Review of *The Cardinal*. *Reporter*, Vol. 30 Feb. 13, 1964. p. 44.

2864   "But not the greatest movie." Review of *The Greatest Story Ever Told*. *Reporter*, Vol. 32 Apr. 22, 1965. pp. 36+.

2865   "Puppets adrift." Review of *Ship of Fools*. *Reporter*, Vol. 33 Nov. 4, 1965. pp. 48-49.

2866   "St. Matthew without passion." Review of *The Gospel According to St. Matthew*. *Reporter*, Vol. 34 June 30, 1966. pp. 39-40.

2867   "Sons and fathers." Review of *The Graduate*. *Reporter*, Vol. 38 Feb. 8, 1968. pp. 38-39.

2868   "Black and white minstrels." Review of *Guess Who's Coming to Dinner*. *Reporter*, Vol. 38 Mar. 21, 1968. pp. 40+.

2869   "Classy stuff." Reviews of *Bedazzled*; *Charlie Bubbles*; *Up the Junction*; *Here We Go Round the Mulberry Bush*. *Reporter*, Vol. 38 May 16, 1968. pp. 33-34.

2870   "Blasphemy or artistry?" Review of *The Last Temptation of Christ*. *New York Times*, Aug. 14, 1988. Sec. II pp. 1+.

CHAPTER SEVEN

UNPUBLISHED PAPERS AND THESES

2871   "A Bishop looks at total education." n.d. 13 pp.

2872   "The 'Catholic Action' ideology: a non-nostalgic reappraisal." n.d. 19 pp.

2873   "The 'Catholic ethic' and social policy: a melancholy reflection." n.d. n.p. *

2874   "The 'Catholic sexual revolution' and religious behavior." n.d. 10 pp.

2875   "Changing intellectual standards in American Catholic colleges and universities." n.d. n.p.
Presented at the 28th annual meeting of The American Catholic Sociological Society, Miami Beach, FL, Aug. 27-29 [1965 or 1966].

2876   "The dynamics of Catholic opinion." n.d. 15 pp.

2877   "The future of Catholic education." n.d. 17 pp.

2878   "Graduate training in the traditional academic disciplines." n.d. 13 pp.

2879   "Grand-dukes in Siberia: the faculty as a social system." n.d. 11 pp.

2880   "Grounds for hope." n.d. 6 pp.

2881   "*Humanae Vitae* and the sense of the faithful--some questions for theologians." n.d. 21 pp.

2882   *et al.* "Immigration: the second American dilemma." n.d. 45 pp.

2883   and William C. McCready. "The Irish personality--some 'hard' data." n.d. 11+ pp.

2884   "Issues in the teaching of religion in Catholic colleges and universities." n.d. 22 pp.

2885   "Loyalty--commitment under pressure." n.d. 21+ pp.

2886   "Making it: a reconstruction of the demographic history of religio-ethnic groups in the 20th Century." n.d. n.p. *

2887   "November: last chance for the system." n.d. 11 pp.

2888   "On top of the heap and no place to go." n.d. 7 pp.

2889   and William C. McCready. "Personality patterns of American ethnic groups." n.d. n.p. Center for the Study of American Pluralism, NORC. *

2890   "Postwar social trends and the Catholic Action Movements." n.d. 59 pp.

2891   "Prayer and the psychedelic world." n.d. 11 pp.

2892   "Priest, church and the future from a sociological viewpoint." n.d. 15 pp.

2893   "Reflections on 'ethnicity and the pluralist fallacy'." n.d. 4 pp.

2894   "Religion and ethnicity." n.d. 11 pp.

2895   "Social problems of the American family and the role of family ritual." n.d. 12 pp.

2896   "Social turf." n.d. 9 pp.

2897   "Subjective religiousness." n.d. 9 pp.

2898   "Theological principles." n.d. 12 pp.

2899   "A time for reappraisal?" n.d. 15 pp.

2900   "Some aspects of interaction between religious groups in an upper
        middle class Roman Catholic parish." 1961. M. A. thesis
        submitted to Dept. of Sociology, Univ. of Chicago, Feb. 1961.
        Published in *Social Compass*, Vol. 9 1962.

2901   "The influence of religion on the career plans and occupational
        values of June 1961 college graduates." 1962. Unpublished
        dissertation, Univ. of Chicago, 1962.
        Thesis No. 9005. Microfilmed by Univ. of Chicago Library.
        Published version *Religion and Career: a study of college
        graduates*.
        Using data from a NORC survey of 35,000 students in 135
        colleges and universities, G deals with two major concerns: "an
        investigation of the alleged anti-intellectualism of American
        Catholics, and an explanation of the differences among the three
        major American religious groups on certain dependent variables."
        Includes NORC questionnaire. Tables. Bibliography.

2902   "Mixed marriages in the United States." 1964. 34 pp.

2903   Peter H. Rossi and Leonard J. Pinto. "The social effects of
        Catholic education." 1964. n.p. Chicago: NORC, 1964. *

2904   "Academic growth in Catholic higher education." 1966. 21 pp.
        Presented to the American Catholic Sociological Society
        Convention, Aug. 1966.

2905   "Ethnicity in the social sciences." Apr. 1967. 8 pp.

2906   "A new urbanity." July 1967. 11 pp.

2907   "A social organizational view of the Catholic Church?" July
        1967. 13 pp.

2908   "The wandering critic goes to the missions." July 1967. 12 pp.

2909   "American Catholicism at the crossroads." Nov. 1967. 19 pp.

2910   "Collegial leadership: a sociologist's point of view." Nov. 1967.
        13 pp.

2911   "The Catholic priest in contemporary American society." Nov. 1967. 21 pp.
Presented at a symposium sponsored by the Assn. of Chicago Priests, Nov. 20, 1967.

2912   "Student stress because of moral change." Mar. 1968. n.p.
Presented at the 23rd Annual National Conference on Higher Education, Chicago, IL, Mar. 3-6, 1968.

2913   "The denominational society." June 1968. n.p. *
Presented at the Annual Meeting of the Religious Research Assn., Columbus, OH, June 1968.

2914   "The future of the Church." Apr. 1969. 5 pp.
Presented to the Assn. of Chicago Priests, Apr. 15, 1969.

2915   "Needed research on white ethnic groups." 1969. 18 pp.

2916   "Reunion all around." Nov. 1969. 6 pp.
Presented at the Annual Lotke-Hammentash Debate, Nov. 25, 1969.

2917   "Sense and sensitivity in the Catholic Church." Jan. 1970. 19 pp.

2918   "The positive contribution of ethnic groups in American society." May 1970. 27 pp.
Presented at a meeting sponsored by the American Jewish Committee, May 1970.

2919   "Some notes on the war and white ethnic groups." May 1970. n.p. Chicago: NORC, 1970. *

2920   "The academy and the world outside." July 1970. 14 pp.

2921   "Faculty and the epistemological revolution." Aug. 1970. 12 pp.

2922   "Essential structures for the church of the future." Sept. 1970. 24 pp.
Presented at the Congress of Theology, Brussels, Sept. 15, 1970.

2923   "Commentary on: William Birenbaum 'Something for everybody

is not enough'." Oct. 1970. 6 pp.
Presented at the Annual Meeting of the American Council on
Education, Oct. 7-9, 1970.

2924   and Joe L. Spaeth. "Alumni reactions to college student protest."
        Nov. 1970. 15 pp.

2925   "Ethnic politics and the liberal heartland." Nov. 1970. 13 pp.

2926   "State of the union, black and white." Nov. 1970. n.p.
        Presented at the Leadership Conference of the Institute of Public
        Affairs, St. Mary of the Lake Seminary, Mundelein, IL, Nov. 4-
        6, 1970.

2927   "White ethnics for fun and profit." Jan. 1971. 6 pp.

2928   "American priests." Mar. 1971. n.p. Chicago: NORC, 1971. *

2929   "Intellectuals and the working class." May 1971. 5 pp.

2930   Norman Nie and Barbara Currie. "Ethnics and coalition." Sept.
        1971. 17+ pp. Chicago: Center for the Study of American
        Pluralism, NORC, 1972.

2931   "Thoughts after the Synod." Nov. 1971. 12 pp.

2932   "Religion, ethnicity, and the scientific enterprise." Dec. 1971.
        n.p. *
        Presented at the California Institute of Technology Symposium on
        Women and Minority Groups in American Science and
        Engineering, Pasedena, CA, Dec. 8, 1971.

2933   "The church, the national parish and immigration: same old
        mistakes." 1972. 8 pp. Staten Island, NY: Center for Migration
        Studies, 1972. *

2934   "Report to the Ford Foundation of the Center for the Study of
        American Pluralism of N.O.R.C." 1972. n.p. Chicago: Center
        for the Study of American Pluralism, NORC, 1972. *

2935   "An epitaph for the movement?" Jan. 1972. 16 pp.

2936   "The present state of American Catholicism." Jan. 1972. 16 pp.

2937   "The importance of a neighborhood." Jan. 1972. n.p. *
        Presented at the Beverly Community Relations Council, Chicago,
        IL, Jan. 17, 1972.

2938   "Friendship and marriage: a prolegomenon for a theology of
        sexuality." Jan. 1972. 19 pp.
        Presented at the 25th Anniversary of the Cana Conference,
        Archdiocese of Chicago, IL, Jan. 21, 1972.

2939   "Comments of Andrew M. Greeley to the Ad Hoc committee on
        the Implementation of the Priesthood Study, Chicago, Feb. 7-8,
        1972." Feb. 1972. 43 pp.

2940   "The present condition of American Catholics." Apr. 1972.
        22 pp.

2941   "The eschatology of B. F. Skinner." Apr. 1972. 15 pp.
        Presented at the B. F. Skinner Symposium, Yale Univ., New
        Haven, CT, Apr. 19, 1972.

2942   "The future of the ethnic revival." May 1972. 15 pp.
        Presented at the National Conference on Ethnicity, Cleveland
        State Univ., Cleveland, OH, May 12, 1972.

2943   "Consensus and infallibility: sociological perspectives." July
        1972. 9 pp.

2944   "A clear choice for whom?" Aug. 1972. 15 pp.

2945   "Political participation among ethnic groups in the United States:
        a preliminary reconnaissance." Aug. 1972. 34 pp.
        Presented at the American Sociological Assn. meeting, New
        Orleans, LA, Aug. 28 - 31, 1972.

2946   "Towards understanding America." Nov. 1972. 15 pp.
        Presented to the Rockefeller Foundation, New York, NY, Nov.
        22, 1972.

2947   "Response to urban unrest--the case of the Jews and the Poles."

1973. n.p. Chicago: Center for the Study of American Pluralism, NORC, 1973. *

2948   "An alternative perspective for studying American ethnicity." Jan. 1973. 30 pp.

2949   "The demography of ethnic identification." Mar. 1973. n.p. Chicago: Center for the Study of American Pluralism, NORC, 1974. *

2950   "Remarks on demographic research of American ethnic groups." Mar. 1973. 31 pp.

2951   "The socioeconomic status of American ethnic groups." Mar. 1973. n.p. *

2952   and William C. McCready. "The sociology of mystical ecstasy: some preliminary notes." Oct. 1973. 56 pp. Chicago: NORC, 1973.
        Presented at the meetings of the Society for the Scientific Study of Religion, San Francisco, CA, Oct. 26, 1973.

2953   and William C. McCready. "The mystical, the twice born and the happy: an investigation of the sociology of religious experience." 1974. n.p. Chicago: NORC, 1974. *

2954   and William C. McCready. "A preliminary report to the Henry Luce Foundation." 1974. n.p. Chicago: NORC, 1974. *

2955   "The neighborhood and the big world." Mar. 1974. 18 pp.

2956   "The ethnic revival." Sept. 1974. 33 pp.

2957   "Catholic social action a great debate?" Jan. 1975. 30 pp.

2958   "Ethnicity and inequality, or Max Weber eat your heart out." Jan. 1975. n.p. *
        Presented at the meeting of the American Assn. for the Advancement of Science, New York, NY, Jan. 27, 1975.

2959   "Horizon-experience, symbols, language." Jan. 1975. 32 pp.

2960 "A 'semi-pelagian' view of the American people." Jan. 1975. 86 pp.

2961 *et al.* "Catholicism 1963-1974." Feb. 7, 1975. 86 pp.

2962 "The triumph of the romantic." Mar. 1975. 33 pp.

2963 "A church for the communal Catholic: a position paper?" Apr. 1975. 31 pp.

2964 "Pluralism and the American Catholic Church." June 1975. 9 pp.

2965 "Changing attitudes toward other groups, 1965-1973: a confidential note." June 30, 1975. 5+ pp.

2966 "An address to the Catholic Committee on Urban Ministry." Oct. 1975. n.p.
Presented at the Catholic Committee on Urban Ministry, Univ. of Notre Dame, Notre Dame, IN, Oct. 28, 1975. Reply *National Catholic Reporter,* Nov. 21, 1975 (3111).

2967 "Sociology and the law." Apr. 1976. 16 pp.
Presented at the Conference of the Bicentennial of American Law, New York Univ. School of Law, New York, NY, Apr. 27-May 1, 1976.

2968 "So what have you done for us lately?" May 1976. 17 pp.
Presented at a meeting of the American Jewish Committee, Washington, DC, May 12, 1976.

2969 "Organized religion in the United States." Mar. 1977. n.p.
Commissioned by the U. S. Information Agency, Mar. 1977.

2970 "Catholic schools and the two churches." Apr. 1977. n.p.
Presented at the 74th Annual Convention and Religion Education Congress of the National Catholic Educational Assn., San Francisco, CA, Apr. 11-14, 1977. *

2971 "Factors affecting Roman Catholic satisfaction with their parish: a personal report to Monsignor Richard Malone." June 1977. 10+ pp.

2972   "Some notes on 'evangelization' among American Catholics."
June 1977. 50 pp.
Presented at the Bishops' Ad Hoc Committee on "Evangeli-
zation," Arlington Heights, IL, June 22, 1977.

2973   and William C. McCready. "Societal influences on drinking
behavior." Oct. 1978. n.p. *
Presented at the International Medical Advisory Conference of the
Brewing Assns., Toronto, ON, Oct. 1978.

2974   "On teaching religion." Mar. 1978. 31 pp.
Keynote address at the East Coast Conference on Religious
Education, Washington, DC, Mar. 3, 1978.

2975   "An address to the American Society of Newspaper Editors."
Apr. 1978. 6 pp.
Presented to the American Society of Newspaper Editors,
Washington, DC, Apr. 9, 1978.

2976   "New models of ethnic pluralism." Apr. 1978. 16+ pp.
Presented at an Interdisciplinary Symposium, Univ. of Nebraska,
Lincoln, NE, Apr. 4-7, 1978.

2977   "Intimacy in Catholic family life." June 1978. n.p. *
Presented at the Social Science/Theology Colloquium, Barat
College, Lake Forest, IL, June 1978.

2978   "Activism in a voluntary organization: geography versus
function." Apr. 1980. n.p. *
Presented at the 1980 Annual Meeting of the Population Assn. of
America, Denver, CO, Apr. 10-12, 1980.

2979   "The Madonna in North America. . . . " Apr. 1980. n.p.
Chicago: NORC, 1980. *
Presented at the National Education Assn. Symposium, "In Her
Image," Univ. of California at Santa Barbara, CA, Apr. 23,
1980.

2980   "Moral problems in the use of social science data in areas of
political controversy." Mar. 1981. n.p.
Presented at the Social Sciences and Public Policy Analysis

Meeting, The Hastings Center, Hastings-on-Hudson, NY, Mar. 19-20, 1981.

2981 "Religious imagery as a predictor variable in the General Social Survey." Oct. 1984. n.p.
Presented at the Plenary Session of the Society for the Scientific Study of Religion, Chicago, IL, Oct. 26, 1984.

2982 "The muse: handmaiden or partner?" Dec. 1986. n.p.
Commencement address presented at Bowling Green State Univ., Bowling Green, OH, Dec. 20, 1986.

2983 "Religion and values: three English-speaking nations." 1987. n.p. Chicago: NORC, 1987. *

2984 "Notes toward the sociology of prayer." 1991. n.p. *
Presented at the ISSP meeting in Dublin, 1991.

2985 "The faith we have lost." 1992. n.p. Chicago: NORC, 1992. *

2986 "Sex after sixty: a report." Aug. 1992. 9+ pp.

2987 "Address to the First Annual Conference of Victims of Clergy Abuse Linkup (VOCAL)." Oct. 1992. n.p. *
Presented at the First Annual Conference of Victims of Clergy Abuse Linkup (VOCAL), Arlington Heights, IL, Oct. 1992.

CHAPTER EIGHT

NEWSLETTERS

These newsletters, written by Andrew Greeley, and published by the Thomas More Press in Chicago and by Greeley himself, are of a somewhat ephemeral nature. For help with the documentation of the first four the compiler is indebted to the staff of the Thomas More Association and Press, in particular John Sprague.

2988   *Markings.*
        First issued Mar. 22, 1970. G wrote it every week until Jan. 29, 1984, and thereafter, the following: Dec. 15, 1985. Jan. 26, Feb. 23, Mar. 30, May 25, June 29, Aug. 10, Sept. 14, Nov. 2, Dec. 25, 1986. Mar. 1, Apr. 12, May 17, June 28, Aug. 2, Sept. 13, 1987. Apr. 10, July 3, Oct. 16, 1988.

        Portions of these issues have been reprinted in *Jesus Now: meditations by a modern pilgrim, Good News: further reflections by a modern pilgrim, Fifty-Two Gospel Meditations: by a modern pilgrim, Love in the Gospels: by a modern pilgrim,* and *When Life Hurts.*

        This newsletter is a homily resource which provides priests with scriptural reflections for every Sunday and Holy Day of the year. For some Holy Days issues were reprinted from the previous year "because the liturgical readings were the same from year to year and after doing them seven, eight, nine times, there wasn't too much different to say." (John Sprague).

2989   *Jesus Lives: personal meditations on Christ in today's world.*
        First issued Fall 1973. Nos. 1 to 30 written by G. Nos. 31 to 48 by G and Nancy McCready. There were 48 issues in all, 2 per month, 24 per year until Fall 1975.

Portions of these issues have been reprinted in *Christ for All Seasons: fifty-two personal meditations.*

2990   *Bottomline: a study course in basic Catholic beliefs.*
First issued Fall 1979. 21 issues published, written by G, to Fall 1980.

Reissued, in question and answer format, in *The Bottom Line Catechism for Contemporary Catholics.*

2991   *A Catholic Theology of Popular Culture.*
Written exclusively by G, Nos. I - IV issued in 1987. Nos. V-XX issued in 1988.

The fifth of the newsletters was originally entitled *Mail Box Parish.* The title was changed in the Passover issue, 1990, to *Mailbox Parish.* It was changed again in Vol. 2, No. 6 to *Andrew M. Greeley's Mailbox Parish.* All issues to date were written and published by Andrew Greeley, and distributed free of charge by Rosner & Liss Public Relations, Chicago, to whom the compiler is indebted for back issues and the following documentation.

As nearly as can be determined, the eighteen issues to date appeared as follows:

2992   *Andrew M. Greeley's Mailbox Parish.*

1989
Summer (as *Mail Box Parish*)
Christmas

1990
Vol. 1:   No. 4 Valentine's Day
          No. 5 Passover (as *Mailbox Parish*)
Vol. 2:   No. 2 Halloween

1991
Vol. 2:   No. 4 Voices from the Mailbox

No. 5 Mid Summer's Night
No. 6 Harvest Stories (as *Andrew M. Greeley's
    Mailbox Parish*)

Vol. 3:   No. 1 Autumn Songs

1992
Vol. 3:   No. 2 Epiphany--Darkness and Light
No. 3 March, St. Patrick and Other Saints
No. 4 May, Spring Again?
No. 5 August, Senior Lovers?
No. 6 Fall, Two Traditions on Marriage

1993
Vol. 4:   No. 1 New Year
No. 3 Holy Week
No. 4 Creation
No. 5 Noel!

In the first issue G made the following statement: "Mail Box Parish is a response to suggestions that have been made in many letters. It's an experiment, a mix of poetry and prose, story and nonfiction, reflections and hints of what's to come." And that is exactly what it has been so far.

CHAPTER NINE

MISCELLANEA

EDITORIALS

2993   "Editorial." *Ethnicity*, Vol. 1 Apr. 1974. pp. iii-iv.

2994   "Editorial." *Ethnicity*, Vol. 1 July 1974. pp. 109-110.

2995   "Editorial: ethnicity and politics." *Ethnicity*, Vol. 1 Oct. 1974. pp. 207-208.

2996   "Editorial: religion and ethnicity." *Ethnicity*, Vol. 2 June 1975. p. 123.

CONFERENCE PROCEEDINGS

2997   "Dynamic theology--today and tomorrow." *Theology in Revolution* ed. by George Devine. Staten Island, NY: Society of` St. Paul, 1970.
Proceedings of the College Theology Society Convention, Chicago, IL, Apr. 6-8, 1969. pp. 11-28.

2998   and Paul B. Sheatsley. "Trends in U. S. racial attitudes: changing attitudes of whites toward blacks."
Proceedings of the Twenty-seventh Annual Conference on Public Opinion Research. Public Opinion Quarterly, Vol. 36 Fall 1972. pp. 432-433.

2999   "Sociology and theology: some methodological questions."
Proceedings of the Catholic Theological Society of America, Vol. 32, 1977 ed. by Luke Saln. Toronto, June 15-18, 1977. pp. 31-54. (Reply Vol. 32, 1977.)

3000   Coleman, John A. "A response to Andrew Greeley."
            Proceedings of the Catholic Theological Society of America, Vol.
            32, 1977. pp. 55-71. (Reply to Vol. 32, 1977.)

3001   "The American achievement: a report from Great Ireland."
            *America and Ireland, 1776-1976: the American identity and the
            Irish connection* ed. by David N. Doyle and Owen D. Edwards.
            Westport, CT: Greenwood, 1980. pp. 231-246.
            Proceedings of the United States Bicentennial Conference of
            Cumann, Merriman, Ennis, Aug. 1976.

3002   "Immigration   and   religio-ethnic   groups: a   sociological
            reappraisal." *The Gateway: U. S. immigration issues and policies*
            ed. by Barry R. Chiswick. Washington: American Enterprise
            Institute for Public Policy Research, 1982. pp. 159-192.
            AEI Symposia: 811. Proceedings of a conference cosponsored by
            the American Enterprise Institute for Public Policy Research and
            the College of Business Administration, Univ. of Illinois at
            Chicago Circle, UICC, Chicago,IL, Apr. 10-11, 1980.

SOUND RECORDINGS

3003   "How to be a sociologist." Chicago: Thomas More Assn., 1972.
            n.t. Meditapes 89. *

3004   "Capital sins of the 70's." Chicago: Thomas More Assn., 1973.
            57 mins. Meditapes 145. *

3005   "Renewing the message." n.p. Thesis Theological Cassettes,
            1973. 22.5 mins. 4 no. 7. *

3006   "A contemporary examination of conscience." Chicago: Thomas
            More Assn., 1975. 30 mins. M2. *

3007   "Sex and religion." Chicago: Thomas More Assn., 1975. 30
            mins. M9. *

3008   "Spirituality for modern man." Chicago: Thomas More Assn.,
            1975. 29 mins. M17. *

3009 "Reflections on a priesthood for our time." Chicago: Thomas More Assn., n.d. 3 hours. M19. *

3010 "The joys of being Irish." Chicago: Thomas More Assn., 1975. 27 mins. M35. *

3011 "The sensuous Christian." Chicago: Thomas More Assn., 1975. 28 mins. M47. *

3012 "Why God: religion and the modern world." Chicago: Thomas More Assn., 1975. 6 hours. M127. *

3013 "What a modern Catholic believes about God." Chicago: Thomas More Assn., 1975. 3 hours. M153. *

3014 "First be reconciled." Chicago: Thomas More Assn., 1975. 16 mins. Meditapes 180. *

OTHER

3015 pseud. Laurence Moran. "Murder in the golden gardens." n.d. n.p. (Unpublished novel.) *

3016 "Liam and the new dog." n.d. n.p. (Unpublished children's story.)

3017 *The Magic Cup.* n.d. n.p. (Libretto.) *

3018 "Testimony with regard to H. R. 14910." Before the Committee on Education and Labor, General Subcommittee on Education, U. S. House of Representatives, Mar. 23, 1970. ("A bill to provide a program to improve the opportunity of students in elementary and secondary schools to study cultural heritages of the major ethnic groups in the Nation.")
Inserted into *Congressional Record.*

3019 "Appropriate images." *America*, Vol. 142 Feb. 23, 1980. p. 137. (Poem.)

3020 *Blessings: 1985 engagement calendar--an original blessing for each week in your year.* Chicago: Thomas More, 1984.

3021   "Dilemmas: Ethics." (Regular Feature.) *Woman's Day*, n.v.
        Sept. 4, 1990. p. 12; Oct. 2, 1990. p. 14; Oct. 30, 1990.
        p. 18; Nov. 27, 1990. p. 21; Dec. 25, 1990. p. 15.

3022   *"Chicago, the city that works."* n.d. n.p. (Unpublished play.)
        Performed May 16, 1991 at Quigley Preparatory Seminary,
        Chicago, IL. *

PART TWO:

SECONDARY SOURCES

CHAPTER TEN

BOOKS

3023   Kotre, John. *The Best of Times, the Worst of Times: Andrew Greeley and American Catholicism 1950-1975.* Chicago: Nelson-Hall, 1978.
Reprint. Chicago: Nelson-Hall, 1978. Paperbound.
In this "intellectual" biography, Kotre, associate professor of psychology, University of Michigan, deals exhaustively with G's more important writings, up to and including *The Mary Myth* (1977). He explores the underlying motivations and beliefs, and the circumstances surrounding the controversial works. In so doing he also presents a picture of the times in the American Catholic Church. Included is a listing of G's books published from 1959 to 1977. Bibliographical References. Index.

3024   Shafer, Ingrid H. *Eros and the Womanliness of God: Andrew Greeley's romances of renewal.* Chicago: Loyola Univ. Press, 1986.
Using extensive quotations, Professor Shafer (University of Science and Arts of Oklahoma) analyzes themes and symbols from G's novels from *The Magic Cup: an Irish legend* to *Rite of Spring.* She reflects on the analogical imagination, God as female, the passion of human sexuality, and symbols such as the boat, the lake and the Grail which G employs so often in his stories. Extensive Notes. Bibliography. Index.

3025   Shafer, Ingrid H. ed. *The Incarnate Imagination: essays in theology, the arts and social sciences.* In honor of Andrew Greeley, a festschrift. Bowling Green, OH: Bowling Green State Univ. Popular Press, 1988.
Reprint. Bowling Green, OH: Bowling Green State Univ. Press, 1988. Paperbound. *
Friends, colleagues and one relative, among them David Riesman,

Hans Kung, Jacob Neusner, Mary Durkin and Martin E. Marty
contribute essays in celebration of G's 60th birthday. All of them
deal in some way with creativity and the imagination. The various
sections link this creative imagination with the individual, society,
higher education, the institutional church, art, literature,
scripture, theology and play. Included is a "pictorial tribute," four
pictures of G by Chicago sculptor and artist John David Mooney.

3026   Shafer, Ingrid H. ed. *Andrew Greeley's World: an anthology of
        critical essays 1986-1988.*   New York: Warner, 1989.
        Paperbound.
        Many of these essays are reprinted with minor revisions, seven
        from *Journal of Popular Literature*, Spring/Summer 1988 and
        four from *Midwestern Miscellany* Vol. 15, 1987.
        A collection of essays by American scholars which explore
        Greeley's writings and their "theoretical context." Almost all have
        appeared elsewhere or were presented at conferences in the late
        1980s, many at the Popular Culture Assn. Meeting devoted to G's
        fiction in New Orleans, Louisiana, March 25, 1988. Contributors
        include Jacob Neusner, David Tracy, Michael T. Marsden and
        Roland E. Murphy.

CHAPTER ELEVEN

ESSAYS, PARTS OF BOOKS, DIRECTORIES

ESSAYS

3027   Chomsky, Noam. "On the limits of civil disobedience." *The Berrigans* ed. by William V. Casey and Philip Nobile. New York: Avon, 1971. pp. 37-59.
Chomsky argues that the war in Vietnam is illegitimate and, in a democracy, should be opposed by civil disobedience. He also contends that this form of protest, as made by the Berrigan brothers, does have an impact on government policy and public opinion. He refutes G's discussion of the Berrigans in general (the source of this discussion is not cited), calling it "frivolous and irresponsible. . . . " He also disagrees with G's assertion that such protests may have actually prolonged the war.

3028   May, John R. "The demonic in American cinema." *Religion in Film* ed. by John R. May and Michael Bird. Knoxville, TN: Univ. of Tennessee Press, 1982. pp. 79-100.
May begins his essay with a discussion of G's *New York Times* article "Why Hollywood Never Asks the God Question" (Jan. 18, 1976.) His answer to Greeley is that "It is more in the American cultural tradition . . . to raise the 'demon' question."

3029   Spencer, William D. "God as lover/God as sadist: Andrew Greeley's Blackie Ryan Series." *Mysterium and Mystery: the clerical crime novel* by William D. Spencer. Ann Arbor, MI: UMI Research, 1989. pp. 173-190 and *passim*.
Spencer analyzes two of G's novels, *Virgin and Martyr* and *Angels of September*, and the mystery, *Happy Are the Meek*, as well as the role of Blackie Ryan in the solving of their puzzles. He compares and contrasts him with other famous fictional detectives such as Father Brown and Nero Wolfe. Finally, he

considers Ryan's theology, which he finds ambivalent at times, and the philosophy of his ethics.

3030   Hoch, Edward D. "The priestly sleuths." *Synod of Sleuths: essays on Judeo-Christian detective fiction* ed. by Jon L. Breen and Martin H. Greenberg. Metuchen, NJ: Scarecrow, 1990. pp. 1-17.
Hoch outlines the development of the mystery story featuring detective-priests, or nuns, from Chesterton's Father Brown to G's Father (Monsignor, Bishop) Blackie Ryan. He briefly describes five Blackie Ryan stories (three novels: *Virgin and Martyr*, *Angels of September*, *Patience of a Saint;* and two mysteries: *Happy Are the Meek, Happy Are the Clean of Heart*) and judges *Virgin and Martyr* to be the best.

PARTS OF BOOKS

3031   "Greeley, Andrew M(oran)." *Current Biography Yearbook* ed. by Charles Moritz. New York: Wilson, 1972. pp. 189-192. Reprinted from *Current Biography*, Dec. 1972.

3032   Buenker, John D. and Nicholas C. Burckel. *Immigration and Ethnicity: a guide to information sources*. Vol. 1 in the American Government and History Information Guide Series. Detroit: Gale, 1977. *Passim*.
There are thirteen Greeley entries in this bibliography, five books and eight journal articles, in two sections headed "Old Immigration" and "Acculturation, Assimilation and Restriction."

3033   Hay, David. *Exploring Inner Space: scientists and religious experience*. Harmondsworth, Eng.: Penguin, 1982. *Passim*.

3034   "Greeley, Andrew M(oran) 1928--." *Contemporary Authors: a bio-bibliographical guide to current writers in fiction, general nonfiction, poetry, journalism, drama, motion pictures, television and other fields* ed. by Ann Evory. New Revision Series, Vol. 7. Detroit: Gale, 1982. pp. 199-204.

3035   "Andrew M(oran) Greeley 1928--." *Contemporary Literary Criticism: excerpts from criticism of the works of today's novelists, poets, playwrights, short story writers, filmmakers, script-writers, and other creative writers* ed. by Jean C. Stine. Vol. 28. Detroit: Gale, 1984. pp. 169-178.

3036   Kennedy, Eugene. *Tomorrow's Catholics Yesterday's Church.* New York: Harper & Row, 1988. *Passim.*

3037   Kennedy, Eugene. *Cardinal Bernardin.* Chicago: Bowes, 1989. pp. 87-90, 169-173, 178-182, 187-222 and *passim.*

3038   Fanning, Charles. *The Irish Voice in America: Irish-American fiction from the 1760s to the 1980s.* Lexington, KY: Univ. Press of Kentucky, 1990. pp. 325-326.

3039   Sipe, A. W. Richard. *A Secret World: sexuality and the search for celibacy.* New York: Brunner/Mazel, 1990. *Passim.*

3040   Frisbie, Margery. *An Alley in Chicago: the ministry of a city priest.* Kansas City, MO: Sheed & Ward, 1991. *Passim.*

3041   Harpur, Tom. *Life after Death.* Toronto: McClelland & Stewart, 1991. *Passim.*

3042   Ryan, Bryan, ed. *Major 20th-Century Writers: a selection of sketches from Contemporary Authors.* Detroit: Gale, 1991. pp. 1258-1261. *
Reprinted from *Contemporary Authors: a bio-bibliographical guide to current writers in fiction, general nonfiction, poetry, journalism, drama, motion pictures, television, and other fields.*

3043   Berry, Jason. *Lead Us Not into Temptation: Catholic priests and the sexual abuse of children.* New York: Doubleday, 1992. *Passim.*

3044   Burkett, Elinor and Frank Bruni. *A Gospel of Shame: children, sexual abuse and the Catholic Church.* New York: Viking, 1993. *Passim.*

DIRECTORIES

3045   *American Men of Science: a biographical directory*. Vol. 1 The Social and Behavioral Sciences A-K. 11th ed. New York: Bowker, 1968. p. 596.

3046   *World Who's Who in Science*. Chicago: Marquis Who's Who, 1968. p. 696.

3047   *Contemporary Authors: a bio-bibliographical guide to current authors and their works* ed. by Barbara Harte and Carolyn Riley. Vols. 5-8 First Revision. Detroit: Gale, 1969. p. 473.

3048   *Who's Who in America*. Vol. 1. 37th ed. 1972-1973. Chicago: Marquis Who's Who, 1972. p. 1227.

3049   *American Men and Women of Science*. Vol. 1 The Social and Behavioral Sciences A-K. 12th ed. New York: Bowker, 1973. p. 863.

3050   *Who's Who in America*. Vol. 1. 38th ed. 1974-1975. Chicago: Marquis Who's Who, 1974. p. 1217.

3051   *Who's Who in America*. Vol. 1. 39th ed. 1976-1977. Chicago: Marquis Who's Who, 1976. p. 1226.

3052   *Who's Who in Religion*. 2d ed. 1977. Chicago: Marquis Who's Who, 1977. p. 249.

3053   *American Men and Women of Science*. Social and Behavioral Sciences. 13th ed. New York: Bowker, 1978. p. 469.

3054   *Who's Who in America*. Vol. 1. 40th ed. 1978-1979. Chicago: Marquis Who's Who, 1978. p. 1278.

3055   *The American Catholic Who's Who*. Vol. 23 1980-1981. Washington, DC: National Catholic News Service, 1979. p. 306.

3056   *Who's Who in America*. Vol. 1. 41st ed. 1980-1981. Chicago: Marquis Who's Who, 1980. p. 1332.

3057 *Who's Who in America*. Vol. 1. 42d ed. 1982-1983. Chicago: Marquis Who's Who, 1982. p. 1290.

3058 *Who's Who in America*. Vol. 1. 43d ed. 1984-1985. Chicago: Marquis Who's Who, 1984. p. 1278.

3059 *Who's Who in Religion*. 3d ed. 1985. Chicago: Marquis Who's Who, 1985. p. 138.

3060 *Who's Who in America*. Vol. 1. 44th ed. 1986-1987. Wilmette, IL: Marquis Who's Who, 1986. p. 1097.

3061 *Who's Who in America*. Vol. 1. 45th ed. 1988-1989. Wilmette, IL: Marquis Who's Who, 1988. p. 1211.

3062 *Who's Who in Religion*. 4th ed. 1992-1993. Wilmette, IL: Marquis Who's Who, 1992. p. 193.

3063 *Who's Who in the Midwest*. 23d ed. 1992-1993. Wilmette, IL: Marquis Who's Who, 1992. p. 261.

CHAPTER TWELVE

PERIODICAL ARTICLES

3064   O'Gara, James. "Criticizing the critics." *Commonweal*, Vol. 77 Oct. 26, 1962. pp. 110. (Reply Dec. 7, 1962.)

3065   Greeley, Andrew. "Catholic self-criticism." *Commonweal*, Vol. 77 Dec. 7, 1962. pp. 280+. (Reply to Oct. 26, 1962.)

3066   Herr, Dan. "Priest of tomorrow?" *St. Jude*, Vol. 29 May 1963. pp. 7-11. *

3067   McNamara, Robert J. "Intellectual values: campus and seminary." *Sociological Analysis*, Vol. 25 Winter 1964. pp. 200-211.

3068   "Are the schools worth it?" *America*, Vol. 111 Sept. 19, 1964. p. 286.

3069   "If, then, on the other hand, it is interesting to note." *Ave Maria*, Vol. 100 Sept. 19, 1964. p. 17. (Catholic education.)

3070   Donovan, John D. "Creating anti-intellectuals?" *Commonweal*, Vol. 81 Oct. 2, 1964. pp. 37-39. (Reply Dec. 18, 1964.)

3071   Grant, Edward J. "Parochial schools." *Commonweal*, Vol. 81 Dec. 18, 1964. pp. 423-424. (Reply to Oct. 2, 1964.)

3072   Callahan, Daniel. "The schools." *Commonweal*, Vol. 81 Jan. 8, 1965. pp. 473-476. (Replies Feb. 5, 1965.)

3073   Fleming, Thomas J. "Most intelligent." *Commonweal*, Vol. 81 Feb. 5, 1965. pp. 594-595. (Reply to Jan. 8, 1965.)

3074 Sister Teresa Mary. "Unscientific, prejudiced." *Commonweal*, Vol. 81 Feb. 5, 1965. p. 594. (Reply to Jan. 8, 1965.)

3075 O'Gara, James. "An editorial dissent." *Commonweal*, Vol. 81 Feb. 19, 1965, p. 657. (Catholic education.)

3076 "Using the Greeley-Rossi report." *America*, Vol. 115 Aug. 13, 1966. p. 150.

3077 Cross, Robert D. "The Greeley-Rossi report." *Commonweal*, Vol. 84 Sept. 16, 1966. pp. 577-579.

3078 O'Gara, James. "Adolescent Catholicism." *Commonweal*, Vol. 85 Nov. 25, 1966. p. 217.

3079 "Fr. Greeley's lesson." *Triumph*, Vol. 3 Jan. 1968. p. 8.

3080 Means, Richard L. "A funny thing happened on the way to the faculty forum." *America*, Vol. 118 May 25, 1968. pp. 702-703. (*The Changing Catholic College*.)

3081 "Slandering the Poles." *American Polonia Reporter*, Vol. 13 Autumn 1968. n.p.

3082 Cogley, John. "The youngest old Irish pastor." *National Catholic Reporter*, Vol. 5 Dec. 18, 1968. p. 8.

3083 "Roman Catholics: clouded future." *Time*, Vol. 93 Jan. 10, 1969. p. 63.

3084 Cogley, John. "American Catholic backgrounds." *National Catholic Reporter*, Vol. 5 Feb. 26, 1969. pp. 8-9.

3085 Steinfels, Peter. "Andrew Greeley, divine sociologist." *Commonweal*, Vol. 92 June 12, 1970. p. 286.

3086 Hoyt, Robert. "Notes for the record: in explication of A. Greeley." *National Catholic Reporter*, Vol. 7 Mar. 5, 1971. p. 12.

3087 Hickey, John. "Greeley gains status among English." *National Catholic Reporter*, Vol. 7 Mar. 5, 1971. p. 13.

3088 "Bishops' election urged as priority." *National Catholic Reporter,* Vol. 8 Feb. 28, 1972. pp. 1+.

3089 "Greeley: ask new questions." *National Catholic Reporter,* Vol. 8 Apr. 21, 1972. p. 6.

3090 "Greeley, Andrew M(oran)." *Current Biography,* Vol. 33 Dec. 1972. pp. 11-13.

3091 Dominick, Abel. "The four-foot bookshelf by Father Greeley." *Chicago,* Vol. 22 Mar./Apr. 1973. pp. 44+.

3092 Segal, Andrew and Don Rose. "Why no protests over Andy Greeley?" *Hyde Park-Kenwood Voices,* Vol. 8 July 1973. p. 1.

3093 Sutor, David. "Greeley denied tenure for 8th time." *National Catholic Reporter,* Vol. 9 Aug. 31, 1973. p. 16.

3094 Baum, Gregory. "The theology of Andrew Greeley." *Ecumenist,* Vol. 11 Sept./Oct. 1973. pp. 85-90. (Excerpted from the foreword to *The New Agenda: a proposal for a new approach to fundamental issues in contemporary times.*)

3095 "Andrew Greeley, Inc." *Time,* Vol. 103 Jan. 7, 1974. pp. 75+.

3096 McNamara, Patrick H., Martin E. Marty and Samuel A. Mueller. "Review symposium: the sociology of religion of Andrew M. Greeley." Ed. by Jeffrey K. Hadden. *Journal for the Scientific Study of Religion,* Vol. 13 Mar. 1974. pp. 75-97. (Reply June 1974.)

3097 "The Andrew Greeley popularity poll." *Catholic Messenger,* Vol. 92 Apr. 25 1974. p. 8. (Letters to the editor asking for column back.)

3098 "Welcome back, Fr. Greeley." *Catholic Messenger,* Vol. 92 Apr. 25, 1974. p. 8. (Editorial.)

3099 Greeley, Andrew. "Andrew Greeley replies to his critics." *Journal for the Scientific Study of Religion,* Vol. 13 June 1974. pp. 228-231. (Reply to Mar. 1974.)

3100   Star, Jack. "Greeley the go-go priest." *The Chicagoan*, Vol. 1
        July 1974. pp. 46-49.

3101   "Our man for all seasons." *Chicago Tribune*, July 12, 1974. p.
        18.

3102   Taylor, James A. "Giants of our faiths." *U. S. Catholic*, Vol.
        39 Dec. 1974. pp. 18-23.

3103   Novak, Michael. "The communal Catholic." *Commonweal*, Vol.
        101 Jan. 17, 1975. pp. 321+.

3104   Porvaznik, Pamela. "Priest in print: his biting column is defying
        taboo." *The Sunday News Magazine* (Detroit), Feb. 2, 1975.
        pp. 16-18+.
        Reprinted in *Biography News*, Mar./Apr. 1975 as "His biting
        column is defying taboo."

3105   Royko, Mike. "Fr. Greeley and the Poles." *Chicago Daily
        News*, Mar. 11, 1975. p.3.

3106   "Greeley-Royko: a feud or a put on?" *Chicago Tribune*, Mar.
        16, 1975. Sec. 2 p. 4.

3107   Porvaznik, Pamela. "His biting column is defying taboo."
        Biography News, Vol. 2 Mar./Apr. 1975. pp. 338-340.
        Appeared in Sunday News Magazine (Detroit), Feb. 2, 1975 as
        "Priest in print: his biting column is defying taboo."

3108   Robison, James. "Cody is lashed as 'madcap tyrant': letter by
        Father Greeley." *Chicago Tribune*, July 24, 1975. p. 5.

3109   Enright, Vincent L. "Father Greeley rattles the cages: liberation
        theology." *The Priest*, Vol. 31 Oct. 1975. pp. 28-33.

3110   Zutter, Albert de. "Catholic left called impotent." *National
        Catholic Reporter,* Vol. 12 Nov. 7, 1975. p. 2.

3111   "Sister-sociologist chides Greeley for suggesting end to world
        view." *National Catholic Reporter,* Vol. 12 Nov. 21, 1975. p.
        2.

Reply to "An address to the Catholic Committee on Urban Ministry" (2966).

3112   Brown, Robert M. "Father Greeley and the WCC." *Christianity and Crisis*, Vol. 35 Dec. 22, 1975. pp. 306-307.

3113   "Greeley *et al.*" *Commonweal*, Vol. 103 Apr. 23, 1976. pp. 261-262. (*Catholic Schools in a Declining Church.*)

3114   Harris, T. George. "Nothing but a loud-mouthed Irish priest." *Psychology Today*, Vol. 10 June 1976. p. 46.

3115   "Raising Catholic consciousness." *National Review*, Vol. 28 July 23, 1976. pp. 774-775.

3116   Beckwith, Barbara. "Greeley's study on Catholic schools: where do we go from here; an overview by Barbara Beckwith." *St. Anthony Messenger*, Vol. 84 Aug. 1976. pp. 20-23. (*Catholic Schools in a Declining Church.*) (Replies Aug. 1976.)

3117   Harper, Mary-Angela. "A response by Mary-Angela Harper." *St. Anthony Messenger*, Vol. 84 Aug. 1976. pp. 25-26. (Reply to Aug. 1976.)

3118   Sullivan, Walter F. "A response by Bishop Walter Sullivan." *St. Anthony Messenger*, Vol. 84 Aug. 1976. p. 24. (Reply to Aug. 1976.)

3119   Fox, Thomas C. "The company priest who discovered (and told) why half America's Catholics no longer attend mass." *The Free Press* (Detroit), Sept. 5, 1976. pp. 15-17.

3120   Kotre, John N. "Andrew Greeley and the recurring dream." *National Catholic Reporter*, Vol. 13 Feb. 25, 1977. pp. 7-9+.

3121   McCourt, Kathleen. "The place of parochial schools in the Church: discussion of a study of American Catholics by the National ORC in 1974." *Origins*, Vol. 6 Apr. 28, 1977. pp. 709+. (*Catholic Schools in a Declining Church.*)

3122   "Fr. Greeley's broadsword." *Catholic Messenger*, June 9, 1977.

p. 8. (U. S. bishops bicentennial Call to Action program.)

3123 "Andy's answers." *Time*, Vol. 112 July 10, 1978. pp. 70+.

3124 Gleason, Philip. "Review article: Greeley watching." *Review of Politics*, Vol. 40 Oct. 1978. pp. 528-540. (Review of G's writing, particularly *The American Catholic: a social portrait*.)

3125 Larson, Roy. "3 Popes tried to fire Cody: priest." *Chicago Sun Times*, Apr. 12, 1979. pp. 5+.

3126 Larson, Roy. "Cody source of reports on ouster, Greeley says." *Chicago Sun Times*, June 6, 1979. p. 10.

3127 Deedy, John. "American letter." The Tablet (London), Vol. 234 Jan. 26, 1980. pp. 80-81.

3128 Jones, E. Michael. "Vox populi vox Dei: Father Greeley's sociological theology." *Homiletic & Pastoral Review*, Vol. 81 Apr. 1981. pp. 65-69.

3129 Beifuss, Joan T. "Priests hit Greeley's opinion of Maryknoll." *National Catholic Reporter,* Vol. 17 May 22, 1981. p. 24.

3130 "A priestly novelist, gluttony, and other cardinal sins." *Chicago*, Vol. 30 June 1981. p. 12.

3131 Ryan, Michael. "In the fictional church of Father Andrew Greeley, even the Cardinal sins." *People*, Vol. 15 June 8, 1981. pp. 32-35.

3132 McDowell, Edwin. "Behind the best sellers." *New York Times Biographical Service*, Vol. 12 July 1981. pp. 941-942. From the *New York Times Book Review*, July 19, 1981.

3133 McDowell, Edwin. "Andrew M. Greeley." *New York Times Book Review*, July 19, 1981. p. 22. (Reply Aug. 16, 1981.)

3134 Coburn, Randy Sue. "Greeley: priestly author breaks cardinal rule?" *Washington Star*, July 26, 1981. p. ?.

3135   Scott, Ernest L., Jr. "Previous works." *New York Times Book Review*, Aug. 16, 1981. p. 30. (Reply to July 19, 1981.)

3136   Mullen, William. "Greeley denies being behind investigations of Cody." *Chicago Tribune*, Sept. 26, 1981. p. 3.

3137   "Greeley: he's a 'marginal man'." *Chicago Tribune*, Sept. 27, 1981. p. 14.

3138   Mullen, William. "Article charges Greeley plotted Cody 'scandal'." *Chicago Tribune*, Sept. 27, 1981. pp. 1+.

3139   "Text of Greeley statement." *Chicago Tribune*, Sept. 27, 1981. p. 14.

3140   Warden, Rob. "The plot to get Cody." *Chicago Lawyer*, Vol. 4 Oct. 1981. pp. 3-6.

3141   McClory, Robert J. "'Greeley tapes' tangle Chicago web." *National Catholic Reporter*, Vol. 17 Oct. 2, 1981. p. 3.

3142   McClory, Robert J. "Greeley tried press campaign against Cody." *National Catholic Reporter*, Vol. 17 Oct. 9, 1981. p. 3.

3143   Woodward, Kenneth L. and Frank Maier. "The power of the prelate." *Newsweek*, Vol. 98 Oct. 12, 1981. pp. 117-118.

3144   McDowell, Edwin. "Greeley: new novel, new controversy?" *New York Times Biographical Service*, Vol. 13 Mar. 1982. pp. 339-341. *
        From the *New York Times*, Mar. 22, 1982.

3145   McDowell, Edwin. "Father Greeley: new novel, new controversy?" *New York Times*, Mar. 22, 1982. Sec. III p. 11.

3146   Buursma, Bruce. "The many faces of Andrew Greeley." *Chicago Tribune*, Apr. 4, 1982. Sec. 9 pp. 10-14+.

3147   Roberts, Eleanor. "A priest and his sexy novels." *Herald American* (Boston) Apr. 18, 1982. p. ?.

3148   Klein, Frederick C. "Contentious cleric: Andrew Greeley wins fame as a priest who writes steamy novels." *Wall Street Journal*, Apr. 20, 1982. pp. 1+.

3149   Farrell, Michael J. "The resilient Father Andrew Greeley." *National Catholic Reporter*, Vol. 18 Apr. 30, 1982. pp. 9-11+.

3150   Lessner, Richard. "It is written." *Arizona Republic* (Phoenix), May 15, 1982. p. ?.

3151   McConnell, Frank. "Boiling the Irish Catholic pot." *Commonweal*, Vol. 109 June 4, 1982. pp. 342-344.

3152   Mohs, Mayo. "The luck of Andrew Greeley." *Time*, Vol. 120 July 12, 1982. pp. 70+.

3153   Buursma, Bruce. "Libel suit filed against Greeley." *Chicago Tribune*, July 22, 1982. Sec. 2 p. 3.

3154   Varacelli, Joseph A. "The future of U. S. Catholicism." *Ecumenist*, Vol. 20 July/Aug. 1982. pp. 71-75.

3155   Emswiler, James P. "How to pray as a couple: most couples don't pray together, even though they wish they could." *U. S. Catholic*, Vol. 47 Aug. 1982. pp. 26-29.

3156   Woodward, Kenneth L. "Trials of a novelist-priest." *Newsweek*, Vol. 100 Aug. 16, 1982. p. 61.

3157   Bryk, Anthony S. and Peter B. Holland. "The implications of Greeley's latest research." *Momentum*, Vol. 13 Oct. 1982. pp. 8-11.
Condensed in *Education Digest*, Mar. 1983.

3158   "Priest-novelist." *The Tablet* (London), Vol. 236 Oct. 23, 1982. p. 1062.

3159   Higgins, George. "Greeley's aim was off in picking on this man." *Catholic Messenger*, Jan. 13, 1983. p. 9.

3160   Bryk, Anthony S. and Peter B. Holland. "Catholic high schools

and minority students." *Education Digest*, Vol. 48 Mar. 1983. pp. 26-28.
Condensed from *Momentum*, Oct. 1982.

3161   Dunlap, John R. "Andy's ego." *American Spectator*, Vol. 16 Mar. 1983. pp. 26-28. (Includes reviews of *The Cardinal Sins* and *Thy Brother's Wife*.)

3162   Petosa, Jason. "Priestly vocations: options and antidotes." *National Catholic Reporter*, Vol. 19 Mar. 4, 1983. p. 12.

3163   Woods, Richard. "'What has changed is us.'" *National Catholic Reporter*, Vol. 19 Apr. 1, 1983. p. 13.

3164   McDowell, Edwin. "Prolificity." *New York Times Book Review*, June 12, 1983. p. 46.

3165   Whalen, William J. "How Catholic prayer became a Mass movement." *U. S. Catholic*, Vol. 48 Sept. 1983. pp. 32-39.

3166   Guinn, John. "He leadeth us beyond the blond to a priestly drama." *Detroit Free Press*, Sept. 4, 1983. Sec. B p. 5. *

3167   Kelly, Brian J. "A question of sex and the single priest." *Macleans*, Vol. 96 Oct. 17, 1983. pp. 14-18.

3168   Brune, Tom. "Successful author-priest uses sociology in fiction." *Boston Globe*, Dec. 18, 1983. p. 18.

3169   Granger, Bill. "Greeley's lofty sermon from Mt. Hancock." *Chicago Tribune*, Jan. 4, 1984. p. 2. (Reply Jan. 29, 1984.)

3170   Buursma, Bruce. "Greeley gives $850,000. for U. of C. chair." *Chicago Tribune*, Jan. 24, 1984. p. 9.

3171   Greeley, Andrew. "Rev. Greeley's response to Bill Granger." *Chicago Tribune*, Jan. 29, 1984. Sec. 5 p. 2. (Reply to Jan. 4, 1984.)

3172   Green, Laura. "Who is Father Andrew Greeley?" *Chicago Sun-Times* Feb. 5, 1984. pp. 1+.

3173 O'Hare, Joseph A. "Of many things." *America*, Vol. 150 Mar. 3, 1984. p. 140.

3174 "Dancing with Father Greeley and his Lord." *Chicago*, Vol. 33 May 1984. p. 14.

3175 Harris, Mark. "Novelist, journalist, sociologist, priest: Andrew Greeley." *New York Times Biographical Service*, Vol. 15 May 1984. pp. 652-658. *
From the *New York Times Magazine*, May 6, 1984.

3176 Harris, Mark. "Andrew Greeley: novelist, journalist, sociologist, priest." *New York Times Magazine*, May 6, 1984. pp. 34-37+.

3177 Harris, Mark. "The sexy work of a writer-priest." *San Francisco Chronicle*, May 8, 1984. p. ?.

3178 Smith, Sam. "Big talkers." *Chicago Tribune Magazine*, May 20, 1984. pp. 16-21+.

3179 Barr, Donald. "Sin and salvation--the novels of Andrew M. Greeley." *New York Times Book Review*, June 17, 1984. pp. 12-13. (Reply July 15, 1984.)

3180 Johnston, James E. "Priests, prose, and preachment." *Theology Today*, Vol. 41 July 1984. pp. 161-170.

3181 Greeley, Andrew M. "Sociology, religion and the novel." *New York Times Book Review*, July 15, 1984. p. 31. (Reply to June 17, 1984.)

3182 Weatherby, W. J. "The priest with a passionate pen." *Guardian*, Aug. 23, 1984. p. 10.

3183 Sheehan, Thomas. "Greeley's agnosticism: have story, will travel." *Commonweal*, Vol. 111 Sept. 21, 1984. pp. 500-501. Discussion of "The ways of knowing," Aug. 10, 1984 (742).

3184 Buursma, Bruce. "More gospel according to Father Greeley." *Chicago Tribune*, Jan. 5, 1985. p. 6.

3185   Langan, John. "Andrew Greeley vs. the bishops." *America*,
        Vol. 152 May 4, 1985. pp. 354-355.
        Discussion of "The bishops and the economy: a 'radical' dissent,"
        Jan. 5, 1985 (748).

3186   Evans, Fallon. "The convent wall and the connubial bed: a
        literary history." *New Catholic World*, Vol. 228 July/Aug. 1985.
        pp. 153-156.

3187   O'Rourke, William. "Catholics coming of age: the literary
        consequences." *New Catholic World*, Vol. 228 July/Aug. 1985.
        pp. 148-152.

3188   Shafer, Ingrid H. "The Catholic imaginative universe in the
        novels of Andrew Greeley." *Quarterly Journal of Ideology*, Vol.
        10 n.m. 1986. pp. 71-83. *
        A version appears in *Andrew Greeley's World: an anthology of
        critical essays 1986-1988.*

3189   Shafer, Ingrid H. "Catholic priests on Andrew Greeley."
        Chicago Studies, Vol. 25 Aug. 1986. pp. 188-197.

3190   "A non-fiction Greeley drama." *Chicago Tribune*, Sept. 23,
        1986. Sec. 3 pp. 1+.

3191   Deedy, John. "Andrew Greeley, this is my life!" *Commonweal*,
        Vol. 113 Oct. 24, 1986. pp. 560-561.

3192   McCann, Dennis P. "New face on an old criticism."
        Commonweal, Vol. 113 Dec. 26, 1986. pp. 707-709.

3193   Anderson, David D. "The Greeley phenomenon, or some parish!
        some priest!" *Midwestern Miscellany*, Vol. 15 1987. pp. 7-10.
        *
        A version appears in *Andrew Greeley's World: an anthology of
        critical essays 1986-1988.*

3194   Bresnahan, Roger J. "The sacramental body: Andrew Greeley's
        autobiography." *Midwestern Miscellany*, Vol. 15 1987. pp. 11-
        18. *
        A version appears in *Andrew Greeley's World: an anthology of
        critical essays 1986-1988.*

3195 Julius, Patricia W. "Andrew M. Greeley: ethnic historian or social reformer." *Midwestern Miscellany*, Vol. 15 1987. pp. 19-24. *
A version appears in *Andrew Greeley's World: an anthology of critical essays 1986-1988.*

3196 Rout, Kathleen. "Renew your people, O Lord: Andrew Greeley's Passover trilogy." *Midwestern Miscellany*, Vol. 15 1987. pp. 25-32. *
A version appears in *Andrew Greeley's World: an anthology of critical essays 1986-1988.*

3197 Finley, Mitchel B. "What makes Andrew Greeley tick?" *St. Anthony Messenger*, Vol. 95 June 1987. pp. 34-40.

3198 Conroy, John. "Cardinal sins." *Reader*, Vol. 16 June 5, 1987. pp. 1+.

3199 Stange, Mary Z. "Little shop of horrors." *Commonweal*, Vol. 114 July 17, 1987. pp. 412-417. (Replies Oct. 9, 1987.)

3200 Achenbach, Anne D. "Enchanting heroines." *Commonweal*, Vol. 114 Oct. 9, 1987. p. 546. (Reply to July 17, 1987.)

3201 Gallagher, Michael. "A clear-eyed view." *Commonweal*, Vol. 114 Oct. 9, 1987. p. 546. (Reply to July 17, 1987.)

3202 Maran, Linda. "Unmasking fantasy." *Commonweal*, Vol. 114 Oct. 9, 1987. pp. 546+. (Reply to July 17, 1987.)

3203 Marsden, Madonna P. and Michael T. Marsden. "Women in control." *Commonweal*, Vol. 114 Oct. 9, 1987. p. 546. (Reply to July 17, 1987.)

3204 Taylor, Robert. "Authors appearing." *Boston Globe*, Nov. 15, 1987. p. 102.

3205 Neusner, Jacob. "Andrew M. Greeley at sixty." *America*, Vol. 158 Jan. 23, 1988. pp. 63+.

3206 Becker, Allienne R. "'Virgin and Martyr': a story of God?"

Journal of Popular Literature, Vol. 4 Spring/Summer 1988. pp. 49-58. *

A version appears in *Andrew Greeley's World: an anthology of critical essays 1986-1988.*

3207   Browne, Ray B. "Expanding parameters of crime fiction: George C. Chesboro and Andrew Greeley." *Journal of Popular Literature*, Vol. 4 Spring/Summer 1988. pp. 59-76. *

A version appears in *Andrew Greeley's World: an anthology of critical essays 1986-1988.*

3208   Kaler, Anne K. "The 'Legenda Aurea' lives again: Andrew Greeley's use of the saints' lives in his novels." *Journal of Popular Literature*, Vol. 4 Spring/Summer 1988. pp. 77-106. *

A version appears in *Andrew Greeley's World: an anthology of critical essays 1986-1988.*

3209   Kelly, Philip H. "Sin, guilt and forgiveness in Greeley's Passover trilogy." *Journal of Popular Literature*, Vol. 4 Spring/Summer 1988. pp. 37-48. *

A version appears in *Andrew Greeley's World: an anthology of critical essays 1986-1988.*

3210   Lowry, Mary Ann. "Parables of love: the fiction of Andrew M. Greeley." *Journal of Popular Literature*, Vol. 4 Spring/Summer 1988. pp. 25-36. *

A version appears in *Andrew Greeley's World: an anthology of critical essays 1986-1988.*

3211   Marsden, Michael T. "The feminine divine: a search for unity in Andrew Greeley's Passover trilogy." *Journal of Popular Literature*, Vol. 4 Spring/Summer 1988. pp. 13-24. *

A version appears in *Andrew Greeley's World: an anthology of critical essays 1986-1988.*

3212   Shafer, Ingrid H. "The dance of creation and incarnation: God, woman, and sex in the novels of Andrew Greeley." *Journal of Popular Literature*, Vol. 4 Spring/Summer 1988. pp. 107-124. *

A version appears in *Andrew Greeley's World: an anthology of critical essays 1986-1988.*

3213 McClory, Robert. "The trial: the case of the Greeley 'plot' and the 'hotshot' reporter." *National Catholic Reporter,* Vol. 24 Mar. 4, 1988. pp. 9-11.

3214 Reich, Howard. "Greeley on the Grail: two priests turn Irish legend into an opera." *Chicago Tribune,* Mar. 13, 1988. Arts Sec. p. 12. (Opera *The Magic Cup.*)

3215 Lowe, Charlotte. "Greeley's passionate prose." *Citizen* (Tucson, AR), May 3, 1988. p. ?.

3216 Garascia, Anthony. "Forum: the RCIA as conversion therapy." *Worship,* Vol. 62 July 1988. pp. 360-365.
Comment on "Empirical liturgy: the search for grace." *America,* Nov. 21, 1987 (777).

3217 McClory, Robert. "The Winters vs. Greeley libel suit." *Columbia Journalism Review,* Vol. 27 Sept./Oct. 1988. pp. 39-40.

3218 Scaglione, Donna. "A priest cut from different cloth: author Andrew Greeley has his own ideas about the Catholic church." *Enterprise* (Brockton, MA), May 19, 1989. p. ?.

3219 Woods, Richard. "Clerical celibacy has never been a well-kept discipline." *National Catholic Reporter,* Vol. 26 Mar. 2, 1990. p. 14.
Comment on "Bishops paralyzed over heavily gay priesthood." Nov. 10, 1989 (806).

3220 Bering-Jensen, Helle. "Catholic soul-searching in America." *Insight,* Vol. 6 May 14, 1990. pp. 52-54.

3221 Higgins, Richard. "High-powered priest cites opinion polls to defend faith." *Boston Globe,* May 26, 1990. p. 4.

3222 Seaver, Lynda. "World according to Greeley: sex, sins and sermonizing." *Tribune* (Oakland, CA), June 6, 1990. p. ?.

3223 Donohoe, Cathryn. "The devils and angels of Andrew Greeley." *Washington Times,* June 12, 1990. p. ?.

3224   Martinez, Demetria. "Eroticism: reconnecting faith and flesh for God's sake and ours also." *National Catholic Reporter,* Vol. 27 Mar. 22, 1991. p. 25.
Comment on "Healthy marriages are romantic ones, requiring mix of religion and sex." Jan. 25 1991 (832).

3225   Waznak, Robert P. "How Andrew Greeley can improve the quality of the Sunday homily." *New Theology Review*, Vol. 4 Aug. 1991. pp. 70-81. *

3226   Wind, James P. "Clergy lives: portraits from modern fiction." *Christian Century*, Vol. 108 Sept. 4, 1991. pp. 805-810.

3227   McBrien, Richard P. "If conservative Catholics are few, whom do the bishops lead?" *National Catholic Reporter,* Vol. 27 Oct. 11, 1991. p. 2.
Comment on "Who are the Catholic 'conservatives'?" *America*, Sept. 21, 1991 (843).

3228   Murnion, Philip J. "A peaceful reflection on a modest proposal." *America*, Vol. 166 June 20, 1992. pp. 528-529.
Comment on "A modest proposal for the reform of Catholic schools." Mar. 21, 1992 (860).

3229   Sipe, A. W. R. and B. C. Lamb. "Chesterton's Brown & Greeley's Blackie: two very different detectives." *Commonweal*, Vol. 119 Aug. 14, 1992. pp. 18-19+.

3230   Grossman, Ron. "Publish and parish." *Chicago Tribune*, Aug. 18, 1992. Sec. 5 pp. 1-2.

3231   Woodward, Kenneth L. and Karen Springen. "Better than a gold watch." *Newsweek*, Vol. 120 Aug. 24, 1992. p. 71.

3232   Fein, Esther B. "A priest polls the public." *New York Times*, Mar. 24, 1993. Sec. III p. 20.

3233   Sprague, Stephanie. "Church won't face issue of abuse: author." *The Gazette* (Montreal), May 13, 1993. p. 7.

3234   McCarthy, Tim. "Stories are Fr. Quixote's bread and wine." *National Catholic Reporter*, Vol. 29 May 28, 1993. pp. 24-26.

CHAPTER THIRTEEN

NEWS REPORTS

3235 "Father Greeley finds parochial schools do influence religious behavior." *Catholic School Journal*, Vol. 64 Nov. 1964. pp. 14+.

3236 Conley, W. "The effects of Catholic education." *Catholic School Journal*, Vol. 64 Dec. 1964. p. 4.

3237 Leo, John. "News and views." *Commonweal*, Vol. 83 Feb. 25, 1966. p. 596. (Excerpts from *The Education of Catholic Americans*.)

3238 "Study evaluates Catholic schools." *New York Times*, July 25, 1966. p. 29.

3239 "Roman Catholics: degrees of devotion." *Time*, Vol. 88 July 29, 1966. p. 49.

3240 Fiske, Edward B. "A hard look at religious education." *New York Times*, July 31, 1966. Sec. IV p. 10.

3241 "Parochial benefits." *Newsweek*, Vol. 68 Aug. 1, 1966. p. 77.

3242 "The Greeley-Rossi report on Catholic schools." *America*, Vol. 115 Aug. 6, 1966. p. 128. (Editorial.)

3243 Leo, John. "News and views." *Commonweal*, Vol. 84 Aug. 19, 1966. p. 514. (Greeley-Rossi report.)

3244 Currivan, Gene. "Priest criticizes Catholic schools." *New York Times*, Feb. 25, 1968. p. 14.

3245 "Roman Catholics: clouded future." *Time*, Vol. 93 Jan. 10, 1969. p. 63.

3246 "Whites' hostility laid to insecurity." *New York Times*, May 17, 1969. p. 40.

3247 "A comment by Fr. Greeley." *America*, Vol. 121 Sept. 6, 1969. p. 129.

3248 "Catholics are shaken by the Berrigan case." *New York Times*, Feb. 6, 1971. p. 34.

3249 Fiske, Edward B. "Most U. S. priests found to oppose birth curb ban." *New York Times*, Apr. 15, 1971. pp. 1+.

3250 "To save a bankrupt." *Time*, Vol. 99 Feb. 21, 1972. p. 79.

3251 "Greeley defends ethnics." *National Catholic Reporter*, Vol. 9 Nov. 10, 1972. p. 20.

3252 "Rev. Greeley named Loyola sociology prof." *Chicago Tribune*, July 4, 1973. p. 4.

3253 Dugan, George. "Church council scored on stand." *New York Times*, Oct. 16, 1973. p. 21. (Names G as supporter of Israel in Israeli-Arab conflict.)

3254 "Catholic churchgoing still declining." *New York Times*, Nov. 12, 1973. p. 3.

3255 "Catholics find more support for abortions in certain cases." *New York Times*, Nov. 14, 1973. p. 22.

3256 Fiske, Edward B. "Graduates of Catholic schools found more 'hopeful' in study." *New York Times*, Jan. 8, 1974. p. 36.

3257 Maeroff, Gene I. "White ethnic groups in nation are encouraging heritage programs in a trend toward self-awareness." *New York Times*, Jan. 28, 1974. p. 11.

3258 "Shapers and shakers." *Time*, Vol. 104 Sept. 9, 1974. p. 66.

3259   "Greeley charges FBI visit is 'intimidation'." *National Catholic Reporter,* Vol. 10 Oct. 11, 1974. p. 18.

3260   Briggs, Kenneth A. "Despite drop in parochial schools, 89% of laity in poll say they're needed." *New York Times,* Dec. 29, 1974. p. 12.

3261   Deedy, John. "Catholicism and cultural shock." *New York Times,* Jan. 19, 1975. Sec. IV p. 11.

3262   Robison, James. "Mystics in U. S. profiled: Black male, in 40s." *Chicago Tribune,* Feb. 1, 1975. p. 19.

3263   "Greeley criticism challenges plan as elitist manipulation." *Catholic Messenger,* Feb. 13, 1975. pp. 1+. (Catholic bicentennial observance.)

3264   Blau, Eleanor. "Extent of anti-Catholicism is debated; issue linked to abortion and school aid." *New York Times,* Apr. 11, 1975. p. 33.

3265   Farrell, William E. "Cardinal Cody is assailed for closing 4 schools in Chicago ghetto." *New York Times,* July 27, 1975. p. 25.

3266   Robison, James and Jeff Lyon. "W. Side school closing big issue for Cody critics." *Chicago Tribune,* Aug. 24, 1975. p. 12.

3267   Robison, James. "Jews, Irish Catholics tops in wealth: survey." *Chicago Tribune,* Oct. 19, 1975. Sec. 2 p. 27.

3268   "Birth control ban hurt Catholic Church: study." *Chicago Tribune,* Mar. 24, 1976. p. 1.

3269   Briggs, Kenneth A. "Papal birth stand found to hurt Church." *New York Times,* Mar. 24, 1976. pp. 1+.

3270   Robison, James. "Cody aide rebuts birth control study findings." *Chicago Tribune,* Mar. 30, 1976. p. 5.

3271   "Blame encyclical for decline in Catholic practice." *Catholic Messenger,* Apr. 1, 1976. pp. 6+.

3272   "New study by Greeley blames Pope's encyclical for decline of Catholic practice in the U. S." *Our Sunday Visitor*, Vol. 64 Apr. 4, 1976. p. 1. *

3273   "Greeley report criticized by Washington archbishop." *Our Sunday Visitor*, Vol. 64 Apr. 11, 1976. p. 2. *

3274   Maher, J. "Jesuit theologian questions approach of Greeley study." *Our Sunday Visitor*, Vol. 64 Apr. 11, 1976. p. 2. *

3275   "See Greeley study as 'contribution to Church'." *Catholic Messenger*, Apr. 22, 1976. p. 10.

3276   Robison, James. "Fewer turn to God for aid." *Chicago Tribune*, June 6, 1976. p. 16.

3277   "Greeley's study is examined." *Catholic Messenger*, June 17, 1976. pp. 1+.

3278   "Blaming the Pope." *Time*, Vol. 107 Apr. 5, 1976. p. 56.

3279   Maeroff, Gene I. "Catholic schools slowing decline." *New York Times*, Apr. 25, 1976. pp. 1+.

3280   McCready, William C. "American Catholics want Catholic schools." *Momentum*, Vol. 7 May 1976. pp. 15-25.

3281   Kinzie, John, Jr. "Royko calls Greeley 'constipated twirp' Greeley appeals with carbon copy to God." *Near North News* (Chicago), May 1, 1976. p. 1.

3282   Briggs, Kenneth A. "Jews urged to fight anti-Catholicism." *New York Times*, May 13, 1976. p. 18.

3283   Deedy, John. "American flock strays beyond Catholicism." *New York Times*, May 23, 1976. Sec. IV p. 9.

3284   Briggs, Kenneth A. "Brown brings spirituality to political ideas." *New York Times*, June 4, 1976. p. 12. (Edmund G. Brown.)

3285   Briggs, Kenneth A. "Priest and Rabbi exchange charges on anti-

Catholicism among Jews." *New York Times*, Oct. 5, 1976. p. 43. (Replies Nov. 10, 1976.)

3286 Angell, Charles. "Interfaith dialogue." *New York Times*, Nov. 10, 1976. p. 28. (Reply to Oct. 5, 1976.)

3287 Neusner, Jacob. "Interfaith dialogue." *New York Times*, Nov. 10, 1976. p. 28. (Reply to Oct. 5, 1976.)

3288 Dugan, George. "Priest and Rabbi patch up dispute over a charge of anti-Catholicism." *New York Times*, Mar. 13, 1977. p. 48.

3289 "Catholic schools OK, leadership Not OK in diverging Church, says Father Greeley." *Catholic Messenger*, Apr. 21, 1977. pp. 1+.

3290 "Greeley says anti-Catholic bias influences educators." *Our Sunday Visitor*, Vol. 66 July 17, 1977. p. 2. *

3291 "Government definitions of 'minorities' growing to involve more groups." *New York Times*, July 30, 1978. p. 1.

3292 Cornell, George W. No title. *New York Times*, Aug. 14, 1978. p. 28-?. (Report of G's "Papal job description" from the New York Times News Service and The Associated Press. *New York Times* on strike.)

3293 "John Paul's warm beginning." *Chicago Sun Times*, Aug. 29, 1978. p. 39. (Editorial.)

3294 Green, Laura. "A special day for city's Poles." *Chicago Sun Times*, Oct. 22, 1978. p. 7.

3295 "Greeley sees 'stewpot' in America's ethnic mix." *Catholic Messenger*, Nov. 9, 1978. pp. 1+.

3296 "Inadequacies of evangelization." *Society*, Vol. 16 Mar./Apr. 1979. p. 2-3.

3297 "Cody won't discipline priest critic." *Chicago Sun Times*, Apr. 19, 1979. p. 56.

3298   "Story of two Popes, as told by 'Deep Purple'." *New York Times*, June 8, 1979. Sec. III p. 32.

3299   "U. S. Catholics find prejudices waning." *New York Times*, Oct. 2, 1979. p. 9.

3300   Hunter, Marjorie.   "New Coleman study is defended and criticized by 500 educators." *New York Times*, Apr. 8, 1981. p. 12.

3301   Middleton, Lorenzo.   "Coleman study says private schooling superior to public: social scientists attack his findings." *Chronicle of Higher Education*, Vol. 22 Apr.13, 1981. pp. 1+.

3302   "The bright flight." *Newsweek*, Vol. 97 Apr. 20, 1981. p. 66-73. (Private schools.)

3303   Shanker, Albert. "Where we stand." *New York Times*, July 19, 1981. Sec. IV p. 7.

3304   "The Cardinal's sin?" *Newsweek*, Vol. 98 Sept. 21, 1981. p. 44.

3305   Schmidt, William E. "Editor's use of Cody critic's notes focus of dispute." *New York Times*, Sept. 21, 1981. p. 16.

3306   Larson, Ray, William Clements and Gene Mustain. "Greeley denies role in prompting probe of Cardinal John Cody." *Chicago Sun Times*, Sept. 25, 1981. p. 16.

3307   Briggs, Kenneth A. "Attention focuses on critic of Cody." *New York Times*, Sept. 27, 1981. p. 26.

3308   Larson, Ray, William Clements and Gene Mustain.   "Ohio prelate denies alleged conspiracy in Cardinal Cody case." *Chicago Sun Times*, Sept. 27, 1981. p. 18.

3309   "Ohio Archbishop denies reports of Cody scheme." *New York Times*, Sept. 28, 1981. p. 14.

3310   "Indiana editor sues Greeley for libel in dispute on files." *New York Times*, July 22, 1982. p. 18.

3311   Blechman, Barbara. "Personalities." *Washington Post*, July 22, 1982. Sec. E p. 2. (James Winter's libel suit.)

3312   McDowell, Edwin. "About books and authors: a song and a 'dance'." *New York Times Book Review*, Mar. 6, 1983. p. 38.

3313   Sweet, Lynn. "Father Greeley's $1.25 million gift." *Chicago Sun-Times*, Jan. 24, 1984. pp. 1+.

3314   Buursma, Bruce. "Greeley gives $850,000 for U. of C. chair." *Chicago Tribune*, Jan. 24, 1984. p. 9.

3315   "Novelist plans to sponsor a chair in Catholic studies." *New York Times*, Jan. 29, 1984. p. 12.

3316   McClory, Robert J. "Greeley donates $1.5 million." *National Catholic Reporter*, Vol. 20 Feb. 3, 1984. p. 12.

3317   Garcia, Guy D. "People." *Time*, Vol. 123 Feb. 6, 1984. p. 63. (Gift to Univ. of Chicago.)

3318   "Generous gifts." *Christian Century*, Vol. 101 Feb. 29, 1984. p. 217.

3319   "Shop talk: life with Father." *Wall Street Journal*, Mar. 28, 1984. p. 35.

3320   Kenkelen, Bill. "Greeley huffs off TV show to avoid questioner." *National Catholic Reporter*, Vol. 21 Dec. 7, 1984. p. 23.

3321   Peters, Edward N. "Greeley walks off TV show." *National Catholic Register*, Vol. 60 Dec. 9, 1984. p. 3. *

3322   Castelli, Jim. "Catholics (and others) less hawkish than they used to be." *National Catholic Reporter*, Vol. 21 June 21, 1985. p. 20.

3323   Buursma, Bruce. "Don't revoke reforms, Rev. Greeley says." *Chicago Tribune*, Aug. 28, 1985. p. 3.

3324 McClory, Robert J. "Study says U. S. Catholics fear Vatican II retrenchment." *National Catholic Reporter,* Vol. 21 Sept. 6, 1985. pp. 1+.

3325 Dowd, Maureen. "New York Irish grasp new image and power." *New York Times*, Aug.1, 1986. pp. 1+.

3326 "Priest offering $1 million from his books for Chicago schools." *New York Times*, Sept. 12, 1986. p. 10.

3327 "Greeley sets up private fund for Chicago inner-city schools." *National Catholic Reporter,* Vol. 22 Sept. 26, 1986. p. 3.

3328 "Church declines million-dollar gift." *National Catholic Register*, Vol. 62 Sept. 28, 1986. p. 2. *

3329 "Greeley turned down." *Christian Century*, Vol. 103 Oct. 8, 1986. p. 855.

3330 Eisenstadt, Todd. "Church urged to try credit card donations." *Chicago Tribune*, June 10, 1987. p. 8.

3331 Johnson, Dirk. "Catholics giving less to church, report says." *New York Times*, June 10, 1987. p. 22.

3332 McClory, Robert J. "Greeley ties dwindling donations to church stand on birth control." *National Catholic Reporter,* Vol. 23 June 19, 1987. p. 3.

3333 Delloff, Linda-Marie. "Old St. Patrick's new art." *Christian Century*, Vol. 105 June 1, 1988. p. 534.

3334 Schmidt, William E. "Valentine in a survey: marital fidelity." *New York Times*, Feb. 12, 1990. p. 18.

3335 Goldman, Ari L. "New gauge on prayer." *New York Times*, June 29, 1991. p. 10.

3336 Goldman, Ari L. "Nontraditional Catholics." *New York Times*, Sept. 21, 1991. p. 5.

3337   "Support for euthanasia growing, sociologist says." *Toronto Star*, Dec. 28, 1991. Sec. H p. 14.

3338   Johnson, Steve. "Sex and seniors: flesh weak, but not that weak." *Chicago Tribune*, Aug. 12, 1992. Sec. 2 pp. 1+.

3339   "Many 'playful' seniors enjoy frequent sex, study says." *Toronto Star*, Aug. 12, 1992. p. 2. (Reply Aug. 21, 1992.)

3340   Kennedy, Laura. "Lovemaking reduced to mere touch." *Toronto Star*, Aug. 21, 1992. p. 26. (Reply to Aug. 12, 1992.)

3341   "Happiest couples in study have sex after 60." *New York Times*, Oct. 4, 1992. p. 23.

3342   "Happiest couples over 60 enjoy sex often, survey finds. *Toronto Star*, Oct. 6, 1992. Sec. F p. 1.

3343   "Holy war." *USA Today*, Mar. 23, 1993. Sec. D p. 1. (Diocesan newspapers refuse to advertise *Fall from Grace*.)

3344   "Clergy sex abuse widespread, says priest." *Christian Century*, Vol. 110 Apr. 14, 1993. pp. 392-393.

3345   Hirsley, Michael. "13-nation survey finds strong belief in God." *Chicago Tribune*, May 18, 1993. p. 2.

3346   Goldman, Ari L. "People do believe." *New York Times*, May 22, 1993. p. 25.

3347   Gibeau, Dawn. "Religious belief remains vital around the world, study says." *National Catholic Reporter*, Vol. 29 May 28, 1993. pp. 4-5.

3348   "Religious revival grips Russia, study says." *Toronto Star*, Dec. 18, 1993. Sec. J p. 17.

CHAPTER FOURTEEN

SELECTED REVIEWS OF BOOKS

All comments below are direct quotations from the reviews.

NON-FICTION

The Church and the Suburbs.

3349   Review. *American Catholic Sociological Review,* Vol. 21
        [Summer] 1960. p. 174. *

Strangers in the House: Catholic youth in America.

3350   Rosanna, M. Review. *American Catholic Sociological Review,*
        Vol. 23 Fall 1962. pp. 277-278.

Religion and Career: a study of college graduates.

3351   Demerath, N. J. III. Review. *American Sociological Review,*
        Vol. 29 Aug. 1964. pp. 628-629.

3352   Carlson, Leland H. Review. *Journal of Higher Education,* Vol.
        35 Dec. 1964. pp. 518-519.
        The exciting conclusion is that Catholics are leaving behind an
        immigrant mentality, abandoning their ghetto defensiveness,
        and assuming a normal share of the intellectual heritage.

3353   Wilson, Bryan R. "Essay review." *School Review,* Vol. 73
        Summer 1965. pp. 156-172.

3354   Vernon, Glenn M. Review. *Journal for the Scientific Study of*

Religion, Vol. 5 Fall 1965. pp. 161-162.
The study provides valuable information about the religious factor as it is involved in the American way of life, not only the intellectual-scientific aspects, but also such phenomena as conversion patterns, correlates of "marriage conversions," ethnic differences, and alienation.

3355   Lenski, Gerhard. Review. *American Journal of Sociology*, Vol. 71 Sept. 1965. pp. 200-201.

And Young Men Shall See Visions: letters from Andrew M. Greeley.

3356   Evans, John W. Review. *America*, Vol. 110 Mar. 7, 1964. p. 319.

3357   Burger, Nash K. "In the field of religion." *New York Times Book Review*, Mar. 22, 1964. pp. 26-27.

Letters to Nancy: from Andrew M. Greeley.

3358   Burger, Nash K. "In the field of religion." *New York Times Book Review*, Nov. 8, 1964. p. 22.
The discussion . . . is meaningful and practical, and keenly alive to the special conditions of contemporary life.

3359   Phillips, Gene D. Review. *Review for Religious*, Vol. 24 Mar. 1965. pp. 313-314.

3360   Golinvaux, Jeanne. Review. *Cross and Crown*, Vol. 17 Sept. 1965. pp. 365-366.
Without flowery phrases or too much theorizing, he inspires fidelity to one's vision, and arouses a desire to answer God's call with a resounding "Yes!"

The Education of Catholic Americans.

3361   Ryan, Mary P. Review. *The Critic*, Vol. 25 Dec. 1966/Jan. 1967. pp. 76-79.

3362 Callahan, Daniel. Review. *Commentary*, Vol. 43 Jan. 1967. pp. 81-83.

3363 Hassenger, Robert. Review. *American Journal of Sociology*, Vol. 72 Jan. 1967. pp. 444-445.
The results of this study are suggestive, not conclusive. That they are the best presently available makes the volume indispensable for anyone who would discuss Catholic education intelligently.

3364 Bressler, Marvin. Review. *American Sociological Review,* Vol. 32 Feb. 1967. pp. 147-148.
The authors furnish us with an instructive example of how stimulating empirical sociology can be when disciplined intelligence confronts major problems of social science and public policy.

3365 Fichter, Joseph H. Review. *Harvard Educational Review*, Vol. 37 Summer 1967. pp. 499-500.
The authors seem determined to avoid the charge that they "claim too much" either for their data or for the Catholic school system. In this, they probably frustrate both the proponents and opponents of the Catholic schools who are seeking definitive "proofs" for their particular position in this continuing controversy. Yet, for both the educator and the religionist, this is by far the most useful study that has been attempted in the area of American Catholic education.

3366 Moberg, D. O. Review. *Journal for the Scientific Study of Religion*, Vol. 6 Fall 1967. pp. 304-307.

3367 Erickson, Donald A. "Review essay." *School Review*, Vol. 75 Winter 1967. pp. 425-436.

The Hesitant Pilgrim: American Catholicism after the Council.

3368 Evoy, John J. Review. *America*, Vol. 115 Nov. 26, 1966. p. 713.

3369 Vanderpot, Maurice P. Review. *Review for Religious*, Vol. 26 Mar. 1967. pp. 375-376.

3370 McCabe, Bernard. Review. *Catholic World*, Vol. 205 May 1967. pp. 118-119.
This loosely-organized book covers a wide, well-informed range of contemporary Catholic preoccupations.

The Catholic Experience: an interpretation of the history of American Catholicism.

3371 Morrison, Michael. Review. *America*, Vol. 118 Mar. 2, 1968. pp. 297-298.

3372 O'Brien, David J. "Andrew Greeley and American Catholicism." *Catholic World*, Vol. 207 Apr. 1968. pp. 36-38.

3373 McManamin, Francis G. Review. *Theological Studies*, Vol. 29 June 1968. pp. 386-387.
. . . the historian will recognize that more co-ordinated work must be done between the sociologists and the historians in the presentation of the American Catholic story.

3374 Ellis, John T. Review. *Catholic Historical Review*, Vol. 56 Apr. 1970. pp. 151-157.
As previously mentioned, there is much of value in this volume, e.g., the chapter entitled "The Chicago Experience" (pp. 247-274), which is, in my judgment, an excellent essay in the contemporary Catholicism of the largest and in many respects the leading diocese of the Middle West out of which there have come so many worthwhile features of the American Church in our time.

The Changing Catholic College.

3375 Callahan, Daniel. "Academic standards are secular." *Saturday Review*, Vol. 51 Mar. 16, 1968. p. 77.

3376 Schlesinger, Bruno. "Assimilate or perish." *The Critic*, Vol. 26 Apr./May 1968. pp. 91-92.

3377 Review. *Choice*, Vol. 5 Jan. 1969. p. 1482.
Lucid, disturbing, challenging; candid but hopeful.

3378   McGee, Reece. Review. *American Sociological Review,* Vol. 34
        Apr. 1969. p. 286-287.

3379   Locigno, Joseph P. "The college and the Catholic." *Catholic
        World,* Vol. 209 June 1969. pp. 132-133.

*The Crucible of Change: the social dynamics of pastoral
practice.*

3380   Review. *The Critic,* Vol. 27 Feb./Mar. 1969. p. 94.

3381   Casey, Thomas M. Review. *American Ecclesiastical Review,*
        Vol. 160 June 1969. p. 420.
        It should be required reading for any concerned Catholic
        who desires the Church to develop dynamic structures
        instead of stumbling into the twenty-first century with a
        tired gasp.

Uncertain Trumpet: the priest in modern America.

3382   Whitehead, James. Review. *America,* Vol. 118 Feb. 17, 1968.
        pp. 236+.

3383   Heaney, Thomas W. "The priesthood." *Catholic World,* Vol.
        207 June 1968. pp. 132-133.

3384   Streng, William D. Review. *Lutheran Quarterly,* Vol. 20 Aug.
        1968. p. 316.

*From Backwater to Mainstream: a profile of Catholic higher
education.*

3385   Hassenger, Robert. Review. *Saturday Review,* Vol. 53 May 16,
        1970. pp. 83-84.

3386   Cass, James. "Ultimate questions." *The Critic,* Vol. 28
        July/Aug. 1970. pp. 69-70.

3387   O'Byrne, E. M. Review. *Journal of Higher Education*, Vol. 41
         Oct. 1970. pp. 579-580.

A Future to Hope In: socio-religious speculations.

3388   Stanton, Edward S. Review. *America*, Vol. 120 May 3, 1969.
         p. 540
         The style is light; the observations are sober; the tone is
         optimistic.

3389   Raines, Robert A. "Shell-shedding." *Christian Century*, Vol. 86
         May 28, 1969. pp. 753-754.

Life for a Wanderer.

3390   Tittiger, Niles. Review. *Spiritual Life*, Vol. 16 Spring 1970. p.
         81.

3391   Hovley, Vincent E. Review. *Review for Religious*, Vol. 29 Mar.
         1970. p. 313.
         The updating is so radical, the categories of contemporary
         science and philosophy so boldly and exclusively used that
         the suggested vision may well be as offensive to some as
         it will be inspiring to others. If, then, only to provoke a
         thorough reconsideration of essential Christian concepts, I
         recommend this book to all who are actively interested in
         the spiritual life.

3392   Pennington, M. Basil. Review. *Theological Studies*, Vol. 31
         Mar. 1970. p. 231.
         One likes the joy and optimism that comes through
         throughout.

Religion in the Year 2000.

3393   Byron, William J. Review. *America*, Vol. 121 Oct. 11, 1969.
         p. 304.
         A serious empirical examination of the secularization hypo-
         thesis is long overdue. Careful data collection and sophisticated

analysis are required; there is little evidence of either in this book.

3394   Furfey, Paul H. Review. *Commonweal*, Vol. 91 Nov. 28, 1969. pp. 284-285.

3395   Christopher, Michael. "Ever changing, ever same." *U. S. Catholic and Jubilee*, Vol. 35 Feb. 1970. pp. 47-48.

Why Can't They Be like Us? Facts and fallacies about ethnic differences and group conflicts in America.

3396   Berger, Peter L. "Inventing the ethnics." *Commentary*, Vol. 52 July 1971. p. 82-83.

3397   Bliven, Naomi. "E pluribus what?" *New Yorker*, Vol. 47 Nov. 20, 1971. pp. 225-229.

3398   Larrabee, Harold A. Review. *New England Quarterly*, Vol. 46 Dec. 1973. pp. 643-644.
        His candor extends to the mystery of ethnicity itself, remarking that "the primordial ties of land ancestry and common faith interact in American society in ways which we do not begin to understand." He has made a ground-breaking move in that direction, and his combination of modesty and daring commands respect.

3399   "The week's worth." *Chicago Tribune*, Apr. 13, 1975. Sec. 7 p. 6.

Can Catholic Schools Survive?

3400   Chamberlin, J. Gordon. Review. *Journal of Ecumenical Studies*, Vol. 8 n.m. 1971. pp. 877-879.

3401   Clancy, Thomas H. "Youth: education, drugs, religion. Some recent fiction." *America*, Vol. 124 Apr. 10, 1971. p. 382.

The Friendship Game.

3402   Christopher, Michael.   "Tradition and friendship."   *U. S. Catholic and Jubilee*, Vol. 35 Nov. 1970. pp. 49-51.
. . . it is written in clear, readable prose; it seeks a middle way between the extremes of contemporary approaches; it offers practical help to the reader who is persuaded that Father Greeley's point of view is reasonable and compelling.

3403   O'Shea, Daniel G.   "Spouses and other strangers."   *Catholic World*, Vol. 213 June 1971. p. 155.
Greeley's approach is generally based on the sexuality of love and friendship, which are, in his view, the same thing. If love and friendship are the same, and love is sexual, then obviously, friendship is sexual. With Greeley, the prototype of all friendship is marriage, and the setting of sexuality against the concept of a game leads him to some interesting conclusions.

New Horizons for the Priesthood.

3404   McBride, Alfred.   Review.   *Worship*, Vol. 44 June/July 1970. pp. 379-380.

3405   Dorff, Francis.   Review.   *American Ecclesiastical Review*, Vol. 163 Nov. 1970. p. 350.
Father Greeley writes hopefully of hope, respectfully of self-respect, cordially of friendship, light-heartedly of hilarity, enthusiastically of enthusiasm, courageously of integrity and intelligently of all he considers.

Come Blow Your Mind with Me.

3406   Matzek, Richard A.   "The new religion, with caution, alarm and hope."   *New York Times Book Review*, July 25, 1971. pp. 6+.

3407   Nobile, Philip.   Review.   *Spiritual Life*, Vol. 17 Fall 1971. pp. 232-233.
Come Blow Your Mind With Me, as the Legion of Decency

used to put it, is objectionable in part for all. But if you like
Andrew Greeley, you'll love this book.

3408   Smith, Sheldon M. "Whiff of oxygen." *National Review*, Vol.
        23 Sept. 10, 1971. pp. 999-1000.

3409   Naver, Barbara. "The church: past, present, future the ethics of
        development." *America*, Vol. 125 Sept. 11, 1971. pp. 153-154.
        Greeley is level-headed, cheerful and passionately loyal to the
        ministry and the Church, which makes it a bit hard to figure
        out why his views have long tended to raise hackles--as
        Come Blow Your Mind will surely do--among both progres-
        sive and conservative Catholics.

3410   Hotze, Mary H. Review. *Review for Religious*, Vol. 30 Nov.
        1971. pp. 1157-1158.

3411   Review. *Choice*, Vol. 9 May 1972. p. 382.

The Jesus Myth.

3412   Matzek, Richard A.   "Three new ventures in the continual
        rephrasing of faith." *New York Times Book Review*, Nov. 14,
        1971. pp. 44+.
        Greeley's most pointed commentary is directed against those
        who preach a theology of radical political action. As a social
        scientist, he finds such action counterproductive; as a Chris-
        tian he links it to the Zealot tradition which Jesus criticized for
        diverting our attention from the kingdom of God.

3413   Schroth, Raymond A. Review. *America*, Vol. 126 Feb. 5, 1972.
        pp. 126-127.
        Reading this kind of a book is like having a five-beer conver-
        sation with a strong, intelligent, but preoccupied friend who
        keeps glancing around the room while telling you with great
        earnestness something you already know.

3414   Lyons, James. "A Greeley view of biblical studies." *National
        Catholic Reporter*, Vol. 8 Feb. 25, 1972. p. 15.

3415   MacRae, George. Review. *Commonweal*, Vol. 96 Mar. 10,
        1972. pp. 18-19.

        The Touch of the Spirit.

3416   Donnellan, Michael. "Helpful book for (Roman) Christians."
        National Catholic Reporter, Vol. 8 Feb. 18, 1972. p. 20.
        The book's inspirational value is marred, however, by a
        distressing tendency to take potshots at those who don't
        reflect the virtues portrayed. . . .

        *The Catholic Priest in the United States: sociological
        investigations.*

3417   Fichter, Joseph H. Review. *America*, Vol. 127 Oct. 7, 1972. p.
        270.
        The result is a dull and ponderous tome which stands in a
        sociological and historical vacuum, waiting to be interpreted
        and fleshed out by scholars. Nevertheless, the facts are there,
        and the bishops got what they paid for.

3418   Fleming, David A. Review. *Review for Religious*, Vol. 31 Nov.
        1972. p. 1059.

3419   Angilella, Joseph T. Review. *Theological Studies*, Vol. 34 Mar.
        1973. pp. 129-131.

        *The Denominational Society: a sociological approach to religion
        in America.*

3420   Marty, Martin E. "Religious books." *The Critic*, Vol. 31
        Sept./Oct. 1972. pp. 94-95.

3421   McKenna, Edward E. Review. *Review of Religious Research*,
        Vol. 14 Spring 1973. pp. 201-202.
        Many of Greeley's conclusions are debatable; but from a
        functional standpoint this only increases his book's value.

3422　Review. *Choice*, Vol. 10 June 1973. p. 637.
A refreshing and scholarly book, readable in style and content, it should rank with Gerhard Lenski's *The Religious Factor* (1972) and Will Herber's *Protestant, Catholic, Jew* (rev. ed. 1955).

3423　Payne, David E. Review. *American Journal of Sociology*, Vol. 79 Nov. 1973. p. 784.

Priests in the United States: reflections on a survey.

3424　Sweeney, Francis. "The Roman Catholic Church--three reports on trouble." *New York Times Book Review*, Apr. 2, 1972. pp. 5+.

3425　Fichter, Joseph H. "Andrew Greeley reflects on a survey." *America*, Vol. 126 May 20, 1972. pp. 532-534.
Fr. Greeley sheds the scientific mantle of value-free objectivity, bares his gut reactions to the public and is at his controversial best. I think he is brilliant and provocative--probably because I am so much on his side--but some are sure to find him irritating and patronizing and generally outrageous.

3426　Murnion, Philip J. Review. *Commonweal*, Vol. 96 June 16, 1972. pp. 341-342.

3427　Baker, Kenneth. Review. *Homiletic & Pastoral Review*, Vol. 72 July 1972. pp. 74-76.
But throughout the book there is a sense of the dignity of the priesthood and the importance of the priesthood for the Church, though one might disagree with him on many particular points.

3428　Noll, Ray R. Review. *Theological Studies*, Vol. 34 Mar. 1973. pp. 131-133.

The Sinai Myth.

3429　Harrington, Daniel J. Review. *America*, Vol. 127 Nov. 25,

1972. p. 455.

3430   Spina, Frank A. Review. *Christian Scholar's Review*, Vol. 5
n.m. 1976. pp. 312-313.

That Most Distressful Nation: the taming of the American Irish.

3431   Clancy, Thomas H. Review. *America*, Vol. 127 Aug. 5, 1972.
p. 73.

3432   O'Neill, William L. "The contradictory ethnics." *New Republic*,
Vol. 167 Sept. 9, 1972. pp. 25-26.
So long as ethnicity remains a fact of American life it needs
to be studied, and Greeley has approached it with real inven-
tiveness. He is not maudlin, boastful or self-serving, and
breaks new ground in ways that other historians and social
scientists would do well to exploit.

3433   Horgan, John. Review. *The Critic*, Vol. 31 Nov./Dec. 1972.
pp. 77-78+.

3434   Carroll, James. "From Greeley, polemic with passion."
National Catholic Reporter, Vol. 9 Dec. 15, 1972. p. 16.
Greeley tells the grand story well, from the ancient and on-
going resistance to English oppression to the drab suburban
sell-out of the Chicago Irish, who in "making it" lost it, too.

3435   Duff, John B. Review. *Journal of American History*, Vol. 59
Mar. 1973. pp. 1001-1002.
As usual, he writes with wit, verve, and clarity; and no one
can accuse him of not having a feel for his subject.

3436   Cross, Robert D. Review. *American Historical Review*, Vol. 78
Apr. 1973. pp. 496-497.
Truly Father Greeley is the James Cagney of ethnic studies.
The blows come in flurries, and he usually saves one mystery
punch for the bell.

3437   Greene, Robert W. "Lost identity." *Commentary*, Vol. 55 Apr.
1973. pp. 100+.

Unsecular Man: the persistence of religion.

3438   Berger, Peter L. Review. *New York Times Book Review*, Nov.
        19, 1972. pp. 22+.
        Secularization theory, in this its central proposition, is not
        demolished by Greeley's argument. Greeley does make a very
        plausible case that this theory has been wrong about the degree
        of secularization. Even more important, he shows that most pro-
        ponents of the theory have been misled by evolutionary bias to
        assume, without warrant in the evidence, that secularization is
        progressive and irreversible.

3439   Kelly, James R. Review. *America*, Vol. 128 Feb. 17, 1973. pp.
        148-150.
        But here Greeley does not disguise his own religious sensi-
        bilities and political judgments, and his special contribution
        is one of championing a legitimate and frequently ignored
        perspective in the unending discussion about contemporary
        religious consciousness.

3440   Robbins, Richard H. Review. *Sociological Analysis*, Vol. 34
        Spring 1973. pp. 75-78.

3441   Review. *New Yorker*, Vol. 49 Mar. 3, 1973. pp. 114-115.

3442   Eller, Vernard. Review. *Christian Century*, Vol. 90 Apr. 18,
        1973. pp. 459-461.

3443   Mintz, Alan L. "Religion and modern man." *Commentary*, Vol.
        56 Aug. 1973. pp. 83-86.

3444   Murray, John J. Review. *Annals of the American Academy of
        Political and Social Sciences*, Vol. 409 Sept. 1973. pp. 230-231.

3445   Hamnett, Ian. Review. *Clergy Review*, Vol. 59 Feb. 1974.
        pp. 153-155. (Review of *The Persistence of Religion*, English
        edition.)

3446   Kelley, Dean M. Review. *Social Forces*, Vol. 52 Mar. 1974.
        p. 422.

3447   Mounce, Robert H. "Same as the ice age." *Christianity Today*, Vol. 18 May 24, 1974. pp. 38-39.

3448   McNamara, Patrick H. Review. *Journal of the American Academy of Religion*, Vol. 43 Mar. 1975. pp. 116-118+.
Yet Greeley is unmatched by any contemporary writer, in my opinion, in his ability to marshall scholarship and evidence to refute easy journalistic assumptions about "modern man's emancipation from the shackles of religion."

What a Modern Catholic Believes about the Church.

3449   Murphy, Francis X. "What does a Catholic believe?" *National Catholic Reporter*, Vol. 8 Apr. 28, 1972. p. 10.

3450   Coogan, Daniel. Review. *America*, Vol. 126 May 27, 1972. p. 576.

3451   Schlitzer, Albert L. Review. *Commonweal*, Vol. 96 July 14, 1972. pp. 389-390.

The New Agenda: a proposal for a new approach to fundamental issues in contemporary times.

3452   Fiske, Edward B. "Books of the times: old symbols, new situations." *New York Times*, Nov. 30, 1973. p. 35.
While many would no doubt like to dismiss this effort outright for his lack of credentials, the fact is that he has produced the most provocative book on religious belief for the intelligent layman in the last few years. It is a vindication of the widely spoken but not very widely applied dictum that theology is too important to be left to theologians.

3453   Fleming, Peter J. "Christian dilemmas: sex, religion and Jesus." *America*, Vol. 129 Dec. 8, 1973. pp. 450-452.

3454   Callahan, Daniel. "A live future?" *New Republic*, Vol. 169 Dec. 29, 1973. pp. 27-28.

3455   Hejja, Julius. Review. *Library Journal*, Vol. 99 Feb. 1, 1974.
       p. 371.

3456   McNamara, Patrick H.   "Review Essay. The Churches:
       reflection, reassessment, and reform." *Sociological Analysis*,
       Vol. 35 Autumn 1974. pp. 216-221.

3457   Baum, Gregory L. Review. *Frontier*, Vol. 18 Autumn 1975.
       pp. 176-178.

3458   Tracy, David. "Greeley's new agenda: 'a generous, intelligent
       theology'." *National Catholic Reporter,* Vol. 10 Nov. 16, 1976.
       Christmas Book Report p. 1.
          It is a delight to see theology worked out by a professional
          social scientist who, because of his commitment to the
          questions raised in all serious theology, can write a believable
          modern theology.

The Persistence of Religion.

3459   Nichols, Francis W. Review. *Review for Religious*, Vol. 32
       Sept. 1973. p. 1178.

3460   Review. *Catholic Library World*, Vol. 45 Dec. 1973. p. 217.

Sexual Intimacy.

3461   Driver, Tom F. Review. *America*, Vol. 129 Dec. 8, 1973. pp.
       448+.

3462   Garvey, John. Review. *Commonweal*, Vol. 99 Dec. 14, 1973.
       pp. 298-300.

3463   De La Bedoyere, Quentin. "Understanding sexuality." *The
       Month*, Vol. 7 Mar. 1974. p. 522.
          I liked his positive approach to fidelity--seeing it as a constant
          search to know and to please the other, rather than the negative
          legalistic perspective we are more familiar with.

3464   Prewitt, Charles B. Review. *Journal of Pastoral Care*, Vol. 31
        Mar. 1977. pp. 71-72.

Building Coalitions: American politics in the 1970's.

3465   Reeves, Richard. "Common sense and too much dictation." *New
        York Times Book Review*, Feb. 24, 1974. p. 5.
        Father Greeley was one of the first observers of the almost
        willful isolation of American ethnics from the national thought
        processes in places like New York, Cambridge, and
        Washington. Here he returns to their defense, a defense both
        rational and passionate, against those who would dismiss
        hyphenated Americans as selfish, bigoted and warlike know-
        nothings.

3466   Dreyer, Edward C. Review. *Library Journal*, Vol. 99 Apr. 1,
        1974. pp. 1015-1016.

3467   Grumbach, Doris. Review. *New Republic*, Vol. 170 Apr. 13,
        1974. p. 31.

3468   Review. *Choice*, Vol. 11 May 1974. p. 508.

3469   Sundquist, James L. Review. *Political Science Quarterly*, Vol.
        89 Fall 1974. pp. 657-658.

3470   Novogrod, R. J. Review of *American Politics in the 1970s* [sic].
        Annals of the American Academy of Political and Social Sciences,
        Vol. 415 Sept. 1974. pp. 252-253.
        His surveys are tight and exact. Myths are assaulted with
        logic. Problems are solved with insight and reason. It truly is
        most rewarding reading.

3471   Wentz, Richard E. Review. *Christian Century*, Vol. 92 June 25,
        1975. pp. 634-636.

3472   Sheerman, Barry. Review. *Political Studies*, Vol. 24 Sept.
        1976. pp. 343-344.

The Devil You Say! Man and his personal devils and angels.

3473   Review. *Publisher's Weekly*, Vol. 206 July 29, 1974. p. 49.

3474   Connolly, Paul H. Review. *America*, Vol. 131 Nov. 30, 1974.
        p. 352.
        A number of the "demons" sound like Greeley's pet peeves,
        and make their homes in the particular academic and clerical
        worlds he inhabits. Some of the angels strongly favor their
        left wing, while others bear a striking resemblance to
        Greeley's favorite authors.

3475   Christopher, Michael. "Clouds of evil, light of faith." *U. S.
        Catholic*, Vol. 39 Dec. 1974. pp. 48-50.
        In a sense Father Greeley is writing an examination of
        conscience for contemporary men and women or at least
        relevant reflections that should make most readers pause.

3476   Frye, Roland M. Review. *Theology Today*, Vol. 32 Apr. 1975.
        pp. 119-120.

Ecstasy: a way of knowing.

3477   Review. *Publishers Weekly*, Vol. 205 Mar. 4, 1974. p. 78.

3478   Verene, D. P. Review. *Annals of the American Academy of
        Political and Social Sciences*, Vol. 416 Nov. 1974. pp. 254-255.

3479   Keeley, Benjamin J. Review. *Sociological Analysis*, Vol. 35
        Winter 1974. p. 297.
        It is almost a trigger for a mystical experience. Here is a
        book on mysticism containing brilliant passages and ingenious
        insights written with a remarkable clarity and literary skill by
        a hard-nosed rational empiricist, a skeptical survey-research
        sociologist, who happens to be blessed with the free-flowing
        uninhibited imagination of a scholar as well as the courage and
        commitment of a priestly man.

3480   Dittes, James E. Review. *International Journal of Comparative
        Sociology*, Vol. 16 Sept./Dec. 1975. pp. 303-304.

3481 Rue, Loyal D. Review. *Journal of the American Academy of Religion*, Vol. 43 Dec. 1975. pp. 827-828.

3482 Navone, John. Review. *Gregorianum*, Vol. 57 n.m. 1976. pp. 172-173.

Ethnicity in the United States: a preliminary reconnaissance.

3483 Raffaele, Joseph A. Review. *Annals of the American Academy of Political and Social Sciences*, Vol. 423 Jan. 1976. pp. 201-202.

3484 Schnall, David J. "Ethnicity and American society." *Judaism*, Vol. 25 Spring 1976. pp. 242-250. (Review essay.)
Its author is meticulous in his methodology, clear in his hypothesis and guarded in his conclusions, all essential qualities in social scientific literature.

3485 Weiner, Terry S. Review. *Social Forces*, Vol. 55 Sept. 1976. pp. 208-209.

3486 Yinger, J. Milton. Review. *American Journal of Sociology*, Vol. 82 Mar. 1977. pp. 1116-1118.

3487 Cummings, Scott. Review. *Sociology and Social Research*, Vol. 62 Jan. 1978. pp. 318-319.
As a source book and a resource for generating new hypotheses, the book is excellent.

Love and Play.

3488 Doyle, Kevin. Review. *Commonweal*, Vol. 104 Dec. 9, 1977. p. 796.

3489 Oppenheimer, Helen. "Celebrations of the couple." *Times Literary Supplement*, No. 4,248 Aug. 31, 1984. p. 973.
The author's originality lies in firmly attaching the delightfulness of play, not to transient relationships, but to deep-rooted ones.

The Sociology of the Paranormal: a reconnaissance.

3490   White, Rhea A. Review. *Journal of Parapsychology*, Vol. 40
        Mar. 1976. pp. 81-85.

3491   Van Valey, Thomas L. Review. *Journal for the Scientific Study
        of Religion*, Vol. 16 Dec. 1977. pp. 435-436.
        To summarize, this monograph (which should have been an
        article in the first place) clearly indicates that there could and
        probably should be a "sociology of the paranormal." Such
        experiences appear to be pervasive and interesting forms of
        social as well as personal behavior.

3492   Young, Gay. Review. *Contemporary Sociology*, Vol. 7 Mar.
        1978. p. 229.

Catholic Schools in a Declining Church.

3493   Woodward, Kenneth L. "Birth-control factor." *Newsweek*, Vol.
        87 Apr. 5, 1976. p. 57.

3494   Kelly, James R. "*Catholic Schools in a Declining Church*: a
        review article." *America*, Vol. 134 May 15, 1976. pp. 425-426.
        (Reply June 5, 1976.)

3495   Greeley, Andrew. "Friendly persuasion." *America*, Vol. 134
        June 5, 1976. p. 485. (Reply to May 15, 1976.) (Rejoinder
        June 5, 1976.)

3496   Kelly, James R. "Friendly persuasion." *America*, Vol. 134 June
        5, 1976. p. 485. (Rejoinder to June 5, 1976.)

3497   Elford, George. Review. *Commonweal*, Vol. 103 June 18,
        1976. pp. 409-410.

3498   Garvey, John. Review. *Commonweal*, Vol. 103 July 16, 1976.
        pp. 472-473.

3499   Keefe, Donald J. "Catholic Schools in a Declining Church: a
        theological reflection." *Review for Religious*, Vol. 35 Nov.
        1976. pp. 801-812. (Review essay.)

3500 Van Allen, Rodger. Review. *Horizons*, Vol. 4 Spring 1977. pp. 155-157.

3501 Neal, Marie A. Review. *Sociological Analysis*, Vol. 38 Summer 1977. pp. 181-184.

3502 Vaillancourt, Jean-Guy. Review. *Social Forces*, Vol. 56 Sept. 1977. pp. 294-296.

3503 Nelsen, Frank C. Review. *Christian Scholar's Review,* Vol. 8 n.m. 1978. pp. 77-78.

3504 Arroyo, Edward B. "More Catholic research than title suggests." *Journal for the Scientific Study of Religion*, Vol. 17 Mar. 1978. pp. 65-67.
This is obviously an important and sophisticated piece of research on American Catholicism. The frequent appeals to religious authorities, that they take social science more seriously in the formation of policies, could provide a beginning of a new style of leadership in American Cathollicism.

3505 Wood, James R. Review. *American Journal of Sociology*, Vol. 84 Jan. 1979. pp. 1038-1040.
However, the data are solid and the evidence for most of the interpretations is convincing. Greeley et al. should not be faulted for treating sociology as though it mattered.

The Communal Catholic: a personal manifesto.

3506 Review. *Kirkus Reviews*, Vol. 44 Apr. 15, 1976. p. 507.

3507 Cunneen, Joseph. Review. *Commonweal*, Vol. 104 May 13, 1977. pp. 312-314.

3508 Lederer, Norman. Review. *Review of Religious Research*, Vol. 20 Fall 1978. pp. 107-108.

Death and Beyond.

3509   Casey, Genevieve. Review. *Library Journal*, Vol. 101 May 1,
        1976. p. 1127.

3510   Gastonguay, Paul R. Review. *Linacre Quarterly*, Vol. 43 Aug.
        1976. pp. 216-217.

Ethnicity, Denomination and Inequality.

3511   Review. *Choice*, Vol. 14 Apr. 1977. p. 220.

3512   Featherman, David L. Review. *Sociological Analysis*, Vol. 38
        Summer 1977. pp. 176-179.

The Great Mysteries: an essential catechism.

3513   Rohrbach, Peter T. Review. *America*, Vol. 135 Nov. 6, 1976.
        pp. 308-309.

3514   Dulles, Avery. Review. *The Critic*, Vol. 35 Spring 1977. pp.
        79-81.
        He cites no creeds, no councils, no papal documents, nor
        even any biblical proof texts. He is not interested in
        establishing the coherence or the truth of the Christian
        message, but simply in showing its meaningfulness--i.e., its
        capacity to disclose authentic dimensions of common human
        experience.

3515   Ryan, John. "An epitome of American Catholicism?" *Cross
        Currents*, Vol. 27 Fall 1977. pp. 351-354.

3516   Kaufman, Philip. Review. *Worship*, Vol. 51 Sept. 1977. pp.
        468-469.

3517   Thomas, Joseph R. "Greeley's new catechism views nitty-gritty
        of belief." *Catholic Messenger*, Oct. 21, 1976. p. 11.
        The truth is that here we have Fr. Greeley at his literary best,
        writing easily without vituperation, bitterness or know-it-all
        smugness.

The American Catholic; a social portrait.

3518   Cuddihy, John. "Not the stereotype at all." *New York Times Book Review*, Mar. 6, 1977. pp. 3+.

3519   Sohran, M. J., Jr. "A shrinking militant." *National Review*, Vol. 29 Apr. 15, 1977. pp. 444-445.

3520   Briggs, Kenneth. "Books of the times: upheaval in the church." *New York Times*, May 28, 1977. p. 17.
        I like him best in this book when he is unempiricically, [sic] undefensivenly [sic] in love with his Catholic heritage. He has brought together many strands and forged a book that can be both maddening and greatly fascinating.

3521   Blasi, Anthony J. Review. *Sociological Analysis*, Vol. 38 Summer 1977. pp. 171-173.

3522   Neal, Marie A. Review. *Commonweal*, Vol. 104 Aug. 19, 1977. pp. 541-543.

3523   Wright, Richard A. Review. *Annals of the American Academy of Political and Social Sciences*, Vol. 435 Jan. 1978. pp. 319-320.

3524   Paroni, Adele S. Review. *Dissent*, Vol. 25 Spring 1978. pp. 239-241.

3525   Davidson, James D. "Fifteen years of Catholic research: a challenge for all." *Journal for the Scientific Study of Religion*, Vol. 17 Mar. 1978. pp. 63-65.
        The book challenges the leadership of the Catholic church to establish deeper roots among the Catholic people, to recognize the people's real attributes and needs, and to use these attributes and needs (not particularistic and secondary personal motivations) as the primary bases for their decisions.

3526   Nelsen, Hart M. Review. *American Journal of Sociology*, Vol. 84 July 1978. pp. 205-207.

3527   Frankovic, Kathleen A. Review. *American Political Science Review*, Vol. 72 Sept. 1978. pp. 1059-1061.

3528   Clignet, Remi. Review. *Society*, Vol. 15 Sept./Oct. 1978. pp.
        87-89.

3529   Ebaugh, Helen R. Review. *Contemporary Sociology*, Vol. 8
        May 1979. p. 445.

Ethnicity.

3530   Lal, Barbara B. "Shared sense of peoplehood." *The Month*, Vol.
        10 Sept. 1977. pp. 323-324.
        Andrew Greeley's editorial summary of part one does not
        organise the many interesting observations and ideas presented
        in these essays in an especially original or insightful way,
        which is surprising given his first-class work in the sociology
        of ethnicity.

3531   Newman, William M. Review. *Review of Religious Research*,
        Vol. 20 Fall 1978. p. 108.

The Mary Myth.

3532   Gaffney, J. Patrick. Review. *Horizons*, Vol. 4 Fall 1977. pp.
        252-253.

3533   Bruns, J. Edgar. Review. *Theological Studies*, Vol. 38 Dec.
        1977. pp. 816-817.

3534   Review. *Choice*, Vol. 14 Jan. 1978. p. 1516.

3535   Suchocki, Marjorie. Review. *Theology Today*, Vol. 34 Jan.
        1978. pp. 448-452+.

3536   Christ, Carol P. Review. *Journal of the American Academy of
        Religion*, Vol. 46 Sept. 1978. pp. 416-417.
        . . . one searches in vain in his book for a clue about the
        significance of Marian symbolism for women, or even for a
        clear indication that Greeley is aware of the limitation of his
        perspective.

Neighborhood.

3537   Blei, Norbert.   "Greeley's credo: up with people and
        neighborhoods." *Chicago Tribune*, Nov. 20, 1977. Sec. 7 p. 3.
        And if you give a damn at all about the city, your old or new
        neighborhood, you must give Greeley's "Neighborhood" all
        the concern and respect it is due.

3538   McWilliams, Carey. "There's trouble in ethnicity." *Nation*, Vol.
        225 Dec. 31, 1977. pp. 729-731.
        Greeley provides an excellent account of the process of
        neighborhood disruption: panic peddling of homes, redlining,
        the emergence of a dual real estate market, ill-conceived urban
        renewal and high-rise projects, the abandonment of tenements
        and large-scale arson.

3539   Pasquariello, Ronald D.   "Yans-McLaughlin's *Italians* might
        inhabit Greeley's *Neighborhood.*" *National Catholic Reporter*,
        Vol. 14 Jan. 20, 1978. p. 12.
        The drift of Greeley's argument is that neighborhoods are
        perennial, neighborhoods are possible, neighborhoods are for
        people.

3540   Review. *Choice*, Vol. 15 July/Aug. 1978. p. 758.

No Bigger Than Necessary: an alternative to socialism,
capitalism and anarchism.

3541   Review. *Publishers Weekly*, Vol. 212 Sept. 5, 1977. p. 69.
        . . . his book is heavy going until the closing chapters in
        which he adopts a pragmatic and refreshingly outspoken style.

An Ugly Little Secret: anti-Catholicism in North America.

3542   Fisher, Eugene J. "Greeley study confuses an issue." *Catholic
        Messenger*, Feb. 9, 1978. p. 9.

3543   Hitchcock, James. Review. *The Critic*, Vol. 36 Spring 1978.
        pp. 77-79.
        This leads to one of my major criticisms of Father Greeley's

book, namely, his generally unfriendly stance towards the anti-abortion movement, which is noticeable in some of his other writings even more. This is short-sighted because the Church's position on abortion and the militancy of so many Catholics on the subject, has been the greatest single occasion for the resurgence of respectable anti-Catholic feeling. There has been a massive effort--in the media, in academic life, in government agencies--to deny Catholics even the right to have a position on this subject, to discredit what they say simply because it is Catholics who are saying it.

3544   Christopher, Michael. "Did you hear about the Catholic who . . . " *U. S. Catholic*, Vol. 43 Mar. 1978. pp. 48-50.
I sometimes wonder that he is not stoned to death by his fellow sociologists and fellow theologians who seemingly are unable to duplicate or even come close to his stylistic achievements.

3545   Review. *Choice*, Vol. 15 May 1978. p. 418.

3546   Conlin, James J. Review. *Theological Studies*, Vol. 39 June 1978. p. 392.

3547   Kelly, James R. Review. *Thought*, Vol. 54 June 1979. pp. 208-210.

Everything You Wanted to Know about the Catholic Church But Were Too Pious to Ask.

3548   Dick, Jack. "For Greeley gourmets: a Catholic smorgasbord." *National Catholic Reporter*, Vol. 14 June 30, 1978. p. 15.
It's no high point of popularized theology, but it offers thinking Catholics a lot of common sense and quite a few chuckles.

3549   Gartland, Joan W. Review. *Library Journal*, Vol. 103 Aug. 1978. p. 1521.
Greeley has approached a monumental task with the tone of a talk-show host overly chummy both with his material and his audience.

Crisis in the Church: a study of religion in America.

3550   Bernard, Anne E. Review. *Library Journal*, Vol. 104 Apr. 15, 1979. p. 967.

3551   Van Allen, Rodger. Review. *Horizons*, Vol. 6 Fall 1979. pp. 321-322.
        I found Greeley's discussion of "communal Catholics" to be marked by more precision than in his other works. His data on the results of mixed marriages was quite interesting. The book's analysis of evangelization turns into a fascinating analysis of religion in America.

3552   Arroyo, Edward. "'Look sideways, as it were, on all done in this world'." *America*, Vol. 141 Sept. 15, 1979. pp. 117-118.

3553   Faase, Thomas P. Review. *Social Forces*, Vol. 58 Mar. 1980. pp. 992-993.

The Family in Crisis or in Transition.

3554   Clanton, Gordon. "Social-scientific study of religion." *Journal of the American Academy of Religion*, Vol. 49 Mar. 1981. pp. 158-159.

3555   Miller, Donald E. Review. *Religious Studies Review*, Vol. 7 Apr. 1981. p. 138.

The Making of the Popes 1978: the politics of intrigue in the Vatican.

3556   Thomas, Joseph R. "Greeley isn't White, but he's entertaining." *Catholic Messenger*, Apr. 26, 1979. p. 9.
        As for brilliance, in the light of the election of first Cardinal Albino Luciani and then Cardinal Karol Wojtyla as Popes John Paul I and II, it is impossible to top Fr. Greeley's before-the-fact analysis of the need for "a hopeful holy man who smiles." Bullseye.

3557   Hughes, John J. "The making of popes: a passionate insider's view." *America*, Vol. 140 May 26, 1979. p. 437.
        The book is a remarkable achievement. Flawed, but always fascinating, it will be read by tens of thousands whom the rest of us will never reach. We are fools, and guilty fools, if we dismiss it as unworthy of serious consideration."

3558   Schroth, Raymond A. "The vicars of Christ on earth." *New York Times Book Review*, June 24, 1979. pp. 11+.

3559   Wills, Gary. Review. *New Republic*, Vol. 181 July 21, 1979. p. 36.

3560   Maier, Paul L. Review. *Christian Century*, Vol. 96 Aug. 29, 1979. pp. 827-828.

3561   McBrien, Richard P. Review. *Commonweal*, Vol. 106 Aug. 31, 1979. pp. 472-474.

3562   Cornell, George W. Review. *The Critic*, Vol. 38 Sept. 1, 1979. pp. 4-5+.

Ethnic Drinking Subcultures.

3563   Blane, Howard T. Review. *Social Science and Medicine*, Vol. 16 n.m. 1982. pp. 346-347.

3564   Hill, Thomas W. Review. *Medical Anthropology Newsletter*, Vol. 13 May 1982. pp. 19-20.
        Given such fundamental theoretical and methodological difficulties, most anthropologists will not find much in this book to interest them.

The Young Catholic Family: religious images and marriage fulfillment.

3565   Gardiner, Anne M. Review. *Catholic Messenger*, Aug. 7, 1980. p. 9.

3566   Reese, Thomas J. Review. *America*, Vol. 143 Oct. 11, 1980.
        p. 216.

        The Irish Americans: the rise to money and power.

3567   Taliaferro, Frances. Review. *New York Times Book Review*,
        July 26, 1981. p. 12.

        Parish, Priest and People: new leadership for the local church.

3568   Casey, A. Robert. Review. *America*, Vol. 145 Dec. 5, 1981.
        pp. 364+.

3569   Varacalli, Joseph A. "A plea for the local church." *Cross
        Currents*, Vol. 32 Spring 1982. pp. 116-119.
        The most irritating aspect of the volume is the arrogant,
        falsely elitist, tone of some of the essays, especially those in
        which Greeley played a major part. Greeley constantly "talks
        down" to his readers, informing them that the overwhelming
        percentage of pastors are utter failures--and that he (Greeley)
        just happens to have all of the answers. This is all the more
        ironic in the light of Greeley's oft-made criticisms of the 1976
        Call to Action Assembly and the Bishops Bicentennial
        Celebration that it was run by a group of elitists out of touch
        with rank-and-file Catholics.

        The Religious Imagination.

3570   Navone, J. Review. *Gregorianum*, Vol. 64 n.m. 1983. pp.
        389-390.
        Greeley makes an important contribution to the theology of
        story with this thought-provoking and well-documented study
        of the factors that promote religious faith.

3571   Stack, Steven. Review. *Journal for the Scientific Study of
        Religion*, Vol. 22 Mar. 1983. p. 97.
        On the whole, this book is a solid contribution in the study of
        the causes and consequences of religious belief. It measures
        religiosity in an innovative way.

3572   Faase, Thomas P. Review. *Contemporary Sociology*, Vol. 12 July 1983. pp. 444-445.

Young Catholics in the United States and Canada: a report to the Knights of Columbus.

3573   McNamara, Patrick H. Review. *Sociological Analysis*, Vol. 43 Winter 1982. pp. 381-383.

3574   Wimberley, Dale W. Review. *Journal for the Scientific Study of Religion*, Vol. 22 June 1983. p. 198.
       The reader should keep in mind, however, that a number of this work's conclusions rest on assumptions which are questionable if not actually implausible.

The Bottom Line Catechism for Contemporary Catholics.

3575   Watts, Richard S. Review. *Library Journal*, Vol. 107 July 1982. p. 1334.

3576   Kinast, Robert L. Review. *Theological Studies*, Vol. 44 June 1983. pp. 314-316.
       Greeley is brimming with bias, energy, investment, flippancy, edges, provocation.

Catholic High Schools and Minority Students.

3577   Hassenger, Robert. Review. *Commonweal*, Vol. 109 Nov. 5, 1982. pp. 596-598.

3578   Review. *Choice*, Vol. 20 Dec. 1982. p. 626.

3579   Tavel, David. "Minority education and Catholic schools." *Social Education*, Vol. 47 Mar. 1983. p. 220.

3580   Hannaway, Jane. Review. *Journal for the Scientific Study of Religion*, Vol. 22 June 1983. pp. 198-200.

Religion: a secular theory.

3581   Armstrong, Edward G. Review. *Sociology and Social Research*, Vol. 67 Oct. 1982. pp. 91-92.

3582   Hunt, George L. Review. *Theology Today*, Vol. 39 Jan. 1983. pp. 481-482.
        The book is stimulating reading for anyone who is interested in religion, not as a series of propositions or proofs, but as a human experience.

3583   Lane, Ralph. Review. *Sociological Analysis*, Vol. 44 Spring 1983. p. 73.

3584   Christiano, Kevin J. Review. *Journal for the Scientific Study of Religion*, Vol. 22 Mar. 1983. pp. 88+.

3585   Faase, Thomas P. Review. *Contemporary Sociology*, Vol. 12 July 1983. pp. 444-445.

3586   Hillery, George A., Jr. Review. *Society*, Vol. 21 Nov./Dec. 1983. pp. 117-119.

3587   Hargrove, Barbara. Review. *Review of Religious Research*, Vol. 25 Dec. 1983. pp. 174-175.

3588   Jenkins, Pamela. Review. *Social Science Quarterly*, Vol. 64 Dec. 1983. pp. 915-916.

The Catholic WHY? Book.

3589   Review. *Library Journal*, Vol. 108 Oct. 15, 1983. p. 1966.

The Dilemma of American Immigration: beyond the golden door.

3590   Moore, Joan. Review. *Contemporary Sociology*, Vol. 13 July 1984. pp. 434-435.

3591   Jorgensen, Carl C. Review. *Social Forces*, Vol. 63 Mar. 1985.
        pp. 864-865.

3592   Tienda, Marta. Review. *American Journal of Sociology*, Vol. 91
        Jan. 1986. pp. 1023-1024.
        It is well written in nontechnical prose and contains no statis-
        tical tables. The latter feature is both an asset and a liability. It
        is an asset in that the book is more accessible to a broader
        audience; it is a liability in that readers are forced to rely on the
        authors'interpretation of the facts. . . .

A Piece of My Mind . . . on just about everything.

3593   Review. *Kirkus Reviews*, Vol. 51 Mar. 1, 1983. p. 283.
        Like any other successful columnist, Greeley writes pieces
        that are short, pithy, and upbeat.

3594   Review. *Publishers Weekly*, Vol. 223 Mar. 25, 1983. p. 41.

3595   Rockwood, D. Stephen. Review. *Library Journal*, Vol. 108
        May 1, 1983. p. 912.

3596   Breslin, John B.   "Andrew Greeley: piety and prurience."
        Washington Post Book World, July 10, 1983. pp. 3+.

*Angry Catholic Women: a sociological investigation Andrew M.
Greeley a theological reflection Mary G. Durkin.*

3597   Flynn, Eileen. P. Review. *Theology Today*, Vol. 41 Oct. 1984.
        pp. 363-365.
        While not the last word, it is a thoughtful commentary on a
        very pressing problem.

3598   Wallace, Ruth A. Review. *Sociological Analysis*, Vol. 46 Fall
        1985. pp. 335-336.

How to Save the Catholic Church.

3599   Imbelli, Robert. Review. *Commonweal*, Vol. 111 Oct. 19,

1984. pp. 563+.

3600 Nocera, Joseph. "Greeley's grail." *New Republic*, Vol. 191 Dec. 17, 1984. pp. 35-38. (Reply Feb. 25, 1985.)

3601 Gewen, Barry. "Two roads to Rome: writers and writing." *New Leader*, Vol. 67 Dec. 24, 1984. pp. 12-13.

3602 Schroth, Raymond A. "Sacramental encounters all over." *New York Times Book Review*, Jan. 6, 1985. p. 18. (Reply Mar. 17, 1985.)
More significant in a book that purports to chart the future of Catholicism is its silence on the so-called life issues--nuclear disarmament, abortion, capital punishment, race, world hunger, social and economic justice.

3603 Costello, Gerald M. "Church change: you ain't seen nothing yet." *U. S. Catholic*, Vol. 50 Feb. 1985. pp. 48-51.

3604 Durkin, Mary G. "Touchy Greeley." *New Republic*, Vol. 192 Feb. 25, 1985. p. 2. (Reply to Dec. 17, 1984.)

3605 Greeley, Andrew M. and Mary G. Durkin. "Sexual love as a sacrament." *New York Times Book Review*, Mar. 17, 1985. p. 32. (Reply to Jan. 6, 1985.)

3606 Cavanaugh, Michael A. "Two from Greeley." *Sociological Analysis*. Vol. 47 Summer 1986. pp. 173-174.

American Catholics Since the Council: an unauthorized report.

3607 Eykamp, Muriel C. Review. *Library Journal*, Vol. 110 Nov. 15, 1985. p. 104.

3608 Adriance, Madeleine. "Two from Greeley." *Sociological Analysis*, Vol. 47 Summer 1986. pp. 174-175.

3609 Kelly, Timothy I. "Review essay: American Catholics." *Journal of Social History*, Vol. 23 Fall 1989. pp. 155-166.
The strength of Greeley's work lies not in his overall

interpretation, however, but in the richness of the data upon which he reports. The historian can go to any chapter and glean valuable information about American Catholics' attitudes and beliefs over the past twenty years as reported in various national [*sic*] Opinion Research Center polls, including the General Social Survey and the University of Michigan American National Election Surveys.

Confessions of a Parish Priest: an autobiography.

3610   Toth, Susan A. "Don Quixote in the trenches." *New York Times Book Review*, Sept. 14, 1986. p. 14.
But his autobiography does reveal a man of depth, intense feeling and abiding belief. Readers looking for racy "confessions" may be disappointed, but those wanting to know more about this complex priest--and his church--will be well rewarded.

3611   Blotner, Joseph. "'for a happy life is joy in the truth'." *America*, Vol. 155 Oct. 4, 1986. pp. 170-173.
This book, says Father Greeley, is the first part of his story, Volume One. It is to this reader an admirable story, and he will do his best to wait in patience for Volume Two.

3612   Deedy, John. "Andrew Greeley, this is my life!" *Commonweal*, Vol. 113 Oct. 24, 1986. pp. 560-561.
Many people write autobiographies who needn't have. That's not Andrew Greeley's case. His is a life and self-view which should be on the record, if only for the narrower denominational world of Roman Catholicism.

3613   McCarthy, John R. Review. *Catholic Historical Review*, Vol. 74 Jan. 1988. pp. 141-142.

Catholic Contributions: sociology and policy.

3614   Review. *Christian Century*, Vol. 104 Sept. 30, 1987. p. 836.

3615   Novak, Francis A. "Church support: winning back the laity." *The Priest*, Vol. 44 Jan. 1988. pp. 10-15.

God in Popular Culture.

3616   Griffin, William. Review. *Publishers Weekly*, Vol. 235 Mar. 17, 1989. p. 73.
It is a dazzling performance, and impossible not to agree as often as disagree with Greeley's thesis.

3617   Watts, Richard S. Review. *Library Journal*, Vol. 114 Apr. 15, 1989. p. 79.

3618   Brunkhorst, Christine L. Review. *America*, Vol. 160 May 13, 1989. pp. 459-461.

3619   Sequeira, Isaac. Review. *Journal of Popular Culture*, Vol. 23 Summer 1989. pp. 137-140.
Greeley's discussion is always sharp, penetrating, catholic and syncretic because of his range of scholarship across a variety of disciplines.

When Life Hurts.

3620   Finley, Mitch. Review. *St. Anthony Messenger*, Vol. 96 Jan. 1989. pp. 49-51.
Among Father Greeley's many talents is a knack for getting to the heart of the matter in language that cuts out all foolishness and says this is how it is.

3621   Griffin, William. Review. *Publishers Weekly*, Vol. 237 Mar. 9, 1990. p. 47.
Vintage Greeley!

Religious Change in America.

3622   Coleman, John A. Review. *Commonweal*, Vol. 116 Oct. 20, 1989. pp. 568-569.

3623   Olson, Daniel V. Review. *American Journal of Sociology*, Vol. 95 Jan. 1990. pp. 1099-1101.
Those unfamiliar with the data Greeley cites will find the

book provocative and challenging. Those familiar with these data will find his analyses helpful. Those looking for a general interpretation of American religion will find the theoretical speculations of the last eight pages interesting but incomplete.

3624   Kelly, James R. Review. *Contemporary Sociology*, Vol. 19 Mar. 1990. pp. 285-286.

3625   Byrne, Harry J. Review. *America*, Vol. 162 June 16, 1990. pp. 611-613.

3626   Glenn, Norval D. Review. *Public Opinion Quarterly*, Vol. 54 Fall 1990. pp. 444-447.

3627   Roof, Wade C. Review. *Journal for the Scientific Study of Religion*, Vol. 30 Mar. 1991. pp. 122-124.
        He makes his point without unnecessary verbiage, and his data have a way of jumping out at you in new and refreshing ways.

3628   Martin, Steele W. Review. *Anglican Theological Review*, Vol. 73 Winter 1991. pp. 88-89.

The Bible and Us: a priest and a rabbi read scripture together.

3629   Woodward, Kenneth L. "The priest and the rabbi: do Jews and Christians have anything to discuss?" *Newsweek*, Vol. 116 July 30, 1990. p. 46.

3630   Zaleski, Philip. "The priest, the rabbi and the best of intentions." *New York Times Book Review*, Sept. 2, 1990. p. 9.
        Like all successful collaborations, this one works because the partners scuffle as often as they nuzzle.

The Catholic Myth: the behavior and beliefs of American Catholics.

3631   Rutler, George W. "Popular opinion." *National Review*, Vol. 42 Apr. 16, 1990. pp. 51-52.

3632   Warner, R. Stephen. "Here is the church, here are the people."
        New York Times Book Review, Apr. 22, 1990. p. 9.
        . . . and it must be said that he expects the sacramental-
        imagination construct to do more work than the sociologist,
        wanting to inspect the tables, or the general reader, looking
        for imagery from other Catholic novelists, can easily accept.

3633   Wycliff, Don. Review. *Commonweal*, Vol. 117 May 18, 1990.
        pp. 323-324.

3634   Sullivan, Andrew. "Incense and sensibility: the spiritual con-
        fusions of American Catholicism." *New Republic*, Vol. 203 Sept.
        24, 1990. pp. 33-38.

3635   Yanitelli, Victor R. Review. *America*, Vol. 164 June 1, 1991.
        pp. 604-606.
        Backed by some 30 years of intensive monitoring of move-
        ments within and without the Catholic Church, this
        professional sociologist sets about shooting down a whole host
        of mass-media-created so-called popular "facts" about the
        U. S. Catholic Church.

Year of Grace.

3636   Review. *Christian Century*, Vol. 108 Mar. 20, 1991. p. 345.

3637   Forrester, David. "The human condition." *The Tablet* (London),
        Vol. 245 May 25, 1991. p. 651.
        Alternately trenchant or perceptive and occasionally lyrical,
        he is never dull. For him "pure astonishment" is the heart of
        the religious experience and it is this quality which crops up
        time and again in the pages of *Year of Grace*.

A Book of Irish American Blessings & Prayers.

3638   Hillenmeyer, Kathleen. Review. *St. Anthony Messenger*, Vol.
        99 Mar. 1992. pp. 50-52.
        These blessings and prayers will relieve the doldrums.

3639   Forrester, David. Review. *The Tablet* (London), Vol. 246 Sept.
        26, 1992. p. 1200.
        Clearly Irish-American in style, they [the blessings and
        prayers] also respond to our deepest needs.

Faithful Attraction: discovering intimacy, love, and fidelity in American marriage.

3640   Review. *Kirkus Reviews*, Vol. 58 Dec. 15, 1990. p. 1721.
        A few flashes of vintage Greeley wit, but for the most part
        this is a dry report; the pleasure lies in contemplating the
        (mostly) good tidings it relays.

3641   Review. *Publishers Weekly*, Vol. 238 Jan. 4, 1991. p. 64.

3642   Yanitelli, Victor R. Review. *America*, Vol. 164 June 1, 1991.
        pp. 604-606.
        . . . *Faithful Attraction* is a book written with relish. A joyful
        spirit seems to surface every now and then, especially when
        another shibboleth is being demolished.

3643   Doyle, John. "Father Greeley explains it all for you." *Globe
        and Mail*, July 13, 1991. Sec. C p. 13.
        Faithful Attraction is intended as a benchmark against which
        all future pronouncements on marriage in America can be
        measured.

Love Affair: a prayer journal.

3644   Thompson, Joanna M. Review. *Library Journal*, Vol. 117 July
        1992. p. 89.

3645   Review. *Publishers Weekly*, Vol. 239 July 20, 1992. p. 242.

3646   Finley, Mitchel B. Review. *St. Anthony Messenger*, Vol. 100
        Feb. 1993. pp. 52-53.
        Readers will discover, or rediscover, Father Greeley's unique
        ability to identify religious concepts that many of us
        understand but vaguely and his gift for restating them in terms
        that make good sense.

NOVELS

The Magic Cup: an Irish legend.

3647   Review. *The Critic*, Vol. 38 Mar.-I, 1980. p. 7.
There are some out there who would ardently like to see him
overreach himself just once. They'll have to wait for another
day because *The Magic Cup* makes remarkably good reading
and reveals a solid base of research on the social trauma that
accompanied the change from pagan to Christian ways.

3648   Christopher, Michael. Review. *U. S. Catholic*, Vol. 45 May
1980. pp. 49-50.

Death in April.

3649   Pradt, Mary A. Review. *Library Journal*, Vol. 105 Sept. 15,
1980. p. 1878.

3650   Review. *The Critic*, Vol. 39 Oct. 1, 1980. p. 8.
Greeley knows his Chicago well, and the world of Irish-
Catholic power and politics even better.

The Cardinal Sins.

3651   Review. *Kirkus Reviews*, Vol. 49 Mar. 1, 1981. p. 302.

3652   Nobile, Philip. "Steamy sex and the celibate novelist." *National
Catholic Reporter*, Vol. 17 May 1, 1981. p. 17. *See* reply
Catholic Messenger, May 14, 1981 (1714).

3653   Shea, John. Review. *The Critic*, Vol. 39 July-I & II, 1981.
p. 5.
The subject matter is the eternal mix of human obsessions--
religion, sex, politics, friendship, requited and unrequited love,
violence, vindication, death and hope. Always hope. If you
don't find what you want, wait a page, it will turn up.

3654   McKean, Margaret K. "Towering 'Cathedral' lowly 'Cardinal'."
Los Angeles Times Book Review, July 19, 1981. p. 10.

3655   Mohs, Mayo. "Fighting Irish." *Time*, Vol. 118 Aug. 10, 1981. p. 69.

3656   Firth, Brian. "Change and intrigue." *The Tablet* (London), Vol. 235 Oct. 24, 1981. pp. 1045-1046.
. . . his emphasis on intrigue means that the process of change [in the Church] is presented not in terms of changing experience, but in terms of a series of challenges to political and moral decision.

Thy Brother's Wife.

3657   Champlin, Charles.   "Beneath the passions, a message of morality." *Los Angeles Times Book Review*, Mar. 28, 1982. pp. 1+.
The book will not necessarily be read for its message instead of the melodrama, but the message is there.

3658   Schott, Webster. "Sacred and secular love." *New York Times Book Review*, Apr. 11, 1982. pp. 7+.
Andrew Greeley's novel makes strong statements about important matters--love, morality, power, belief and human frailty under the pressure of animal drives.

3659   Moore, Benita.   "Greeley's priests are still very human." *Catholic Messenger*, Apr. 22, 1982. p. 9.
Fr. Greeley is doing his part to hold the mirror of art up to culture. If some illusions are shattered while deeper truths are revealed, so be it.

3660   Gallagher, Michael. "'No authentic Christian vision'." *National Catholic Reporter,* Vol. 18 Apr. 30, 1982. p. 16.

3661   Mohs, Mayo. "The luck of Andrew Greeley." *Time*, Vol. 120 July 12, 1982. pp. 70+.

Ascent into Hell.

3662   Schott, Webster. "A priest's indulgence." *New York Times Book Review*, July 3, 1983. p. 8.

Still, I enjoy reading Andrew Greeley. He is never dull, he
spins wondrous romances and he has an admirable ideal for
what his church should become.

3663   Breslin, John B.   "Andrew Greeley: piety and prurience."
        Washington Post Book World, July 10, 1983. pp. 3+.

3664   Browne, Joseph.   "'Stories, like whiskey, must be allowed to
        mature in the cask'." *America*, Vol. 149 Oct. 22, 1983.
        pp. 236-237.

Lord of the Dance.

3665   Review. *Kirkus Reviews*, Vol. 52 Jan. 1, 1984. p. 5.

3666   Vogel, Christine B. "The high priest of pulp." *Washington Post*,
        Apr. 6, 1984. Sec. D p. 8.
        It is probably the most hopeful of Greeley's novels
        (appropriate, considering its Easter symbolism) and the least
        unkind to the Catholic Church.

Happy Are the Meek.

3667   Review. *Publishers Weekly*, Vol. 228 Aug. 9, 1985. p. 71.
        Blackie Ryan is a character who could definitely become
        habit-forming.

3668   Stasio, Marilyn. Review. *New York Times Book Review*, Sept.
        29, 1985. p. 46.

3669   Christie, David. "Paper crimes." *Armchair Detective*, Vol. 19
        Spring 1986. p. 210.
        It will surprise no one that Greeley is considerably more
        liberal than his church, and that his theology is therefore
        unorthodox. As a result, Greeley's explanation of meekness and
        the book's religious content generally are fascinating, even for
        a reader raised in another faith.

Virgin and Martyr.

3670   Review. *Kirkus Reviews*, Vol. 52 Dec. 15, 1984. p. 1157.

3671   McCarthy, Abigail. "Gospel according to Greeley: sex and money." *Chicago Tribune*, Mar. 3, 1985. Sec. 14 p. 33.

3672   Cooney, John. "St. Cathy of Chicago." *New York Times Book Review*, Mar. 10, 1985. p. 13.

3673   Breslin, Patrick. "Confessions of a novelist." *Washington Post Book World*, Mar. 24, 1985. p. 6.

3674   Ames, Carol. Review. *Los Angeles Times Book Review*, Apr. 7, 1985. p. 4.

Angels of September.

3675   Review. *Kirkus Reviews*, Vol. 53 Dec. 1, 1985. pp. 1276-1277.

3676   Dooley, Susan. "The gospel according to Greeley." *Washington Post*, Jan. 27, 1986. Sec. B p. 9.

3677   Akst, Daniel. Review. *Los Angeles Times Book Review*, Mar. 16, 1986. p. 4.
         Stereotypes and bad dialogue abound, and while the story unfolds nicely, the outcome is preposterous.

3678   Polak, Maralyn L. "A passion born in kindergarten." *New York Times Book Review*, Mar. 30, 1986. p. 10. (Reply Apr. 20, 1986.)

3679   Greeley, Andrew. "'Angels of September.'" *New York Times Book Review*, Apr. 20, 1986. p. 34. (Reply to Mar. 30, 1986.)

God Game.

3680   Sladek, John. "Andrew Greeley's Messianic mess." *Washington Post*, July 21, 1986. Sec. D p. 4.

This is what comes of Bailey's Irish Cream. Greeley needs to fire this character [the narrator] and replace him with a good honest whiskey priest.

3681   Geis, Richard E. Review. *Science Fiction Review*, Vol. 15 Aug. 1986. p. 37.

3682   Kennedy, Veronica M. "Hubris, computer-enhanced." *Fantasy Review*, Vol. 9 Sept. 1986. p. 24.

3683   Jonas, Gerald. Review. *New York Times Book Review*, Sept. 21, 1986. p. 31.
        It is Father Greeley's point that all writers are less-than-omnipotent creators whose struggles to control their creations can teach us something about the theological concept of grace.

Happy Are the Clean of Heart.

3684   Review. *Publishers Weekly*, Vol. 230 July 18, 1986. p. 84.

The Final Planet.

3685   Collins, Bill. Review. *Science Fiction & Fantasy Book Review Annual 1988*, ed. by Robert A. Collins and Robert Latham. Westport, CT: Meckler, 1988. pp. 193-194.
        Also appears in *Fantasy Review*, July/Aug. 1987.

Happy Are Those Who Thirst for Justice.

3686   Review. *Kirkus Reviews*, Vol. 55 Aug. 1, 1987. p. 1115.

Patience of a Saint.

3687   Review. *Kirkus Reviews*, Vol. 54 Nov. 1, 1986. p. 1603.
        Although it suffers from the Greeley hallmark of a self-consciously naughty emphasis on shocking prose and sexual situations, this novel ultimately succeeds through its

supercharged central character, prose so energetic it fairly
bounces off the page, and the audacity of the central premise.

3688   Sullivan, Jack. "Oh, to be sexually indifferent." *New York
Times Book Review*, Feb. 8, 1987. p. 31

3689   Leopold, Wendy. Review. *Los Angeles Times Book Review*,
Feb. 15, 1987. p. 4.

Rite of Spring.

3690   Review. *Kirkus Reviews*, Vol. 55 Sept. 1, 1987. p. 1259.
A Mickey Finn of a book, a knockout brew of spilled blood,
ripe bosoms (one of Fr. Greeley's favorite images), sizzling
suspense, and swirls of Irish mist, by the tart-tongued imp of
American letters.

3691   McDaniel, Maude. "Greeley's Irish stew." *Washington Post*,
Nov. 16, 1987. Sec. B p. 4.

Angel Fire.

3692   McCully, William C. Review. *Library Journal*, Vol. 113 July
1988. p. 92.

3693   Teal, Alison. Review. *New York Times Book Review*, Aug. 14,
1988. p. 16.

3694   Lowry, Mary A. Review. *Science Fiction & Fantasy Book
Review Annual 1989*, ed. by Robert A. Collins and Robert
Latham. Westport, CT: Meckler, 1990. pp. 285-286.

Love Song.

3695   Steinberg, Sybil. Review. *Publishers Weekly*, Vol. 234 Oct. 14,
1988. p. 50.

3696   Olson, Kiki. Review. *New York Times Book Review*, Jan. 22,
1989. p. 23.

3697   Graham, William C. "Andrew Greeley's new one, and many others." *National Catholic Reporter,* Vol. 25 June 16, 1989. p. 20.

St. Valentine's Night.

3698   Schulman, Donna L. Review. *Library Journal,* Vol. 114 June 15, 1989. pp. 79-80.

3699   Paulos, Sheila. Review. *New York Times Book Review,* Sept. 17, 1989. p. 24.
        The most entertaining aspects of this book are its author's perceptive remarks on topics ranging from the Afghan freedom fighters to the ethics of television news reporting--which, unfortunately, don't have all that much to do with advancing the plot or fleshing out the characters.

The Cardinal Virtues.

3700   Review. *Kirkus Reviews,* Vol. 58 Feb. 15, 1990. p. 207.

3701   Steinberg, Sybil. Review. *Publishers Weekly,* Vol. 237 Mar. 23, 1990. p. 66.
        While the plot is plausible, Greeley simply fails to engage us; with the possible exception of Lar, the characters remain two-dimensional, serving Greeley's nostalgia for those who believed in Vatican II and his revulsion for those who fought the reforms.

An Occasion of Sin.

3702   Finn, Peter. Review. *New York Times Book Review,* June 30, 1991. p. 20.

3703   Kanfer, Stefan. Review. *Time,* Vol. 137 July 1, 1991. p. 71.

3704   Doyle, John. "Father Greeley explains it all for you." *Globe and Mail,* July 13, 1991. Sec. C p. 13.

It's a rapid read thriller full of references to real events and
real people.

The Search for Maggie Ward.

3705   Steinberg, Sybil. Review. *Publishers Weekly*, Vol. 237 Nov.
        23, 1990. p. 55.

3706   Ramsland, Katherine. Review. *New York Times Book Review*,
        Dec. 30, 1990. p. 14.

Happy Are the Merciful.

3707   Review. *Publishers Weekly*, Vol. 239 Feb. 3, 1992. p. 75.
        . . . the dialogue is lean and the plotting appropriately
        convoluted yet logical.

Wages of Sin.

3708   Review. *Kirkus Reviews*, Vol. 60 May 15, 1992. p. 627. (A
        Kirkus "book of special note.")

3709   Review. *Publishers Weekly*, Vol. 239 June 22, 1992. p. 46.

3710   Finley, Mitchel B. Review. *St. Anthony Messenger*, Vol. 100
        Feb. 1993. pp. 52-53.
        If your own exposure to preaching leaves you in danger of
        cracking your head solidly on the back of the pew in front of
        you, the preaching in this novel is an outstanding remedy.

Fall from Grace.

3711   Review. *Publishers Weekly*, Vol. 239 Dec. 14, 1992. pp. 38-39.
        Greeley maintains suspense by not revealing all of the con-
        nections between characters and events until the denouement,
        but the clues are there and the ending is satisfying.

3712   Shapiro, Susan. Review. *People*, Vol. 39 May 3, 1993. p. 36.
. . . his novel trenchantly depicts the intricate machinations of an attempted Church cover-up.

Happy Are the Peacemakers.

3713   Review. *Publishers Weekly*, Vol. 240 Mar. 8, 1993. p. 73.
. . . the inevitable love affair between the detective and Nora is both realistic and tension-provoking.

SHORT STORIES

All about Women

3714   Kaganoff, Penny. Review. *Publishers Weekly*, Vol. 236 Dec. 8, 1989. p. 50.

3715   Solomon, Andy. Review. *New York Times Book Review*, Jan. 7, 1990. p. 18.
These are cumbersome, antiseptic tales whose sentimentality is reminiscent of Hollywood movies in the 1930's and television comedies in the 1950's.

INDEXES

AUTHOR INDEX

References are to entry numbers, not page numbers.

TITLE INDEX

References are to entry numbers, not to page numbers. Book titles are shown in italics.

Dynamics of Catholic opinion, The 159

Ecstasy 50 (Reviews 3477-3482)
Editorial research note 642
Education of Catholic Americans, The 8, 57 (Reviews 3361-3367)
Effectiveness of self-administered questionnaires, The 358
Effects of Catholic education, The. Part I 324, Part II 351, Part III 354
Ellis Peters 758
Emerging Coalitions in American Politics 189
Empirical liturgy 777
Encyclopedia of Social Work Vol. 2 187
End of American Catholicism? The 515
End of Catholicism, The 741
End of religion? The 529
Entering the mainstream 348
Eros and the womanliness of God 3024
Ethnic America 2814
Ethnic and religious origins of young American scientists and engineers,
    The 511
Ethnic and Social Segregation in the New York Metropolis 2780
Ethnic Chauvinism 2812
Ethnic divergences 869
Ethnic domestic architecture in Chicago 690
Ethnic Drinking Subcultures 76 (Reviews 3563-3564)
Ethnic Enterprise in America 2768, 2787
Ethnic Families in America 2797
Ethnic group which vanished--the strange case of the American Irish, An
    492
Ethnic Groups in the City 160
Ethnic Identity 2852
Ethnic minorities in the United States 639
Ethnic miracle, The 621
Ethnic Politics in America 2759
Ethnic variations in religious commitment 191
Ethnicity 65, 184 (Reviews 3530-3531)
Ethnicity and nationality in alcoholism 197
Ethnicity and racial attitudes 575
Ethnicity as an influence on behavior 160, 431
Ethnicity, Denomination and Inequality 60 (Reviews 3511-3512)
Ethnicity in the United States 51 (Reviews 3483-3487)
Evangelization in the American Context 2810

From Backwater to Mainstream 16 (Reviews 3385-3387)
Frustrating fifties, The 265
Full life, The 223
Future Forms of Ministry 163
Future of an ailing church, The 631
Future of Catholic Leadership, The 2839
Future of the Christian Churches in the 1970's 17
Future to Hope In, A 18 (Reviews 3388-3389)

Games are not enough 230
Gateway, The 3002
General Theory of Secularization, A 2811
Give them back their revolutionary 286
Gloom and doom don't fit into the Good News 415
God as lover/God as sadist 3029
God Game 123 (Reviews 3680-3683)
God in Popular Culture 98 (Reviews 3616-3619)
God who plays it by ear, A 838
God's Warriors 2857
Going their own way 724
Going whose way? 249
Good liturgy is little more than a good weave 812
Good News 52
Good Society, The 2856
Good worship 424
Gospel of Shame, A 3044
Graced interludes of wonder 687
Great Mysteries, The 61, 93 (Reviews 3513-3517)
Greeley: it's faddish on revolution 399
Greeley on Fichter 380
Guide to conferencemanship 516, 520

Habits of the Heart 2825, 2856
Hail Mary 571
Hair of the Dog, A 2801, 2807
Hallucinations among the widowed 771
Handful of tinsel, A 925
Hanukkah, Christmas--in the same light 831
Happy Are the Clean of Heart 124 (Review 3684)
Happy Are the Meek 119 (Reviews 3667-3669)
Happy Are the Merciful 136 (Review 3707)

APPENDIX

SUBJECT CATEGORIES

To locate the entry for a title please consult the title index on page 349.

AMERICAN CATHOLICISM

Books

The Church and the Suburbs.
The Hesitant Pilgrim: American Catholicism after the Council.
The Catholic Experience: an interpretation of the history of American Catholicism.
The Future of the Christian Churches in the 1970's.
Come Blow Your Mind with Me.
The American Catholic: a social portrait.
An Ugly Little Secret: anti-Catholicism in North America.
Communication in the Church.
Crisis in the Church: a study of religion in America.
Young Catholics in the United States and Canada.
Angry Catholic Women.
American Catholics since the Council: an unauthorized report.
Confessions of a Parish Priest: an autobiography.
Catholic Contributions: sociology and policy.
The Catholic Myth: the behavior and beliefs of American Catholics.

Essays

"The urban church."
"American Catholics: the post-immigrant century."
"Why Catholics stay in the church."

Articles

"Some information on the present situation of American Catholics."

"U. S. Catholicism: growth or decline?"
"Theories of American Catholicism."
"The real problems of the American Church."
"Catholicism Midwest style."
"What's right with American Catholics?"
"Anti-clericalism in the American church."
"The church in the suburbs: some afterthoughts."
"The church as "new community.""
"U. S. Catholics '72."
"The end of American Catholicism."
"Drop in churchgoing 'catastrophic'."
"Rate of catastrophe may drop."
"The 'Catholic action' ideology: a non-nostalgic reappraisal."
"The next 10 years."
"American Catholics: ten years later."
"Birth control--a bitter pill for Catholics."
"Catholics loyal to their schools, cite lack of them."
"Supply of priests drops."
"The crisis in American Catholicism":
    "Ten years of declining loyalty and religious devotion in U. S."
    "Part II: The disastrous effect of Pope Paul's encyclical."
    "Part III: Fewer schools a mistake; CCD no substitute."
    "Part IV: Respect for the priesthood has been diminishing."
    "Part V: Despite what you hear, donations are down."
    "Part VI: Scenarios show some bad news on the horizon."
"Catholicism in America: two hundred years and counting."
"Dispelling myths about Catholics."
"The future of an ailing church."
"Little impact from 9 U. S. cardinals."
"Scant say by Yanks on pontiff."
"U. S. Catholics grow up: a letter from America by Andrew Greeley."
"A profile of the American Catholic family."
"U. S. Catholics' crisis."
"Message from Chicago."
"Catholics at the end of the century."
"Going their own way."
"The year of the Catholic."
"American Catholicism: 1909-1984."
"Why Catholics stay in the church."
"Defection among Hispanics."
"Where have all the contributions gone? And why?"
"Is there an American Catholic elite?"

"Challenges facing U. S. Catholics: the next ten years."
"Parish priest holds key to solution of financial difficulties."
"Actions speak louder than doctrine in fueling dissent."
"Angry Catholics: Poll finds key issues affect their generosity."
"Catholics speak out: Many are angry, but few leave."
"Family and faith are key reasons most Catholics remain in church."
"Toughest church critics: Catholic women over 40."
"Bernardin has favorable image with 70 percent."
"Who are the Catholic 'conservatives'?"

CATECHISMS, MEDITATIONS, PRAYERS

Books

Complaints Against God.
Jesus Now: meditations by a modern pilgrim.
Good News: further reflections by a modern pilgrim.
May the Wind Be at your Back: the prayer of St. Patrick.
The Great Mysteries: an essential catechism.
Christ for All Seasons: fifty-two personal meditations.
Fifty-Two Gospel Meditations: by a modern pilgrim.
The Bottom Line Catechism for Contemporary Catholics.
Love in the Gospels: by a modern pilgrim.
When Life Hurts.
The Irish.
Year of Grace: a spiritual journal.
A Book of Irish American Blessings & Prayers.
Love Affair: a prayer journal.

EDUCATION

Books

Religion and Career: a study of college graduates.
The Education of Catholic Americans.
The Changing Catholic College.
The Student in Higher Education.
From Backwater to Mainstream: a profile of Catholic higher education.
Can Catholic Schools Survive?

Recent Alumni and Higher Education: a survey of college graduates.
Catholic Schools in a Declining Church.
Catholic High Schools and Minority Students.

Essays

"Non-public schools and metropolitanism."
"The teaching of moral wisdom."
"Catholic high schools and the secular city."
"Catholic scholars witness to freedom: a symposium."
"The religious effects of parochial education."
"Rethinking urban religious education."
"Freedom of choice: our commitment to integration."
"School desegregation and ethnicity."
"Catholic high schools and minority students."

Articles

"Catholic scholars of tomorrow: report on a survey."
"Do they lose the faith at secular colleges?"
"Anti-intellectualism in Catholic colleges."
"Catholic colleges: system in transition."
"The effects of Catholic education. Part I."
"Conventional wisdom and the Catholic schools."
"Correlates of parochial school attendance."
"The impact of the Roman Catholic denominational school."
"The contribution the behavioral sciences can make in seminary training."
"The new debate--I: entering the mainstream."
"The effects of Catholic education. Part II."
"The effects of Catholic education. Part III."
"Catholic education."
"Criticism of undergraduate faculty by graduates of Catholic colleges."
"The place of religion."
"Parochial school origins and educational achievement."
"The Catholic campus."
"Campus community: experiment in living."
"Issues in the teaching of religion in Catholic colleges and universities."
"The facts about Catholic schools."
"'Laicization' of Catholic colleges."
"Myths and fads in Catholic higher education."
"The college blight on idealism."

"Academe, my academe."
"Comparative financial and employee data on Catholic institutions of higher education."
"The new urban studies: a word of caution."
"Between 'tenuously in' and 'solidly in': a view from the borderland."
"The Newman report: four comments."
"Public and nonpublic schools--losers both."
"Catholic schools are committing suicide."
"Catholic education produces 'hopefuls'."
"Is this suicide necessary?"
"Intellectuals."
"A school report."
"Is the American educational enterprise anti-Catholic?"
"Who controls Catholic education?"
"Neighbourhood and downtown."
"A preliminary investigation: the 'profitability' of Catholic schools."
"The need for leadership: an outsider's viewpoint."
"Schooling in the U. S. A."
"Why Catholic higher learning is lower."
"Catholic high schools: an effective inner-city ministry."
"Catholic intellectual life."
"Achievement growth in public and Catholic schools."
"Community as social capital: James S. Coleman on Catholic schools."
"Catholic schools: a golden twilight."
"Don't sell Catholic schools short."
"My research on Catholic schools."
"A modest proposal for the reform of Catholic schools."

ETHNICITY

Books

Why Can't They Be Like Us? Facts and fallacies about ethnic differences and group conflicts in America.
Ethnicity in the United States: a preliminary reconnaissance.
Media: ethnic media in the United States.
Ethnicity, Denomination and Inequality.
Ethnicity.
Ethnic Drinking Subcultures.
Catholic High Schools and Minority Students.
The Dilemma of American Immigration: beyond the golden door.

Essays

"White against white: the enduring ethnic conflict."
"Ethnicity as an influence on behavior."
"Take heart from the heartland."
"'We' and 'they': the differences linger."
"What is an ethnic?"
"Attitudes toward racial integration."
"New ethnicity and blue collars: cultural pluralism in the working class."
"The transmission of cultural heritages: the case of the Irish and the
    Italians."
"Why study ethnicity?"
"Minorities: white ethnics."
"Ethnic variations in religious commitment."
"School desegregation and ethnicity."
"Catholic high schools and minority students."
"Immigration and religio-ethnic groups: a sociological reappraisal."
"Ethnicity and nationality in alcoholism."

Articles

"The Negro and his middle class leadership."
"What about this Negro community?"
"American sociology and the study of ethnic immigrant groups."
"Ethnicity as an influence on behavior."
"A note on political and social differences among ethnic college graduates."
"The misunderstood minority."
"Take heart from the heartland."
"The alienation of white ethnic groups."
"The rediscovery of diversity."
"For a black vice president in 1972."
"Portrait of a neighborhood, changing."
"Attitudes toward racial integration."
"Political attitudes among American white ethnics."
"The new ethnicity and blue collars: cultural pluralism in the working
    class."
"The civil religion of ethnic Americans: the viewpoint of a Catholic
    sociologist."
"Civil religion and ethnic Americans."
"Reflections on politics and pluralism: a response to jeremiads."
"Making it in America: ethnic groups and social status."
"Does ethnicity matter?"

"Catholics and Democrats: an ethnic manifesto."
"Political participation among ethnic groups in the United States: a
preliminary reconnaissance."
"Notes on a theology of pluralism."
"Political attitudes among American ethnics: a study of perceptual
distortion."
"Ethnicity and racial attitudes: the case of the Jews and the Poles."
"A model for ethnic political socialization."
"Is ethnicity unAmerican?"
"The ethnic miracle."
"Ethnic minorities in the United States: demographic perspectives."
"Editorial research note."
"Attitudes toward racial integration."
"After Ellis Island."
"Ethnic domestic architecture in Chicago."
"The persistence of diversity."
"Social determinants of racial prejudice."
"Attitudes toward racial equality."
"The persistence of diversity."

THE IRISH

Books

That Most Distressful Nation: the taming of the American Irish.
The Irish Americans: the rise to money and power.
The Irish: photographs by Andrew M. Greeley . . . along with poems,
proverbs, and blessings.

Essays

"The Irish."
"The American achievement: a report from Great Ireland."

Articles

"The last of the American Irish fade away."
"The American Irish since the death of Studs Lonigan."
"A most distressful nation: a portrait of the American Irish."
"An ethnic group which vanished: the strange case of the American Irish."
"Occupational choice among the American Irish: a research note."

"A most distressful nation: the American Irish."
"The meaning of being Irish-American."
"The unwanted who proved indispensable."
"The American Irish: a report from Great Ireland."
"Creativity in the Irish family: the cost of immigration."
"The success and assimilation of Irish Protestants and Irish Catholics in the
    United States."
"'Development' and tolerance: the case of Ireland."

THE PRIESTHOOD

Books

Priests for Tomorrow.
Uncertain Trumpet: the priest in modern America.
New Horizons for the Priesthood.
The Catholic Priest in the United States: sociological investigations.
Priests in the United States: reflections on a survey.
Parish, Priest and People: new leadership for the local church.

Essays

"Priesthood."
"Andrew M. Greeley: sociologist, author, novelist."

Articles

"Going whose way?"
"Letter to a seminarian."
"Parish priest as administrator."
"The lonely pastor and the expendable curate."
"The problems of ex-priests."
"A question of identity."
"Leadership."
"Overkill on celibacy."
"A fresh look at vocations."
"Why they leave."
"Priest, church and the future from a sociological viewpoint."
"The state of the priesthood."
"The sexual revolution among Catholic clergy."

"Why priests stay."
"Role commitment processes and the American Catholic priesthood."
"Proposed: limited terms of priesthood."
"Do priests fall in love? Of course they do."
"We priests owe a debt of gratitude to Robert Blake."
"Bishops paralyzed over heavily gay priesthood."
"Some married men aren't faithful, but we don't say marriage is a failure."
"Priestly silence on pedophelia."
"But Father, they're priests! Clerical culture and pedophilia."
"How serious is the problem of sexual abuse by clergy?"
"A view from the priesthood: it's bigotry to blame celibacy for church problems."

THE RELIGIOUS IMAGINATION

Books

The Religious Imagination.
Religion: a secular theory.
How to Save the Catholic Church.

Articles

"The religious imagination: a sociological approach."
"Fiction and the religious imagination."
"The Catholic imagination of Bruce Springsteen."
"Protestant and Catholic: is the analogical imagination extinct."
"The Catholic imagination and the Catholic university."
"Theology and sociology: on validating David Tracy."

SOCIAL AND POLITICAL COMMENTARY

Books

The Church and the Suburbs.
Building Coalitions: American politics in the 1970's.
Neighborhood.
No Bigger Than Necessary: an alternative to socialism, capitalism and anarchism.

Faithful Attraction: discovering intimacy, love, and fidelity in American marriage.

Essays

"The new American religion."
"The redeeming of America according to Charles Reich."
"Contemporary American romanticism."
"Catholics and coalition: where should they go?"

Articles

"The myth of machine-made leisure."
"Suburbia: a new way of life."
"The Catholic suburbanite."
"The suburban novel."
"Beat, cool--and lonely."
"The changing city."
"Conformity or community?"
"Organization man: hope for a halo."
"The frustrating fifties."
"Pioneers in suburbia."
"The vanishing hero."
"The neurotic city."
"Suburbia revisited."
"An upper middle class deviant gang."
"The church in the suburbs: some afterthoughts."
"The psychedelic and the sacred."
"The sacred and the psychedelic."
"There's a new-time religion on campus."
"The overcommitted man."
"Turning off 'the people': the war and white ethnic groups."
"Intellectuals as an 'ethnic group'."
"Malice in Wonderland: misperceptions of the academic elite."
"The redeeming of America according to Charles Reich."
"War, morality and error."
"The 'new politics' was big loser in elections."
"A scrapyard for the Daley organization?"
"More long weekends: a relatively modest proposal."
"Leave John Kennedy in peace."
"Theological table-talk: politics and political theologians."

"Antiwar fictions."
"What is a liberal: who is a conservative."
"Debunking the role of social scientists in court."
"The state of the nation's happiness."
"The Pope and TV: why their relationship is a 'terrible mess'."
"Today's morality play: the sitcom."
"The best 30-minute sermon on TV."
"The declining morale of women."
"Religion and attitudes towards AIDS policy."
"How just a war?"
"Live and let die: changing attitudes."
"The neglected Catholic vote is big one and may be returning to the Democrats."
"The abortion debate and the Catholic subculture."
"Necessity of feminism."

SOCIOLOGY OF RELIGION

Books

The Denominational Society: a sociological approach to religion in America.
Unsecular Man: the persistence of religion.
The Mary Myth.
Religious Change in America.

Essays

"Sociology and church structure."
"A social science model for the consideration of religious apostasy."
"Implications for the sociology of religion of occult behavior in the youth culture."
"Religious musical chairs."
"Why Catholic stay in the church."

Articles

"Areas of research on religion and social organizations."
"New horizons in Catholic thought--II: sociology of religion."
"American religious pluralism and social organization."

"Influence of the 'religious factor' on career plans and occupational values
   of college graduates."
"A note on the origins of religious differences."
"The Protestant ethic: time for a moratorium."
"After secularity: the neo-gemeinschaft society."
"Religion and academic career plans: a note on progress."
"The sociology of knowledge and the sociology of religion in the Catholic
   university."
"Continuities in research on the 'religious factor'."
"Superstition, ecstasy and tribal consciousness."
"The bread of faith."
"Religion still has tenure."
"Comment on Hunt's 'Mythological-Symbolic religious commitment: the
   LAM scales'."
"The uses of sociology."
"The end of religion."
"The 'religious factor' and academic careers: another communication."
"Religion in a secular society."
"The sociology of American Catholics."
"The center doesn't hold: church attendance in the United States, 1940-
   1984."
"Musical chairs: patterns of denominational change."
"Evidence that a maternal image of God correlates with liberal politics."
"Sociology and the Catholic church: four decades of bitter memories."
"A model of religious choice under uncertainty: on responding rationally
   to the nonrational."
"Religion and attitudes toward the environment."
"Religion not dying out around the world."

YOUTH MINISTRY

Books

Strangers in the House: Catholic youth in America.
And Young Men Shall See Visions: letters from Andrew M. Greeley.
Letters to Nancy: from Andrew M. Greeley.
Youth Asks, Does God Still Speak?
*Young Catholics in the United States and Canada: a report to the Knights
   of Columbus.*

Articles

"Should your daughter go to college?"
"The parish, the teenager, and the liturgy."
"Treat them like people."
"Prepare your child for college."
"Why they cheat."
"Let them make their own decisions."
"Why they go steady."
"The teen years: spiritual difficulties."
"Don't push them into marriage."
"Letter to a young man."
"Letter to a young woman."
"Youth in the age of renewal" (series).
"A new breed."
"The new young people."
"The temptation of the new breed."
"Social-medical problems of youth."
"A farewell to the new breed."
"Vandalism, suburban style."
"A post-Vatican II new breed?"

ABOUT THE AUTHOR

Elizabeth Harrison holds degrees from McMaster University (Political Economy) and the University of Toronto (Library Science). She worked for some years as a reference librarian in the Metropolitan Toronto Library System before taking early retirement to pursue a career as a bibliographer.